Great Irish Reportage

Great Irish Reportage

Edited by

JOHN HORGAN

Foreword by Olivia O'Leary

PENGUIN

IRELAND

PENGUIN IRELAND

Published by the Penguin Group
Penguin Ireland, 25 St Stephen's Green, Dublin 2, Ireland
(a division of Penguin Books Ltd)
Penguin Books Ltd, 80 Strand, London WC2R 0RL, England
Penguin Group (USA) Inc., 375 Hudson Street, New York, New York 10014, USA
Penguin Group (Australia), 707 Collins Street, Melbourne, Victoria 3008, Australia
(a division of Pearson Australia Group Pty Ltd)
Penguin Group (Canada), 90 Eglinton Avenue East, Suite 700, Toronto, Ontario, Canada M4P 2Y3
(a division of Pearson Penguin Canada Inc.)
Penguin Books India Pvt Ltd, 11 Community Centre,
Panchsheel Park, New Delhi – 110 017, India
Penguin Group (NZ), 67 Apollo Drive, Rosedale, Auckland 0632, New Zealand
(a division of Pearson New Zealand Ltd)
Penguin Books (South Africa) (Pty) Ltd, Block D, Rosebank Office Park,
181 Jan Smuts Avenue, Parktown North, Gauteng 2193, South Africa

Penguin Books Ltd, Registered Offices: 80 Strand, London WC2R 0RL, England

www.penguin.com

First published 2013
001

Selection and editorial text copyright © John Horgan, 2013
Foreword copyright © Olivia O'Leary, 2013

The Sources on pages 443–6 constitute an extension of this copyright page

Typeset in 12/14.75pt Bembo Book MT Std
by Palimpsest Book Production Ltd, Falkirk, Stirlingshire
Printed in Great Britain by Clays Ltd, St Ives plc

A CIP catalogue record for this book is available from the British Library

ISBN: 978–1–844–88321–9

www.greenpenguin.co.uk

Contents

Foreword

What makes a good report? Is it the typical front-page story about the fall of Saigon in 1975 which begins: 'National Liberation Front troops rolled into the South Vietnamese capital unopposed'? Or is it the eyewitness piece, like that of the *Guardian*'s Martin Woollacott from Saigon, with the famous line: 'There had to be a first tank – just as there had to be a first tank in Paris in 1944.' One tells you the facts. The other tells you what it's like to live those facts.

Nell McCafferty put it well in her introduction to *The Best of Nell*, explaining how she came to the realization that she'd never be able to write the front-page story:

I discovered this particularly on Bloody Sunday in Derry, when I was lying on the street while people around me got shot dead. I saw everything, while the other reporter was at the back. He, rightly, wrote the front-page story because somebody had to establish the name of the officer in charge, interview him and provide all the deadly details. Had it been up to me to phone the officer, the row would still be going on and the story would never have been written. My version appeared on the inside pages. I wrote about how the rest of us felt, lying on the ground.

Descriptive writing has always been a central part of the best and most serious journalism. Its power lies in its ability to bear witness and to be subversive of the hard facts as they are agreed by an establishment consensus, either within society or within the newspaper or magazine itself. Most important of all, descriptive writing returns the human dimension to journalism. It goes behind the headlines and the statistics, and puts people and their quirks and their lives at the centre of the story.

We're not talking about whimsy here. Nor are we talking about the totally personalized New Journalism, as practised by Tom Wolfe and Hunter S. Thompson. But there is room for pieces that reach out to make human and emotional connections with the reader. What we are talking about includes the pen-picture, that mixture of description, anecdote and comment which makes up the parliamentary or party conference sketch. It includes the descriptive piece on great occasions, whether that is famous funerals or royal marriages. It includes the profile/interview. It includes the essay. It also includes some of the greatest and most vivid journalism of all, the descriptions by foreign correspondents of intractable conflict, of wars and of pestilence.

Hubert Butler, the Kilkenny essayist, was a particularly useful witness because he was not part of the great Roman Catholic consensus. In the 1950s, Protestants in Fethard-on-Sea, Co. Wexford, were the target of a Roman Catholic boycott because a local woman, Sheila Cloney, married to a Catholic, left home with her children rather than have them educated in a Catholic school. In his essay 'Boycott Village', reprinted in this anthology, Butler not only describes the petty details of the boycott, which was supported by the Catholic Hierarchy; he also points out what it tells us about the wider fault lines in Irish society:

It is now fifty years since the *Ne Temere* decree, which condemns the Irish nation to live in two mutually distrustful camps, was first applied to Ireland. It has broken up many homes beside the Cloneys' and brought an element of hypocrisy and perjury into every marriage between Irish people of different faith. Yet never until now did the whole Irish nation observe and deplore the cruel tensions which it has created.

What Butler identified was one of the main reasons why even still we have failed in this country to develop a common sense of Irishness, an active citizenship, a real civic society.

As the years of the Troubles dragged on in Northern Ireland, and reader fatigue set in, it was a challenge to maintain interest. Fine reporters like Fionnuala O Connor met that challenge. Reporting from the Official Unionist Party Conference in 1984, she wrote one of her brilliantly perceptive pieces. She had been sitting on an almost deserted press bench in a half-empty hall while a delegate spoke about the voices he was hearing on BBC Radio Ulster. She quotes him thus:

There is a deliberate attempt to introduce a foreign culture. How often I have been irritated as I'm sure you must be, by that dreadful pronunciation 'Haitch'. Laughter. (Explanation for those unaccustomed to the fine points of Northern anthropology: the pronunciation is deemed to denote Catholics, much as shifty eyes do, or coal in the bath.)

'Where did it come from? I hate the haitch,' beamed Councillor Ward, buoyant on a sea of happy chuckles, the best audience of his life. 'Give me the native Ulster aitch.'

He had them laughing and then produced something better. 'I'd like to point out some of the names that have crept into the BBC and I make no apology for reading them out.'

He proceeded, O Connor reports, to read out eight or nine names of broadcasters, including Frank Delaney and Terry Wogan. They were all identifiably Irish and Catholic. This little episode showed sharply, as perhaps nothing else could, the level of prejudice even within the moderate Unionist party, despite the conciliatory line being adopted by its leaders.

Foreign correspondents have to fight for their space all the time. After risking his life to get a story once, Robert Fisk, the legendary Middle East correspondent of the London *Times* (and, later, the *Independent*), found his report buried at the back of the paper. He telexed the office wryly to say that he didn't mind risking his life for the *Times*, but please, please, please, could it be on Page 1?

A thousand killed, a million homeless, camps full of orphaned children: these are statistics, too big to take on board. So any foreign correspondent has to bring the story down to human dimensions, to introduce us to things we can relate to about people: what their names are, what their houses are like, how many children are in their families, whether they play football, what they are proud of, or afraid of. Sometimes correspondents will deliberately turn the tables on us, as Conor O'Clery of the *Irish Times* did reporting on the war in Afghanistan in 1980. Along with two colleagues, he had to dress up

as an Afghan tribesman to get through the roadblocks, and this caused
their guides some merriment:

Their amusement was derived not so much from the sight of myself and a
Canadian freelance companion, Keith Leckie, dressing in baggy pyjama
bottoms and turbans but from the Othello-like dash cut by the third member of our group, Mark August, a tall reporter from *New Africa Magazine*
and one of the first black men many of the Afghan tribesmen had ever seen.
  'Oh my God,' said Jamal, looking at the bespectacled black face topped
by a magnificent white turban. 'How will we ever get you through the
checkpoints?'

There was much more about mountain passes and Russian missiles and
rebels praying to Mecca. But by putting himself and his colleagues in
the picture, by allowing us to see how ridiculous they looked in the
eyes of their Afghan guides, Conor was allowing us to see through
Afghan eyes, so that when we came to hear of the Afghan wish for an
Islamic state, of their firm belief that Allah and the Afghan landscape
would beat the Russians, we would understand a bit better.
  Books survive for years. Newspapers don't. So it is a challenge to
collect into a book pieces written for tomorrow's newspaper. Put
together under pressure, often with imperfect information, in the
middle of danger and distraction, they were never meant to endure.
But miraculously, many of them do.
  Some of the writing collected here is of the highest quality because
it is the work of established novelists, short-story writers, poets and
essayists. Sometimes the pieces stand out because they are the result
of dramatic events and particular journalistic skill. Those of us in
journalism regard what we do as an honest trade, at best a craft. And
every so often, as well as the serviceable kitchen chairs and the bed-
side lockers we turn out, maybe luck or a bit of inspiration allows us
to produce a lacquered cabinet or a fine rosewood chest or two.
  Because a good, even a useful, journalistic writer is a great thing to
be. And those of us lucky enough to practise my trade don't ask for
much more.

                                             Olivia O'Leary

Introduction

We tell ourselves stories in order to live.

Joan Didion, *The White Album*, 1979

Reportage: The describing of events (typically by an observer); *spec.* the reporting of events for the media. Also: a piece of journalistic or factual writing; a literary style or genre that imitates or resembles such writing. Also in extended use.

The Oxford English Dictionary

Most journalism, done at high speed to demanding deadlines, is of its nature ephemeral: locked into a momentary or otherwise limited frame of reference and intended for daily consumption. Some exceptional pieces of reportage, however, speak to us across the years. How do they do it?

Often the answer lies in the sheer skill and ambition of the author: in the way a Myles na gCopaleen or a Nell McCafferty can look around, talk to people, and produce a piece of writing that does not (or does not merely) tell us who, what, where, when and how, but that evokes the human climate and sensibility of a place and time. The pieces gathered in this anthology were produced by writers who are good at journalism and by journalists who can really write. And they were published, for the most part, in newspapers and periodicals that gave them the time and resources they needed to dig deeper into a subject than journalists are usually able to do.

It is something of an accident that the first piece in the anthology dates from 1922, the year that saw the establishment of an independent Irish state and the copper-fastening of partition. There is much fascinating reportage from earlier periods, but I eventually concluded that the tone, language and sensibility of the excellent earlier pieces I came across did not have quite enough in common with those of the pieces included here. Nor is this book a shadow history of Ireland since 1922, covering all major events and phenomena through the lens of contemporary journalism: some major topics are not dealt with at all, while others receive disproportionate attention. There is chronological disproportion, too. The 1980s, for example, are represented far more heavily than any other decade, owing in part to the temporary prosperity of magazines during a period when they, unlike the newspapers, were able to run high-value colour advertising. This gave gifted writers and editors the resources they needed to produce some remarkable long-form reportage.

The vast majority of the pieces published in this anthology were written for newspapers or periodicals, or for books that drew their material directly from their authors' practice of daily journalism, but a few have different origins: Denis Johnston's diary; Colm Tóibín's account of his walk along the Irish border; Mary Raftery and Eoin O'Sullivan's exposé of the industrial schools; and three official dispatches that were not intended for public consumption at all but are no less revelatory for that.

This anthology defines 'Irish' broadly. It contains a number of pieces about Ireland by non-Irish journalists, including reflections by Alex Comfort on Dublin in 1943 and by Andrew O'Hagan on Dublin in 2002; V. S. Pritchett's portrait of Belfast in 1923; Honor Tracy's controversial evocation of clerical influence in a small Cork town in 1950; and Michael Lewis's 2011 account of the causes and consequences of the property crash. The other side of that coin is represented by Irish writers reporting from abroad. The Second World War is bracketed here by R. M. Smyllie's portrait of Hitler's pre-war Berchtesgaden idyll and Denis Johnston's experiences of Buchenwald. Much later, in a different era with different sensibilities, the incisiveness and sheer style of writers like Maeve Binchy (about a royal wedding), Kevin Myers (on famine in Ethiopia) or Joseph O'Connor (on the ability of Irish football fans to travel halfway around the world without ever leaving their own cultural bubble) helped to widen the horizons of a sometimes self-absorbed Irish public.

Selection decisions, inevitably, were very difficult, and I have had to omit many excellent pieces, by superb journalists, that would have found their places in a lengthier collection, or in one with slightly different criteria. This book is thus presented as a sort of a tasting menu; and if discussion of omissions leads readers to other great works of reportage, so much the better.

An anthology of Irish reportage produced twenty or thirty years from now would no doubt look rather different from this one, and not just because a different anthologist would inevitably make different choices. Writing about current events will have been transformed by the rise of digital media in ways we can only guess at. Space is not a problem in the digital realm, but money is. The old economic model of the print media is under intense pressure, and it is not clear how it will evolve, or what might replace it. But the pieces gathered here – produced in often challenging cultural, economic and technological circumstances – give us reason to feel confident that the urge to observe and to report, and to do so with precision, artistry and commitment, will survive.

JH

The Taking of Cork

FRANK GEARY (1922)

Anti-Treaty forces – referred to here as 'irregulars' – occupied Cork in July 1922, shortly after the commencement of the Civil War, and retained control until 10 August, when Emmet Dalton of the National Army retook the city for the Provisional Government. Frank Geary, a Kilkenny-born journalist who would go on to serve as editor of the *Irish Independent* from 1935 to 1961, had come close to being shot as a spy by anti-Treaty forces while covering earlier hostilities in Limerick. This diary could not be published until 12 August, after Geary – the only national newspaper reporter in Cork – had escaped from the city.

Cork has fallen. The National Army are now in possession. The irregulars fired all the barracks they occupied and evacuated. I have now reached Waterford from Cork after a 12-hour journey. How I did it I don't know, but it has easily beaten anything I have ever experienced from the point of view of thrilling and dangerous experiences.

Sunday, August 6th. This is my third day in Cork. It has rained practically all the time since my arrival. The weather seems to be in keeping with the times. The people are still patiently waiting – waiting for the coming of the war. They await it with conflicting emotions. They are nervous at its coming. They have had too much war, they say, and they want no more of it, particularly this kind, they remark, with emphasis on the last two words. And yet though fearful of the consequences and the sufferings they may have to endure, they are welcoming its coming. With all the tension they have endured, they have reached that stage when they think that the reality cannot be worse than the imagination. I am not so sure that they are wrong. It is a city of contradictions this. The tension of the people has been spoken of as a living, a real thing. I repeat it. It is terrible. It is in fact overpowering.

And yet as I write hundreds, nay thousands of people, men, women and children, all decked out in their best summer finery, are dashing away to the seaside. There they go, happy, joyous, buoyant parties in brakes, cans, jaunting cars, row-boats, motor-boats. Hundreds are going to the railway stations, for the local trains are still running. You will notice I did not say anything about motor cars. Occasionally you see a motor car, but it belongs to a doctor and carries the red cross. For the rest, the only other cars on the road have as passengers armed men. Such is Cork today. Almost within hearing of the sound of the guns thousands are flocking to the seaside. Momentarily expecting the advent of, perhaps, the most awful kind of war, tens of thousands are seeking enjoyment.

It is midnight. The streets are long since silent. Cork retires early these nights. Suddenly there is a burst of music. You can call it music if you like, or perhaps I should say sound. The holidaymakers are returning, and they are evidently in a happy mood. The day was not an ideal one but, apparently, it has not damped the ardour of these pleasure-seekers. The streets echo and re-echo with a medley of wary sounds. War-pipes, mouth-organs, melodeons, concertinas, to say nothing of the conglomeration of choruses and the loud and oft-repeated fare-wells. The war may be here tomorrow; but it is not yet, not yet.

Monday, August 7th: The August Bank Holiday. The shops are all closed today. The war has not yet come. It is raining again. I seem to have struck a very wet patch, but the rain does not deter that rush to the sea. It is even more pronounced today than yesterday. The same programme is gone through, except that the participants are more enthusiastic. There was little or no activity among the irregulars today. There is the usual coming and going. There are no signs of defensive work around the positions they occupy. At Union Quay barracks there is nothing but one sandbag. Perhaps the National forces are a long way off; there will be ample time before they come – perhaps! They're coming back – the holidaymakers, drenched, bedraggled, tired – they return. But they come with a smile and a song. They sing their way through the heavy downpour. The war may be here tomorrow, but it is not yet.

Tuesday, August 8th. There is a certain liveliness in the city this morning. Motors are whizzing past, leaving clouds of bluish smoke. Armed men are coming and going. There is something afoot. Just now I have seen half a dozen men with Red Cross armlets and white haversacks also red-crossed. Sinister signs, these men, these things. Groups of people in the streets, at street corners, are eagerly and excitedly discussing some happening, whatever it was, or happenings, whatever they were. What can it be all about? One hasn't long to wait for the news and when it comes, it comes as with an avalanche. The National troops have landed at Passage!

The city is throbbing with interest. The news has spread and is spreading through the streets like fevered blood through men's veins. The city is excited. People are pulsating with expectancy that almost borders on pain – mental and physical pain. In the street, the shops, everywhere – everywhere you can hear them talk – short, sharp, rapid sentences . . . 'They're in Passage, five or six miles from the city; they landed last night; they captured the place.' 'They are marching on Cork,' and so on; sometimes incoherent in their frantic mutterings. There is great activity among the irregulars. Bands of them are going and coming. Others are flying to and fro. I have just seen a big lorry going by which was laden with land mines, and armed men sit all around the side of the car. In the places the irregulars occupied all is hurry and excitement. Today, as hour succeeds hour, the excitement becomes more ·intense. The National forces have landed at Youghal and taken the town without firing a shot. They will soon be in Cork. So everyone is saying. There were also landings at Glandore and Castletownbere. The National forces are also in possession of Cobh. The irregulars have vacated it, but before they left they fired and destroyed Admiralty House and other buildings. The railway bridge at Carrigaline, on the Cork, Blackrock and Passage Railway, was blown up this morning.

I have just heard an interesting story of the landing of the National forces at Passage this morning. The surprise created by the coup was only equalled by the successful, daringly brilliant manner in which it was accomplished. Here is how it was done. Yesterday evening at the turn of the tide the SS *Classic* of Cork Steampacket came out from the dock to Penrose's Quay with passengers for Fishguard. In passing, may I say that through the instrumentality of a friend I was able to get a despatch by a passenger on this boat. All went well with the *Classic* as she ploughed her way into the cloudy deep. After a few hours' steaming, she sighted some strange-looking craft. One – two – three of them! Soon she drew near, and was hailed. There were three sloops, with scarce a sign of life. One of them drew alongside, and some men boarded the steamer. There was a parley with the captain, and then an order to the passengers to come on deck, and bring their baggage with them.

Then, as if from nowhere, came men – men – men: hundreds of National soldiers being transferred from the sloops to the steamer. Up they came, clambering over the sides of the boat like a phantom army from the vasty deep. Men and guns, and guns and men; and when they were all on board the passengers were transferred to sloops to finish their journey. One could easily visualise the strange scene that was being enacted. One could feel the excitement, the mystery, the utter weirdness of the whole thing; and with grim, mechanical silence, the task is completed, and, like ships that pass in the night, they have gone!

But the final episode of this thrilling story has to come. Back towards Cork the *Classic* steamed silent, mysterious. Coming into the harbour she showed signals of distress. The *Classic* returning! 'Twas about midnight. She should have been near the Welsh coast now. What was the matter? More signals of distress. Engine trouble! What a sensation! Slowly, silently, she limped, as it were, up the Channel, as if she were gasping for very breath and fearful lest she should not make the shore. It was past 1 o'clock now. She was opposite Passage. All was quiet, dead quiet, save for the snorting of the engines below.

She docked at Passage. The hawsers were made fast. A brief period of death-like silence and then a signal. In a twinkling the whole ship was a mass of humanity, with scarce a sound. They were up and over and on the land. Hundreds of them in the gloom. They lined along, like ghost-like figures, and then, at a muffled word of command, they melted away into the darkness, as mysteriously as they had come.

When Cork woke up this morning it learned that the National troops had landed at Passage, and had taken the little town.

Tuesday. The activity of the irregulars has become greater. Motors are careering all over the city from barracks to barracks. A large force of men have just gone to the office of the *Cork Examiner*, and, as I write, they are wrecking the machinery. A curious crowd has gathered outside. But armed guards are stationed all round. One can hear the hammering and the smashing inside. After some hours they leave the whole place in a wreck. All the machinery has been smashed. Up to now the *Examiner* has published under the censorship imposed by the irregulars. The wrecking of the place today gives one furiously to think, as they say in France. Three members of the staff have also been arrested, it is said. From the *Examiner* offices the band of irregulars proceed to the offices of the *Cork Constitution*. These premises have been closed down for some time past, but the machinery and fittings have, of course, remained intact. They meet with a fate similar to that of the *Examiner*. Here also everything in the way of machinery was wrecked. Practically all the machines being reduced to scrap iron, Cork is now without any paper or even the means to print one.

News of doings outside the immediate vicinity of Cork is slowly trailing through. All people coming into the city are being held up and marched by irregulars' outposts. The Nationals, I am told, hold all points of strategic value on the Cork side of Passage. There is feverish excitement in and around Union Quay barracks, which apparently is the headquarters. Crowds of people have congregated around the building, and view the preparations for what nobody seems to know. When motoring through the city today, Mr Grace, manager at the Ford Works, was held up by a force of irregulars, and despite his protests his car was taken from him. Mr Grace, who, by the way, is an American, subsequently walked to the works and ran up an American flag on the flagstaff.

This is not his first encounter with irregulars. A few weeks ago they visited the plant and asked him if he had certain moulds and castings. He replied that he had. They said they wanted them. 'Very well,' he is reported to have said, 'you can take them if you like, but if you do I will walk out through that gate and I will bring 1,960 other men with me.' The moulds were not removed.

I have also heard just now that one of the old hulks in the channel was blown up this morning, blocking the fairway. This closes the entry to, and the exits from, the city docks. Several explosions have been heard outside the city, but impossible to locate. Huge posters have been posted up this evening announcing a meeting of unemployed for Sunday next, giving the condition of things, which was causing such enforced unemployment in the city.

The excitement has grown within the past few hours. Thousands of people have flocked into the streets. A dense throng has gathered outside Union Quay, where numberless motors continue to arrive. Just now three immense lorries laden with hundreds of bicycles drove up to the barracks. They have evidently come from Ballincollig, which is also occupied by irregulars. After disposing of their load they leave, but return again, this time laden with large barrels of petrol and oil. A short time ago the fire escape was removed from the fire station. The telephone exchange has also been dismantled. Barrels of petrol! No fire escape! No telephone! Are all this rush and hurry of the day and night the beginning of the end? Who can tell? Are these preparations for evacuation? Will it be like the collapse of Limerick? Who can tell?

There have been a couple of revolver shots. We thought it was the beginning, but all is quiet again. Not a sound but the soft swish of the water over the weir a short distance away, and the occasional rattle of a passing motor. 'Watchman, what of the night?'

Wednesday, August 9th. [. . .] Today there is the same ceaseless activity in and around Union Quay barracks. There is the same interminable coming and going of motor cars, motor lorries, motor cycles etc. There are, too, not a few motor ambulances on the move. Small light Raleighs have been hastily converted and fitted up with stretchers etc. The excitement, which was manifest yesterday amongst the people, has diminished considerably today. There is no slackening, however, of the crowds that congregate along the quays and watch the coming and going of the irregulars.

There were no fewer than 35 cars outside this morning – from the heavy steam ferry and the char-a-banc to the motor car. Included in the number were heavily built armoured cars, evidently of local manufacture, but they look substantial and bullet worthy. The landing of the National troops at Passage is still being talked about. Yesterday, when the news got around, housewives made a rush to the grocery and provision shops and bought up practically all the stocks available. They were preparing for a siege. This morning a force of irregulars visited the city markets and seized large quantities of fresh meat etc. There were no newspapers of any kind in the city today. We are now completely isolated.

Wednesday evening. Still the same activity. Still the same coming and going. Still the same crowd of curious onlookers. This evening I have seen dozens of lady nurses in and around the irregular headquarters, coming out with haversacks bulging with dressings etc., and driving away in motor cars. I don't know where they are going, but it looks as if there is an engagement somewhere. The channel has been cleared of sunken barges, and many ships are again arriving and leaving. The SS *Classic* left again for Fishguard this evening. She sailed from Cobh, and not from the city docks. It was feared if she came to the docks she would have been burned. I was also told this evening that the banks in the city were to close, but I could not verify this.

Wednesday night. I have just got another bit of exciting news. Picking up news under present circumstances is lively enough, but not altogether a pleasant occupation. The greatest difficulty, however, will be getting it away. Sometimes that appears insurmountable – however, that is another day's work. The big viaduct bridge on the Cork, Bandon and South Coast Railway was blown up this evening. Situated about 3½ miles from the city, it was an immense structure, towering over 100 feet high. It was badly damaged, and it will take an infinite amount of time and money to repair it.

Further reinforcements of National troops arrived today at Passage. The big guns were in action down the river this evening. National guns shelled Fota, the beautiful mansion and demesne of Lord

Barrymore, situated opposite Passage on the far side of the river. The irregulars were in possession, occupying the mansion, and having large forces in the woods adjoining. The whole place has been sub-jected to a heavy fire, and the irregulars have had many casualties. I was told that two boat-loads of wounded have been brought up the river, but verification of the incident was not possible. It is said that fighting is also taking place at Maryboro Hill, Douglas, and Roches-town, Belvedere Bridge, and Dunkettle Bridge, between Cork and Cobh, have also been blown up. The number of casualties on both sides have been admitted to the South Infirmary. It is impossible as yet to estimate the number.

Thursday morning, August 10th. Last night was quiet. There is less energy today amongst the irregulars, but the incessant coming and going continues. Raids have been made on shops again this morning, and quantities of goods seized. A number of men this morning entered the Imperial Hotel and took over possession. They also took possession of the Co. Club and the premises of the League of Ex-Soldiers. In the latter place the members who were present refused to leave on request, the menace of revolvers notwithstanding. Other members of the organisation in the city, hearing of the incident, went to the club and they also trooped into the rooms. A guard of armed irregulars took up a position opposite the building.

I have just heard details of the fight which took place yesterday evening at Rochestown. It seems to have been a bloody affair, and, at one time, the opposing forces came into hand-to-hand conflict. The place was strongly held by the irregulars, but it was subjected to heavy machine and rifle fire by the National forces. Perhaps the best description of the ferocity of the fight was given by one of the National forces who was wounded. He received terrible abdominal injuries and when asked how he got them replied, 'Well, I saw a fel-low behind a machine-gun. I went for it. I rushed at it, and was just going to grab for it when he turned it on me, and I got seven or eight bullets.' It is feared that his wounds may terminate fatally. Another young fellow, a National soldier, when asked where he was wounded replied, 'Punchestown', meaning, of course, Rochestown. Another

National soldier who was wounded said: 'I am the transport driver. I just stood up, and a bullet hit me in the arm, breaking it.' The wounded from both sides were brought to the city by boats. So far as is known there was nobody killed during this encounter. Another boat, a big corn boat, was stuck in the channel again this morning, blocking the fairway.

Thursday, noon. There is renewed activity of irregulars all over the city. Bands of men with rifles flung over their shoulders are marching around. The Imperial Hotel, the County Club and the Ex-Soldiers League have again been vacated. News is being spread that the Nationals are advancing on the city. The people are wondering when they will come. A *Republican War News* has been published by irregulars today and is being sold on the streets. It consists of three or four pages of typewritten matter. The excitement of the past few days appears to be dying down. How long will it continue so?

Thursday afternoon. It is now 2 o'clock. Things have quietened down to a dead calm. Stopped the coming of the motors, ceased the going of the lorries. The last one went about half an hour ago, loaded with land mines, red, cylindrical things which made one shudder. Outside Union Quay barracks there is a collection of motor vehicles of all kinds and descriptions – lorries, five-seaters, two-seaters, and bicycles and sidecars. Still dead calm. There is a slight flutter of excitement. Big crowds still gather around the quays. A messenger has just arrived at the barracks. Rushing excited, almost breathless, he gives a message with frantic haste. Immediately the storm bursts. Men run here and there into the building and out of it.

I am standing at the opposite side of the quay. Everyone is excited. A number of the irregulars rush on to the road. They get around a big five-ton lorry. They push it and get it going, and then, splash, it is into the river. There is a shout of consternation from the assembled hundreds. Was it an accident? The men rush to another car, a fine five-seater. They push it into the river. Another and another and another and yet another meet with similar fates before the horrified gaze of the crowd. Several motor cycles, many of them with sidecars, were pushed into the water. One pretty little two-seater motor car just gets caught in the woodwork on the quay and doesn't fall. It hangs there, betwixt and between, a funny-looking sight. The whole quayside is now cleared.

Everybody has now come out of the barracks. It is an immense and imposing red brick structure. Suddenly a volley of rifle and revolver shots ring out. How the crowd scatters! Another volley. People run helter skelter, seeking refuge in every open door. Women shriek with very fear. Everybody thinks the National forces have arrived and that they have engaged the irregulars in the streets. They are wrong.

The volleys have apparently been fired as a warning for, just now, there is a loud resounding boom, a dense volume of black smoke bursts up from the barracks, followed by the crash of falling masonry. There is another terrific crash. Another cloud of bluish smoke rushes up. In the midst of it, tongues of flame can be seen. Then the crackle of countless explosions, ammunition bursting.

Thursday, 3.00 p.m. The building is doomed. Smoke is issuing from every window, from every chimney, even from between the very slates. In other parts of the city there are explosions followed by smoke and fire. Elizabeth Fort, off Barrack Street, is in flames. The Bridewell in Cornmarket Street is blazing. Tuckey Street police barracks is a mass of fire. Empress Place police barracks way up on Tuckey Hill is belching forth mountains of smoke and, further up, what seems like the very hell itself seems on fire. The latter is Victoria barracks, which is completely in the grip of the flames. No words can adequately picture such weird and horrifying scenes. I have had experience now of four of them; I have seen them in Belfast, Dublin, Limerick, and now Cork, and, God knows, I don't want to see any more of them. One does not get accustomed to this kind of thing. It is the end. Cork has fallen.

3.15 p.m. The irregulars are evacuating. As it was in Limerick they are going, going, going!

3.40 p.m. Explosion follows explosion with terrifying rapidity. Cork has been my worst experience from this point of view. Like the waters of many rivers converging into a big lake, the smoke of many fires has converged into one dense mass which hangs like a deadly pall over the whole city. The air below, as it were, is imprisoned and one stifles with the heat, the oppressive heat, and the acrid smell of burning buildings. The sun is darkened; one can see it through the smoke, a red, almost a bloody disc. Showers of charred papers and other debris are falling everywhere and litter the streets. Ever and anon, gusts of wind carry clouds of smoke through the streets. Union Quay barracks is now a mass of flame and the roof has fallen in.

3.45 p.m. Looting has begun, and processions of men, women and children flock to the burning buildings and take everything they can lay their hands on. One had a motor-bicycle, another a wardrobe, and beds, chairs, tables, everything. Braving the danger of exploding bullets and bombs, they actually go into the burning buildings and carry away various articles of furniture. 'If we don't take them, they will be burned,' they say.

4.00 p.m. There is another big explosion, perhaps the loudest yet. This one is an attempt made to blow up the Parnell Bridge. It was only partially successful. A big gaping hole was blown in the wooden groundwork and part of the steel work was rent asunder and twisted like a piece of paper. Pedestrian traffic over the bridge is still possible.

4.10 p.m. The party which has acted as a rearguard leaves. All the buildings are now doomed.

4.30 p.m. The streets are crowded with people who are going around viewing the burning places. When I viewed Tuckey Street barracks it was only a smouldering ruin. Shortly after the outbreak here, this was the scene of a very exciting incident.

The flames were making rapid headway, and when the ground floor and second storey were well involved, the onlookers were horrified to see two young men appear at a top-storey window of the burning building. They had evidently been asleep when the building was fired, for they were only partially dressed. One of the unfortunate men was so terror-stricken that he attempted to jump to the ground. Encouraging shouts from those around that help was coming helped to prevent their jumping. The floor on which they stood was now in flames, and volumes of smoke were issuing from the window. A number of men then arrived with ladders and rescued the unfortunate fellows from their perilous position. They were black with smoke and their hair was actually singed. Shortly after their rescue the floor collapsed.

5.00 p.m. Large crowds of sightseers still throng the streets. There is not a shop open in the city. At the first explosion all the shops were quickly shuttered and closed down. All the factories and workshops in and around the city were also closed. The tramway service, too, was suspended, and was not resumed this evening. Just before the irregulars left they also visited the post office and wrecked the telegraphic department. They also smashed up other things. The telephone exchange was also visited and here the apparatus was also wrecked. The damage in both cases is so considerable that it will take many days before any telegraphic or telephonic communication can be established. Several bridges on the main line to Dublin have also been blown up. Railway communications will also be impossible for some time.

6.00 p.m. The fires are continuing unabated. There is the rattle as of machine gun fire all over the city and people are becoming alarmed. It is only boxes of ammunition that are exploding in the burning buildings. Searching among the ruins, some young men discovered a quantity of bombs. One youth pulled the pin out of one, and was killed, several others being injured. One young fellow in whose hand another bomb exploded received frightful injuries. Every bit of his clothing was blown away except one boot. All the skin from his head, neck and hands has gone, and splinters inflicted terrible injuries in every part of his body.

7.30 p.m. Cork is again excited, but this time it is the excitement of relief. A thrill of sensation has run through the city with the spread of the announcement that National troops had arrived and were actually in the city – they were crossing Parnell Bridge. There was a rush, a veritable stampede. Practically every resident in every street flocked out, and all made their way to the south quays, along which the troops were coming.

8.00 p.m. Amazing scenes are being witnessed. The troops have arrived, the first of them preceded by an armoured car. The advance guard comes slowly. They come almost struggling. They are tired but the warmth of their reception lights the light of gladness in their eyes. The people are almost frantic with delight; they cheer and shout and wave handkerchiefs. They give the soldiers biscuits, sweets, cigarettes, fruit. They shower them on them. How glad they look. Another batch has come and they too are cheered to the echo. Unshaven, mud-stained they plod along. They were all wearing badges of the Sacred Heart in their caps and on their coats. The view along the Mall as they passed baffles description. Tens of thousands of citizens thronged the thoroughfares to view the unusual scene and all the time the smoke from six fires in the city ascended to the heavens and above the cheering could be heard the boom of another explosion and the crackle and bursts of ammunition. I have had a talk with some of the Nationalist soldiers, who have made the Bandon Railway their headquarters for the night. They have told me more of the bloody night in Rochestown. Four or five of their men were killed, but the irregulars lost nine. At times the fighting was almost hand-to-hand.

10.00 p.m. The streets were quietening down somewhat now, yet crowds of people still walk about viewing the damage. Beyond the destruction of the buildings there is not much injury to the city. All the windows of the houses at Morrison's Quay were smashed as well as those of the Provincial Bank and the Savings Bank. They were broken from the force of the explosions in their localities. A party of young people have passed by my window and they gave vent to their relieved feelings in no uncertain manner. They have a melodeon, and it too, apparently, has caught the spirit of the city. Isolated explosions here and there serve as grim reminders. All is quiet. Cork has retired after one of its most eventful days. My work to get away begins tomorrow. No trains, no motors, no clear roads. The sea is the only way open but there are no boats tonight.

Friday, August 11th
From early morning I have been plodding about looking for a way out. Everything blank. There are a few cars, but none would take the risk. I tried to charter a motor boat to bring me to Youghal. Another blank. Nobody would attempt any journey, and everyone was

advising me not to do so either. By a stroke of luck I got my man. I told him my errand. He hesitated. He must have been a 'sport'. 'It is worth the chance,' he said, 'and I will drive you to Waterford.' I am sure he regrets it. [. . .] It was some drive, too. Through fields, over ditches, through places which to call them 'boreens' would be as ludicrous as comparing them to O'Connell St. At some time or other there might have been a car track down there, but now . . . And that for miles! Then through rivers where bridges had been blown down. Three times we drove through water, in one place about 100 yards, and sometimes the water covered the splashboard. We got to Midleton in two hours. It is 13 miles from Cork and we were going all the time. The driver says he knows the way he came. I doubt it.

In Midleton I found that the irregulars had evacuated last night and burned the barracks. It was still smouldering as I passed this evening. We ran into a bunch of them outside the town but they let us pass. Then to Castlemartyr, which was also evacuated last night. Here they blew up the bridge, which was being repaired, and we were obliged to ford the river. And then into Youghal, which is occupied by National troops. The capture of Youghal was as amusing as it was clever. In the dead of the night the National forces landed. The garrison of irregulars in the pleasant little seaside resort was isolated and when they awoke they were all prisoners. Not a single shot was fired. There is no telegraph, telephone or railway communication with the city this evening.

From Youghal to Dungarvan – a delightful run through a delightful country – and then the old borough by the sea. Peaceful and beautiful it nestles by the ocean. It is in the hands of the irregulars. We ran into some of them in the town. They wanted petrol. I got to the post office and was met with the notice that it was 'completely isolated'. Completely isolated – will I ever get this message tonight? It was 6 o'c.

Now, the last bid for Waterford, 30 miles away. How far off it seems! I hope I will never get anything to remind me of that journey. A couple of miles out we met a big batch of irregulars. They, too, looked tired and worn. We were questioned, and such questioning: I had the bulk of my copy with me. We were allowed to pass and were directed as to the road.

The man who called where we had to go a road is a damned liar: but we were lucky to get through [...] On by Kilmacthomas, Kilmeadon and then to Waterford at last! The post office. It is 7.30. And here let me pay a tribute to the courteous manner in which I was received. Anything, everything, that it was possible for them to do, was done.

Poetry Drives No Rivets

V. S. PRITCHETT (1923)

After escaping from drudgery as a shop assistant in Paris, a young
V. S. Pritchett, the son of a Christian Scientist, worked as a reporter
for the *Christian Science Monitor* in Spain and Ireland. He visited Belfast
in 1923, aged twenty-two, with his career as an author of short stories,
novels and essays still ahead of him. His impressionistic report was
written in the context of the recent partition of Ireland.

If you are minded to see all things Irish through political or religious
spectacles – which I am not – you will no doubt have thought of
Belfast as the home, par excellence, of loyalty and of all those virtues of empire about which a patriotic Englishman is most flattered
to hear. It is a good theme and though six counties await their
Kipling, I admit I see Belfast with cockney rather than with imperial
eyes.

It is a city of red trams and barefooted newsboys. As they hum and
sway down the streets, one feels there is something prosperous, well-
fed and municipal about the trams; so that one may be excused
finding delight in the newsboys getting free rides on the steps, in spite
of the conductor. All day long and halfway through the night the
keen-eyed urchins cry their papers and dart about the streets and
the pavements, and you are a fortunate person if you can escape the
excitement of the evening news.

There are crowds of people in the streets. Belfast may not be very
polite; it may not have the charm of the south; but it certainly has all
the hurry and noise and pre-occupation which seem to go with commercial prosperity. There is energy in the shoulders of the Ulsterman,
a steely keenness in his eyes, a bluffness in his bearing. He is proud of
his achievements; and indeed he has achieved much. He believes in
business. 'We work some,' said one of them as we passed the docks.
Then, remembering I came from the south, he added, 'Writing
poetry don't drive many rivets.'

As I looked round the docks, the moored steamers, the expectant cranes, the warehouses, and beyond all, at the fantastic derricks of the shipyards pencilled against the sky, I realized the case for poetry was a poor one. Under a sky dulled by the smoke of 50 chimney stacks, and in the city of shops, rope and linen, how could I plead the measures of the Gael? How could I have ever whispered to a gigantic, red-faced, clear-eyed Ulsterman who was, besides, a magistrate and a member of Parliament, that 'A.E.' and 'John Eglinton' were northerners? I am afraid that it would not have driven many rivets!

Mind you, I would not grant Belfast all the virtues. The Liffey may be despicable, but the Lagan can hardly be called beautiful. I confess to a thoroughly decadent and sentimental weakness for Merrion Square, mainly because Yeats lives at No. 82. I prefer the faded Abbey to the very electric opera house. It may be a significant fact that Belfast bricks are fiercely red, while those of Dublin are warm and lazy in the afternoon sun. The fact is northern virtues are more apparent than southern virtues.

The northerners seem more unanimous about themselves. Each Ulsterman seems to be his own publicity department. The Government is everywhere anxious that you take away a picture of a happy, prosperous and very loyal Ulster. One is plied with pamphlets, with statistics – which carry with them the subtle conviction of figures – with illustrations, and all so thoroughly well done that one would have to be exceptionally hard of heart not to be influenced by them. At the luncheon given by the Belfast Chamber of Commerce to Sir Philip Lloyd Greame, one felt one was in the midst of a body of business men who believed in their own solidarity. It makes one ask if hard-hearted visitors to Dublin might not take away a far better picture of the Irish Free State if southern publicity methods approached the thoroughness of northern methods.

In the obvious differences, racial and temperamental, which exist between the north and the south, may there not lie the seed of mutual help and ultimate reunion? The progressive nature and briskness of the north should be an incentive to the south. One feels the north will take the lead; the south will be impelled to follow. One is inclined to make a virtue of necessity, and to find what benefit may be gained by the separation of the two parts of the country. Competitive work may be good for the southern character. And perhaps the northerners will go more happily to their rivet driving after reading the southern poetry!

The Fuehrer's Unpretentious Villa

R. M. SMYLLIE (1936)

In Ireland, Hitler's rise to power in Germany in 1933 was at first perceived as intriguing rather than menacing. R. M. Smyllie, who was
appointed editor of the *Irish Times* in 1934, was a fluent German-
speaker: as a young graduate he tutored children in a family in
Germany, and as a British subject spent the First World War in an
internment camp there. The following is one of a series of fourteen
articles that appeared in the *Irish Times*, with the byline 'Nichevo', in
November 1937; they were later published together as a pamphlet and
sold for threepence. This article appeared midway through the series;
only the final two were more darkly shaded than this one.

What is there to do in Berchtesgaden? This question has been put to
me several times since I came back to Ireland, and it is very difficult
to give a satisfactory answer. From the point of view of the ortho-
dox, sight-seeing tourist, there really is little to do. There are a few
nice little churches in the neighbourhood. I have been told that the
Schloss is worth a visit; but I admit that I gave it a miss. The salt
mines also constitute a great attraction for visitors during the season:
but here again I was a heretic. The fact is that I found so much to do
outside the beaten track that I had no time for the things that everybody is supposed to see.

Of course no visit to Berchtesgaden would be complete without a
pilgrimage to the Hitler house. As I have said already, I shall be sufficiently grateful to Herr Hitler, since it was the fact that he had
chosen it as his home from home that led me originally to go to Berchtesgaden. Long before he ever became Chancellor of the Third
Reich – in fact, when he was a very humble individual, indeed – Herr
Hitler acquired a little shack on Obersalzberg, about a thousand
metres above sea level, to which he used to repair with some of his
cronies for occasional week-ends. When the National Socialist Party
came into power it presented its leader with a villa in the same

neighbourhood, and now he spends every available minute of his time at Obersalzberg.

It is an indescribably lovely spot. The house itself is anything but pretentious – just an ordinary Bavarian villa, such as one sees in thousands in that part of the world; but it commands one of the most glorious views in Europe. It looks right across the broad valley to the Watzmann, whose lofty peaks dominate the whole countryside, and there is an air of brooding peace about the place that must be experienced to be understood. My respect for Herr Hitler has increased since I visited Obersalzberg. One may not be enamoured of his politics, but there must be something at least unusual about a man who chooses to live and do his work in such heavenly surroundings.

Herr Hitler generally flies from Berlin to Munich, and then drives by car to Obersalzberg. Sometimes he takes the train, and his arrival at Berchtesgaden railway station invariably is the occasion for a popular demonstration. For the ordinary visitor there are two ways of getting up to Obersalzberg. He can go with the Post 'bus, or he can walk. The road from Berchtesgaden up to the Hitler house must be one of the steepest in existence. Very wisely private motor cars are not allowed to make the ascent, which goes up in a series of hair-raising corkscrew bends, and the gradient is so fierce that even the powerful Post 'bus finds some difficulty in its negotiation. To do it on foot is the best part of a day's march; but it really was remarkable to see how many corpulent Germans of both sexes contrived to toil up that dreadful hill merely in order to have a look at their Fuehrer's house. We compromised, taking the 'bus up, and walking down; but the hill is so steep that it is almost as difficult to come down as it is to go up, and woe betide you if you do not mind your step.

Up at the house there were a couple of black uniformed S.S. men on duty at a large wooden gate on the roadside; but they were cheery individuals, and chatted brightly with the little knot of pilgrims who had foregathered in the hope that they might be vouchsafed a glimpse of the Fuehrer. When Herr Hitler is in residence he usually strolls down the avenue once or twice in the course of the day to shake hands and exchange a few words with his admirers. Certainly he seems to be very democratic in his attitude towards the general public, and, of course, every visitor to Obersalzberg with whom he converses goes back to his town or village more firmly convinced than ever that Adolf Hitler is a demi-god.

I was thirsty after the trip to Obersalzberg, so I made my way to a little restaurant just across the road from the Hitler house, and got into a conversation with the *Wirtin*. She at any rate is a Hitler 'fan' and is likely to remain so while the Fuehrer continues to have his house in Obersalzberg. She told me that the increase in her business was so great that she had to make extensive additions to her premises to cope with the rush of tourist traffic, and the whole district of Obersalzberg must have been coining money during the last few years.

Naturally, Obersalzberg is the show place of the Berchtesgaden area; but for the visitor who does not particularly wish to spend his time waiting for Herr Hitler to emerge, there are many far more interesting places in the neighbourhood. For instance, there is Ilsank. There really is nothing much in Ilsank, which is the starting point of the ascent of the Watzmann; but there is a little inn there which is a real delight. I started off one day from Berchtesgaden to walk to the Hintersee, about fifteen kilometres from the village; but when I reached Ilsank it began to rain rather heavily, and being without a coat, I took refuge in this wayside inn.

I spent some hours there, and it was a fascinating experience. On the way down I had met a burly peasant with an ox wagon carrying wood up a hill to his cottage, and when I asked him how far we were from the Hintersee he burst into loud peals of laughter, and told me that I had still two hours' walk ahead of me. He seemed to think it a huge joke that anybody should want to walk at all in the rain, and the idea of a trip to the Hintersee in such conditions was just too comic. He had the bluest pair of eyes I ever have seen in a man's head, and his laughter was so infectious that in a few moments we all were in fits. We were only a couple of yards from the Ilsank Inn, so by common consent, we all adjourned thither to enjoy some excellent beer at twopence halfpenny a pint.

Here was the real Bavaria. We were in a largish room, with a colossal green stove and a half a dozen deal tables, scrubbed to a spotless whiteness. On the walls were a couple of photographic enlargements of a twenty-stone Bavarian, holding a great *Maas* of beer in his hand, apparently the deceased spouse of the buxom hostess, who, despite his great bulk, must have been an active sportsman; for the room was full of stags' heads, testimony to his prowess as a shot. Seated round a circular table were seven or eight middle-aged peasants, all wearing native costume, with their quaint hats decorated with either long black and white plumes, or those large shaving-brush pom-poms, which give their wearers such a picturesque appearance.

Mutatis mutandis, the whole party might have been lifted straight from the stage of the Abbey Theatre. All the men were of the same type; yet they were entirely different. One was a great hulking brute of a fellow, who must have weighed well over twenty stone, and still did not appear to be fat. He had a pair of the most gigantic knees that I have ever seen, and his tiny hat, perched on the top of a closely cropped head, gave him an almost grotesque appearance. Another was a little wizened gnome-like creature, who apparently was trying to compensate for his lack of inches by a lofty shaving-brush, which kept on nodding over his left ear in disconcerting fashion. Some of them had beery, rubicund faces, bursting with good humour; others had faces like pieces of old wrinkled leather, while there was one who was the living image of a famous Dublin surgeon.

They were all drinking beer in generous quantities, and then the hostess decided that the time had come for a diversion, and produced a pack of cards. My friend from the mountain seemed to be the crack player. What the game was, heaven only knows; but it certainly gave the players great amusement. The hostess ignored any other customers who happened to be in the establishment to join in the school, and, what was more important, to join in the incessant argument that accompanied the game. They all were speaking in the broadest Bavarian dialect – which is entirely incomprehensible even to a North German, let alone a foreigner – but although we could not understand a word of what they said, their gestures were so amusing, and their excitement was so intense, that our little party was kept in continuous laughter for the better part of an hour.

I never have seen more natural people than those Bavarian

peasants. They have a joy in life that seems to derive from their mountain homes, and have an immense capacity for fun. Even the serving maid joined in the card game, leaving the table at intervals to inquire if our party would like another jorum of beer; and although two of us manifestly were foreigners from the back of beyond, our presence seemed to be taken as a matter of course. No questions were asked. The old men at the table did not even turn round to have a look at the curious strangers who had broken in upon their afternoon peace, and we might just as well have been bits of furniture for all the notice that was taken of us.

After a while the serving maid disappeared, to return with a huge bowl of steaming soup. The card game was interrupted. Great dishes were placed before the players, and very rapidly they were tucking in to a hearty meal. After the soup came gargantuan sausages with large plates of potatoes, and every man was served with his full litre of heavy beer. They certainly have fine appetites in Bavaria; their thirsts are beyond description.

This was just at the end of September. The weather had been wettish, but warm, and it never had been sufficiently wet to keep us indoors. That evening, however, as we left the inn at Ilsank to walk the five or six miles back to our hotel in Berchtesgaden we noticed that the rain had assumed a quality of unusual softness, and realised to our astonishment that it was snowing. When we had arrived the snow line on the mountains had dropped to about a thousand metres, which was unusually low for the autumn; now it was right at our feet. It snowed solidly for two and a half days. When we woke up on the following morning the whole place was covered, and by the time when the snowfall had ceased there were between two and three feet of snow on the ground.

The effect was simply wonderful. Snow-tipped mountains always have a queer fascination for me. Even the sight of the snow on the Three Rock always gives me a thrill; but to see Berchtesgaden under snow is an unforgettable experience. Most of the mountains are covered with pine trees to the height of about 1,500 metres, and when these trees are laden with snow they give the impression in the distance of Gothic architecture, looking for all the world like huge cathedrals. We trudged for miles through that Berchtesgaden snow, watching the little peasant boys dashing about on snow shoes, and tobogganing down the hills in reckless fashion. Actually, although there was no frost, and the snow, accordingly, was as soft as wool, we came across a platoon of Alpine Jaegers practising skiing on the slopes of the mountain near Bad Reichenhall. The Germans lose no opportunity of making their army efficient, and the Austrian frontier is only a stone's throw away.

The Death Knell of the Working Woman

GERTRUDE GAFFNEY (1937)

The political debate surrounding the framing and passage of the 1937 Constitution was largely concentrated on three issues: a suspicion that Éamon de Valera wanted to endow himself with quasi-dictatorial powers; a fear that the new constitution would facilitate censorship; and, among female trade unionists and activists, a well-founded sense that it was designed to push women out of the workforce. Gertrude Gaffney was an unexpected convert to the latter cause. She had extolled Franco in dispatches from Spain the previous year, and in all other respects her articles and political attitudes had appeared to mirror the deeply Catholic priorities of the *Irish Independent*, of which she was a star reporter. Her feminist opposition to de Valera's constitution was, in this context, remarkable.

The death knell of the working woman is sounded in the new Constitution which Mr de Valera is shortly to put before the country. If the average woman in this country is going to vote for a Constitution containing certain of the clauses in Articles 40 and 41, then she is going to be up against it for the rest of her life in supporting her daughters, for there will be no work for them here.

Mr de Valera has always been a reactionary where women are concerned. He dislikes and distrusts us as a sex, and his aim ever since he came to office has been to put us in what he considers is our place, and to keep us there. He has gone about it in such a clever way that he has got his way before anybody realised it. He showed his hand for the first time in the Conditions of Employment Bill, which gives him power to exclude women from any industries in which he does not need them. Now he finishes the job in his new Constitution. Listen to this.

'All citizens shall, as human persons, be held equal before the law. This shall not be held to mean that the State shall not in its enactments have due regard to differences of capacity, physical and moral, and of social function.'

And again: 'In particular, the State recognises that by her life within the home, woman gives to the State a support without which the common good cannot be achieved.' Highly significant, that.

Consider these reactionary clauses side by side with that in the Proclamation of 1916: 'The Republic guarantees religious and civil liberty, equal rights and equal opportunities to all its citizens.'

Article 3 in the Saorstát Constitution, which is now to be disregarded, gave this guarantee: 'Every person without distinction of sex, dominated in the area of the jurisdiction of the Irish Free State – is a citizen of the Irish Free State and shall within the jurisdiction of the Irish Free State enjoy the privileges and be subject to the obligations of such citizenship.'

The clauses from Articles 10 and 11 quoted in the first two paragraphs are clearly designed to deprive women of their right to work for their living, and give the President powers to exterminate others of their right by degrees. We are to be no longer citizens entitled to enjoy equal rights under a democratic constitution, but laws are to be enacted that will take into consideration our 'differences of capacity, physical and moral, and of social function'.

Mr de Valera has been driven to this by the nightmare of unemployment that has been hanging over him for the past few years, and as I have already stated, by his own innate prejudice against women anywhere outside the kitchen.

He thinks that by driving women out of the jobs they are in because they must, like their brothers and fathers, earn their livelihood and that of their dependents, that he will create employment for men. There he is making the mistake of his life.

There is one way, and one way only, of driving women out of competition with men in the comparitively few kinds of work in which they are really in competition, and it is by raising the status of the woman by the enactment of a law that will provide equal pay for equal work. In the event the average employer will employ a man in preference to a woman in practically every kind of work, except office work.

Mr de Valera never has been in contact with, and never will

descend to, the realities of life. He lives in a remote and distant political world of his own where his plans look exceedingly well on paper, and everybody around him is nice and well-ordered and agreeable and rifts in the lute are not discernible.

If he had more contact with the average working man and woman he would know that ninety per cent of the women who work for their living in this country do so because they must. It is only the exceptional woman who prefers working for others to marriage, and she is found to be among the well-off classes rather than among the poor, whom this new legislation is bound most to affect.

Neither do the women of the working classes work after marriage if they can help it: the married woman who continues her work for preference after marriage in conjunction with running a home because she can pay maids to look after it, belongs to a class that will in all probability be comparatively unaffected by the proposed curtailment of women's rights as a citizen.

Since Mr de Valera is so completely out of touch with ordinary people, it would be a bad mistake on his part to judge the general world of women by those in his immediate surroundings, for women who go on working after marriage are the exception and not the rule.

These clauses are obviously aimed in the first instance at women in industry, at the working girl and woman who earns anything from fifteen shillings to a couple of pounds per week. And if you are going to throw these girls out of employment, what are you going to do with them; who is going to feed and clothe them?

Mr de Valera thinks that throwing them out of other work will send them into domestic work . . . In England . . . For we have, as it is, as many girls for domestic service as we require in this country. What is wrong with them is not their quantity, but the quality of their work. There are already as many girls in the domestic service as the country can absorb, unless large fortunes are to be made for a great many people in some mythical way in order to enable them to employ large staffs of maids.

The vast majority of these working girls are only too willing to get married when they have the opportunity, and they are going to have fewer opportunities of marriage if they are badly clothed, badly nourished, and without the means to help either themselves or the mothers and sisters who may be depending on them.

By creating an artificial situation in thrusting men into industries for which they have not the hands or natural taste – and I don't believe it can be done if the time comes to try the experiment – you are not going to force men into marrying when they do not want to marry unless Mr de Valera is to follow the course of Herr Hitler, of whom he appears to be so ardent a disciple, in banning them from certain jobs unless they are married.

Instead, what will actually happen, if the exclusion of women from certain types of work [. . .] comes to pass, is that the larger section of those thrown out of work will go to England, and a certain number of those who remain will be forced into the streets.

These considerations together are too serious for any man who professes to have a moral outlook on life to ignore. The trouble is that Mr de Valera will not face this reality. All his talk about preserving the sanctity of the home is sheer window-dressing: the best way to preserve the sanctity of the home is by giving the daughters as well as the sons a chance to live decently and earn the wage to pay for living decently.

But for the women of Ireland, Mr de Valera would not be in the position he holds today. He was glad enough to make use of them to transport guns and munitions, to carry secret dispatches, and to harbour himself and his colleagues when it was risking life and liberty to do any of these things. If the women had not stood loyally behind the men we might be today no further than we were before 1916. It is harsh treatment, this, in return for all they have done for their country.

It would do well to recall, too, that all the social services we enjoy today were achieved by the fight women made for them, and not by men. Do you think we should have school meals, free milk, school medical inspection, organised welfare help for mother and child, old age pensions, widows' pensions, and so forth if it were not that the demand of these things came from women pioneers who organised the agitation for them? If it were left to men, our social services would be in a sorry state and welfare work non-existent.

It took a Florence Nightingale to organise sick nursing so that it cured rather than killed patients. It took an Elizabeth Fry to bring common humanity into prisons. It took a Josephine Butler to rescue women from being the victims of commercialised vice. Men had made no attempt to tackle any of these things until women not only showed them the way but kept pricking them on from behind to make them do their duty.

If you are going exclude women from the normal participation in affairs for which her particular experience fits her, take from her her God-given right to work for her living, and thrust her back into her status of the Middle Ages when she was little more than a chattel, then the whole life of the country is going to suffer for it.

Apart altogether from the effect on the well-being of the community, and in particular of women and children, any curtailment of women's rights as citizens is going to send the whole body of intelligent women eventually into the arms of communism, which at least promises them fair play. If the Constitution passes with the clauses to which I refer intact, that is going to be the most serious danger of all that will almost certainly result.

Already, the Saorstát is on the black list at Geneva as one of the countries where women have been accorded the worst treatment, despite the supposed equality of our present status. If we are to be relegated to a new status that saddles us with physical and moral incapacity as bread-winners, a new class of country in a category all by itself will have to be created at Geneva, and a nice laughing-stock will be made of us.

I met at the Spring Show an ardent follower of Mr de Valera who was holding forth of what a marvellous person he is and calling him 'the darling'.

I said that he must be a darling all right, but that I had no use for this attitude to women, and I cited the Conditions of Employment Act as an example.

She was an intelligent woman, but she confessed that she had never known about the Act, and had not known what the Constitution was going to do to us and, being a working woman herself, she was extremely and unpleasantly surprised. She said she had never known this side of Mr de Valera's policy.

There you are! The whole thing may be through before the unthinking masses of women realise what has happened. This is not a party question. It is something that every woman in the country will have to watch for herself, and to try to step through the members of her own party by promising her vote only to those who will start forthwith to work to have those clauses amended, giving women the same rights as citizens as men.

Women are in the majority in this country, and if they let themselves be robbed of the rights that it has taken so long to win they are not only themselves going to suffer for their indifference, but their daughters will suffer more for their chances of securing work in the future will be reduced by more than half of what they are at present, and bringing them up at all will be a sheer liability.

When I talked about this to the lady I have mentioned above, I said that the great fault I had to find with Mr de Valera was this reluctance of his to come down to reality, and she sighed and said, 'Ah, but all men run away from reality. I have never yet met a man who would face reality unless he was made to face it.' She was married, and she had grown-up sons, so she ought to know it!

It is up to the women of the country to see that they are not permitted to run away from it in this for them vital instance.

A Difficult Man to Interrupt

JOHN MAFFEY (1939)

The outbreak of the Second World War concentrated British minds on the strategic significance of Ireland and on the uncertainties created by its policy of neutrality. John Maffey, a veteran civil servant, was appointed as the United Kingdom's diplomatic representative to Dublin in 1939 – though, as the following report shows, 'representative' was not a designation with which his interlocutor, Éamon de Valera, was comfortable. Aside from the questions of nomenclature which occupied much of the conversation, the two men were mainly concerned with the delicate state of play in Ireland's territorial waters. Maffey would be an invaluable interpreter of de Valera's somewhat Byzantine mind for the entire period of hostilities. This report, in common with many others prepared by Maffey, was addressed to the Foreign Secretary, Sir Anthony Eden. 'Mr Chamberlain's letter', to which Maffey refers, contained a request for a formalized agreement on British–Irish co-operation to counter U-boats in Irish waters.

Wednesday, 20th September. I did not arrive in Dublin till the evening, my journey via Stranraer and Belfast having taken nearly twenty-four hours from London owing to various delays. I established touch with Mr Walshe, Secretary for External Affairs, by telephone and was told that Mr de Valera would see me that same evening at 8 p.m. if convenient. Mr Walshe came to drive me round.

I was alone with Mr de Valera from 8 p.m. till 9.45. After our first greeting I handed him Mr Neville Chamberlain's letter. I said that I understood that our Prime Minister had addressed him as 'Dear Prime Minister' and that I had learnt that this was not the mode of address which found favour. If incorrect it was an unintentional mistake. He smiled and said that he did not mind and gave me a constitutional lecture, which I did not follow entirely, explaining why 'Prime Minister' was inappropriate. Dominions Office should note this. 'President' is not a good alternative, since the President is President Hyde. 'Mr de Valera' is the best solution.

After asking me whether the letter was germane to our discussion he proceeded to open it with extraordinary difficulty, holding it close to his nose. The reading of it was even more laborious. He obviously made no progress and kept looking away. Finally he said: 'Excuse my difficulty in reading. My sight is very bad and my trip to America, which I have had to cancel, was intended to benefit my eyes.' I asked if I might read it out aloud to him and he gratefully accepted.

When I had finished, he at once turned on the old arguments as to why 'Minister' was a possible title for a United Kingdom agent in Dublin and why 'Representative' was impossible. He is a difficult man to interrupt. But interrupt him you must. He shows no resentment when this happens and his nimble mind is quickly lifted on to the new line you have started.

However, to start with he had a good run on the old scent.

Though he fully saw our difficulties, etc., etc., he could not face the danger and embarrassment resulting from a new and unusual title applied to a new British post. To do so would be to more than undo any possible good results. Every action he took in any matter affecting neutrality or relationship with Great Britain was watched by most critical eyes. He was known to be pro-British in sentiment on the question of the war. No doubt, half or more of his people shared this sentiment. But it was a delicate balance. A clumsy step on his part would lose him much of that support. The striking German successes in the war had produced a good many waverers. That was the way of the world. However, he said, early successes do not mean everything. The way in which suspicion could be excited and susceptibilities aroused in Ireland was beyond belief. For instance, a most natural and proper suggestion had been put forward that some of the women and children evacuated from danger zones in England should be offered hospitality in Éire. It had at once provoked outspoken opposition, as suspicion was aroused that there was 'something behind it'.

It was now time for me to intervene. I said that Mr Chamberlain was concerned somehow or other to find a practical solution to a very grave problem, which would day by day grow more insistent. Éire was pursuing a path of neutrality. She had proscribed submarines in her waters and we acquiesced. But the whole thing was in reality an empty gesture. The last war and German methods generally showed plainly what might and what probably would happen in the secret places of the Irish coast. Already tongues were beginning to wag. [De Valera] must surely see that unless a closer relationship was established in Dublin, unless the Admiralty felt that through that relationship they had established a real liaison with and source of information in the Irish system of watch and ward, any happenings off the Irish coast would start a justifiable outcry and our two Governments would meet in headlong collision simply because we had not established reasonable contacts and collaboration. The same considerations applied to other questions.

The President agreed to this but said that the solution proposed was not acceptable. His Government was not strong enough to take such a step and risk the consequences. If he went, who would come in? There was a delusion in some people's minds that if he went a government of the right would come in. This was utter nonsense. The only alternative to his Government was a government of the left.

I intervened again to say that if he could swallow the word 'Minister' it seemed difficult to see the enormous difference between that and the term 'Representative'. A stand on that point would make it look as if a side issue was being exploited in order to gain a point in the constitutional game. This stung. He exclaimed that any such view was quite unjustified. He could assure me that there was no such thought in his mind. And after all, if it came to a question of quibbles, what were the objections to using the term 'Minister' for a post which would, like that of a High Commissioner, be mainly diplomatic in character. I said that if the King appointed a Minister it could only be done by the procedure applicable to foreign countries, by exequatur, etc. The King could not appoint a Minister to himself. He then went off on the line that he would not expect the same formal methods of appointment to be applied in this case. Let the name be Minister or Ambassador, and he could explain away to his people

the difference in the accrediting on the score that it was a post established to balance his High Commissioner in London and that the
appointment was of a special character as from Government to
Government. I said that we only knew one way of appointing a Minister and a Minister to us had a certain defined meaning. However, in
his reply to Mr Chamberlain's letter he could explain the difficulties
and make his suggestion. I gave no encouragement to the idea, though
it may not be as repellent to some people as it is to others. Therefore
I did not kill it then and there.

I went on to make one or two other points. I said that if representation here in some form was to be arranged it could not be long
delayed. A debate in the House of Commons might at any moment
reveal the natural anxiety in England at seeing other countries,
enemy countries too, represented in Dublin, while we with our old
traditions and our many links today, commercial, cultural and
social, were not represented at all. As it would be doubly difficult
for him to act after such a debate, he would no doubt bear that in
mind.

I also said that in times of grave emergency it was important for
London to know what was in *his* mind. Did we know at present? We
had our doubts. He fully agreed as to this and said where Mr Dulanty
[*the Irish High Commissioner in London: what is being referred to is unclear –*
Ed.] succeeded and where he failed, though I had not intended my
comment to be a criticism of Mr Dulanty. Having so far failed to get
any sign of yielding to the request put forward in Mr Chamberlain's
letter, I turned the conversation in search of a consolation prize.
Whatever happens on the question of a representative, the problem
of *liaison* with our Admiralty in regard to watch and ward along the
coast and the difficulties to be anticipated from the Éire policy of
neutrality remain to be tackled. They would be greatly helped by the
presence of a representative. But they cannot be allowed to drift,
even if we have no representative. I therefore put the Admiralty
difficulty to the President and said: 'It is obvious beyond all dispute
that there must be liaison and information. Otherwise your neutrality will be non-operative and will be a positive danger to us. Do you
agree to the appointment in some unobtrusive way of a liaison officer

representing the Admiralty and having under him in the watch and ward service three or four men, Royal Navy Irishmen preferably, who will be his active agents in promoting the efficiency of your coastal service?'

After some consideration Mr de Valera said that he thought such an arrangement possible. And I said: 'If a submarine is reported in your territorial waters what happens?' He said: 'Information of its whereabouts will be wirelessed at once, not to you specially. Your Admiralty must pick it up. We shall wireless it to the world. I shall tell the German Minister of our intention to do this.' (I am certain *his* wish is to make it thoroughly unhealthy for a German submarine to use Irish waters.)

I said: 'You realise that on receipt of such information our destroyers, if available, would attack wherever the submarine happened to be.' He said: 'We do not want you to take action in our territorial waters.' I said: 'It will happen and you will have to turn the blind eye.' He did not know what to say to this except that if they had information they should find it easy to lie up outside and deal with the enemy. I said that there was too many a slip between the cup and the lip. A submarine could create many perils once having dived out of view.

He said that they needed swift patrol boats, and gear of various kinds in order to deal with these matters themselves. I agreed and said that the Admiralty would certainly help. A patrol of civil aircraft would also greatly help him to gain his objective. He was interested in this suggestion. He spoke of the delay in the supply of anti-aircraft guns and said that though he understood it the delay gave a bad impression in Éire. Could we not hurry matters up?

More than once he asked that these military and naval requirements which are to serve the British should not be charged up against Éire at a high price. I must emphasise his repeated request for consideration in this matter of price. He said that people think they are out of the war and do not approve of the expenditure. Besides, with falling tariffs, we are hard-hit financially. A low scale of prices is of great moment to us.

He turned now to the general questions arising under Eire's neutrality. He had put in the ban on submarines to please us. To balance that he had put a ban on military aircraft. I said that he must not suppose that the ban on our submarines meant nothing to us. Submarines were a weapon in anti-submarine measures. However, we accepted the ban because obviously, broadly speaking, it was to our advantage.

He then reverted to military and naval aircraft. Cases had already occurred of their alighting in the territorial waters of Éire. I said that it would happen again. This upset him somewhat and he asked why. I said: 'Because, no longer having the facilities of the Irish coast, they have to take a longer flight out and back and this lands some of them like "exhausted birds" on your shores. I hope you will go slow with any specific rules about aircraft.' Then he said: 'Shall I leave out all mention of submarines? But I have already communicated with the German and French Governments.' I suggested fuller consultation with London. The whole fabric of neutrality was beginning to look healthier from our point of view. Indeed, at the moment it seems to be in a tangle and the longer it remains so the better. Still an attempt will be made to introduce rules or make a statement. I suggested a vague formula (vide my instructions), viz., a neutrality in general accordance with the practice of international law and a specific formula as to submarines. But the difficulty over the submarine point persists in his mind if he cannot balance it in some way to prove his basic neutrality.

I gathered from Mr Walshe that any mention at present of facilities at Berehaven would upset the applecart. [*This is a reference to British frustration at no longer having the use of the port of Berehaven, in Co. Cork, one of the 'treaty ports' that had been ceded back to the Irish state in 1938 – Ed.*] As progress was being made by me on certain other lines, I thought it best not to jeopardise this progress at present and I hope the First Lord will understand this. Action at Berehaven would undoubtedly shake the President's position. If such action is vital we shall have to take it. But we must think twice and count the gain and the loss. Generally speaking, he revealed to me a much warmer pro-British attitude than on the last occasion. I am sure that he greatly appreciated the fact that Mr Neville Chamberlain had written a personal letter to him. The more that kind of thing can be done, the better.

But, apart from that, in his actions he is definitely showing a bias in our favour, and we must be most careful not to deflect it.

He spoke of his Red Cross campaign. Of course, it is entirely neutral in constitution and aims but everyone knows that it is only the British who can benefit. He said: 'Recruiting is active here for the British forces. We place no obstacle whatsoever in the way. I believe there are as many men recruited here now as in 1914 in spite of all Redmond's big talk. But you would help us and help yourselves if the men did not come into Éire in uniform.'

It is again one of those unreasoning prejudices to which attention must be paid. He had no particular feelings himself about it, except in so far as here lay a source of possible trouble. Perhaps the War Office and Admiralty will take note of this in an understanding spirit.

I now rose to leave and most surprisingly he said: 'I am turning over in my mind the question of "Minister" or "Representative". I shall make a choice after discussion with my constitutional lawyers. I want to examine the case for each of them from every point of view.' This was much more forthcoming than anything I had dared to hope for and shows that some of the seed sown has not been wasted. However, it may well all be reversed again before I leave Dublin.

As I left the room he led me to his black map of Éire with its white blemish on the North East corner and said: 'There's the real source of all our trouble.' He could not let me go without that.

The Trade

MYLES NA GCOPALEEN (1940)

The year 1940 saw the launch of Sean O'Faolain's magazine *The Bell* and, in the pages of the *Irish Times*, the first instalments of Myles na gCopaleen's satirical column 'Cruiskeen Lawn'. In this, his first essay for *The Bell*, the 29-year-old Myles (pseudonym of the civil servant Brian O'Nolan), already author of the extraordinary novel *At Swim-Two-Birds* (of which most of the stock had been destroyed by a German bomb in London), wrote about the place where he was to spend far too much of his time: the pub.

In the last ten years there has been a marked change in the decor of boozing in Dublin. The old-time pub was something in the nature of the Augean stable (it is true that Pegasus was often tethered there) with liberal lashings of sawdust and mopping-rags to prevent the customers from perishing in their own spillings and spewing. No genuine Irishman could relax in comfort and feel at home in a pub unless he was sitting in deep gloom on a hard seat with a very sad expression on his face, listening to the drone of bluebottle squadrons carrying out a raid on the yellow sandwich cheese. In those days a definite social stigma attached to drinking. It was exclusively a male occupation and on that account (and apart from anything temperance advocates had to say) it could not be regarded as respectable by any reasonable woman. Demon rum was a pal of the kind one is ashamed to be seen with. Even moderate drinkers accepted themselves as genteel degenerates and could slink into a pub with as much feline hug-the-wall as any cirrhotic whiskey-addict, there to hide even from each other in dim secret snugs. A pub without a side-door up a lane would have been as well off with no door at all.

Up to recent times the only improvement was the bar parlour, a dark privacy at the rear where any respectable bowler-hatted gentleman from the counting house of a large drapery concern could tinkle

in peace at his hot mid-day whiskey. Such places were clean and comfortable enough, though often equipped with forbidding furniture
of the marble-topped and iron-legged variety usually found in
morgues and fish-shops. Latterly, however, we have had the Lounge,
the Lounge Bar, the Select Lounge, the Oak Lounge, and Octagonal
Lounge, and still more refined booze-shops called brasseries and but-
teries where obsequious servers in white coats will refuse point-blank
to give you beer, even if your doctor has certified under his own hand
that you will drop dead after one glass of spirits.

It is in such places that one can perceive in its full force the Reformation which has been spreading throughout the public house
congregations. The old-fashioned curate, the drinker's confessor and
counsellor, is disappearing. His honest country face, his simple black
clothes, his coatlessness, his apron, and the gleaming steel armbands
on his shirt-sleeves were almost supernatural symbols which invested
the lowliest pub with a feeling of being-with-friend, a homeliness
which many men fail to find in their own houses. He was the repository of every grain of knowledge which could be gathered from a
lifetime of other people's drink-loosened conversations. In one small
head he could contain an incomparable compendium of every known
fact about politics, women, the GAA, and, tucked away in a separate
compartment by itself, a thesaurus of horse-lore not entirely to be
independently unearthed from the Form Book or the Calendar.
Sensing the innate spiritual character of his calling, he served humanity well in his licensed parish.

The white-coated server who has ousted the curate in some pubs
may be taken as a sign of the decline of faith. The Irish brand of
humanity, expansive and voluble, is hardening and contracting under
the hammer-blows of international mammon, dealt through the
radio, press and cinema. Among the stupider section of the younger
generation a shabby and rather comic 'smartness' may be discerned,
even in the simple task of dealing with a bottle of brown stout.

Their cinema-going has taught them the great truth that William
Powell does not walk up to a counter, bellow for a schooner or a
scoop and ask Mick whether the brother is expected up for the match

on Sunday. William is modern and drinks out of glasses with long stems in a cushioned corner with his doxy. His many imitators (what could be more flimsy than an imitation of a flat two-dimensional picture-house ghost?) have insisted on something similar, since they, too, have to go out with Myrna Loy. The Select Lounge has been the handsome answer of the trade in Dublin.

Today there are many of these lounges in the city, even in those areas which people living elsewhere call 'tough quarters'. Some are very good, many are curious travesties of what may be regarded as the publican's conception of paradise. The better places are quiet and comfortable, softly lighted, and a boon to any sensible, tired person who wants a stimulant without being jostled and who does not concern himself with social trends or think that a well-dressed woman in a pub is an outrage that imparts a sourness to the drink.

The other places afford a pathetic insight into the meaning attached to the word 'modern' by many publicans. They think that it means just tubes – tubular chairs, repellent alike to eye and seat, tubular lighting, tubular effects in decoration. Those who have been to a prison immediately recognise the lamentable simplicity of the decor and the severity of the furnishings. The ugliness of such a tavern cannot be completely offset by the fact that most of the customers appear to be film-stars or that the man who serves you is a bell-hop from New York.

Here let us digress to touch upon a very important irrelevancy. The lower orders (non-car-owners and the like) are excluded from all these lounges, sometimes by an impudent surcharge on the already extortionate price of drink, nearly always by outlawing the pint, which is the only cheap nourishing light beer that can be had. Although probably more than half of the money amassed by any publican has been made from selling pints of porter, the pint-drinker is rigidly confined to his outer corral, far away from the heat and the soft seats; he never even sees the fancy clock that has no numbers on its face, only a dot for each hour. Some publicans, equipped with the odious sham-gentility which money earned by astute trading confers on humble folk, justify this nonsense by a process of reasoning too torturous to record. One well-known argument is that 'the lads would not go in there if you paid them'. In a country which is held to be democratic and in which writers and labourers are on the same economic place, it is an impertinence which should be challenged by some public-spirited person at the annual licensing sessions, if only to make 'himself' explain his quaint social theories in public.

One wonders what Mr James Montgomery would think of it all. Mr Montgomery is one of the select band of Dublin gentlemen who knew the Dublin pub-life of the old days and who contributed his own big share of whatever ambrosial vitamin made that generation of drinkers and thinkers immortal. (We cannot help wondering, myself, the printer and the Editor, whether a compliment can also be libel.) Other veterans, happily still encounterable, are Seamus O'Sullivan and famous Martin Murphy of the Gaiety Theatre. If they could be persuaded to tell the tale (or 'write it down' in a manner of people who summon their neighbours for using unmentionable language) they could fill *The Bell* for many issues with material that would make it a standard work of reference for anybody who wants to dig under the callused skin of Dublin.

They could tell about the beginnings of the United Arts Club, conceived in Neary's snug (or maybe in MacCormack's of South King Street) by the boisterous Count Markievicz. If you turn into Chatham Street today and mount the stairs inside the Neary hall-door, you will find yourself in a seductive den (Select Lounge is the correct term) probably never dreamt of by the Count. Here the authorities had the sense to employ a real artist, Miss Bradshaw, rather than a distant Japanese technician, to enliven the walls with pictures.

The only other public-house that comes to mind in this connexion is Higgins's Waterloo Bar at the bottom of Waterloo Road. Here the far-sighted proprietor, who also owns another pub in Pembroke Street and in person resembles [Fritz] Kreisler, had the enlightenment within him to retain Mr Brendan O'Connor to design his lounge and Mr Desmond Rushton to leave his mark upon the walls. The result is a combination of utility (functional something-or-other architects call it), comfort and restraint – but no pints. All sorts may be seen here of an evening, front and rear.

> Sometimes carters slacken rein,
> Sometimes exiles come again,
> Or a pilgrim you will see
> On the way to Mellary.

Davy Byrne's in Duke Street, the Bailey Restaurant nearly opposite, and the underground Bodega in Dame Street are licensed tabernacles sanctified by the past attendances of people with names like Orpen, Gogarty, Griffith, Murphy, Furlong, Montgomery, McKenna, even Joyce, not to mention the Toucher Doyle, the Bird Flanagan and his relative, the Pope. (Who will pretend that these are not ordinary surnames that can be borne by anybody?) All three still open their doors at ten o'clock and possibly shelter today the makings of a second fame – the same again. They are run by new if cognate personalities and none has found any necessity to have recourse to the blandishments of the Select Lounge. The premises bear openly the marks of their departed guests, like traces of fresh stout found in a glass by a policeman after hours; but they still look prosperous, not like banquet-halls deserted.

The bar of the Ormond Hotel and Barney Kiernan's down the quays were other centres of intellectual sodality. Barney's was a dim and venerable backwater where an argument could be pursued hour by hour without interruption, with casks all around to receive the resounding fist. Fanning's of Lincoln Place had and has a similar fame. Some of the distinguished guests in Fanning's, guzzling the uniformly good drink, will tell you that the intransigence of the distinguished boss's political beliefs can sometimes lend an unwelcome uniformity to his conversation.

Today, as in the past, birds of a feather tend to flutter into the same snug. Grogan's of Leeson Street and Higgins's of Pembroke Street are noted for the punctilious attendances of students from 'National'; Trinity students have their names marked on the roll at Davy Byrne's. Mulligan's in the narrow street which runs alongside the Theatre

Royal caters for painted ladies and painted men – the theatrical kind, often straight from the stage. Most people connected with show business make their way here, and Mr Mulligan has recently provided a new Lounge for their further entertainment and approval.

The Palace Bar in Fleet Street is the main resort of newspapermen, writers, painters and every known breed of artist and intellectual. Porter is served willingly everywhere in the house, and in fancy tankards. The clients range from the tiniest elfin intellectual to a large editor, alive and in good condition. [*Presumably R. M. Smyllie, editor of the* Irish Times – *Ed.*] Looking at the editor, one frequently sees the left hand flung out as if in demonstration of some wide generous idea; actually, however, it is merely a claw in search of a cigarette, a modest tax that is gladly paid by listening neophytes. The editor is unconscious of this mannerism; he is king in this particular Palace and merely exercises a ruling-class prerogative.

The portioning-off idea which dominates the scheme of the lounges at Doran's of Marlboro' Street and O'Mara's of Aston's Quay seem to attract clients who have weighty secrets to exchange – lovers and the like. The Scotch House on Burgh Quay is famous for the mellowness and good colour of its whiskey and civil servants. It was stated officially recently in the newspapers that the Dolphin Hotel is noted for its 'sporting crowd' and 'racing people'; whatever about the horses, it bounds in suede shoes and jackets with two splits. Probably the oldest licence and the oldest pub in Dublin is the Brazen Head Hotel, an old coaching house down the quays, one-time resort of Robert Emmet and the United Irishmen. Here the most random spit will land on ten centuries of antiquity. 'Professional gentlemen' as they are called by landladies – doctors, lawyers, architects, and that ilk – do a lot of their drinking in the Metropole. The Red Bank, the Wicklow Hotel, the various Mooney's, Madigan's of Earl Street, and McArdle's of South King Street are popular with all creeds and classes.

When many of Ireland's staid rulers of today were younger and on the run, they ran sometimes towards Rathfarnham, frequently in the Parnell Street direction. Devlin's, Kennedy's and Kirwan's in that thoroughfare were places where Miss Ní-h-Uallacháin was served without question, even though the lady no longer lived in her guardian's house and was wanted by the police. Michael Collins often drank a bottle of stout in the bar of Vaughan's hotel. In Dan Dunne's of distant Donnybrook, as Batt O'Connor relates, he once, leaning back, touched a hanging bell-push with his head. The man of the house promptly cut down the bell-push and proudly showed it afterwards to customers as his most famous and cherished possession. Not even the jagged wire can be seen today, for Time, that bedfellow of all publicans, has erased the whole public-house.

At ten o'clock on week nights and at half-nine on Saturday the tide ebbs suddenly, leaving the city high and dry. Unless you are staying at a hotel or visiting a theatre, you may not lawfully consume excisable liquors within the confines of the county borough. The city has entered that solemn hiatus, that almost sublime eclipse known as the Closed Hours. Here the law, as if with the true Select Lounge mentality, discriminates sharply against the poor man at the pint counter by allowing those who can command transport and can embark upon a journey to drink elsewhere until morning. The theory is that all travellers still proceed by stage-coach and that those who travel outside become blue with cold after five miles and must be thawed out with hot rum at the first hostelry they encounter by night or day. In practice, people who are in the first twilight of inebriation are transported from the urban to the rural pub so swiftly by the internal combustion engine that they need not necessarily be aware that they have moved at all, still less comprehend that their legal personalities have undergone a mystical transfiguration. Whether this system is regarded as a scandal or a godsend depends largely on whether one owns a car. At present the city is ringed round with these 'bona-fide' pubs, many of them well-run modern houses, and a considerable amount of the stock-in-trade is transferred to the stomachs of the customers at a time every night when the sensible and the just are in their second sleeps. Coolock, Tallaght, Templeogue, Santry, Lucan, Ballydown, Cabinteely, Shankill, Fox-and-Geese and Stepaside are a few of the villages where there is revelry by night. Stepaside in recent years has been notable for the engaging personality of Mr James Whelan, who has now, however, forsaken the dram-shop for the farm. The Lamb Doyle's nearby, cocked high up near Ticknock, was a favourite point of pilgrimage of a summer Sunday for the boys of Casimir Markievicz's day. It is still there, though under new and female management.

To go back to the city: it appears that the poor man does not always go straight home at ten o'clock. If his thirst is big enough and he knows the knocking-formula, he may possibly visit some house where the Demand Note of the Corporation has stampeded the owner into a count of illicit after-hour trading. For trader and customer alike, such a life is one of excitement, tip-toe and hush. The boss's ear, refined to shades of perception far beyond the sensitivities of any modern aircraft detector, can tell almost the inner thoughts of any policeman in the next street. At the first breath of danger all lights are suddenly doused and conversation toned down, as with a knob, to vanishing point. Drinkers reared in such schools will tell you that in inky blackness stout cannot be distinguished in taste from Bass and that no satisfaction whatever can be extracted from a cigarette unless the smoke is seen. Sometimes the police make a catch. Here is the sort of thing that is continually appearing in the papers:

Guard —— said that accompanied by Guard —— he visited the premises at 11.45 p.m. and noticed a light at the side door. When he knocked, the light was extinguished, but he was not admitted for six minutes. When the defendant opened eventually, he appeared to be in an excited condition and used bad language. There was nobody at the bar but there were two empty pint measures containing traces of fresh porter on the counter. He found a man crouching in a small press containing switches and a gas-meter. When he attempted to enter the yard to carry out a search, he was obstructed by the defendant, who used an improper expression. He arrested him, but owing to the illness of his wife, he was later released.

Defendant: Did you give me an unmerciful box in the mouth?
Witness: No.
Defendant: Did you say that you would put me and my gawn of a brother through the back wall with one good haymaker of a clout the next time I didn't open when you knocked?

Witness: No.

Justice: You look like a fine block of man yourself. How old are you?

Defendant: I'm as grey as a badger, but I'm not long past forty. (*Laughter*.)

Justice: Was the brother there at all?

Defendant: He was away in Kells, your worship, seeing about getting a girl for himself. (*Laughter*.)

Justice: Well, I think you could give a good account of yourself.

Witness: He was very obstreperous, your worship.

Witness, continuing, said that he found two men standing in the dark in an outhouse. They said they were there 'for a joke'. Witness also found an empty pint measure in an outdoor lavatory and two empty bottles of Cairnes.

Defendant said that two of the men were personal friends and were being treated. There was no question of taking money. He did not know who the man in the press was and did not recall having seen him before. He had given strict instructions to his assistant to allow nobody to remain on after hours. There was nobody in the press the previous day as the gasman had called to inspect the meter. The two Guards had given him an unmerciful hammering in the hall. His wife was in ill-health, necessitating his doing without sleep for three weeks. A week previously he was compelled to send for the Guards to assist in clearing the house at ten o'clock. He was conducting the house to the best of his ability and was very strict about the hours.

Guard —— said that the defendant was a decent hard-working type but was of an excitable nature. The house had a good record. Remarking that defendant seemed a decent sort and that the case was distinguished by the absence of perjury, the Justice said he would impose a fine of twenty shillings, the offence not to be endorsed. Were it not for the extenuating circumstances he would have no hesitation in sending the defendant to Mountjoy for six months. He commended Guards —— and —— for smart police work.

Not many publicans, however, will take the risk. If they were as careful of their souls as they are of their licences, heaven would be packed with those confidential and solicitous profit-takers and, to please them, it might be necessary to provide an inferior annex to paradise to house such porter-drinkers as would make the grade.

Paddy of the RAF

A. J. LIEBLING (1941)

A. J. Liebling joined the staff of the *New Yorker* in 1935, and moved to Europe in October 1939 to cover the Second World War. His famous profile of the Irish RAF pilot Brendan Finucane was published on 6 December 1941 – the day before the bombing of Pearl Harbor, which drew the US into the war. Finucane, whose father had fought alongside Éamon de Valera in 1916, was the RAF's most successful fighter pilot until his death in action in 1942, when his plane went down in the English Channel after a sortie over France.

The few British fighting men who have become popular legends during this war have done so without the connivance of His Majesty's Government. German and Russian communiqués are studded with the names of individual heroes, but even the RAF, although garrulous compared to the British Army and Navy, believes fliers should be almost anonymous. Whereas the Luftwaffe would announce that the late Werner Molders had shot down his ninety-ninth plane – and, incidentally, British airmen would take no stock in his score – the Air Ministry says merely that a pilot attached to one of its squadrons scored his eleventh victory. Weeks later, perhaps when the pilot is due for a decoration, his name will appear in the *London Gazette*, a government newspaper few civilians read. For this reason, a high score is not enough in itself to make a fighter pilot a new personality. He has to have some particularity that the public can remember.

Flight Lieutenant Brendan Finucane – Distinguished Service Order and Distinguished Flying Cross with two bars – has established himself in the public mind by being profoundly Irish, so Irish that strangers spontaneously address him as Paddy, which is also what his friends call him. He is neither Ulster Irish nor Anglo-Irish nor public-school-and-Oxford denatured Irish but middle-class Dublin Irish, and so proud of it that he has a big shamrock painted on his

Spitfire. It is a shamrock designed by the adoring Yorkshire rigger and Canadian fitter who look after his plane. The shamrock has the initials 'B. F.' in the centre and is surrounded by thorns. The rigger says he knows that thorns belong on a rose, but he feels they are appropriate, and Paddy agrees with him. The same rigger once, after the pilot had shot down his twenty-first plane, thought he would please him by painting twenty-one little swastikas around the periphery of the shamrock. Paddy got angry at this, saying they were an affectation of elegance, and made the rigger remove them. Paddy is twenty-one years and a couple of weeks old, and has a boyish eagerness to avoid any implication of swank. The way he got his most serious war injury fits in almost miraculously with his public personality; he broke his right foot jumping over a wall at a wake.

Being Irish is not itself a rare distinction in the RAF. At least five hundred citizens of Éire wear pilots' wings on their tunics and about fifty have been decorated. What made Paddy identifiable even before the public knew his name was his being both Irish and attached to an Australian squadron. When the Londoner at his breakfast table reads, for example, about a Polish pilot in the RAF shooting down a plane, he has no way of knowing whether or not it is the same Pole he read about last Thursday, but the designation 'an Irish pilot officer attached to an Australian squadron', which began to thread its way through the communiqués last June, gave Paddy his public identity. Subsequently the Londoner could follow Paddy's promotions as well as his triumphs, because the communiqués, which early last summer mentioned him as an Irish pilot officer (a pilot officer being the equivalent of an American second lieutenant), later spoke of him as a flying officer and then as a flight lieutenant. The last rank is like our captaincy. Finucane's decorations piled up even faster. He began the summer with a Distinguished Flying Cross left over from 1940, when, as a comparative novice, he had shot down five 'certains', as the unquestionably disposed-of planes are called, in the Battle of Britain. As the summer progressed, he added two bars to the cross, and then, just before his birthday, he received the Distinguished Service Order. A couple of days later he broke his foot. By that time he had accumulated twenty-three 'certains' and about a dozen 'probables'. He doesn't try to remember the planes he damages but does not bring down.

There are a good many men in the RAF who think Flight Lieutenant Finucane is the most accomplished fighter pilot of the war, although he has not actually downed the most planes. In support of their argument, they point out that he made almost all his kills last summer and that 1941 was a poorer season for German planes than 1940 had been. Firth, Paddy's Yorkshire rigger, holds this point of view. In 1940, he says, there were 'hoondreds of Jerries – all you'd to do was fly oop in air and poosh booton. But this year, when Paddy wants one, he has to go to France for it.' Also, the technique of air fighting has been much refined since 1940. As there has been no general melee this year, German and British veterans alike have had time to teach the new pilots their tricks. None of the other pilots in Paddy's outfit, Squadron 452, had fought before last June, though they were the pick of the first lot to enter training in Australia. They had continued their training in Canada and Scotland. Paddy, who had been in the RAF since 1938, joined them last spring at their first fighter station, which was in England, with the assignment of teaching them by example. They were the high-scoring squadron in England in August and September. They were nosed out by the American Eagle Squadron in October, while Paddy was nursing his foot, as he still is.

The wake at which Paddy broke his foot was expressly an Australian fliers' variant of the rite. All squadron members leave a couple of extra shillings in a kitty each time they settle their mess bills; then, when a pilot goes missing, the survivors drink up what he has left. The day before this particular observance, a sergeant pilot had been shot down over France. He had left two pounds ten, which was enough to finance only a modest wake. That, Paddy says, is why it was emotion and not drink which was responsible for his accident. The sergeant had been a close pal of his, and when, at the party, Paddy came upon a wall, he decided to jump over it, as a gesture of respect. There was a blackout, he says, and the wall looked like any other wall in the same circumstances. However, there happened to be a twenty-foot drop into an areaway on the other side, so he broke his foot. He was consoled a couple of days later by the news that the sergeant was safe in a prison camp. 'In a way, the whole party was a waste,' he says, 'but I don't bear him any hard feeling.' The hospital ward to which he was immediately afterward assigned was devoted entirely to RAF leg injuries, and every pilot present, except himself, had been hurt either in a motorbike accident or a rugby match. This excess of animal spirits may result in the loss of some flying hours, but it is also a sign that the men are in prime condition.

Paddy Finucane is an unusually serious young fighting man except when he is actually in the midst of the Australians, which is perhaps why he likes them so much. One Australian flight lieutenant, called Blue because he has such red hair, says, 'We had to teach Paddy to play the fool when he came to us. The poor man had been with an English squadron so long he was trying to act dignified.' The Australians, though few of them are older than Paddy – one pilot officer with a magnificent drooping mustache is nineteen – are relatively worldly types. One, upon returning recently from what the fliers call a sweep, remarked that he had shot a German into the Channel and that after the plane had struck, a bright-green stain had appeared on the surface of the water, something he had never seen before. 'Heavy creme-de-menthe drinker, no doubt,' he concluded. Most of them, before joining the Force, were university undergraduates or students in Australian public schools, whereas Paddy, right before he enlisted in the RAF, was an assistant bookkeeper in an office in London. Yet today, on all questions pertaining to air fighting, the Australians defer to Paddy's advice and obey his instructions. When he is flying with them, he sometimes, by radio-telephone, directs four dogfights simultaneously. 'Has one of those beautifully efficient minds that work along just one line,' a disciple of his says. 'He can remember the positions of a dozen planes at once, although they change by the split second. And he has phenomenal eyes. Some fellows say Paddy smells Messerschmitts, but what really happens is that he sees them before anybody else can.'

This exceptional vision may be the one quality all great pilots have in common. Once Paddy's mates saw him going after two Messerschmitt 109 F's, of which he downed one. The second plane flew into a cloud and was lost to view. Finucane flew in after it, opened fire while in the cloud, and a moment later flew out of the other side as the German fell out of it, trailing flames. Another time, when the Australians and a New Zealand squadron were taking part in a sweep, Paddy, three miles away, saw some Messerschmitts flying near the New Zealanders and warned them before they were aware of their own danger. He isn't a 'suicide fighter', his comrades say. He will sometimes maneuver his section for five or ten minutes before he sends it in to the kill, but when he does, every Spitfire is apt to be on a German plane's tail. 'The idea isn't just to get a plane for yourself,' Finucane himself says. 'You want to see the other fellows get some shooting, too.' He derives more pleasure from helping a new pilot to his first certain than out of increasing his own bag. Paddy thinks his squadron is perfect. 'All the Australians are mad,' he says in a tone of heartiest approbation. 'Waggle your wings, and they'll follow you through hell and high.'

Paddy is of almost exactly medium weight and height; he is probably an inch too short for the New York police force. He boxed as a welterweight on the RAF team in a match against the combined Scottish universities just before the war began, which means he weighed a hundred and forty-seven pounds, or ten stone seven in the national jargon. He is a few pounds heavier when he isn't in boxing trim, and he has the strong neck, the wide cheekbones, and the broad jaw of a good Irish ring type. He has wavy dark-brown hair, blue eyes, and a pink-and-white complexion that looks like a soap ad; he reddens to his ears when flustered. He was wild about boxing until he turned to air fighting, which he thinks a more exhilarating form of competition, and constantly draws analogies between the two. 'Some pilots roll better to their right than to their left,' he may say, 'the way some boxers move better to one side.' Or he says, 'You have to take the play from the other fellow, just like boxing. I don't let them dither around.' It isn't that Paddy is frivolous or brutal; in his direct way, he has made a mental adjustment that he couldn't have bought from a psychoanalyst for under a million dollars. 'The personality never enters my mind,' he says. 'I always think to myself, I'm just shooting down a machine. Some things get you rather angry, though,' he adds. 'For instance, if they shoot at our chaps after they've bailed out. That's like hitting a man when he's down.' He has never seen this happen, he explains, but he has talked to fellows who say they have. He used to like rugby almost as well as boxing. When the Army beat the RAF at rugby this fall, 30–3, Paddy took it as hard as missing three Germans. He watched the game on crutches.

He has never been shot down or wounded or forced to bail out, although during the 1940 hurly-burly he got a number of bullets through various Spitfires he was piloting. All last summer his planes went unscathed, a proof of his skill at maneuvering. Pilots like to find a couple of bullet holes in their planes after they get safely back to the airdromes, because it gives them something to talk about at mess. Once this year Paddy landed with holes in the tail fin of his plane, but they proved to have been made by the branches of a tree he had scraped. His rigger and fitter say he was much disappointed. He has never fought in anything but Spitfires, and has had them in all their editions. During the summer he ran through five planes – three early Spits and two of the latest Spit fives. He cracked up two machines on his own airdromes, stunting near the ground. Stunting is an officially discouraged but universal custom among fighting pilots. He is very careful about selecting a plane; he not only puts it through all the tricks he knows but he fires several trial bursts with its cannon and machine guns. If a cannon jams, he gets out instantly and walks away from the machine. Once he has picked a Spit, he leaves it in the care of his rigger and fitter, who work with an armorer, an electrician, and a radio man. Aircraftsmen in the last three categories take care of three planes apiece, so they are not identified with one pilot as a rigger and a fitter are. Finucane does not fancy himself an engineering shark. When he comes in from a sweep, he may say to his retainers, 'She's flying left wing down,' or 'right wing down', but he leaves the remedy to the ground crew. This delights them. Firth, the rigger, who is dark, solid, and snaggle-toothed, says, 'When Spit's been in dogfight, she's oopsey.' His tone implies that the ordeal is rather like a childbirth for a delicate woman. Moore, the fitter, who is small and blond, says, 'Some officers get a big head when they down one or two planes, but not

Paddy.' They both carry decks of snapshots of Finucane in their pockets.

After Paddy has chosen a plane, his shamrock and the letter 'W' are painted on it. Each plane in a squadron is identified by a letter, as moviegoers who saw *Target for Tonight* know. Senior pilots usually get low letters, but Finucane insists on his 'W', for sentimental reasons. It stands for Wheezy Anna, a nickname he gave his first Spit because its engine made such strange sounds. In those days the RAF was short of planes and young pilots took what they could get. 'Wheezy was a good old girl,' Paddy says. 'I cracked her up so hard I had the mark of the stick on my chest for a month.'

When Paddy is on leave, as he is now on account of his foot, he lives with his parents, a small brother named Joseph, and two sisters, Monica and Claire, aged eleven and seven, in Richmond, the London suburb south of Kew. He has another brother, Raymond Patrick, who is nineteen and a sergeant air gunner in the Bomber Command. The house looks like several thousand others in suburban London and America. It is Tudor of a recent vintage, complete with the part of irregular concrete flagstones from gate to front door. Paddy's father is a night office manager at an airplane-parts factory that works the clock around. He is black-haired, energetic, witty, and a firm teetotaller. He looks a good deal younger than his forty-nine years and used to be an amateur soccer star in Ireland. Mr Finucane pronounces his surname 'Finewcan', but Paddy says 'Finoocan'. Paddy, who admires his father, has never developed a taste for beer or whiskey. Recently, in an effort to keep up with the Australians, he has learned to order a bottled drink called Pimm's No. 1, which is like a sweet Tom Collins. Mrs Finucane is good-natured and hospitable. When Joe, the small brother, gets home from school, his favorite reading is a monthly publication called *Rockfist Rogan of the RAF*, the adventures of a British Superman with a war slant. Rockfist, typically, will jump from his flying plane into that of a wounded brother pilot, drag him from the cockpit, and make a double parachute jump to safety, perhaps lassoing the propeller of a Heinkel on the way down and hauling the crew into captivity. This serial greatly increases Joe's respect for his older brothers. Paddy himself prefers more realistic books about flying. There is a recently published one called 'Fighter Pilot', which he describes as wizard, his favorite adjective of praise. He uses it, too, to describe the two Australian flight lieutenants who roomed with him at the airdrome up to the time of his jumping over the wall. One, the red-haired fellow called Blue, is addicted to mystery stories and the other reads poetry, forms of composition which Paddy runs down at every opportunity, out of a spirit of contradiction. The poetical Australian says he knows Paddy has a poetic soul, a suggestion that drives Paddy into a picturesque fury. The mystery-story Australian, who has downed ten German planes, wears the jacks of spades, hearts, clubs, and diamonds inked on his 'Mae West', as the fliers call their bulbous yellow inflatable life-saving jackets, because these cards are the sign of a fictional detective he admires. The mantelpiece in the Finucanes' dining-sitting room is decorated with cut-outs of Snow White and the Seven Dwarfs made by Monica, a large square clock with an inscription saying it was presented to Flight Lieutenant Brendan Finucane by the night staff at the factory where his father works, and a bronze cigarette-lighter in the form of an aircraftsman spinning a propeller. This last is a gift to Paddy from his girl friend. He doesn't think it a good idea to get married during the war, he says, because 'someday I might be going on a sweep and I would have it in the back of my head that I wanted to get back that night and that would distract me'. Even now, he acknowledges, he sometimes has 'a funny feeling in my tummy' just before he takes off, and he is afraid that marriage might make it funnier. He is a devout Catholic and attends Mass whenever he gets a chance. The Australians, he says regretfully, are 'free and easy' about spiritual matters. He gives you a feeling that this worries him a little. He is always worrying about the fellows he flies with. Blue says that Paddy once woke him at four in the morning by shouting 'Break, Blue! There's a Messerschmitt on your tail!' 'I guess he dreams about air fighting all night,' Blue says.

The Finucanes' move from Dublin to Richmond took place early in 1938. In Dublin, Paddy had attended a wonderful institution of learning called the O'Connell School, where the headmaster was a retired Army officer who had held a service boxing title. Like headmasters the world over, this one believed in his own favorite sport as a character-builder. Every morning at eight-thirty, according to Paddy, the boys were turned out under a large shed in the schoolyard and told to whack each other. Paddy developed such a taste for whacking that the future pattern of his life lay clear before him when he came to England; he was destined to be a fighter pilot. He was too young to enlist in the RAF immediately, so he worked without pleasure at an office job until May, 1938. Then, on the precise day that he became seventeen years and six months old, the minimum age allowed, he enrolled for a course leading to a short-term commission. Richmond had seemed somewhat humdrum after the O'Connell School, and the Finucane brothers, during their first few months there, found the English rather 'standoffish'. After Paddy joined the RAF things went much better. He is still, however, a vocally patriotic Dubliner. Being an RAF officer, he does not go in for political arguments, he explains, but occasionally somebody says something about Éire which betrays a lack of understanding, and then Paddy puts him right.

War News in the Country

ELIZABETH BOWEN (1942)

British intelligence-gathering in Ireland during the Second World War took many forms. The novelist Elizabeth Bowen's dispatches to the UK Dominions Office and Ministry of Information – over her married name Elizabeth Cameron – followed some of her frequent visits to her ancestral home at Bowen's Court in north Cork during the war, and shed light on Ireland's public moods at the time. The unexpected warmth of her pen-picture of John Charles McQuaid, who had been appointed the Catholic Archbishop of Dublin two years earlier, is testimony to the personal magnetism this young reforming prelate (as he then was) must have exercised in those early years. The file name for this dispatch indicates that it was sent to the Dominions Office.

In this rural part of Éire (Co. Cork, approximately 135 miles from Dublin), which is, I suppose, typical, I notice a very much greater degree of cut-offness, since last year, with regard to up-to-date war news. This for two reasons – (1) The scarcity, and late arrival of newspapers; even the local paper, the *Cork Examiner*, does not reach the village until the late afternoon of each day. (2) The difficulty, nearing impossibility, of obtaining new high-tension batteries for wireless sets. Wireless sets, other than those run on electricity (ESB or the plants of the big houses), are gradually going out of commission. Almost all the cottage wireless sets are now silent, and likely to remain so.

The break in the habit of listening in is energetically regretted by the country people. Cottages that had wireless were much frequented by neighbours after working hours. Young men and boys who did not possess a wireless had the habit of walking miles in the evening to listen in at a friend's house – always to the war news.

The virtual suspension of wireless, and the greater difficulty in

obtaining newspapers, only bring into prominence the keen interest felt by rural South Irish people in the progress of the war. I
have gathered opinions on this from many people – employers of
labour. All are struck by the intelligence, the grip and the up-to-
dateness shown, on the subject of war news, by country working
men. The interest would appear to be keener than in many parts of
rural England.

In this, I notice a contrast between the Irish country and Dublin.
Dublin was more apathetic. In the country the men (though not, I
think, the women) are keen readers of newspapers – even when these
are, owing to present conditions, a day or two out of date. The
increasing uselessness of country wireless sets is felt as a deprivation
and injury. At those informal gatherings of country working men
that go on in the evenings, at the crossroads and bridges, I am told
(and can gather from what I have overheard) that 'they talk of nothing else but the war'.

As people from England, my husband and I are constantly, eagerly
questioned by everybody we meet. It becomes impossible to transact
any business, in an office or shop, until there has been about ten minutes' conversation about the war.

The pros and cons of the second front question are eagerly debated.
I would say there was passionate interest in the war as a topic; and
at the same time, there is a dispassionate tone to discussions, as few
people are willing to declare themselves *parti pris* on either side.

I have met, and heard of, almost no explicit pro-German feeling in
this part of Éire. But there continues to be manifest an almost superstitious admiration for the German fighting technique.

One psychological explanation of this interest in the war is that it
is a form of escapism. With regard to Éire domestic affairs the country people are at once bored and depressed. A sense of immediate
dullness, fretted by deprivations, seems to cloud life here. 'The war'
stands for drama, events in a big way, excitement. All this appeals to
the Irish temperament.

The leader in today's (July 31st) *Cork Examiner* appears to give
point to this theory of mine. The leader, headed 'The Uninformed
Citizen', rebukes Irishmen for substituting war interest for interest in

his own local affairs – particularly, the forthcoming local elections. It says: –

The average man nowadays can give quite a good account of himself in any argument concerning the military possibilities in Europe, Africa or the Far East, whereas in matters nearer home he remains dumb and uninformed unless they directly and obviously affect himself or his livelihood. The bend of the Don, the commanding heights of the Ruweizat Ridge, the sinkings in the Caribbean, are everyday topics, and subjects of self-instruction from the daily Press, while the conduct of affairs in the citizen's own town, or his country, is followed with only a hazy interest by no means comparable to the avid consumption of communiqués and the outpourings of military correspondents ... The man who turns his back to glance at the map of Russia and wheels around to discover that in the interim some of his personal rights have been whittled away by some order or other, has nobody to blame but himself. It is his duty to himself and his neighbour to keep in touch, as well as he can, with what is going on around him at home, and to make his voice felt in the Government of the nation. He can do so by paying as much attention to the reading of reports of the meetings of the Dáil, Senate, and local councils as he does to the plans and deeds of foreign generals and soldiers on fields thousands of miles away. Very shortly he will be given one of the very rare opportunities afforded to citizens of voicing satisfaction or dissatisfaction, when he will be asked to go to the polls in the local elections. We wonder whether he will be too busy, engaging in discussions about the Caucasus or the Suez Canal, to spare time to inquire into the qualifications of the candidates and to vote for the man he thinks best fitted to preside over the general conduct of local government in his borough, county, or urban area?

It is to be noted that the *Cork Examiner* is a Cosgravite, or Opposition newspaper. All Opposition people that I have met are suspicious of the devices used by the Government to distract attention while they put something across. (Overtly, the forthcoming local elections are to be non-political in character – or rather, candidates are expected to disassociate themselves from Party issues outside the local field – but a general consensus of opinion seems to regard this as, for Éire,

Utopian. The local elections are, therefore, likely to serve as a straw ballot, and their outcome is being keenly awaited by politicians, who are anxious to stimulate all the interest possible. I subscribe to the *Cork Examiner*'s view that the *ordinary* man, so far, regards the elections with apathy. There are many grumbles at their having been fixed for the middle of harvest time. This, the countryman regards as a bit of typical 'Dublinism'.) The prominence given to war news in the *Irish Press* (the official Government paper) might support the Cosgravite contention that the Government is exploiting the people's interest in 'foreign generals and soldiers on fields thousands of miles away', in order to distract attention from the management (? or mismanagement) of affairs at home.

[. . .]

Mr Dillon's criticisms of his country-people, however tonic, are probably delivered rather too harshly and ruthlessly. Accordingly, they are resented. At the same time, I do notice that the Irish, both in Dublin and in the country, are becoming more self-critical. I notice this change even since this time last year. Self-complacency has waned with self-confidence. People are inclined to say, 'We are getting slack.' This is given point to by the droppings off, and increasing slackness, in the LSF. Also, to an extent, among all voluntary workers for 'Emergency' services. (Though, Dublin continues to man its ARP posts night and day.) The original inspiring sentiment has lapsed. What is more important is that the people seem to be conscious of, and ashamed of, its lapsing.

At the beginning of the war, Éire, prepared to defend her neutrality, claimed the right to regard herself as a land of heroes. Now, most of the heroic illusion has been stripped from Irish neutrality. (Possibly Mr Dillon's speeches may have done something towards this.) Now, neutrality seems to be seen as a dreary and negative state – the sheer negative of 'not being in the war'. Its glory – as being Éire's first autonomous gesture – appears to fade.

The people are candid enough, with regard to themselves, to admit this drop in height. Hence, a good deal of self-dissection that has gone on lately. The atmosphere reminds me a little of the atmosphere in England in the year after Munich. It would be much too much to say that the people would feel relief if they were to be precipitated into the war. But participation in the war is not regarded with the same superstitious horror as it was two years ago. [. . .]

The Archbishop of Dublin

On July 10th I had tea with the RC Archbishop of Dublin, Dr McQuaid, at his house in Glasnevin Road. I had, and have, heard it said that Dr McQuaid is anti-Protestant. But he seems to have taken trouble to keep in touch with Protestant friends of his in Dublin. It was through one of these – Professor Constantia Maxwell, of TCD – that I met him.

Miss Maxwell proposed our visit to the Archbishop on the grounds of my being interested in social work. Dr McQuaid takes a keen interest in technical schools, housing, clubs, people's restaurants, etc. Part of our conversation was on these subjects. The municipal school of cookery (on the north side of Dublin) he strongly supports. He is anxious to raise the Irish standard of living, to improve the amenities of the home. He showed me the curricula of the cookery school, and other technical schools; unfortunately, these had just closed for the vacation, so that, though I could have seen over the premises, I could not have seen the classes at work.

Dr McQuaid said that the Irishwoman had (as a housewife) much to learn from the Frenchwoman. He appeared to believe that she might learn it . . . He is an enthusiast on the subject of France: has lived there, has many French friends. The greater part of our conversation was, in fact, about France.

The Archbishop said that, much as he had felt for the French humiliation, he could not regret (for France's sake) the fall of the Third Republic. As a form of government for France he had regarded this as pernicious because it was not representative. He is in favour of Marshal Petain's work, first of all, as a movement of decentralisation – one calculated to return to the different French provinces their integrity, in which lay the health of France as a whole.

Dr McQuaid said that he would wish to see Éire more decentral-ised. He believed Éire and France to be much alike. He believed in the provincial spirit, in both countries. Would wish to see the Irish provincial cities – Cork, etc. – asserting themselves, expressing them-selves and become centres of life, instead of being drained of their best, most ambitious men, who at present all went to Dublin. (I heard it said in Dublin that the Cork men run Dublin now. The Archbishop did not refer to this. But he evidently feels strongly that Cork men should run Cork, Waterford men Waterford, etc.)

Dr McQuaid's reputation as a man of intellect, and as a live wire, is established – I need not discuss it. In the course of our conversa-tion, that afternoon, I was struck by the balance he kept, in his point of view, between the mystical (we discussed visions) and the practi-cal – belief in good cooking, intelligent domestic life, etc. I was aware that the Archbishop was being both courteous and diplo-matic: he made every allowance for my point of view in any matter we talked about. This, however, made his few assertions of his own point of view – such as his defence, in passing, of M. Laval – all the more interesting.

I shall be sending further Notes in the middle of next week.

Elizabeth Cameron
SECRET

When You Go to Lough Derg

The poet Patrick Kavanagh, whose own religious feelings combined
a visionary streak with an almost pantheistic fascination with nature,
published this piece in the *Standard*, a weekly Catholic newspaper, on
which he later had a staff job.

In the Basilica on Lough Derg the young priest was speaking to a congregation of about two hundred pilgrims. He was speaking about St
Paul and what Paul had said about Christ. Listening to him and observing the congregation, the thing that struck me most forcibly was the
freshness, the recency of Christianity. Lough Derg is no museum piece.
The old stalk of Christianity ends in influences that have both colour
and scent – and thorns too. The absence of thorns, I might remark, is
one of the signs of senile decay in a bush. It might have been ad 100 or
thereabouts and all the excitement of the New Truth was stirring the
imaginations of men and women. Perhaps there were people present
who had seen Christ. From the way they prayed a man could think so.

That was my first and strongest impression of Lough Derg when I
went there for the opening of the pilgrimage last week. I arrived in
the little town of Pettigo in the evening at three o'clock. I had only
time to take a bare look at the village that is half in Northern and half
in Southern Ireland. The village has no bookshop that I could find,
though going on pilgrimage with a book might lessen the tedium of
the place – and reading is not prohibited by the rules. The only book
on sale in Pettigo was a new version of the prophecies of St Colum-
cille, but I didn't come across that piece of fiction until the return
journey. The bus took us up the hill that got barer and bleaker as we
climbed. On one side I caught a glimpse of a pretty stream that must
have some trout in it as there's an anglers' hotel in Pettigo.

At the end of about a four miles' climb we came to the ledge over
the lake. At the pier the boatmen were getting ready the boats. The
sun was shining on the scene as it always seems to do when I go on

pilgrimage. Down below us in the hollow of waters is the holy island. It looked so completely unnatural. Around stood the bleak depressing hills like walls shutting out the green sensual world. The Basilica in the sunlight looked like some fairy castle that had been transported there. The whitewashed cottages might have awakened my poetic imagination. But the place is too real, too valid, to encourage the romantic attitude. As soon as we arrived on the island we had to take off our boots and our pride and commence the Stations. And of course we were fasting from the night before. A most interesting character whom I met on the bus took a deep interest in my spiritual welfare. He explained the Stations to me as well as giving me a leaflet. This man who made the pilgrimage twenty-seven times in twenty years was a mirror reflecting a Christian optimism and fortitude that is unusual in the modern world.

'If I started telling you of my good luck I wouldn't be done talking till tomorrow morning.' And he went on to tell me how he had been sick, on the point of death, and had recovered. A few years later he split his skull 'from there to there'. He pointed to his ears. 'And I'm as fit today as any man here.' Those were only a few of the disasters that had befallen him and the fact that he recovered was due to the mercy of God. The majority of the pilgrims appeared to be of the business class. The reason may be because farmers are busy at this time. I did meet one large farmer, the father of ten children, from whom and his wife and farm he goes every year to Lough Derg, full of confidence that on his return everything will have prospered. I met a well-known ballet-dancer, on the night of the vigil during one of the intervals. I saw her on the concrete pavement at the back of the church having a Scotch dance explained to her by a girl in a tartan skirt.

Although, on paper, St Patrick's Purgatory is not such a terrible punishment, in actuality it almost reaches the limits of human endurance. Most people find the vigil the worst part. For me the worst was the austerity, the prostration of both mind and body that is seldom relieved by any flamboyant life. The coat of heavy protective piety is hard to pierce down to the bare heart.

On the second day we had no Stations to make and so were free to lounge about on the rocky height in the middle of the island. I sat there a while and listened to the conversations. 'Is it down by the lighthouse in Fanad that you live?' That was an old woman speaking to an ascetic-looking young man who had cycled eighty miles . . . 'A bloater's kipper . . . What was the name of the young fair-haired priest that said Mass this morning? . . . Were you "sitting" last night? . . . Why can't you see something good in it? If one soul is made more virtuous, more pure, don't you think that is good?'

It is to be regretted that sinners don't come to Lough Derg any more. As one of the priests on the island said to me, when a modern man sins now he doesn't believe in sin. He rejects the fundamental fact of sin. The ethic has been torn up by the roots. And yet even then there is something in men which compels them to dredge the harbours of the soul in self-denial. Lough Derg is above everything else a challenge to modern paganism. If a man brings his pride with him there's sure to be a fierce battle. The only thing that disturbed me on Lough Derg was the absence of obvious mental or spiritual struggle. I like dramatic conflict, the inner convulsions that erupt the burning lava of the soul through the crust of piety. That is the way of the Catholic Church which has nothing whatever to do with Victorian smugness.

'Why are you here?' I asked an old man.

'I'm practising for the next world,' was his answer.

I remember Lough Derg with pleasure. I remember the old whitewashed cottages with their open hearths and cranes and crooks and a healthy smell of lime. The Basilica has the virtue of usefulness and simplicity. The Stations of the Cross in stained glass are pretty in the way of minor effeminate art, but are too small.

I remember the sunlight on the buildings and the sound of the bell that called us to prayer. I remember the deep seriousness of every official from the Prior down to the humblest maid-servant – their anxiety for the pilgrimage and the pilgrims. And there is one other thing I should like to mention. It is often said that girls go to Lough Derg to pray for husbands and men for wives; if this is true it is a Christian desire. Is there anything more holy than the deep longings of the human heart? Ultimately it means the desire for Reality – for the Holy Grail of God's Truth.

Letter from Dublin

ALEX COMFORT (1943)

Cyril Connolly's magazine *Horizon* (1940–49) had a soft spot for Ireland and Irish writers. In 1942 it published an Irish number, in which Connolly described the atmosphere of the Palace Bar, much frequented by journalists and literary types, as akin to that of a 'warm alligator tank'. Undeterred by the banning of that issue in Ireland (for the inclusion of a section of Patrick Kavanagh's astonishing poem 'The Great Hunger'), Connolly next turned to a young medical student of his acquaintance, Alex Comfort, who was working at the Rotunda Hospital in Dublin as an intern. Three decades later Comfort would become famous as the author of *The Joy of Sex*.

Dear Cyril,

I promised you a letter from Ireland, and a letter I'm afraid it will have to be. I want rather to give you an idea of how we live here than a tourist impression of Dublin. Patients who are in labour do not usually feel ready for an exchange of ideas, and most people whom I have been able to meet in the intervals of eating and sleeping have been hospital patients in labour.

We live in a modern hostel, with polished linoleum (one individual seems to devote his whole life to polishing, beginning at the top and working downwards, which occupies exactly the eight hours for which he is employed), adjoining the hospital. Every landing smells of turf and Dettol, which arrives not in bottles but in Rabelaisian churns. This whole building was devised by Rabelais – quantities of food, particularly stuffed hearts, seem disproportionate when one comes from England: Mooney's bar over the road (known as Dispensary No. 3) is a place where one walks under the butt-ends of enormous tuns with taps like water-mains, built into the wall. Outside the streets are full of polygonal-wheeled growlers, which charge four shillings to drive one any distance, however short. Our windows look down on to Parnell Street and the main entrance of the hospital, where patients come in, and where a small queue of people with stout-bottles is always waiting to buy four pennyworth of the House Medicine. This is a particularly vicious purge, whose popularity for every type of illness is remarkable – two gallons of it are made daily in an enormous kettle and dispensed by the porter out of Winchester quarts.

Our life is regulated by bells. On every landing and in every cor-ridor there are two electric bells side by side. One makes a noise like a sullen hornet and the other like a fire alarm. Whenever one of them rings, everyone ceases talking or eating and counts the peals. Three peals of the buzzer call the 'district', and the two men on duty put down their forks or their playing cards and go for the extern bag. The buzzer is ringing all day on other missions, calling various members of the staff to and from the labour ward and the theatre, and one can follow the progress of awkward cases as first the Clinical Clerk, and then the Assistant Master, and then the Master himself are called in quick succession. The other bell has a quality of blowing one off one's chair or making ex-FAP personnel yell 'Action Stations!' whenever it rings, another baby being born into the world. If it rings twice, the new arrival is making a decent entry head first, and conversation in the common-room begins again. But if it rings once, a peal like a fire-alarm, accompanied by a deafening crackle on the common-room radio, the labour is abnormal. I was going upstairs on the first occasion this happened. Instantly doors flew open everywhere, and students rushed out. Feet begin pounding up the labour ward stairs. A tall narrow metal lift like a sarcophagus delivers loads of people on the labour floor. In a few minutes we are gowned and watching the Assistant Master bring down a foot.

The labour ward was also devised by Rabelais. It is a big sunny room divided up by curtains hung from wires. All its beds are full. Some patients are groaning and working hard, others are asleep, waiting to be sent to the puerperal ward (you can tell which have been delivered, because the polished metal slop-bath has gone from under the bed). Others are clutching rosaries and calling on saints. Nurses go about saying, 'Now bear down. You aren't working.' The patients look up at the students who drift in and out. Next door, in the waiting ward, rows of women are rolling towel swabs. Next to that is the baby room, which I found terrifying. The newly born are wrapped in cloths and placed in two-handled mahogany boxes, holding two, which are stacked in rows like racks of shells in a factory. The notice 'No person may pass through this Arch without a Mask' swings slowly from a nail. Some of the newly born are crying, most of them are sleeping. A few are moving their hands. Presently a trolley is wheeled in, and a dozen boxes are wheeled out to the wards. Rabelais founded this place, and 'Don Leon' described it:

> Come, Malthus, and in Ciceronian Prose
> Tell how a rutting Population grows
> Until the Produce of Land is spent
> And Brats expire for Lack of Aliment . . .

The 'district' is liable to call us at any hour of the day or night, and two students set out with a bag. So much of this work is done between two and three in the morning that there is very little I can tell you about it. The most obvious memories in my mind are of blowing up turf fires with an enema syringe, of one or two actual deliveries, of a coloured oleograph of St Bernadette adoring Our Lady of Lourdes, opposite which I sat for nearly twenty-four hours waiting for a case of inertia to be delivered, the peculiar wet warm surface of the newborn infants, born covered in grease like a new rifle, the after-birth putting out the fire, and the voices of children, late on into the night, sleepless children whom one sees at two and three in the mornings dancing in the fringe of light from a shaded lamp or pushing little carts to destinations in the darkness. I remember burning round polished logs which are the waste wood from Maguire and Patterson's match-factory, delivering the wife of a long-distance engine driver, and helping a fish-porter smash up boxes for fuel, scaly boxes under a gigantic market-roof like sky.

You will realize that I had time for very little else besides the business in hand. I went into the Lane Gallery, just by our back door, a fine gallery filled with assorted art, and a monument to one of the dirtiest tricks ever played by one gallery on another. I wish I could have seen the paintings its founder wished it to hold – 'Les Parapluies', the Ingres, the swashbuckling portrait by Mancini. As it is, the gallery is full of paintings by Lavery. I did not know what I could say of them – Lavery can paint, but my chief reaction was of embarrassment. There are feelings and reactions which are personal, and which a painter must express by painting, but there are also pictures that should not be shown. Works of patriotism, like the picture of Michael Collins lying in state, and works of personal grief, cannot be judged as art. Of the rest of the work in this gallery, there are some queer nebulous groups by AE, two more Mancinis, an unusual reversal of bad Sickerts and quite good Steers, much good sculpture, and one or two utter monstrosities, including an enormous pale distemper mural by Tuohy, and two or three paintings by Keating which give the same sense of embarrassment as Lavery's. The best work in the collection is by Jack Yeats – besides this, there is nothing in the modern manner which is not utterly venomous.

I did not see the National Gallery of Ireland – that is where I should have looked first, I suppose. I did not find the time to meet very many writers, except Maurice Craig who is working on a Life of Landor which ought to make his name. Much of the time which I could spare was spent up and down Moore Street market watching the slaughterman and the greengrocers, and in and out of the beautiful flimsy Regency [*recte* Georgian] houses in Mountjoy Square, which are now turned into tenements. I helped to screw a light-bracket into a magnificent stucco ceiling. The worst of the fuel problem in Dublin is the racket in turf, which is artificially wetted with a hose to make it look heavy, and the turning off of the gas supply, except for stated periods in the day. We live by boiling water in obstetrical practice; it appears that the risk of explosion prevents the company from cutting off the main gas completely, so that a small fitful flame remains at all times. In the streets near the gasworks this is quite bright – it is known as 'the glimmer', and most of the population lives by it. Anyone found making use of the glimmer is in danger of being cut off the gas, and an inspector or sycophant is employed to make rounds, which enable him to enter any room without warning and feel the pots and pans on the stove. I threw him out myself on one occasion – he was a seedy individual in a peaked cap, who looked like Tartuffe, but perhaps I was unduly angry, as the light failed just *in articulo partus*, and I was assisted only by a trembling old lady who dropped and broke the lamp chimney.

Among my patients' friends, who kept me company during the long and exasperating waits, anyone who realized that I was English thought it their duty to talk about neutrality, and expected me to defend the general line of English broadcasts in their entirety. It is hard to talk to people who have listened to Lord Vansittart [a senior British diplomat who opposed the appeasement of Hitler] in cold blood, with none of the background of suspended intellectual function which war entails. As far as possible I tried to talk with an accent which, if not Irish, was at least paradoxical – I did not want to attack neutrality, which is unassailable when one is in Dublin. Most working people have a sense of historical proportion which comes from living in Irish history, and the present time is too full of parallels – the partisans and Michael Collins, Balbriggan and Lidice, Gandhi and McSwiney – and if the British radio assures these people that Germany regressed 250 years into barbarism, the public can reply with conviction that it has not regressed twenty-five. I doubt if you can conceive the excitement – quite genuine excitement – that Gandhi's fast produced. I took a week's holiday in Sligo while its outcome was still in doubt, and the men I met on the roads would stop me to ask if I knew how he was today. I don't think they were ragging the Englishman – the usual comment was: 'makes you think of McSwiney – but he was young and Gandhi's not young at all'. But apart from this, I was back again in a world of home news: the main events were a spectacular murder trial in which the judge constituted himself as an additional prosecutor and a warder was produced in court to testify that the accused had been in prison before; a row over the chair of education in UCD, organized by the Gaelic League, because the new candidate spoke no Irish; and a ghastly fire in which sixty children were burned. They tell me nobody was decorated for starting it. A maid in the hospital told me she had visited New Jersey and would like to have gone back there, 'only the Germans have occupied it now, haven't they?' I had to tell her, with regret, that they have come no nearer than the State Department. Most people are favourably inclined to England, at least when Englishmen are about, though they feel, as with a smallpox patient, that sympathy need not extend as far as catching the disease.

I could not and did not follow Irish politics at all. The language issue is a pretty hollow joke. The letterboxes have still 'BOSCA (BOX)' at the top of the timeplate. A socialist-Republican Party called Córas na Pobhlachta holds meetings in Sean McDermott Street outside a new Italianesque brick church there, and vigorous stump-orators talk about the Beveridge Report from a cart, with a line of little boys dangling legs from the edge of the platform. The main streets have all of them the same absurd rabbit-hutch shelters that were built in London at the start of the blitz, with S signs modelled on ours. These are first-rate hoardings for slogan-painters. In a country where one stays for a few weeks at most, slogans are often a valuable guide to minority thought. I made a collection of them, but got little from it. Inside the first railway carriage I entered there were written up on the left 'Up Hitler!' (prefixed by 'Blow' in a second hand) and some purely personal graffiti; on the right 'B— de Valera' (handwriting of a small boy) and 'B— the bloody jews'. There was also a stencil notice BUY REPUBLICAN BONDS and a sticker 'What Aiséirghe says today, Éire does tomorrow'. Later I saw Aiséirghe's programme. It involves 'the abolition of the foreign system of democracy and the institution of the Gaelic system of leadership and representation of professional and trade bodies': military and labour service for all, with sweeping public work schemes, and liberation of Éire from the influence of 'freemasons and alien elements'. From the pamphlets on all the bookstalls Aiséirghe seems to have plenty of money and support. Meanwhile the Catholic *An t-Iolar* publishes articles on 'Salazar, saviour of his country'. Not all the Churchmen who make speeches have the insight and intelligence of Cardinal McRory. When a public meeting was called, packed with TDs to decide how best to combat the growing scourge of phthisis in Dublin, a telegram arrived from a bishop expressing the opinion that it should be entrusted to the Red Cross. Thereupon the meeting drew stumps without more ado, and the phthisis goes on. The Legion of Mary has a hand-cart which sells pamphlets on *The Menace of Godless Russia*.

While I was in Sligo I visited Yeats's future burial place at Drumcliffe. The site of his grave is submerged under a pile of old plaster flowers and the wire frames of wreaths. I do not know if it was prophecy on his part, but next to him lies a twenty-three-year-old Irish airman killed in action last year. The two great cliffs, Ben Bulben, a sleeping dog, and Ben Whiskin, a petrified wave, stood over all Yeats ever wrote. Sligo town is full of yellow roadblocks and bicycles are worth their weight in gold. Sanctuary oil costs 2s. a pint; one can also buy a fluid called Genuine Grape Brandy. All the Woolworth Stores sell hurleys, and the children use them as weapons from an early age.

Much of this letter is a catalogue of incongruities. It sounds too much like an account of holes in the carpet of a hospitable friend. Perhaps the most striking experience I had was the transition from war to peace in the attitude of the shops. It was a shock to land in Dublin and be civilly spoken to by an assistant in a grocery store. It was even stranger to meet a chemist who refused payment for pills when he discovered I had toothache. Englishmen in Ireland always speak of the hospitality and geniality of the Irish. Coming out of a war is an experience rather like a blow. No patients, except one or two who were better off, would let you leave the house without tea or whiskey. The man who made matches filled my pockets with boxes. The man who worked in Player's sent cigarettes to the hospital. A friend of mine arrived to visit in Corporation Buildings, a strange barrack of rooms built on slippery steel landings, and met the christening party – he was plied with food and drink 'til he could hardly walk home. The poorest people – living in the new 'model flats' at Tigh an Saorse [*sic*], which they cannot afford to furnish, let alone maintain – would offer the doctor pound packets of tea bought for £1 in the black market. I merely put this on record. It is nothing new, but I trust that Englishmen manage to leave an impression which one is glad to remember. I don't think I met a person I regretted having met. The wartime state of London makes me unduly sensitive to friendliness.

I came back from Sligo on the last marriage day before Lent, in a carriage full of confetti with a lachrymose parting at every station. Next night, before I went home to England, I paid ninepence to see the first Irish performance in a hundred years of *Antony and Cleopatra,* at the Gaiety behind Grafton Street. Micheál Mac Liammóir had produced it creditably and without violent introductions. The music was rather more appropriate to a bullfight than to Shakespeare – perhaps the Mediterranean flavour was intended to convey Egypt. Apart from the activities of one horn player, I thoroughly enjoyed the show, and I only mention it for a piece of unconscious humour at the end of Act One. No sooner had the curtain fallen than a safety-curtain of a brilliant yellow descended with horrible velocity. On it was painted,

ODEAREST SANITIZED INNERSPRING MATTRESS
Actively Antiseptic
Self Sterilizing
Permanently Germproof

For ten minutes we inspected this without a murmur. At the end of Act II it reappeared. It finally concealed Cleopatra from us when the band played 'God Save Ireland'.

Next day I went home. I saw a few copies of *Horizon* in Éire. The most widely read English paper is the tabloid *News Review.* The Beveridge Report was out on all the bookstalls.

I trust this finds you well. I have gained ten pounds' weight since I went overseas.

Mise, Le meas,
Alex Comfort

Buchenwald

DENIS JOHNSTON (1945)

The playwright Denis Johnston was present at the liberation of the
concentration camp at Buchenwald in 1945 in his capacity as a radio
reporter for the BBC, with the honorary army rank of captain. Six years
later he published extracts from his diary of this time, in The Bell.

As I drove through the woods the trickle of Displaced Persons grew
in volume, until presently there was a continual stream of them –
filthy, emaciated creatures, many of them in those disgusting striped
pyjamas in which the SS clothe their internees. The concrete road
and the railway track were easy to find, and as I bowled down the
former I passed a bombed-out factory, and then found myself confronted by a great gate in a barbed wire fence surmounted by a large
black flag. An American sentry kept watch over an enormous pile of
rifles, machine guns and other weapons that had been collected by
the side of the road, and the DPs were milling around on both sides
of the fence.

'Say, what's this place?' I asked the sentry.

As usual he didn't know, except that it was some Concentration
Camp that had been overrun by Patton's boys, and that the DPs were
still hunting the SS guards in the woods and lynching them. Indeed
if I cared to look in any of the ditches . . .

'Would you like to see over the camp?' an English voice enquired
at my elbow.

I turned around and found myself facing two internees, dressed in
ragged clothes and holding under their arms bundles wrapped in
sacking.

'Thanks,' I said. 'Are you English?'

'Channel Islanders,' replied the first. He introduced himself as
James Quick and his friend as Emile Dubois.

'Come with us and we'll bring you round by the back. Have you
got a strong stomach?'

Over the main gate I read a defiant inscription:

RECHT ODER UNRECHT — MEIN VATERLAND.

So there had evidently been some doubt in somebody's mind about the rightness or wrongness of this place! On an inner gate a shorter and even more cynical inscription appeared:

JEDEM DAS SEINE

or in a free translation, 'To each what is coming to him.'

By this time I suspected what was coming to me, and I steeled myself for another recital of uncorroborated horrors. But my guides were not so talkative as they might have been. They were bitter, it is true, on the subject of turnip soup and one loaf of bread a day between five, but strangely enough they didn't complain so vigorously about their own lot. They had been in a part of the camp that wasn't too bad, they said, because they were still fit to work. But wait until I saw the fate of those who weren't. At which Dubois stripped the corner of a tarpaulin off a lorry that was standing in the yard, and disclosed the interior piled high with emaciated yellow naked corpses.

Like General Alexander I have not seen many dead in the course of this war; graves by the hundred, and lots of impersonal lumps under covers, but the unsheeted dead have been limited to those waxlike figures in the houses of Ortona and a few more here and there by the roadside. I do not like looking on the dead – not that they move me, so much as disgust me. This was a sight in full measure, and I did not brood on it for long.

'Cover it up,' I said, 'and tell me how it happened.'

'It happened all the time,' Dubois answered. 'This is just a day or two's collection. Come and see inside.'

I had laughed off that camp in Alsace, and what they said of it, but I couldn't laugh this one off, for here it was obvious that most patent efforts had been made to conceal the evidence. In the cellar beneath the crematorium, somebody had been trying to whitewash the walls, but the bloodstains still showed up beneath the new colour. They had taken the hooks out of the walls above each gory splash and had attempted to fill up with plaster the holes that had been left. But the patches still remained, and one great hook had been restored – or left – evidently for some last minute hanging. The stools were there still, and a dented and bloody bludgeon – a couple of the little short narrow nooses, and what to me was probably the most horrible of all – a white coat like that of a hospital attendant, half washed of the blood that had once engrained it.

'They beat us and hanged us here,' said Quick.

And for all I might try, there was no denying the evidence.

'Come and see upstairs.'

Alsace was small-time stuff compared to this place. Instead of one furnace there were half a dozen, and in some of them the charred bones still lay.

'Don't mind those,' said my guide. 'They were put there by some of the prisoners to dress the place up a bit.'

'That seems scarcely necessary,' I answered, my stomach turning within me at the thought of such ghoulish deliberation.

'That's what I thought. But some people can't let bad alone. They've got to fix it up for the photographers.'

But if the prisoners were being business-like in their preparations, it was nothing to the neat organisation of the jailers. For here again I was not so much revolted by the fact of death – which must happen sooner or later – as by a hearty painting of a flaming furnace on one of the end walls of the crematorium, surmounting an inscription that looked for all the world like a religious motto, or a Christmas greeting. But it did not say God Bless Our Home. It translated as follows:

No loathsome worms will feed upon my corpse, but a clean fire will digest it. I always loved warmth and light, therefore burn and do not bury me.

This was the jolly sentiment that was put into the mouths of the wretches who had not died a natural death, but had been beaten to death or hanged in the cellar down below.

'It's quite pretty here in the summer,' said Quick, as we walked through the camp. 'They have a little concrete aquarium just outside the wire there, and trees look nice, don't they? We even had a sort of band that used to play in the evenings over by the gate. It really wasn't so bad – so long as you could work.'

'And if you couldn't?'

'If you couldn't work, or if you got in bad with them, they sent you down to the lower part of the camp.'

'And what happened there?'

'Would you like to come and see for yourself?'

'I fancy somehow that I would not. But I suppose that I had better.'

'Come along then.'

We walked through the camp. Sub-human specimens were tottering around on all sides as we went, most of them dressed in those dreadful striped pyjamas, but all of them in a state of indescribable filth. Some were squatting over the open drains with their pants down.

'Dysentery is the least serious complaint we have here,' explained Dubois. 'It only begins with that.'

'But where did such people come from?' I asked.

'Oh, they were just ordinary people when they came here. In fact most of them were quite well-off people before they fell foul of the party. For instance, that one there was a throat specialist in Vienna, and the one behind him was once the Mayor of Prague, they say.'

'Tell me,' I said, feeling madly around for an explanation, 'this state of affairs isn't normal, of course. This congestion and starvation is a result of the end of the war? – the breakdown of life generally in Germany?'

'To some extent maybe. But it isn't much worse than usual. Normally they kept 70,000 people here, and as soon as your working ability was over, what followed was quite deliberate. It doesn't take you long to get to that state at sixteen hours' work a day; and after you've collapsed physically you're just a useless mouth. The sooner you're dead the better. It's a logical Nazi idea. But surely you knew? Haven't you read their books?'

'Yes, I've read their books. But somehow . . . never mind, tell me what happened when the Yanks got near? Why did they leave you alive to talk?'

'They did their best, but 70,000 people take a bit of killing, you know, and it isn't everyone will do it. As a matter of fact on the 11th they mounted eight machine guns on the gate, and we heard that a killer squad of 500 SS men had been sent from Weimar to exterminate the camp. But the Yanks beat them to it by two hours, and at about four in the afternoon we saw the first tanks coming up. At that, the guards and their dogs ran for the woods and some of the boys have been hunting for them since. In fact I'm afraid they've been beating up the whole countryside.'

I didn't ask what happened to the SS men when they were caught. I had seen signs myself, on the way up, and it was a good killing.

'Here's the block we want you to see,' said Quick. 'Don't come in if you don't want to.'

I went in. At one end lay a heap of smoking clothes amongst which a few ghouls picked and searched – for what, God only knows. As we entered the long hut the stench hit us in the face, and a queer wailing sound came to our ears. Along both sides of the shed was tier upon tier of what can only be described as shelves. And lying on these, packed tightly side by side, like knives and forks in a chest, were living creatures – some of them stirring, some of them stiff and silent, but all of them skeletons, with the skin drawn tight over their bones, with heads bulging and misshapen from emaciation, with burning eyes and sagging jaws. And as we came in, those with the strength to do so turned their heads and gazed at us; and from their lips came that thin unearthly noise.

Then I realised what it was. It was meant to be cheering. They were cheering the [War Correspondent] uniform that I wore. They were cheering for the hope that it brought them.

We walked the length of the shed – and then through another one. From the shelves feeble arms rose and waved, like twigs in a breeze. Most of them were branded with numbers.

'Heil – Heil – Viva – Viva!'

Recht oder unrecht – mein Vaterland.

Through the gates, under this monstrous sentiment, the American Red Cross orderlies were trooping as we came out. As I bade farewell to my two guides one of them bent over the pile of captured weapons on the sidewalk and picked out a Luger.

'How about a souvenir?' he said.

The American sentry casually looked the other way. From the woods around us came the distant sound of a shot. Staring at the gateway and at the white helmets of the orderlies I took the gun and shoved it under my coat.

Recht oder unrecht.

American medicos on a mission in favour of the human race – for that is the issue here, and there is no getting away from it.

This is no fortuitous by-product of the chaos of war. This is no mere passing cruelty or wanton act of destruction. This is deliberate. This is the intentional flower of a Race Theory. This is what logic divorced from conscience can bring men to. This is the wilful dehumanisation of the species, and an offence against Homo Sapiens.

Right or wrong – my Fatherland.

Very well. Have it that way if you insist. Your Fatherland is wrong, therefore your Fatherland must be destroyed. That is logic too. Put it to the test, and if you lose – you must die.

Unconditional surrender is the only answer.

Oh, I have tried so long to fight against this conclusion, but now – as at the thirteenth stroke of a crazy clock – all previous pronouncements become suspect too. Everything else falls into place and acquires a new meaning in the hideous light of Buchenwald. The words of Winston Burdett – the million shoes of Lublin – that camp in Alsace that I laughed at, because I did not want to believe such things of men – because they were not true of men as I had known them.

Cruelty I have known, and sadism, and the villainy of red-hot anger. But mass de-humanisation as a matter of planned policy has not so far come my way.

Worse for me is the fact that I have been made a fool of, in my thirst for fairness and international justice. All the reasonable and sensible things that Hitler has ever said – the virtue of Courage and Order, the justice of self-determination and unity, the fact that we went to war to preserve Danzig for the Poles, the evil of money power, the right of a great people to a place in the sun – all these things were just a cover-up for this!

He has been using our good nature as a means of betraying us; and that is even a greater crime than the degradation of humanity, for it is the degradation of Good itself. It means that Good is not worth while – that Evil is our only means of self-preservation, that like the Vampire, Dracula, he has bitten me upon the throat, and I must either die or be a monster too!

How did I ever dare to doubt that there is an Absolute in Good and Evil?

And what else has he done? He has delivered us bound hand and foot into the power of the Prigs of Ill-will and from now on I am forced to be their ally. This camp will be their war-cry. They will seize upon it with whoops of joy. They will all be here in a day or two, threading their way through its filth – no frozen horror or revulsion in their eyes – nothing but lust and self-righteousness. They will photograph and film it in prepared poses. They will blazon it to the skies as a justification for every crime that will be committed in return. Good nature, they will scream, is folly, and love of justice is only sentimentality. And they will have Buchenwald to prove them right, for all that they will say of Buchenwald is true – every word of it or nearly every word! Buchenwald has buggered up the Master Plan.

Oh Christ! We are betrayed. I have done my best to keep sane, but there is no answer to this, except bloody destruction. We must slay the Oxen of the Sun whatever the Gods may feel about it. We must break the double gates in pieces and fling down the walls, and who-ever tries to stop us, be he guilty or innocent, must be swept aside. And if nothing remains but the stench of evil in ourselves, that cannot be helped!

How terrible that this should be the place that I have been seeking for all these years. I thought that it was Eckartsberga, but it seems that it is Buchenwald. And now, on this terrible – this unforgettable day – I have found it.

Yeats Comes Home

KATE O'BRIEN (1948)

W. B. Yeats died in the south of France in January 1939. According to
his wife George, shortly before his death he told her, 'If I die bury me
up there [at Roquebrune-Cap-Martin] and then in a year's time when
the newspapers have forgotten me, dig me up and plant me in Sligo.'
The outbreak of hostilities in Europe later that year made it impossible to honour Yeats's wish to the letter, but in 1948 his corpse was
exhumed and transported to Ireland by sea. The novelist Kate
O'Brien, who was also an experienced journalist and travel writer,
wrote about the reinterment for the *Spectator*.

It was a fine celebration. He had told us that 'dizzy dreams can spring
from the dry bones of the dead', but we were not in the mood to
speculate thus with him last Friday. There was too much going on;
the day was crowded, and sometimes even clangorous with public
and private pride. And it was both right and easy that the mood of
the occasion was a smiling one; right, because Ireland's very great
son, her immortal, the great poet in English since Wordsworth, was
by his own wish coming home from wide and various wanderings –
home at last from the French Mediterranean shore – to take up his
perpetual rest, completing the bright ring of the poetic life, under
the grey hills of his childhood – a conclusive, right event which must
lift the dullest spirit; and easy, it was easy to enjoy and savour it,
because one knew that nine years would have done their natural
work in the hearts that had loved the man, and because our sense of
the world's loss of the poet has been tempered and even removed by
increasing awareness of all that it gained through his life.

So Friday was something of a festival, and if that word has a free-
and-easy ring, so much the better is it here. For we are not very good
at ceremony in Ireland, and our warmly meant attempts at it in
Galway and Sligo tended to go wrong on us here and there – only
thereby causing us to smile at ourselves and enjoy our occasion by

that much more. Thus, when the corvette *Macha* – first ship of Ireland's own navy to enter Mediterranean waters – sailed into Galway Harbour on the morning's high tide, all of us waiting alongside were delighted with her prettiness and pleased to reflect on the honour she had done herself in this first felicitous commission; but we did not ask, or get, Royal Navy precision in the ritual of bringing the poet ashore; and nobody minded that the city Fathers were gowned or not gowned as their fancies dictated, or that one of them – no doubt with a cold in his head – very splendid from neck to toe in red and purple silk, kept nervously doffing and donning his favourite old brown felt hat. What we did get – the important thing – was a shining Galway morning, a lovely light outlining the noble town and the graceful ship with the still figures on its deck – the poet's wife, his son, his daughter, his famous, white-haired brother – and a communal mood of welcome and gratitude as the great, tall coffin came at last to land.

In Sligo at midday the weather was turning towards sadness, but there was no rain yet, and the people were out from every closed-up house and shop to claim and acclaim their poet. He was met at the city boundary; Sean MacBride, Minister for External Affairs, received him there; so did other members of the Government, so did Éamon de Valera, so did the Mayor and Corporation of Sligo. And the pipers of Sligo piped him into town. As Jack Yeats had said in the Galway hotel the evening before: 'They have a lovely pipers' band in Sligo.' He lay in state an hour before the Town Hall, while Sligo milled delightedly about him, and Dublin, all the thronging, famous Dubliners, a little out of things perhaps at this point, a shade reduced and hungry, sought hastily for lunch.

In the afternoon the rain fell as we turned northward for Drumcliffe. Ben Bulben was draped in cold rain, and the long quays and drained-out waters of Sligo Harbour recalled us to thoughts of his later work, of its unsparing, iron relentlessness – 'that stern colour and that delicate line / That are our secret discipline'. Rain or no rain, the streets and the roads, the grassy banks and hillocks all the way were crowded. There seemed to be children in thousands watching him go past; peering through hazel-branches or over wet stone walls one saw the faces of Crazy Jane and Tom O'Roughley and Red

Hanrahan and Devorgilla; and every signpost that we passed bore some great words from his poems.

Drumcliffe Church and graveyard stand on a little grey-green plateau below Ben Bulben. The landscape all about carries the mist and the grey weather of its natural adornment, and the undulating, dreaming, spacious beauty of this part of Sligo County lays instant claim upon the heart. No wonder indeed, one thought, standing under the tall sighing elms by the open grave, no wonder he desired to be laid down here in this most noble place – he who said that he was 'jealous . . . for those grey mountains that are still lacking their celebration'. He need no longer be jealous; they have been celebrated now and partake henceforward of his immortality.

He was met at his grave-side by a silver-haired bishop with a silver crozier; there were five attendant clergymen, and friends of all kinds and degrees, old friends and young friends – and some ghostly ones, too, maybe, come back for the day – pressed about his family, and tried in vain, against the wind and the sighing of the trees to hear some of the great phrases of the committal service. The rain continued to fall; the turned earth gave up a pungent smell and rooks cawed from the tree-tops. The prayers were over soon, and the grave-diggers began to clank their shovels, but people waited to see the grave filled and the laurel wreath laid on it, and waited on in the rain still to hear the Mayor of Sligo speak his short valediction.

One overheard amusing things: 'O Death, where is thy sting?, sure that isn't in the Burial Service at all! That's from "Abide With Me".' And: 'Stop pushing, man! You'll have me into the grave', 'Sure, wouldn't it be a great honour for you to get a leg in there?' And: 'Did you ever read anything he wrote?' 'Well, I did, mind you. 'Tis high-class stuff, of course – but in my private opinion the most of it is great rambling.'

When the Dubliners got back at dusk to their hotel fires, their tea and toast and glasses of whiskey, they all struck one as singularly peaceful and friendly, as if secretly enriched; the talk on all sides seemed gently and laudatory; there was no malice to be heard, for once. Thoughts ran inevitably on greatness, and most of that lively company of Yeats's mourners were surely thinking without a grudge of what a glorious fate it is, when the earthly end has come, to have been a great poet. 'The years like great black oxen tread the world,' but the poet escapes from them, taking on immortality; and that day in Sligo we enjoyed vicariously his high fortune, and were glad to know that his dreaming bones were home and safe in Drumcliffe. It had indeed been an exhilarating thing to travel the last bit of the road with him, the road that all his life he had resolved to tread.

The New Parochial House

HONOR TRACY (1950)

This artful vignette by Honor Tracy, an English novelist who frequently visited Ireland (and was for a time engaged in an affair with
the writer Sean O'Faolain), was one of a series of pieces commissioned by the *Sunday Times* in London. The waspish tone of Tracy's
perceptive commentary on the relations between priest and people in
Ireland generated two spectacular lawsuits. In the first, the *Sunday
Times* was sued by the parish priest of Doneraile, Co. Cork, whose
identity had been ill-concealed in the piece, and the newspaper had to
pay damages equivalent to what it paid Tracy for a full year's worth of
columns. As part of the settlement, the newspaper also published an
apology, which Tracy subsequently persuaded another jury to decide
had in turn grievously libelled her. She received, in turn, an even
greater sum in damages from the same newspaper.

The village is very small. It is hardly more than one long street that
slopes gently down to a stream and turns at the bridge into a white
road that winds away over the hills into the blue distance. Seven hundred people live here, and three times as many more in the districts
around, forming the parish. There is a big church and a big convent,
two little halls, no library, few diversions and plenty of life. One man
came back to it after twenty prosperous years in Chicago, because he
liked to be where things were happening.

In the ordinary way, the villagers greet you with, 'A glorious
morning, thank God!' if it is not raining much, and 'A lovely soft
morning' if it is. Unless you are known and accepted, that exhausts
the immediate material for conversations.

But now, after the proper exchange of civilities, they all inquire if
you have seen the Canon's new house. 'Oh Lord, it's the size of a
ship!' they say. 'Oh Lord, you'd never forget it!' The large, modern
villa with its glaring red roof and white walls has fired their imaginations completely. The spaciousness of the thing has taken away their

breath. It is so grand to be building at all in this quiet little place, where many of the cottages are without water or light. And the price of it all is said to be nine thousand pounds, which strikes on their ear with a romantic fabulous note, as devoid of real significance as nine million, or the wealth of Araby.

Everyone is busy selling raffle tickets to everyone else. The winners will hand back the prizes as soon as received. The nuns are getting up a sale of work to which all will contribute and from which all will buy. The church dues are increased, the collections multiply and the Canon's voice, so tired and confused at times, rises clear as the Shandon Bells from the steps of the altar as he pricks the faithful on to fresh endeavours.

Before, he lived in the mellow, three-storey, Georgian building where once towards the end of his days, another old Canon [*i.e. Canon Sheehan of Doneraile – Ed.*] sat, writing his tender stories of the people under his care. It is a good house, the best in the neighbourhood apart from those of the gentry, but there is no view from it: nothing can be seen from the windows but the ducks tumbling in the stream, the shaggy donkeys asleep on the kerb, the gay, grubby children at play and the dog that eternally chases his tail: and the Canon wanted a view. The new villa looks out on wide rolling green fields and splendid trees, with hardly a creature in sight.

And so it's great days in the village, with plenty for them to talk about, with all the wit and the bright, vivid phrases and those undertones, so easily missed, which make their conversation the pleasantest thing in the world.

'They do be saying we've built the finest parish priest's home in the country: and isn't it well for us? The Canon was saying on Sunday, not to bother with the Stock Exchange and that, but to lay up for ourselves the unspeakable joys of Heaven: and wasn't he right? Ah, he's a queer old fellow altogether – mind, there's no harm in him, and mind, I didn't say anything, and mind, you didn't have it from me.'

Boycott Village

HUBERT BUTLER (1958)

The boycott by Catholics of Protestant businesses and neighbours in Fethard-on-Sea, Co. Wexford, exposed the deep social and political implications of the Catholic '*Ne Temere*' rule that the children of any Catholic parent must be brought up as Catholics, regardless of the wishes or religious affiliation of the other parent. A sharp-eyed observer of the rural southern Protestant world to which he belonged, the essayist Hubert Butler was perfectly positioned to make sense of the Fethard-on-Sea boycott.

Fethard-on-Sea is a small village of about a hundred houses on the Wexford coast. It is not a seaside resort, for the muddy creek, which brings the houses to an end, can surely only be called 'the sea' to distinguish the village from the less notorious Fethard in Tipperary. The ancient hotel near the creek is now Mr Leslie Gardiner's General Stores, but neither he nor Miss Betty Cooper, who sells cornflakes, sweets and newspapers on the opposite side of the street, expect much from the seaside visitors. Tourists, of course, pass through, but they are mainly the self-sufficient kind with picnic-baskets in the boot. They are bound for Baginbun, a short distance away, where there is a charming secluded shore, rock-pools lined with emerald seaweed and, on most days, no one else. It was at Baginbun that the Normans first landed in Ireland eight centuries ago. They had been invited by Dermot Mac Morrogh, the great chieftain to whom all Wexford belonged. He had stolen another chieftain's wife. There had been unpleasantness and reprisals as a result and so he had asked for English help. The English came and they stayed. So much so that today men of English blood predominate in Wexford.

And now there has been turmoil there again about another truant wife and things have happened that have shocked all Ireland, north and south, and made the hope of unity recede still further. It is not a parochial squabble; it is not exclusively an Irish one. It is a collision between human nature and the 'immutable' principles of the Roman Catholic Church. Such collisions happen somewhere every day, but this one has been watched with such breathless interest, because in Ireland we still have the primitive power of focusing our minds like burning-glasses on tiny patches. Just as bird-watchers go to the Saltees, those three uninhabited islands which lie off Baginbun, so men-watchers should come to Ireland to see how men, not yet trapped in the mental zoo of the television set and the Sunday press, still think and act in a natural untamed state.

In the spring of 1957 Eileen Cloney had reached the age of six. She lived with her parents and her baby sister in a bald grey castle just outside Fethard. It is 600 years old but it has been liberally renovated with concrete and has rather new-looking battlements and a turret. There is a huge barn beside it, whose corrugated iron roof has grown rusty in the salty air. There are elm trees and sprawling hedges, where in late June, when I first saw Dungulph, the blackberries were beginning to flower, the last bells were still clinging to the tips of the foxgloves and the first ones climbing up some stray mulleins. It seemed an enchanted place in which to be six years old. But Eileen Cloney had reached school age and Father Allen and his curate, Father Stafford, were insistent that there must be no further delay. She must go to school. They were emphatic about this, because Mrs Cloney, a strong-minded woman, showed signs of wanting to send Eileen to the small Protestant school, where there were twelve other pupils, children of local farmers and of Leslie Gardiner. Though her husband was a Catholic, Mrs Cloney was the daughter of a Protestant stockbreeder of Fethard. I have never met Sean Cloney or his wife, Sheila, but they seem to be a likeable pair and their marriage appeared to be a happy one. The sudden split, which occurred in the middle of April, arose out of Eileen's schooling. It is disagreeable to discuss the characters and lives of quiet modest people like the Cloneys, who have never courted publicity, but circumstances and, in particular, Father Allen and Father Stafford, have decreed that their private lives are no longer their own. Sean Cloney, in his press photographs, looks a pleasant, good-looking, easy-going young man. He has that amused, cynical, shoulder-shrugging appearance that is common enough in Ireland.

Sheila Cloney, who has hitherto escaped the press photographer, seems to have been more vigorous and dominating. Immediately after her marriage she started to make the 116-acre farm at Dungulph pay, wrestling herself with the tractor and the accounts and achieving such success that last year they bought a combine harvester. She was as devoted to her own Church as to her home and, when she came in from the fields, she often went with broom and scrubbing brush to the Protestant church of Fethard. It was being redecorated this spring and she was among the most tireless of the volunteers, who every night tidied away the builders' debris.

It was on May 13th that the squabble became public property, but it is not yet clear who was squabbling with whom. Was Sheila at war with Sean or was she warring with Father Allen and Father Stafford, while Sean, shrugging his shoulders, looked on? Certain it is that Sheila on April 27th took the car and the children to Wexford, where later it was found abandoned in the street. Three days later a barrister came from Belfast with 'terms of settlement'. They were drastic terms, suggesting an extreme state of feminine exasperation. Sean was to sell Dungulph Castle and they were to emigrate together to Canada or Australia, where the children were to be brought up as Protestants. 'No one influenced her in her decision,' Sean declared to a reporter. 'Once Sheila gets an idea into her head, a regiment of soldiers wouldn't change her.'

The news was received with consternation in Fethard. There was a thunderous pronouncement from the altar, and the next day a boycott started of all the Protestants in the neighbourhood. There was a Catholic teacher in the Protestant school, a Catholic sexton in the Protestant church; they both resigned. The elderly music teacher, Miss Knipe, lost eleven of her twelve pupils, Mr Gardiner's General Store and Miss Cooper's more modest emporium were rigorously boycotted. So were the Protestant farmers who sold milk, and from one of them a Catholic farmhand walked away. The boycott, the priests declared, would continue till Mrs Cloney brought back the children.

For the first week the better-disciplined Catholics refused to greet or to look at their Protestant neighbours, but here and there a rebellious one gave a furtive smile when no one was looking. At the end of the week, either because a breath of Christian charity forced its way through some crack in the united front or because it was better to abate the rigour of the boycott rather than betray any lack of unanimity, the boycotters began to smile and nod. But there was no relaxation of economic pressure.

By this time the newspapers of Dublin and Belfast were headlining the news from Fethard. It was anticipated that very soon a word from the local Catholic bishop, the Bishop of Ferns, would put an end to what was becoming a national scandal. But the ecclesiastical intervention, when it came, was more astounding than what had preceded. On Saturday, June 30th, the Annual Congress of the Catholic Truth Society was being held in Wexford, and at the Church of the Immaculate Conception Cardinal D'Alton was received by the Bishop of Ferns. In front of them and five other bishops of the Roman Church, including the Archbishop of Dublin, the Bishop of Galway preached a sermon defending the boycott.

There seems [he said] to be a concerted campaign to entice or kidnap Catholic children and deprive them of their faith. Non-Catholics with one or two honourable exceptions do not protest against the crime of conspiring to steal the children of a Catholic father. But they try to make political capital, when a Catholic people make a peaceful and moderate protest.

In the same newspaper which reported this apology for a 'peaceful and moderate protest', we read that two of Mrs Cloney's brothers in Fethard had been obliged to seek police protection, because a shot had been fired at one of them near his home. At the same time a young Protestant teacher from Trinity College arrived to take charge of the Protestant school, which had been closed since the teacher had abandoned her pupils. He found a warning nailed onto the school-door:

SCABS! BEWARE OF THE LEAD IN BOYCOTT-VILLAGE!

No prominent Catholic had come forward to condemn the boycott except a barrister, Mr Donal Barrington, who in his address to a

Catholic Social Study Conference in Dublin said that the boycott was doing damage to the cause of Catholicism. 'It is,' he said, 'the most terrible thing that has happened in this part of the country since the Civil War,' and he went on to say that he was only echoing the opinion of all the intelligent Catholics, laymen and priests, with whom he had discussed the matter. But their opinion had been given in private and he felt it his duty to speak publicly. 'There is a time in the affairs of people, when nothing is necessary for the triumph of evil but that good men should maintain what is called a discreet silence.'

No other Catholic made so bold a comment, till a week later Mr de Valera himself declared in the Dáil:

If, as head of the Government, I must speak, I can only say from what has appeared in public that I regard this boycott as ill-conceived, ill-considered and futile for the achievement of the purpose for which it seems to have been intended, that I regard it as unjust and cruel to confound the innocent and the guilty, that I repudiate any suggestion that this boycott is typical of the attitude or conduct of our people, that I am convinced that ninety per cent of them look on this matter as I do and that I beg of all, who have regard for the fair name, good repute and well-being of our nation, to use their influence to bring this deplorable affair to a speedy end.

Mr de Valera was right. The Irish are not by nature bullying or ungenerous; they are indulgent to human weaknesses and disinclined to totalitarian judgments. This essay, therefore, is not about bigotry, but about the ineffectuality of ordinary people with nice intentions and neighbourly instincts. This has often been demonstrated before in totalitarian countries, but only the last stage in the suppression of the amiable, when they are being finished off by threats and violence, has been closely observed. The earlier stages of coercion by 'peaceful and moderate protest' have never had the same attention, yet they are more important. For the handful of free spirits, who in any community are the last-ditch guardians of freedom, are not defenceless till the amiable majority, which forms an inert but not easily negotiable obstacle in the path of tyranny, has first been neutralized. How is this done? It is not difficult. The events in Fethard show how eagerly the amiable will co-operate in their own extinction.

It is now fifty years since the *Ne Temere* decree, which condemns the Irish nation to live in two mutually distrustful camps, was first applied to Ireland. It has broken up many homes besides the Cloneys' and brought an element of hypocrisy or perjury into every marriage between Irish people of different faith. Yet never till now did the whole Irish nation observe and deplore the cruel tensions which it has created. It is doubtful whether de Valera lost a single vote by championing the boycotted. For the Church of Ireland is much more than a vast complex of emptying palaces, rectories, cathedrals. In Ireland it is still the spearhead of the Reformation and few people are ready to renounce the liberties won at the Reformation, even when they repudiate the reformers. Father Stafford and his anathemas are as much an anachronism in Ireland as the Anglo-Irish ascendancy.

Yet this time the Protestant hierarchy made a scapegoat of Mrs Cloney and did not reiterate those protests against *Ne Temere*, which our primate made long ago and more recently re-published. He and others had denied the validity of a promise 'extorted under pressure', and such denials undoubtedly influenced Mrs Cloney in her decision. Weakened perhaps by the emigration of vigour and intelligence, our clergy counselled appeasement and that 'discreet silence', which Mr Barrington saw as the prelude to the triumph of evil. By inference they accepted the *Ne Temere* promises as valid; they deprecated excessive newspaper publicity, condemned any lay attempt to organize aid for the boycotted Protestants as 'senseless retaliation' and, in our diocesan magazine, gave retrospective approval to a strange undertaking given by Mrs Cloney's father, Mr Kelly. Speaking 'on behalf of the Church of Ireland community', he had pledged it to do all it could to bring back his grandchildren to Fethard, and published this promise in the Irish papers. Tactfully he said nothing about the boycott, which is known locally as 'Parish Co-operation' and was described by Father Stafford in the press as 'this grand, dignified, legal profession of our Faith'. By implication Protestants were committed to act as watchdogs for the observance of a decree directed against themselves. It was assumed that, as a *quid pro quo*, the boycott would be called off, but the Church of Ireland bit the dust in vain. The boycott continued and our clergy, returning from their Munich, gave themselves over to exhortation against mixed marriages, and the social intercourse that might lead to them. Canute, rebuking the waves, was not less profitably engaged. In the countryside we have dwindled to two or three per cent of the population (the rector of Fethard controls five amalgamated parishes); if we are to mix exclusively with ourselves, we are condemned to social isolation, to celibacy, inbreeding or dreary marriages of convenience. But can we really believe that our duty to our neighbour is to avoid him socially, lest we love him as ourselves and forget the dangerous contagion of his faith? For that is the way in which the gospel precepts appear to have been revised.

This ecclesiastical advice will not of course be followed, but nor will it be repudiated for, as in the early days of the Brown Shirts in Germany, respectable people put their faith in the healing properties of time. We like to think that, left to themselves, our difficulties will all 'blow over', 'peter out', 'die down'. There is a rich range of synonyms for the spontaneous disappearance of evil and we seldom commit the folly of sticking out our necks or poking in our noses. And, in fact, if we only have patience, the victim of injustice will probably emigrate and cease to embarrass us with his tedious lamentations.

Irish Protestants are generally 'broad minded' about belief. They tend to judge other religions as they judge their own, by its social consequences. Having sometimes a hereditary interest in property, they are impressed by the Catholic defence of property. A true instinct also informs them that the Catholic Church is basically as unsympathetic to Irish nationalism as is the average Irish Protestant and might at any moment barter its support of the Irish Republic for a favoured position in the Commonwealth. This emerged clearly at Fethard. The Bishop of Galway, in his Wexford address, deliberately gave arguments to the Northerners against the abolition of Partition and cannot have been dismayed by the repercussions in Belfast. A united Ireland, in which there would be a twenty-five per cent heretical minority, might seem to present the Church of Rome with problems insoluble, except in the vast dilution of the Commonwealth. But to declaim against Irish unity would be unpopular; the Orangemen could safely be left to do all the declaiming, for Ulster eyes are dim with gazing on far-off imperial horizons and cannot focus clearly on what goes on under the nose. A fund was raised for the boycotted Protestants and a Northern MP sent to distribute it. On July 12th not a single Orange orator failed to mention Fethard, but, as interest on the large 'political capital' derived from the boycott, the dividend that went to Fethard was small.

Some weeks ago Father Allen bought some cigarettes at Gardiner's. This momentous act did not mean the end of the boycott, but it has cast a rose-pink veil over its origins and the responsibility for its continuance. An irreverent person, peering through the veil, would see that the boycott can never now end. The lost customers have found other tradesmen, eager to supply their needs, a new newsagent bicycles round with the papers to Miss Cooper's former clients, a new milkman goes the rounds and the old schoolteacher and the old sextoness will never return. Nor will Miss Knipe's pupils. To end the boycott more unpleasantness and fresh dislocations would be necessary, and these are things which in Ireland we always avoid if we possibly can.

Lessons, Lessons and Then More Lessons . . .

MAEVE BRENNAN (1962)

Maeve Brennan moved to the United States in 1934 at the age of 17, when her father was appointed the Free State's representative in Washington DC. She attended university in the capital, then moved to New York, where she lived the rest of her life. Hired by William Shawn of the *New Yorker*, she contributed a unique series of vignettes about life in New York to that publication, bylined 'The Long-Winded Lady'. The brilliance of her short fiction was not widely recognized until after her death, which followed years of alcoholism and mental illness.

On Eighth Street, in the Village, there is a modest restaurant, humanely lighted, not too bright and not too dark, where I used to spend about two hours every day, sometimes in the afternoon and sometimes in the evening, sitting always at a small table by the large street window. The window was recessed, and half curtained, and it was furnished with an oversized Tiffany lamp and an oversized bronze-colored crock that held artificial flowers or artificial leaves, according to the season of the year. I spent a good deal of time by that window. I remember being there on November nights when it was snowing, and all the people hurrying by were brightened by their white crowns and white epaulets, and then there were afternoons in midsummer when I hardly dared look out for fear of seeing some struggling man or woman become finally embedded in the thick heat, to vanish forever as I watched. I was such a faithful customer that a martini usually appeared on the table while I was still arranging my books in the order in which I would look at them.

There was a small service bar halfway down the room, which was very long and very narrow, but there was no place where people could just sit and drink. It was a decorous place with exactly as much style as a nice, plain tearoom. I used to always carry three or four books with me and, if I had just visited the bookshop across the street, often had six or more to look through when I was not attending to the outside scene.

One afternoon – it was autumn; there was an armful of flaming, papery leaves in the crock beside me – I glanced up to see two nuns walking by, walking west toward Sixth Avenue. All nuns look alike. Their black draperies, their resolute tread, and their remote air – everything about them was familiar to me. I was surprised to see them, as I am always surprised to see nuns abroad in New York, and I thought, as I had thought at other times, that it is out of the ordinary to see nuns here, and a very ordinary matter to see them in Dublin, where I was born. There was a time, during the years I spent in a convent boarding school and for many years afterward, when the sight of a nun would fill me with apprehensiveness and dislike, and I was glad then, sitting by that restaurant window, to know those years were gone.

That afternoon I had arrived at the restaurant when the lunch hour was over, and now, except for two waiters, the place was empty. I like empty restaurants, and I had counted on having all the tables and booths to myself. Even the cash register, by the door, was unguarded. I had taken the afternoon off, but why, what excuse I had offered myself, I can't remember. Perhaps I felt free because it was autumn again. Even so, three o'clock in the afternoon is no hour for anybody to be sitting at a window in a public restaurant with a martini in front of her, or half a martini, as it was by the time the nuns passed, and it seemed miraculous to be able to be so free and independent that I could be in the restaurant I preferred and drink what I liked and eat what I liked and read the books of my choice and see two nuns pass and feel nothing except a slight surprise – no apprehensiveness, no wild survey of a panicky conscience, nothing like that.

The two nuns who ran that boarding school were violent women. The head nun was short and fat and her assistant was tall and thin, and they both had genteel accents, the fat one speaking low, the thin one high. The head taught English and her assistant conducted singing classes, but they spent most of their time looking for sin. Their task was easy because of course we were all filled with sins, but they worked hard at it. They were always on patrol, sometimes together and sometimes separately. They patrolled the silent study hall, and they patrolled the corridors, and they patrolled the classrooms and the washrooms, and they even patrolled the dormitories, often walking between the beds after the lights were out. We knew what they were hunting for, of course, and as soon as one of them appeared in the doorway of a classroom, or anywhere, we all knew that sin had been stalked home and that at least one person in the room was going to have to answer for herself. The only thing was, we did not know which one of us it would be. I always felt I was the sinner, I suppose the others felt the same. The Devil works in mysterious ways, and there was never any way of knowing which of our faces he had chosen to reveal himself in. We never knew where we were.

Those two nuns tracked him down even in the refectory, where we had breakfast, dinner, tea, and supper. They never seemed to notice what was on our plates. Awful food. It was always tea and bread scraped with butter, except at midday dinner, when it was boiled potatoes. And at supper the tea was replaced with vile cocoa. For breakfast on Mondays and Wednesdays and Fridays, the tea and b&b were accompanied by one tablespoonful of dates that had been boiled into a thin soup, or, as the nun who cooked would have said, a jam. On Tuesdays and Thursdays breakfast was emboldened by a wafer of cold porridge damped with blue milk, on Saturdays by a spot of marmalade, and on Sundays by an ugly morsel of bacon. Teatime and suppertime were all bread and butter, except that at teatime we were allowed to bring out the jam and cake we had received in packages from home. Some girls got parcels from home and some didn't. Those who did had the privilege of going around from table to table (there were five long, narrow tables) carrying pots of jam and big cakes and bestowing their favors on the girls they liked and walking past the girls they didn't like. There were about sixty of us, aged from seven to eighteen, and sometimes the room was quite busy at teatime, especially at the beginning of each term, when everybody had something to walk about with. I can't remember Sunday dinner, but on Mondays and Wednesdays it was boiled potatoes with black pudding that was nearly all gray, and on Tuesdays and Thursdays it was said to be corned beef. On Fridays something fishy, and on Saturdays a stew – an end-of-the-week stew.

I was thinking of that Saturday stew and admiring the huge menu the waiter had left on my table when the entrance door of the restaurant opened and the two nuns walked in. They had been looking for a nice quiet place to eat, and they had found it. They walked quickly, without making a sound, straight down the restaurant, and I watched them all the way, and watched until they had settled themselves in a distant booth. Then I went back to my menu. The menu was still in my left hand, tilted up, as I had been holding it, but my right hand, with the empty martini glass in it, had somehow gone under the table and was hiding there behind the tablecloth. It was the moment of no comment. It was the moment of no comment.

Great Summer Sale

LOUIS MACNEICE (1963)

John F. Kennedy's visit to Ireland in 1963 generated a mixture of
Irish self-importance, pro-American sentiment and real or imagined nostalgia, mingled with some genuine emotion around the
issue of emigration. In this report for the *New Statesman*, the poet
Louis MacNeice, a native of Co. Antrim and a long-time resident of
England, cut through these phenomena in a way that built on his
affection for his native island.

The isle was full of Garda. In the Black North the Orangemen were
so anxious not to discuss the President's visit (he, it was implied, having slighted the Six Counties) that they found themselves reduced to
discussing the election of the Pope. The northern Catholics on the
other hand, who felt equally slighted, were pondering the Irish
Derby. I had lunch in Belfast with a Monsignor, all of whose three
brothers are old IRA men, while his mother is the best preserved
93-year-old I have yet met: we talked about modern poetry. And so
to Dublin and the bunting and the loud speakers.

In this country, which is not without a record of violence, nobody
had ever seen such a display of 'security': Queen Victoria must have
been turning in her grave with envy. It was rumoured that for the
progress of the 'motorcade' between Dublin Airport and Dublin
the Americans, not content with their own 280 security men, had
asked for the loan of more native police than the whole Garda
Síochána in the Republic could muster. It was also rumoured that the
individual who drove behind the President in a car with the door ajar
was such a virtuoso that he could jump out while the car was moving
at 25 mph, to take just two paces and start shooting. Some of the
Irish, to start with, were piqued by all this. By the end of the visit,
however, they were beginning to feel sorry for the security men.
'The poor fellows!' one said, 'sure they almost forgot themselves and
waved. And anyhow, one thing in their favour, they failed in their

task, which was to cut him off from humanity.' 'Security men,' another said, 'are like Presbyterian ministers. It takes them some time to relax.'

The first motorcade (an ugly word which we all enjoyed, which sounds especially good in a low-Dublin adenoidal accent) I watched from the window of a small hotel in Parnell Square: there were several nobs present, including the surviving editor of *The Oxford Book of Irish Verse* [i.e. *Donagh MacDonagh – Ed.*]. After the vanguard of motor bicycles, Kennedy himself glided past, standing in an open car and looking just like himself but, we were glad to observe, more so. Or more so at least than his many pictures which plastered O'Connell Street as far as the bridge. Interspersed with the legend 'Céad Míle Fáilte', which, as Kennedy himself later explained to a Galwegian audience, means '100,000 welcomes'. One large shop said: 'Céad Míle Fáilte! Great Summer Sale!' A building opposite said: 'Bingo Nightly'. Left behind in the window, we agreed that the man had a presence. Then we made plans for the morrow and how wrong we were.

I turned up, not too sharp, with my friend DB [Dominic Behan] to keep an appointment 'at 8 a.m. sharp' outside Jury's Hotel in College Green: we were to be driven in a high-powered car to the ancestral Kennedy territory in New Ross, Co. Wexford, nearly 100 miles away. But our driver had overslept. After waiting nearly half an hour DB said: 'Let's go to the Gresham, we'll get it all fixed there.' We went to a bedroom in the Gresham and found one heavy-lidded American reporter and one heavy-lidded American cameraman. They were wearing aggressive pyjamas. We asked for seats in a helicopter, but they said that couldn't be and offered us a drink instead. Keeping up with the President, they explained, was tiring – well, kind of tiring. Now the German visit, they said, they could see the point of that – kind of high policy and strategy and things – but this Irish trip – they'd gotten the idea the President was out to enjoy himself. It would be nice to have time off, they said, but sooner in Frankfurt than in Dublin. 'What the hell can a man do in Dublin?'

They left to catch their helicopter and we went downstairs and got a breakfast-time drink. An Irishman connected with the Press

Centre began to give us the dope. 'A hundred and four of their own,' he said, 'and about 70 foreign reporters. And would you believe it, last night when he arrived, there were only four messages went out through the Centre. The boys had pre-filed their stories. It's only natural of course.' DB looked up contemplatively at a huge chandelier. 'D'ya know,' he said, 'that thing has 96 pieces missing.' 'How do you know?' we naturally asked. 'Because,' he said, 'I was employed one time to wash it. Ammonia it was we washed it with and we had to take it apart. Well, when we came to put it together again, there were these 96 pieces that just wouldn't fit.' And he sang:

> We had wine, porter and Jameson,
> We had cocktails and cocoa and all . . .

Somebody else said: 'Isn't it terrible hard on John Fitzgerald Kennedy that he has to be tethered all the time to the telephone? Even up there in his helicopter sittin' at his walnut writing desk. But that's the American constitution. Suppose now some place like Alabama was to forget itself? Wherever he was, say at his cousin Mrs Ryan's in Dunganstown, he'd have to quell the problem from there.'

The official hand-out had said: '12 noon Lounge Suit Thursday, June 27. President Kennedy arrives at Kennedy homestead, Dunganstown, where he will be a guest at a tea given by Mrs Mary Ryan . . . she has invited 13 other distant relatives to the tea.' We missed it, of course, and the following day's visit to Cork – where the Radio Éireann commentator was so carried away, so his colleagues tell me, by the rapturous crowd that, remembering his race meetings, he said: 'President Kennedy is now well out in front.'

Instead, I got in a train for Galway and read the papers. The Irish *Evening Herald* said helpfully in a special article: 'The role of the President of the USA falls somewhere between that of An t-Uachtarán and the Taoiseach in Ireland.' In the same number were tributes in verse that reminded one that Ireland could always hold her own with England in the broadsheet class:

Heaven direct you safely, and guide you and yours on an even keel,
Never has America had one like you before, you have great appeal . . .
Never despondent, never depressed, never ill at ease;
Nicely illustrating true manhood in the skies, on land, and on seas

While I was indulging myself with such light reading in the train, Kennedy was laying a wreath on the graves of the 1916 martyrs, addressing a joint sitting of the Houses of Parliament and receiving honorary degrees from both University and Trinity Colleges. Of the latter (so long regarded as a Protestant and Saxon garrison) an old man said to me that evening: 'I've just had a terrible shock listening to the radio – beautiful Latin pouring out, better even than you hear from the priests, and, would you believe it, it was Trinity College, Dublin!'

In Galway, Your Man, as they would call him, came down again from the overcast skies, and at last I heard him speak. But not till several dignitaries had spoken at length in the Gaelic. Kennedy replied in the English and did it with wit and charm. Something like this, as he pointed towards Galway Bay: 'If the day were a little clearer and you went down there and your eyesight was good enough, you would see Boston, Massachusetts, and all your relatives working there.' The crowd liked this very much. I decided that Your Man was a fine showman, but also, and more important, happy to be there. *Of course* this was a sentimental visit: you can't have power politics all the time.

When he had helicoptered away I walked round the capital of the Gaeltacht to look at the decorations. Two of them I found original. The usual brace of flags but apparently made of rough bathroom towelling: I crossed the street and found they were made of carnations, all except the stars in Old Glory which were made of cornflowers. But what about the yellows and greens in the tricolour? 'Ah, those ones are dyed,' said the girl in the flower-shop; 'anyhow they're all imported from Holland.' A little further on, in Dominick Street Lower, there was a window full of toys and among them a donkey with a creel of turf on each side of him; out of one stuck the Stars and Stripes and out of the other the Tricolour. But the point was this was a mechanized donkey: he kept nodding his head, but very slowly, like an oriental holy man. It was only later that I remembered that in the US the donkey is the emblem of the Democratic Party.

'Go on!' I said to myself. 'Can't *you* ever say Yes too?' When I got back to Dublin a Dubliner said to me: 'I hope you're not going to send this whole thing up.' When a Dubliner says that, it means his heart has for once got in front of his mind. Well out in front, like the President himself.

The Largest Island

JOHN HEALY (1965)

In 1961, the population of the Republic of Ireland reached its lowest level since the Great Famine. John Healy, a journalist from Charlestown in Co. Mayo, became a spokesman for West of Ireland communities that saw their populations and prospects diminishing amidst the general modernization and relative prosperity of the 1960s. The following piece was published in two parts in the *Irish Times*.

I

The nippy, cream-coloured Triumph sports car comes belting down the road, the hood back, a cream-coloured girl at the wheel, hair streaming in the slipstream. Beside her is another cream-coloured girl, blue-clad, and behind them, sitting on the hood, perched over them like a junior god, is a sun-tanned, handsome young man, shirt billowing in the winds.

The Triumph flashes past the quiet houses, past the lazy pedestrians who no longer look up at passing traffic, past the acreage of caravans and tents, large and small, past the nine-hole golf course, up the snaking road, past the small turf banks where old women, very old men, and very young schoolgirls hump bags of turf from the bank to the roadside, where sheep stare and wonder and take it all for granted.

Excepting the turf banks it all rather looked like a familiar setting for a television commercial. It had all the success symbols, the fast little sports car, the glamorous women, the clean-cut young man: you were missing merely the syrupy commercial urging you to buy cigarettes, beer, or someone's chocolate or toothpaste.

It was actually an everyday scene in Achill island in the month of August last, a month in which this island, the largest off the Irish coast, enjoyed what the local papers like the *Western People* and the *Mayo News* dismissed in a paragraph as 'Boom on Achill'.

Booms are no longer news where Achill is concerned; it is true that each year the island does better and better in the matter of tourism. But to somebody like myself who had not been to Achill for a few years, the size of this year's boom was something I had not expected.

One's background had much to do with it. For four months before that August weekend I had sat in the Press Gallery of Leinster House, listening to speakers dispute statistics, thrusting familiar slide-rules under each other's noses as evidence of the success or failure of the economy. The West was dying or the West was being saved ... the country was in danger of facing a crisis or was already in the grip of a crisis.

Suddenly, with the argumentative words and problems fading with each mile you drove from Dublin, the car rounds the hill and the bend and below you, in brilliant sunshine, is Keel Strand and the Commonage outglistening the sea as hundreds of cars and caravans play back the sun so that it looks like Galway Races on Hurdle Day. You slow down to absorb the scene and caravans pull out and pass you, hustling like beetles down the ribbon road to the snuggle of houses at Keel or further on to Pollagh or Dooagh.

Now you have two miles of cars and caravans in front of you as you drive on again and they are still coming ... cars from Ireland, cars from Britain. You make a mental note that the Ferry is paying off handsomely; noting too the big numbers of Northern Ireland cars, forgiving the cheeky impertinence of the tourist who sports a big GB plate and, underneath it, has the legend 'Co. Fermanagh'. In Achill the Orangeman's pound buys as much as the Dublin man's pound and not to worry.

The next day you find your bearings. The island is jammed full. The Tourist Bureau keeps on taking calls as people look for accommodation. The hotels are fully booked and all their makeshift accommodation is gone. The guest houses are full and the bed and breakfasts are full ... a camp bed here and there is the best that can be done. The camp bed is accepted.

In Westport and Castlebar there will be a shaking of heads at 'crowding people into houses', but the fact remains that the people want to crowd into Achill, and don't mind too much about where they sleep since they'll hardly get any sleep during regular sleeping hours, the night-life being one of the great attractions of Achill.

You meet old friends on the first Tuesday in August. All have the same story: it was a great weekend. Every pub and hotel in the island was drank dry. There had been an exemption until two o'clock in the morning and the last drop of drink was gone at 12.30 on August Monday.

Later someone tells you that one man's bill for drink ordered on his hotel room number for 14 days came to £145 – and this didn't take into the reckoning what he spent in various pubs on the island. You drive through Pollagh and Dooagh at two in the morning and the road is jammed with cars. You realise that you can drive with less frustration through O'Connell Street at the 5.30 evening peak.

But you don't complain for this is Achill, time isn't important and by three a.m. the traffic will have sorted itself out. In the meantime a pub door opens in the dark and the wind carries a lusty chorus of 'Fine Girl Y'Are' before the door is closed on the sing-song and the smoke, and the laughter. A white-belted Garda directs traffic up and down the road and in and out of the parking places.

On Tuesday the first of the big fat beer lorries come snaking in an armada through Achill Sound and on over the unfenced road and through the indifferent sheep to restock and replenish the empty shelves and the growling engines have another long tail of hurrying cars and caravans behind them. More tents mushroom on the Sandy Bank and, in O'Malley's Post Office, and the butcher's adjoining it, the customers are four and six deep and the money flows.

You have a hard time seeing Mr Lemass and his crisis in this hot August sun and all the earnest and sober speeches of all the politicians seem a little unreal in the reality of Achill.

Tonight, you say, you'll eat out and you ring one of the local hotels for a table. They're sorry: they're full. Tomorrow night, then? Sorry. What about the end of the week? Sorry . . .

And still the cars come and the caravans come and on everyone you begin to see the charming almost smug smile of Dr Tim

O'Driscoll [Director-General of Bord Fáilte] who will later in the year count up every one of those cars and wave them triumphantly as all his own work.

Well, you're not going to begrudge Tim O'Driscoll his show of statistics but already you're beginning to wonder what could Achill do if someone took it in hand and gave it a bit of well-planned development.

'Development' is something akin to a dirty word in Achill. Bord Fáilte and Mayo County Council did a magnificent job of laying a clinging road down to Keem Bay so that now you can drive over the shoulder of the mountain and down to the Bay of Sharks and one of the loveliest sights in Europe.

There are some who were annoyed that Keem Bay was made accessible to car-traffic but the drive, as breath-taking as the hairpins of the Pyrenees, *is* dramatic and the sight of the bay so far below, from the top of the road, justifies the work.

It is the old argument again: why 'spoil' a place by developing it? It is an argument used in the main by the people who are entrenched in Achill: who have summer cottages there, or long leases on such accommodation as is available, the people who have been coming here since the late '40s or early '50s and who resent its being discovered because discovery means crowds and crowds mean development.

And yet development in Achill is as inevitable as the tide's ebbing for the flow of tourist traffic is now washing on and over Achill Island with the relentlessness of the waters which break over the Daisy Rocks in the bay. And indeed development might go part of the way to saving the other Achill Island, the island the tourist rarely sees for the cars and the prosperity, the island of the grass widows and the men and women who sneak away into statistics of another kind in the early dawn when the carousing tourists are scarcely in their beds.

II

The morning mist hung over the Minawn Cliffs and there was a great peace on Achill Island. I resented the journey I had to make to

Dublin, but at three p.m. the Senate would sit and there was a job to be done.

The first bus to Dublin rounded by O'Malley's Post Office and halted. The conductor, Mick Lynch, took my overnight bag, pressed the bell, and we were on the way to Dublin. It was also the way to see the other Achill.

The bus was practically empty. Mick Lynch is not so much a conductor as a man who fills the role of a conductor because it allows him to see that people coming to Achill, and leaving, get, and take away, a good impression of his native island, the company with which he is associated (CIE) and generally carries himself as an ambassador for Aran. He is quiet-spoken, dressed like an executive so that you don't see the uniform as much as the man.

Yes, he confirmed, it had been a great season and the island never made as much money. It was said with great sobriety, with no great elation, and you got the feeling (while you rushed on about all the cars and caravans and money-spending you had seen) that Mick Lynch knew something more and it was not quite as pleasant.

Our first two stops were to pick up young girls going to work in Achill Sound or on to shops at Mulranny. They were fourteen or fifteen. Further on a small knot of people stood on the roadside. There were three suitcases, and seven people. Mick opened the door and waited.

'Goodbye again, Maureen, and God send you safe.'

'Look after Mother.'

'And write, Martin James. She do look for your letter.'

There are assurances and Mick Lynch waits. He knows this ceremony and knows the dialogue. Outside, kisses are exchanged . . . the tears which have been held back tremble and break a powdered face and Mick Lynch knows this is the moment to take a case and place it with gentleness in the back seat of the bus. The old man is impassive as his daughter kisses him again and then she turns with her brother and rushes into the bus before the tears well up and fall freely.

Mick Lynch presses the bell. The brother and sister wave back at the knot on the road. Two fields away, in the door etched black against the tidy whitewash, a handkerchief waved.

'There's Mother . . .'

The son puts up a hand. The girl checks herself and her 'Goodbye' dies on her lips as a casual thing. She waves a handkerchief with no animation, and a handkerchief waves back at her. Now you can see the headscarf on the old woman's head and the girl watches the two patches of white, one waving, one still, until the bus climbs round the hill. She will have regained her composure before Mick Lynch punches a ticket for her to Westport and the train to Dublin and the boat for England.

Two miles on it is the same all over again, two daughters off and four suitcases are piled on the back seat. These girls are veterans and yet, although they leave a father and mother dry-eyed, the tears are fought back as the bus gathers speed. Before we reach Newport we have a dozen cases all with the familiar tag, 'via Holyhead'.

One remembers the husband and wife and the two pretty children and the children crying as they said goodbye to a grandmother. They cried into the bus, up the aisle and sobbed into their seats and their father cried with them. Afterwards one was surprised to hear them speak for they were not Irish children but had been born in England of Irish parents.

I have a very distinct remembrance of being choked with a rage I hadn't known for many years. It wasn't as if I hadn't known this. Twenty years ago as a youngster in a small Mayo town I had watched, each morning as I went to collect the daily papers from the morning train, young people go and mothers run after the train as it moved out with its load of human flesh packed as well as the cattle trains on a fair day. But that was wartime and there was great money in the factories in England and none here. But surely that had changed?

Mick Lynch totted his figures and looked up when I said: 'Will it never change?' I didn't have to explain.

He said simply: 'I keep the back seat for the suitcases . . .'

He had statistics . . . smaller classes at the schools in the island, having dwindled down from hundreds to tens and twenties. The all too familiar tale of the West.

We were all right in the '40s for we had the breeding stock. The fathers and mothers were young and could beget more and, while they remained alive, the cheques would flow home and there would be money coming into the country and the family. But now that generation is dying off and in the already empty homes of Achill no cheques come, the once worked land goes sour. And there is no young stock to breed migrants: the final homecoming is to bury the 'old people' or to shutter or sell the 'old place', and be forever lost to this country.

The traffic against us is heavier now and the bus slows down to let the speeding cars and caravans pass by on the way to Achill. The two young English children are laughing now and the father and mother are beginning to pick up again on the threads of their life in Coventry. A little wryly you realise that these too will be ear-marked as tourists by Dr Tim O'Driscoll in the autumn accounting.

They will keep coming until the 'old people' die – and then? They will be the worry and joy and responsibility of a Harold Wilson or a Ted Heath but never of a Charlie Haughey or a Liam Cosgrave or the thing they call 'the old country'.

Five hours later one sits in Seanad Éireann. There is a debate on the Free Trade Area. Sincere young men talk about the dangers of tying ourselves to England. We must be economically and politically independent of England. The debate drags on and on and on and you wonder what Ireland are we talking about.

Statistics are hurled about in the air and you have a very unprofessional desire to cry 'Halt' because in all the thousands and millions of percentages of gains and losses and problematic posings, you keep on hearing the voice of Mick Lynch saying: 'I keep the back seat for the suitcases.'

Instead you leave your seat quietly and slip out for a cigarette, to be joined at the top of the stairs by a politician who has honesty enough to say:

'I couldn't take any more of it, either.'

But we go on taking more of it, for we have statistics, haven't we? Statistical Ireland is doing well, it's Second Progammed and Just Societied and slotted and grooved and State-Industried and Board of Directored and Generally-managed and not to worry.

Next month there will be an innocuous question down on the

Dáil order paper about the slipway at Purteen Harbour in Achill and there will be an innocuous holding answer and Keel and Dooagh and the people who cling to their own way of life will note the ha'penny worth of acknowledgment of their voting power, but will be wholly unimpressed.

It is with a deal of relief that one escapes again to Achill and the sunshine and the midnight traffic jam created by the men and women with the GB cars and the triangled Northern cars and those from Dublin and the South. Mr Brian Faulkner, the Stormont Minister for Commerce, has left the caravan park and his place has been taken by a couple from London. Big-thighed women, berry brown in ridiculous shorts, mince along the strand. Bright young things in toreador tights and provocative sunglasses amble slowly and hopefully on the road from the beach, for an offer of a lift or maybe a date. In a cottage a women salts down fish against the winter, for the summering sun and time of plenty will soon be gone like the tourists and the tourists' money.

Yet in the pubs and the singing lounges of the island the ballads are still going strong and when you think of the women of Achill you realise that of all the apt lines, 'Fine Girl Y'Are' is ironically apt for, without women, Achill island would have no future.

The Exhumation of Roger Casement

SEAN RONAN (1965)

Roger Casement, who had been involved in German-assisted preparations for the 1916 Rising, was hanged in Pentonville Prison for these activities in the same year. For decades thereafter, his execution – and the refusal of successive British governments to repatriate his remains – was an irritant in Anglo-Irish relations. In 1965, the British prime minister Harold Wilson, whose Liverpool constituency included numerous Irish emigrants, decided that repatriation would be an appropriate gesture to mark the fiftieth anniversary of the Rising. The exhumation was officially witnessed, and recorded, by Sean Ronan, a senior official of the Department of External Affairs in Dublin, in order to ensure the authenticity of the remains that were to be transferred back to Ireland.

[. . .] The first sod was removed at about 4.50 p.m. When the top sods were removed two prison officers began to dig the grave using a pick-axe and shovels. As the ground was damp, the prison authorities provided boards on which we could stand against the west wall. As the digging proceeded, it was apparent that the soil was heavy and tightly packed. It was necessary to use the pickaxe constantly to loosen the soil. At 6 p.m. the Deputy Governor sent us coffee. The work proceeded at the rate of about 2 ft per hour, the wardens relieving each other every half-hour or so. Shortly after 6 p.m. the Governor of the prison, Mr A. J. Burnett, who had by this time returned from leave, appeared and introduced himself to us. About this time Mr Cruddas and Mr Kent stated, in response to something said by us in discussion about the effects of quicklime, that lime would not be found in the grave as its use had been discontinued some time before Casement's execution. They said charcoal was used (as an absorbent) subsequently instead. We mentioned that there was a tradition ('That some amends be made / To this most gallant gentleman / That is in quicklime laid') that quicklime was used, but they seemed quite satisfied that this could not be so. (The testimony of Fr McCarroll, who was present at Casement's burial, also indicated that quicklime was thrown into his grave.)

Mr Cruddas had mentioned at the meeting in the Home Office that morning the possibility that water might be encountered in the digging. At about 7.30 p.m., when the workmen had reached a depth of over 5 feet, they reported that the soil was becoming wet. The reason given for this by Mr Cruddas, and later by the prison doctor, Dr Mason, was the water probably came from a culvert carrying away some of the overflow of the old Pen river which had been dammed a long time ago to form a reservoir. During World War II the prison suffered bomb damage and it was thought that in the course of this the culvert had been damaged and so caused seepage. This was related to the fact that some years ago unexplained flooding occurred in the basement of Block B just outside the inner walls of the burial ground and still continues, so that constant drainage by pumping is necessary. At all events, from a depth of over 5 feet the workmen began to encounter wet soil. At a depth of about 6 and 7 feet some lime was unearthed. It was soon discovered that this was a thick layer and that it spread the whole length of the grave. The workmen had at this stage dug vertically down from the head of the grave at the east wall around the two sides but had left steps beginning at a depth of about 4 feet from both the east and west ends of the grave. This facilitated their descent into the grave and their work. At this stage also two long boards of about 1 foot in width were placed on either side of the pit. The prison officers in the grave shovelled the earth onto these boards and this was removed with shovels by the men above the pit.

As lime began to come up shortly before 8 p.m., those present, who up to then had taken turns to move up and down a little, gathered close over the grave and it was quite apparent that a layer of lime had been reached covering the entire area of the grave. At this stage some water appeared and formed a pool in the centre of the grave. As one of the wardens was digging into the lime two small black objects were observed floating in the water. We immediately asked that these be passed up and on examination they appeared to be flint-like in substance and in the shape of small human bones. We were in some doubt because of their colour and weight, whether they were human bones or not so we called for the prison doctor, Dr Mason, and also for pumps to eliminate the water. The coffin, which had been delivered to the prison as scheduled by the undertaker and placed in the engineers' workshop, was wheeled to the grave-side on a small trailer. This was upholstered in white satin, in accordance with our specifications, inside the lead lining. The floor of the coffin was padded and was lined with soft white wool material. There was a white satin pillow at the head of the coffin and the undertaker had supplied all the necessary accessories, including green rubber sheets, a bag of charcoal and a large white plastic covering which we left over the entire coffin as a slight mist was falling.

Dr Mason arrived and identified the two small black objects as human remains, the larger one being a thumb bone and the smaller one part of the bone above the thumb. These were placed on one of the green rubber sheets on the ground. Some delay occurred while the pumping machine was being brought from Holloway prison and the pumping proceeded. During this time Mr Keating, who had arranged to report to the Ambassador around 8 p.m., telephoned him as to the position. At 9 p.m. the Deputy Governor provided coffee and a liberal supply of sandwiches for those present. By about 9.15 p.m. the pumping was completed as best it could but, nevertheless, the prison officers were working in very muddy conditions and water was springing up all the time. The prison officers said there was an unpleasant odour in the grave but this was not apparent to any great extent outside it. (At this stage we noticed from the top of the prison wing, Block B, outside the burial ground wall that a prisoner was observing the proceedings through a mirror on which the light from his cell was reflecting in our direction. The Deputy Governor left immediately, presumably to warn him off.) Within a few minutes one of the prison officers handed up a clearly identifiable human bone which Dr Mason identified as a rib. This was encased with lime.

Some buckets of water were supplied and we had the bone washed and dried and placed with the thumb bones. About this time Mr Kent asked us if we were satisfied that identifiable human bones were being recovered. We replied in the affirmative, whereupon Mr Kent telephoned Mr H. B. Wilson, the Assistant Under-Secretary, who was standing by ready to appear with Sir Charles Cunningham at the burial ground to deal with the situation if, in fact, no remains were being recovered. Later, one of the prison officers working in the grave announced with a note of achievement that he thought he had come upon the skeleton. At this stage the wardens were up to their knees in water and mud in the grave and conditions were extremely difficult. We called for a consultation and asked that the work proceed rather more gently.

From this onwards every shovel-full and bucket of mud was carefully examined for human remains. Parts of a hard calcified-type substance were unearthed. At first Dr Mason thought that these were parts of a cranium but on closer examination some of them appeared to be stones of some kind and others possibly were parts of a calcified shroud as traces of cloth linings were clearly visible under the lights. It had become evident that any bones were going to be recovered singly rather than in the form of an articulated skeleton. By degrees more bones were handed up. These were carefully washed by one of the prison officers, passed to another who dried them and then passed to us, by which stage we were placing them in the coffin in their approximately correct positions according as they were identified by Dr Mason. Fr Keane, the prison Catholic chaplain, had appeared at this stage and he brought his Church of England colleague with him. We estimated that in all there were about fifteen persons who witnessed the vital stages of the exhumation.

Working at the head of the grave, one of the workmen recovered the lower jaw. The four front teeth (the incisors) were missing but there were four teeth on the right-hand side from us (i.e. the lower left canine, the two pre-molars and the first molar teeth) and two on the left (i.e. the lower right canine and first pre-molar). The fourth tooth backwards on the right (lower left molar) contained a lead filling in the centre and the second tooth backwards (first lower left pre-molar) a lead filling down the outer side. By this stage we had recovered about eight ribs, a number of vertebrae, arm bones, shoulder bones, the two pelvic bones and the large bone between them, the two femurs and quite a number of smaller bones. These were all extremely well-preserved perhaps by the action of the lime but very much blackened and encrusted with soil and lime itself. We asked that a special effort be made to recover the skull. One of the prison officers, Mr McKay, up to his knees in water and mud, made a special effort with great care at the head of the grave and with his hands explored in the mud until he located the skull and managed to bring it out not only intact but covered still in some of the shroud which had in some way or other protected it so that there was an element of scalp and hair remaining. The skull was situated in a somewhat lower position than the other bones and was located almost under the chalk vertical line which had been drawn earlier on the east wall of the burial ground.

As the skull was being cleaned one of the prison officers sought to remove the hardened portion of the shroud. In doing so he uncovered part of a very white skull on which there were a few small red dots. Some black hair was clearly visible on the outer part of the skull and Dr Mason warned that the scalp was being removed with the hardened material. We, therefore, asked the prison officer to replace it and we took the entire skull with the material around it, left it to dry for a while, and placed it in position in the coffin with the satin pillow in a vertical position to keep it in place. Judging from the size of the bones which we recovered, especially the femurs, it was quite apparent that these were of a person of exceptionally large size. At this point it was agreed by all that the only remains of any significance that were still unrecovered were the tibias and that there was no real possibility of recovering anything else. A special effort was, therefore, made to recover these bones. The search was, therefore, concentrated on the foot of the grave where some additional digging and scooping was necessary. Eventually, both the tibias were recovered and these we placed parallel to the femurs in the coffin so that all the bones recovered were comfortably distributed on the floor of the coffin as closely as was possible to their normal positions. It may be of interest to record that one of the grave diggers remarked that one of the tibias looked as if it had been broken at some time and reset. This was confirmed by one of his colleagues but the bone was not in fact examined by Dr Mason.

About 10.20 p.m. it was quite apparent to all present, having regard to the extraordinarily difficult conditions in the grave, that there was no possibility of recovering any further bones. Therefore, in response to Mr Kent of the Home Office, we agreed that it was no longer feasible to endeavour to recover any further bones and that the exhumation operation could end.

One feature about the bones as they were placed in the coffin was that they were all black in colour. Dr Mason originally suggested that this was due to putrefaction of the flesh and that the black could probably be scraped off. Subsequently, he thought that the black might be accounted for if pitch were smeared on the corpse prior to burial, which seemed to us and to the Home Office officials as highly unlikely. We covered the bones in the coffin with the charcoal supplied by the undertaker, evenly spread. This was necessary to keep the bones in position and to absorb moisture and gases. Then we placed the white plastic sheet on top of the charcoal and one of the green rubber sheets on top of that.

The coffin was wheeled, at about 10.30 p.m., into the engineers' workshop where the lead top was placed in position and, after some delay, the prison officers lead-soldered the groove between the lead top and the lead sides all the way around the coffin. The mahogany top was then screwed down into position. The Prison Governor, Mr Kent and Fr Keane were present with the prison officers and ourselves. During this time we had an opportunity to clean up, and cups of tea were served. Shortly after 11.30 p.m. six prison officers carried the coffin shoulder-high, and with reverence, from the engineers' workshop into Block D of the prison and into the Catholic Chapel, where silent prayers were said and where the coffin rested, under lock and key, for the night just outside the altar-rails in front of the altar. We took our departure from the Governor and Fr Keane just outside the main gate of the prison and got a taxi to the Embassy where we arrived about 12.30 a.m. and reported to the Ambassador. [. . .]

The Trouble with Larry

MICHAEL VINEY (1966)

The incarceration of children in industrial schools was for a very long time a largely unexplored aspect of Irish life. Many of the inmates had committed no offence, or only very minor infractions; most came from broken homes. The recommendations of a 1936 report on these institutions were ignored or imperfectly implemented. An Abbey play, *The Evidence I Shall Give*, by a district justice who was perturbed by the regime in the industrial schools, created a short-lived sensation in 1961. A report – 'Some of Our Children' (1966) – by Tuairim, a group of young Irish university graduates committed to social and political reform, as well as a series of *Irish Times* articles in the same year by Michael Viney, undoubtedly influenced the appointment in 1969 of the Kennedy Commission, which reported on this topic in 1970. Despite these initiatives, little substantial reform of this sector took place until the creation of the Commission to Inquire into Child Abuse (2000–2009), whose report specifically referenced Viney's work.

Larry first tapped his way to me on a murky afternoon in February. For him it was good weather, because the light tormented his eyes. 'In the brightness of the day I can scarce see a thing at all, but in the dark I can nearly read. Perhaps I'll get black glasses to keep the light out of my head.' He sat stiffly in the chair, gripping his white stick and staring straight ahead of him.

Larry is seventeen, rather thin and frail. He was wearing borrowed clothes and despaired of getting his hair to lie down again after the way they cut it in the reformatory. He wasn't too bitter about that, or indeed about anything much. A bit bewildered, perhaps, and sometimes indignant, but always wanting to be fair. He didn't mind telling his story, if I thought that would do any good.

Parts of it may be distorted, or reflect the partial understanding of his years. And to some of it, undoubtedly, there is another side. But if it matters at all to know how things look to a boy with a 'delinquent' label round his neck, Larry may be listened to with a fair degree of trust. He is very dependent on people just now, and hesitates to alienate a world of blurs and shadows.

'My father and mother,' says Larry, 'was pretty bad on the drink and never had very much happiness. I came in one night and they were arguing and drinking and I couldn't stand it no longer. I got out of the house. I went round to a priest who looks after youths. He gave me the name of a hostel and I went and stayed there for about a week. But I met up with two lads there and one of them was a mechanic and he was great at opening cars. He could borrow one any time. He showed me how to do it and how to start the car and all. And then I got in the habit, any time I'd be stuck for walking anywhere, of hopping in a car and away. I was caught up in a lot of things like that. And when I was brought up in court it was two years in Daingean on account of my background.

'At that time I could see up to two hundred yards away, but I wouldn't know anyone until they came right up against me. I went mainly by voices. When I was in National School I couldn't see the blackboard. I had to go by the other boys' copies and ask them what was written up. Then the master would come down and slap me for talking. I told him I couldn't see the board, but he said: "You just don't want to see it."

'When I went to Daingean there was a medical examination. I told the brother my eyesight was bad and he said: "Why didn't you get glasses outside, what did you wait to come in here for? We haven't got money to be throwing away." And it was months after that, when the eye doctor came visiting, that they gave me glasses. But when I came out on holiday my brother got a hold of them and they was smashed.

'When I went to Daingean first, I was greeted very nicely, shaking hands, but I felt the fear inside me. They asked me about my tattoos, why did I have tattoos. But that first day they was okay and I went out to the square, a great big square with high walls and a few people in it and I started walking up and down. I was just fifteen then.

'They give you black trousers and a coat of sorts, all patches. You might get two odd sleeves up to the elbow. Sunday you have cleaner clothes for church. We got a shower about every month. There was only six showers for all the boys on my side of the school. And we got a haircut a month which left you looking like a Red Indian, you'd be ashamed for anyone to see you.

'The main thing in food was potatoes. Some does be rotten and others good, well, you can't help that. For breakfast there was three cups of tea and a quarter of a loaf and some butter. Dinner was meat and something all mixed up. But the new superior has been improving it a lot by degrees. He did his best in regards of that. And he got teapots and cups for the table, which was a lot better than dipping the mugs in a bucket. But I'd like a bit of cleanliness down there. The rust does sometimes be thick on the knives.

'There was a civics class and a Christian Doctrine class and they was both good. The civics class was about civil rights and how to vote and what to do when you buy a house. If someone comes along and asks you what right you have to be standing on the street, you're able to tell them.

'After dinner you go out to the square and maybe play handball or just sit down and idle away. The walls are very high right round the school and nobody tries to run away for the first three or four weeks. You have to wait until you go out in a batch. And anyone interested in running away asks to get in the farm or the field batch. They're the two hardest and next to that is the bog, footing the turf.

'The field batch is the worst of the lot. You go out there in all sorts of weather with so little clothing on you, just the little short coat, and your hands would be just coiled up and you could beat them against a wall and not feel it. You go out there to the fields and you start picking potatoes, turnips or beet. You have knee-pads on you and you can't move at all, just keep going up and down. Taking them out with your hands and throwing them into the can.

'One of the farmers was very nice to me because I was a long time there. Except for once or twice. There was once he started saying things about my father and no matter how bad your people are you don't like anything said about them. And I jumped at him and he used a fork to me and I used another one to him and then we started to fight. I got a flogging over that. And I got another one for running away.

'We was out in the field batch in January, spreading dung, and it was foggy and snowy and three of us thought we'd had enough. So we jumped a ditch and took off. But you can't tell which way is what from Daingean and we kept going round in circles. And then three of the brothers come up in a car and took us back. They give me a "baldy" haircut as well as a flogging, but maybe they don't do that now. And the new superior, he listens to why you ran away and if it was for worry about home he might not let you be punished.

'I was in eight months when I was let out on holiday. That was July, 1964. And I wasn't going to go back if I could help it. I went away to England until November. And when I was back I kept away from where I might be seen. But someone must have reported me because the police came and took me back. I was arrested in an FCA uniform and back at Daingean they said I looked very cultured in my uniform and where did I get it, did I rob it? And I said no, I didn't, I just went and joined the FCA. They don't ask you anything about eyesight.

'In Daingean they said I could start my time over again, but as it happened I was let go on December 23rd, 1965, which was a very big surprise. I was very excited when I heard about it – I was overjoyed, like. So I got my lecture and I signed a big form.

'The superior asked me what sort of work I would get and I says a builder's labourer. I'd say anything to get out of there. But I didn't have a job and I didn't know how things were at home. I never had a visit. I only had one letter and that was from my mother about my father running away and how she only had thirty shillings to keep herself and my younger brother. I wrote back, but I never got a reply. I often used to worry how she was and whether my brother was getting as much to eat as I was.

'Anyway, my bus fare was paid to Dublin. And I had another pair of glasses by then, but they hurt so much I couldn't wear them. When I got off the bus I jumped into the air and shouted "I'm free!" and everyone must have thought I was mad. I went across the bridge at Capel Street and up George's Street and up into Mount Pleasant Buildings and I knocked at the door.

'And there was no answer. So I put my hand in through the little broken pane of glass and I opened the door to go in. But there was no one there I knew. There was a lady with a load of kids. I said, "Where's me mammy?" She says, "Who are you, coming barging in here?" I says, "Excuse me, ma'am, this is my home."

'The same furniture was there, belonging to us, but different people. I says, "This is my home – that's the dresser over there, that's the table I made." She says, "I'm sorry. Your mammy has gone out of here the past four months. She's gone over to Britain."

'So I didn't know what to do. I'd not a halfpenny in my pocket and nowhere to go. I went to Mrs —— and she suggested a night shelter, but I'd had enough of dormitories and I wanted to keep away from all places like the school. And I was lucky, I got taken in by a family in ——. He's a blind man with twelve kids and two of them are blind. Me and two of his sons slept on a mattress on the floor. And I was happy there, because it was a family and I was welcome. Our meals was bread and tea and only twice a week potatoes, which could not be helped because the money was not in it. And then I went to the blind welfare centre and learned to make baskets. I got 7s. 6d. for a basket and gave the man that and he was thankful for it.'

This arrangement, however, did not last and Larry found himself homeless once again. By this time he had made a few friends in Dublin and they had helped him to get a Corporation blind allotment of 37s. 6d. a week. Now they found him shelter in a hostel, populated mainly by the destitute and derelict. But this made him 'of no fixed address' and lost him his blind allotment. His sight, fortunately, improved with medical attention and he was able to go seeking casual work in the docks and the Liffeyside auction rooms. But he was not very successful, and day after day he was left to wander the city until the night shelter opened for sleep. 'The people in that shelter,' he said, 'they've given up, they're no-hopers. But me, I'm only seventeen.'

A few weeks ago, he was at last in touch with a worker of the Society of St Vincent de Paul, who set about trying to reunite Larry with his mother in Britain. He was put on the boat last night.

Women on the Streets

MARY KENNY (1969)

Mary Kenny, who had worked for the *Evening Standard* in London, became Women's Editor of the *Irish Press* in July 1969. The paper's editor, Tim Pat Coogan, who had been appointed the previous year, recognized that journalism by and for women in Ireland had changed dramatically in the mid 1960s, not least in the rival *Irish Times*. A male journalist would have had difficulty – to put it mildly – in gathering the material for this article.

How do you approach a prostitute? I mean, if you're a girl, and the reason that you want to approach them is to talk to them about their lives. 'Excuse me, Miss, have you got a match?' Surely not. When in doubt, be simple.

The two girls were standing on the corner of a well-heeled street just south of the canal in Dublin. It was Saturday night last, and what with so many people in town for the All-Ireland, business was booming. A line of cars hovered around. I watched from behind a tree; big cars, small cars, young men, middle-aged men, married men, mostly – the only common denominator being that they had £5 to spend on ten minutes' pleasure.

I picked my chance and walked up to the girls. One was a girl, truly: very young, pretty, slim, a blonde, in a mini-skirt. The other was an older woman, in her forties maybe, a motherly figure with an open, nice face. 'Can I talk to you?' I asked. 'I'm a reporter.' The older woman smiled. 'We seen you, we thought you were from the Legion [of Mary].' I offered them a cigarette and we fell into conversation.

They didn't mind talking to me at all, it turned out; their attitude was in fact very easy-going and friendly: in a kind of comradely fashion. No side, as they say. I asked if there were a lot of clients that night; they said there were, they were picking and choosing. The Gardaí came. I said my name and the chief Garda got the message. He said he'd seen me on *The Late Late Show*.

O, media! O, post-McLuhan man! TV: the big identity-giver.

Anyway he said we were trespassing on private property and we'd have to get out. We said nothing and cleared out.

We made our way towards the canal, Kathleen calling down curses on his head, Angela saying ah well, God help them, sure they have their jobs to do too, and it isn't much fun being a Garda on that beat on a Saturday night

'Have you ever tried to come to an arrangement with the Gardaí?' I asked the women. All over the world it is notorious that prostitutes come to some kind of understanding with the police – either by giving the police a rake-off or, quite commonly, by reporting any criminal information that comes their way.

'You couldn't fix this lot,' Kathleen said bitterly. 'They'd have you in a cell before you'd know where you are.'

We found a quiet spot and recorded the interview. Kathleen told me she had been on the street for a bit more than a year; Angela had been at it for rather more than ten years now. Improbably (and yet I feel sure that what she said was the truth) Angela began the game just because she fell behind with the hire-purchase payments. She was a Dublin woman, married, the mother of eight children; everything just got too much for her, financially. She couldn't get financial help from anywhere, she said. Until she discovered that this way you could make it pretty easily. For her, as for nearly all prostitutes, the sex act was a straightforward routine to be got through and got over as quickly as possible, and almost like a separate activity from making love with your husband. She wanted to give it up soon. Her heart was not good now and she had cleared up most of her debts.

Kathleen had a different motive, although money played an important part in it too. She was from the south of Ireland (she asked me not to reveal the name of the town), and she had had a baby. Her boyfriend deserted her. She had had a bad time and she felt that what the hell, what does it matter now . . . she might as well go on the streets. A big consolation was the money coming in. She often made £30 and £40 a night. The least she ever made was £10 a night. One service cost £5 for ten minutes in a car; £10 for ten minutes in a flat (not hers). 'I never stay more than that. I'd never stay a night with a client, even for extra money.' She felt guilty about it certainly, on both social and religious grounds; she wouldn't like her landlord or her neighbours to know how she earned her living. But she cared so little about anything now. 'I feel I've dropped out of everything,' she shrugged.

Angela went to Mass every Sunday. 'You've got to go for the children's sake.'

Their attitude to most of their environment was amazingly compassionate – as is the attitude of most people who have really struck rock-bottom in any way – mentally, morally, physically or spiritually. They didn't mind the Legion of Mary people coming around to talk to them. 'They're good people,' Angela said sympathetically. 'They really are and I know they only want to help us. They have a hard time of it too, you know.' What do the people from the Legion tell them? 'They tell us to go off the streets and to go back to living a straight life.' 'I would do that,' Kathleen said earnestly, 'if I thought that I could earn a decent wage at all. But I couldn't earn anything like the money I'm getting now at anything else.' That was the truth of the matter.

Both of them took contraceptive precautions. Kathleen had had an intra-uterine device fitted in Belfast. Angela said they went to the doctor for check-ups fairly regularly because there was a lot of venereal disease in Dublin these days.

Most of the men that come to them are married, Angela said. You got working men as well as the richer classes. They quite often talked to you about themselves, about their jobs, and about their families. 'You get the impression that with a lot of them, their wives don't treat them right, do you know what I mean?' Angela explained.

My impression was that neither of the women was particularly hard; Kathleen was too young to be really tough, and Angela, for all her ten years' experience, was a tender-hearted kind of Dublin woman. Personally I liked them both as people and if they are blameworthy for what they do, so too are the men who patronise them and so are the social circumstances which drive women onto the streets.

We parted on good terms. 'If you're round here again, come over and we'll go back to the flat for coffee,' Kathleen said to me chattily as I left them. I will.

Visitor to Long Kesh

MARY CUMMINS (1972)

Later the site of the H Blocks of HMP Maze, the disused airfield at Long Kesh was, in 1972, an improvised detention centre in which internees were housed in Nissen huts. At this time, visits to Long Kesh had just resumed after having been banned for three weeks following protests by internees and visitors at searches. The *Irish Times,* in an editorial note accompanying the article, noted that journalists were not allowed in, and justified its decision to send in Mary Cummins under an assumed name because getting information about the camp was 'of public importance'.

You see it, not suddenly. It grows on the pale, February landscape in poles and hangar roofs, an unexpected clutter in an empty space, pastel and grey like the afternoon.

You pass the entrance, and down the road about a quarter of a mile you turn into an open space that is the car park. Through clouds of cold and winter mist the camp is more defined; you can see figures and corrugated roofs and spaces between the buildings.

Last week, day visits were resumed at Long Kesh after about three weeks off, because the internees were protesting against vigorous searches made before and after visits. Internees are allowed one half-hour visit a week. Three adults and two children can visit at that time.

In the car park there's a caravan where if you have a pass, you check in and leave any parcels you have brought. That day, a man had to take away bales of wood; they said they could be used as batons. He had brought them for the internees to carve them into shapes; we saw them later, harps and crosses and wooden lockers with little mirrors on top, carried off by their families. Near the caravan were two wooden huts with yellow doors: toilets. The Ladies was locked, out of order. In the Gents were three lavatories in a row, grubby, no toilet paper. The wind seemed to whistle through. In the large wooden waiting room – steps up to it and a door at either side facing each other – it was warmer. There was a theatre around which we grouped the chairs. In the corner, two Quaker ladies sold containers of tea or orange juice for a penny and little packets of biscuits.

That day, about thirty women and half a dozen children were there. Up to three weeks ago there was no hut for them to wait in. Through the winter months, they waited in all kinds of weather in the open car park for their names to be called. Now they wait in relative comfort, with chairs to sit on and white painted timber walls crying out for a witty or aggrieved pen. Already some of the walls are well covered. 'Up the boys', and 'Up the Tyrone boys', among the graffiti as well as lines of songs and poems.

We sat around sipping our tea and wondering if we would be called. Because it was the first day visits were resumed after the internees' prolonged but successful protest, nobody was sure if it was all over. Somebody had rung Long Kesh in the morning and was told she would be allowed to visit; but they said the same thing had happened in the previous weeks – one had sat until 8 p.m. before being told that she could not see her husband. The army's explanation was that if the men would not accept their visits, it wasn't their fault.

We cracked jokes to cover my nervousness; they said I'd probably only get a year if I was caught. I turned my ring around to look like a marriage band; I was supposed to be the internee's sister-in-law, so I repeated my name and address over and over again to drum it into my head and blot the other one out. My accent? 'Just keep your mouth shut, I'll do all the talking. Just answer any questions and don't raise your voice.'

The woman who was taking me in had been coming since November. She knew the ropes. We waited on for about half an hour, she more patient than I. This is nothing, I was told. You could be here until five or six o'clock. One woman from Ballymurphy with seven young children at home, all under eleven, left at 11.45 a.m. to get to the Falls Road in time for the bus which runs to the camp for five shillings a head. It left there after two. It was now after three o'clock. Almost all the women were in the same boat, having to leave their children in the care of the oldest, usually aged between eleven and fourteen. They talked about the young boy who was electrocuted recently while his mother was away visiting his internee father. They worried about the children coming home from school; they might get shot; they might get run down; they could get hit by a rubber bullet or into a fight.

At last the warden came to the door and started calling names, one by one. We waited. We were almost last, and with another warning to stay behind her and say nothing, the woman and I moved out of the other door, down the steps, and into a Sureline Coach. 'At least we're this far.' We sank back relieved. After about ten minutes the coach moved off, down the road. We sang 'Dublin in the Green' and 'The Men Behind the Wire', and gave the V sign to two passing Saracens.

A tiny, whippet-thin woman with a mass of black, wavy hair led the singing. She knew the ropes too. Her husband is in Long Kesh and her three brothers variously in Magilligan, the Maidstone and Crumlin Road. She makes about three or four visits a week, a half an hour at each one. Between her own and her husband's relatives, near and far, forty are interned. And her house has been raided thirty-one times since 9 August. She laughed, tossing her hair and sang louder as we approached the entrance. A bland, ironic sign, 'No entry beyond this point without a pass.'

We had to wait while an armoured car with soldiers, guns at the ready, pulled out slowly. They looked back unblinking at the tongues stuck out. At either side of the entrance, there's a post covered with green netting and topped with timber. You could just make out a figure in each, but anyone taking a pot-shot would have to be an acrobat.

The coach drove through slowly. Mud, yellow and slimy on the ground. Just inside the entrance are the Army huts – not Nissen like the internees' but spaced out. 'Look at them,' I was told. 'Look at the difference between those and the ones inside.' Soldiers walking around. Young; some of them looked about fifteen. 'Watch that one,' they said, 'you should have heard the language of him to us last week. You wouldn't repeat it.'

The coach stopped outside a wooden building. Wardens and soldiers outside. One soldier called the names one by one. Ours were called. We went in shaking and passed him while he looked us up and down, forty shades of green. Inside two soldiers sat at a desk checking the passes. They gave us a good look but didn't ask anything. We went into another room where there were two youngish girls in green uniforms. We passed them and sat inside. After about ten minutes they came in and went past us through another door. The women started moving in, one at a time. The searches had started. Panic. Once again I went through my bag. Everything identifiable gone except, Christ, a cheque with my name on it. 'Stick it down your bra . . . no, in your boot . . . no, in your knickers.'

Tried them all and none of them safe. Then my motherly friend said to give it to her and hid it in her copious holdall.

Then it was my turn. 'Remember your name and say nothing else.' Inside, they asked the name and wrote it on a large brown envelope. One took my bag, took out keys and matches, and put them in the envelope. The other one said, 'Open your coat.'

Then she started at my head, felt my hair, down to my shoulders, breasts . . . she'd have found the cheque in my bra . . . waist, examined my belt, pulled up my jumper, felt the waistband of my skirt, down to crotch, thighs . . . she'd have found the cheque in my knickers. Asked me if I had anything in my boots, then opened them, felt the toes and tapped the heels. Asked if I had anything in my pockets, then put her hand in. Turned me around, frisked me down the back. And finally – this took about three minutes – let me go.

Inside another room at the far side of the search room, the women were sweating. They thought they'd got one. After about another ten minutes, a warden came to the locked door and started calling names, one by one. They went out. He locked the door again. Opened it again to let other visitors back in. They came carrying harps and plaques and handkerchiefs painted with heads, internee names, and drawings of the wire.

Then it was our turn again, almost last. It was five to four. We went down the steps onto the muddy path. A high wire fence on both sides and a high gate ahead with Long Kesh Internment Centre, white on blue. And barbed wire all around each fence. The compound ahead stretched out of the slush. Guard dogs howled and barked inside somewhere. Lots of soldiers. Trees, muddy green and bare and patches of grass outside the fences.

It was desolate and grim, bitterly cold, and no description except concentration camp seemed proper. Clichés came to mind and fitted . . . cages, pigs, brutality, injustice, victims.

The warden led us down into another wooden hut with a long, narrow corridor. Wardens outside every door; small numbered cubicles. The woman gave her name, a warden told us the number. We went in.

The internee was sitting at a table, four chairs. She whispered who I was in his ear while kissing him, and we smiled without fuss. Outside the warden looked in. There was a whitened out window and it was warm enough. 'But don't let this fool you,' he said.

'It's as cold in the cages as it is outside.' Flagged floors, he said, and a space under the door to let in the wind and rain. They all had to get warm underclothes and layers of jumpers after being put there.

He's a mild-looking, middle-aged man with a lined, worried face and fingers stained dark brown with nicotine. He lit cigarettes, topped them halfway through, and seconds later lit them again.

They hadn't seen each other for three weeks and in hurried fits and starts of conversation they told each other the news. Their fifteen-year-old wanted to leave school, so-and-so was lifted, the house was raided. When he heard that, he jumped up and shook a clenched fist at the door. 'I'll get the bastards, why don't they leave you alone?' She said, 'Pigs!' and then he told her about a fellow they both knew who was put in recently. He was a young fellow with no cigarettes and a blackened ear and a closed eye. He was doing his best for him.

His voice came in short, hurried sentences, as if now that we'd got here he didn't know what to say, then remembered something, then rushed on to another topic. 'Don't keep telling me things I can read in the paper,' he rasped at his wife. 'Tell me things I don't know.' Afterwards she said his nerves were bad since he was put in. In a wondering voice she said, 'He never used to be like that. Never raised his voice to me.'

They are wakened, he said, at 7.30 a.m. Breakfast of an egg, tea and bread and butter at 8.30. Then they do the chores they are allotted, cleaning and such. Each cage has an OC and each compound a Quartermaster and an Adjutant. Lunch of meat, potatoes and another vegetable is at 12.30 p.m. Then they have tea at 4.30 – an egg and tea, bread and butter like breakfast, maybe one sausage. The food, by common admission of the wives I spoke to and the internees, is bad. Tea is the last meal of the day. Usually, at ten o'clock they are locked into the huts and lights out, but this is left at the discretion of each hut. In a grumbling voice he said, 'Some of them are so carried away with the woodwork it's all hours sometimes.'

In this hut they have a kettle and can do a limited amount of heating up of food but he told his wife that the packets of soup she sent were no good. She would have to cook it. She couldn't put it in a flask as flasks aren't allowed. Neither are tins. He asked vaguely what the layout was like on the side we came in. But he didn't look the type who'd get away. He remembered some bars of chocolate in his pocket and gave them to his wife for the children. He showed us a letter she sent him with colourful descriptions of the paratroopers, most of it blackened out, leaving desolately, 'I love you too,' at the bottom of the page.

The worst side of it? His face contorted: worry about the family, the food, being shut up, and fellows getting on your nerves. The endless talk about the 1940s and '50s. He stopped. It seemed too painful. He asked his wife to send more handkerchiefs. 'And write,' he said. 'It's great to get a letter.' At three minutes to half past four the warden knocked at the door. The woman said, 'Take your time, it's not up yet!' and we stood up. They hung on to each other, and the warden told us to move on. Then he was gone, saying, 'Don't forget to write!' with the warden looking backwards down the corridor.

The other cubicles were empty. We went outside again, the gate was opened. We looked for him on his way back to the compound, but he must have been round the other side. No sign of him. And we were the last out. Into the wooden huts again, claimed our matches and keys and other stuff. Into the bus, the women and children more silent now. Back to the car park. Into the waiting room for the bus again. It was getting dark. The road quiet. The field with thirty caravans beside the camp for the English wardens was silent.

The woman from Ballymurphy who had left home at 11.45 a.m. got home at 7 p.m.

The Baby Factories

MARY MAHER (1973)

The *Irish Times* 'Women First' section first appeared in early 1969. Its first editor was Mary Maher, an American who had joined the staff in 1965. Its focus moved rapidly from food and fashion to more feminist-tinged reporting on women's lives. Many of the issues flagged by this article – the third in a series – remain current in the maternity services in Ireland forty years on.

[. . .] The only other method of coping with too many patients is a device which now has a somewhat dreaded familiarity to anyone who's been in a maternity hospital in the past few years: 'The Drip'. This is the intravenous drip of an oxytocic hormone which acts upon the uterus and stimulates it to contract. Originally pitocin, an extract from the pituitary gland, was used, but this has been replaced by its synthetic equivalent, syntocin. The syntocin drip is principally administered to induce labour, usually after an artificial rupture of the membranes of the uterus. More recently, it has been used to accelerate labour in a patient who is progressing slowly.

Virtually all obstetricians defend the syntocin drip on solid medical grounds, because it effects shorter labours; and a shorter labour is a very desirable thing in itself, less exhausting and less dangerous to both mother and infant. Nevertheless, the frequency with which it is used has risen spectacularly in the past few years, and not all consultants are completely happy about it.

It is quite safe, provided both patient and drip are supervised, but this can be a problem in a busy delivery unit. One nurse attending to six women on drips is stretching the safety margin, but it happens. 'The optimum,' one specialist said, 'is one midwife and one pupil nurse per drip.' It is very doubtful if this applies anywhere.

There is no doubt that syntocin drips are a very valuable addition to the battery of weapons science uses to defeat nature at childbirth, just as there's no doubt that nature doesn't always know best: unaided by medical science, human mothers would lose a third or more of their offspring, just as other animal species do, and lose their own lives far more often.

But the delicate question here is when any artificial weapon can be over-used, and something between 30% and 60% of patients in the larger maternity hospitals, especially in Dublin, now meet the drip at some time during their labours. I found only one obstetrician who admitted that expediency was dictating matters to some extent: 'It is true that if I had fewer patients or more staff I wouldn't use the drip as much as I do now.'

In any case, a row of labouring mothers attached by tubes to bottles doesn't alleviate the assembly-line atmosphere so many mothers object to when they talk about 'the baby factories'.

Margaret G., an unmarried mother who described her labour as 'nightmarish', spoke a year after the event as if it had just taken place. 'I was put in a ward with no windows, only a sort of stained-glass partition at one end, and I was in there for 24 hours.' The father of the child was not allowed in to see her. She asked several times how she was getting on, and was met with a cool non-response.

When she finally reached the pushing stage, no one would help her. 'I asked the nurse could I hold her hand, just to have something to push against, and she pulled her hand away. Then the sister came in with the students and they all stood around me. It was because I was unmarried. Then she said, "Come on now, give a big push," and I said – I was so mad – "I fucking well will" and they all laughed. It was horrible. Then she said to the students, "Isn't she pushing very well?" To the students, not to me; why couldn't she have given me a little encouragement?'

When the baby was born, Margaret asked to hold her, but the nurse on duty simply held her up for a moment or two and as Margaret reached, the nurse turned away and hurried off with the baby. It had a very distressing effect on Margaret, who said, 'I got so frightened of the baby, I couldn't bring myself to pick her up for a whole day after that. They ruined my relationship with my own baby for a long time. If I ever have another one I'll lock myself in a room where no one can get at me.'

Maura D., who had two children at home before booking into hospital for her third child, arrived in hospital at 1.30 a.m. on a bank holiday, with contractions coming every five minutes. She was left sitting in the admission office for half an hour before she was eventually taken to be prepared for delivery. She was put to bed for the rest of the night and brought to the delivery room at 7 a.m. when a new nurse came on duty, examined her and said briskly: 'Who told you you were in labour?'

It did not set a good tone for the relationship that had to last, on an intimate basis, for the next six hours. Maura promptly replied that, having had two children, she knew when she was in labour. During the next few hours, the sister commented frequently to her that she was 'not breathing properly', which understandably annoyed Maura, who had delivered her two older children without any drugs, or stitches, and was enthusiastic about the psychoprophylactic method. 'I told her I was breathing as I had been trained to and I'd go on breathing that way, and she said, "You'll do as you're told."'

Maura was eventually put on a drip, and at the final stages she, too, found no one to help her sit upward to push. 'This nurse kept shoving the mask at me and I kept knocking it back; it was a struggle between me and the nurse.' After the baby was born, at 12.30 p.m., Maura was left for nearly an hour, uncovered and shivering, listening to the woman in the next cubicle scream unmercifully.

'I found out later that she had had 20 stitches and she must have been in terrible pain. The nurse never stopped telling her to "shut up" — "shut up", not even "be quiet" — and "you're acting like a child." It was dreadful. I had to go into hospital to find out what labour was really like. They made you feel degraded, disgusting. Never again.'

'Difficult patients,' the doctors would sigh. Neither woman would get far with a complaint on medical grounds, and each went home with babies in perfect health. But for both, the experience of the maternity hospital had been traumatic, and that is a serious failure on the part of the hospital. Rudeness and indifference, and brusque treatment, are common complaints about nurses in maternity hospitals. Insufficient help at the pushing stage is a common grievance, too, especially among women who have faithfully trained in the 'relaxation' classes only to discover that the staff in the delivery unit have apparently never heard of psychoprophylaxis.

The obvious reason why nurses bear the brunt of patients' complaints is that the patients see far more of the nurses than they do of anyone else. It's difficult to find much irritating about the doctors with whom there is only fleeting contact. But it's also true that the nurses carry the burden of hospital work. At the bottom of the hospital oligarchy, they are worked long hours for low pay and treated like slaves themselves.

Rushed and harried, dealing with more patients than the hospital should handle, it is not difficult to see where the temptation to scold, or worse, originates. But during the actual period of labour there is probably no one more important to the patient than the nurse and she can do more to make the experience of childbirth rewarding and happy than the most skilled specialist in the country.

The nurses who are good are worth more than any salary could pay for the morale of the woman whose energy is beginning to flag, and many of them are very good indeed. There are others who should be kept folding the sheets in the linen closet, and there are some whose disposition varies according to the status of the patient. Class attitudes might be no more than a simple choice of language – private patients, for instance, are told to 'bear down in your back passage', and public patients instructed to 'push, missus, push into your bottom like you were constipated'.

[. . .] I don't doubt that public clinic patients are likely to get the best treatment available, in the clinical sense of the word. What they do not get is nursing care, rest and comfort, which are as essential to the whole concept of health as scrupulous testing and examinations. Some of them do not get privacy, courtesy, or even an acknowledgment of personal dignity, and that is a situation we must judge intolerable. No hospital can altogether eliminate the possibility of bedding women down on stretcher beds and mattresses in hallways in an unexpected rush, but why this should invariably happen to the public patients in hospitals is a question that deserves a more honest answer than it normally gets.

[. . .] There are other problems that money cannot put straight, and on these the medical profession will have to come to some conclusions. The area in which I think obstetricians have completely sold women out is in family planning, and it is a serious betrayal, because no one is in a better position to know the toll continuous childbearing takes on mothers and children.

In the first of these articles, I commented at some length on the maternal mortality statistics of this country, which are significantly higher than those of Britain, Scotland or Northern Ireland. I find it a very sad and disturbing fact that not one doctor I spoke to in the course of researching these articles mentioned the death rate among Irish mothers; when I stumbled across the figures myself I was so startled that I checked them several times with the Department of Health.

I also stumbled across some bleak realities – like the woman who has had four caesarean sections in five years and is now pregnant again because her doctor refused to discuss contraception with her; and the mother of 13 who could not be sterilised in Dublin, though it is a perfectly legal operation, because the staff at the hospital refused to cooperate in the operating theatre.

All doctors know that the risk to life and health increases with every pregnancy, especially those after the third and fourth, and that the risk affects both mother and child. They are also aware, or certainly should be, that poor social and economic conditions have a direct bearing on the odds of a woman and her baby coming through pregnancy alive and well.

It is no accident that of the 18 maternal deaths analysed by the Committee on Maternal Mortality, 11 were of women from the lower income group. A recent article in the *Journal of the Irish Medical Association* by Dr Dermot MacDonald, of the National Maternity Hospital, puts the facts on perinatal mortality succinctly:

The labourer's wife has a four times greater chance of losing her baby than the wife of a professional man. Poor obstetrical factors like placental insufficiency or ante-partum haemorrhage may be unaffected by social conditions, yet it is a fact that deaths from intrapartum anoxia and respiratory distress are four times higher in the lower social group than the average. The infant death rate from congenital malformations is six times higher in socio-economic group V than in group I . . .

'In the case of the mother,' Dr MacDonald concludes, 'emphasis on age, height, marital status, parity, occupation and housing must now equal if not surpass that given in the past to obstetrical history and to blood pressure and urine testing.'

I'm prepared to accept – for the purposes of these articles anyway – that the doctors can't do much to promote the social revolution such bald evidence suggests we sadly need. I'm not prepared to believe that they couldn't have done something long ago to focus attention on the fact that excessive child-bearing is dangerous, and that excessive child-bearing is far, far more common among the labourers' wives than the wives of professional men.

I do not believe that it is or was beyond the power of the medical profession to demand contraceptive education and facilities for public patients, especially since private patients of the same doctors have been able to get both for a long time. The fact that this vital task is still being left to a private company subsidised by the Planned Parenthood Federation – a company formed by a handful of concerned doctors and others – and available as a full service only in Dublin, strikes me as a lethal piece of immorality.

Why haven't the doctors assumed this obligation? Is it because Irish maternity hospitals are a fascinating socio-economic obstetrical museum for interested students? We are, after all, obstetrical freaks – there aren't many places left in the world where you can find women over 40 having their first babies and women of 30 having their tenth.

Perhaps the judgment is too harsh. Perhaps the explanation lies in total indifference. But I do rather think it's time that the men who make handsome livings looking after the internal organs of women think about them as women rather than as curious clinical objects.

The Queen Looked Thin and Unhappy

MAEVE BINCHY (1973)

The intermittent love affair between a considerable section of the Irish public and the British Royal Family was, after 1961, intensified by television. In the spectrum between uncritical enthusiasm and republican contempt, there was little space for *lèse-majesté* of a different order. This article provoked a flood of complaints from many upstanding citizens of a democratic republic which, technically at any rate, owed no allegiance or obeisance to its neighbour's hereditary monarchy. Before she became internationally famous as a novelist, Maeve Binchy was a teacher and then, from 1968, a journalist with the *Irish Times*.

The ushers were simply delighted to see me. 'Splendid,' they said, 'absolutely splendid. Let's have a little look. Oh, yes, seat number 17 this way. Super view, and just beside the telly, too. Super!' They could have been brothers of my dearest friend, instead of members of Mark Phillips' regiment examining the press ticket, which had cost £23.

Westminster Abbey was lit up like an operating theatre, the light from the chandeliers was only like candlelight compared to the television lights. Well, since 500 million people, including the Irish, were meant to be looking in, I suppose you had to have it bright enough to see something.

There was plenty to see from the top of a scaffolding over the north transept. Grace Kelly staring into space, looking like she always looked, kind of immaculate. Rainier has aged a bit oddly and looks like Marlon Brando in *The Godfather*. Harold Wilson, all smiles and straightening his tie, his wife looking as if she were about to compose the final poem on the occasion. Jeremy Thorpe was all giggles and jauntiness, Heath looked like a waxwork.

Anthony Barber looked suitably preoccupied, as well he might, with a State-of-Emergency going on outside the Abbey doors, and

Whitelaw looked as if it was his first day off in two years. There were a lot of people whose faces I thought I knew, but it was no help asking for advice on either side. The man from the Manchester *Evening News* seemed to be writing an extended version of *War and Peace* in a notebook and on my right an agency reporter was transcribing a file of cuttings.

And then the royals started to arrive. We could see them on the television set – which was six inches from me – leaving Buckingham Palace in their chariots, and like characters stepping out of a film, they suddenly turned up a hundred feet below our seats. The Queen Mother looked the way she has ever looked – aged 56 and benign. The Queen looked thin and unhappy in a harsh blue outfit. Princess Margaret looked like a lighting devil with a cross face and an extraordinary hideous coat, which may have been some multicoloured fur, but then was there ever an animal or even a selection of animals who would have been given such a coat by Nature?

The Phillips parents looked sick with nerves; nobody in the place was hating it as much as they were. Mother Phillips nearly tore her gloves to shreds, father Phillips let his invitation fall and it struck me as odd that the groom's parents should have had to carry an invitation at all. The son and heir stood smiling and resplendent in scarlet, dimpling and smiling, and you felt that if all else failed and he doesn't become a brigadier or something in six months, he will have a great living in toothpaste commercials.

The Dean of Westminster, who is a very civilised, cheerful sort of man, was sort of happy about it all, and so was the Archbishop of Canterbury. They beamed all round them and extracted a few return grins from the nervous-looking lot in the VIP seats. The choirboys looked suitably angelic and uncomfortable in their ruffs. One of them got his fingers caught behind his neck and had to have it released. The trumpeters were noble and rallying, and the Beefeaters were traditionally beefy. Everything was as it should be in fact, as we waited for the bride.

About three seconds after the glass-coach had left Buckingham Palace with Anne and her father we were all handed two pages of strictly embargoed details about the wedding dress: it would have threatened national security to have had it before, apparently. Journalists all around me were devouring it and rewriting the details of seed pearls and 1,000 threads of 20-denier silk to every inch of the garment. When she arrived at the door of the abbey there was a bit of excitement about arranging the train and adjusting the tiara, and the bride looked as edgy as if it were the Badminton Horse Trials and she was waiting for the bell to gallop off.

Up at the altar all the royals looked out as eagerly and anxiously as if they thought the Duke of Edinburgh and his only daughter might have dropped off for a pint on the way. The Queen actually smiled when they got into sight and Mark gave a matinee-idol shy, rueful smile. Princess Margaret read her programme of the wedding service as if it were the latest Agatha Christie that she had promised to finish before lunchtime.

The Duke of Edinburgh went and sat beside his wife and mother-in-law, and seemed to have a far greater control over his sword than did Prince Charles, who carried his as if it were an umbrella. I was waiting for half his relatives to have their legs amputated but there must have been some kind of plastic top on it because nobody seemed to be maimed or anything when they were leaving.

The service went as planned, and the young voices were clear and loud, as everyone remarked approvingly afterwards, no coyness or nervous stutters. There were a lot of hymns, and I saw the Queen singing her head off, but gloomily, and the Phillips parents sang too, nervously, on their side.

Then off they galloped down the aisle and it was over. And do I mean over! There was no hooley in the palace or anything; the party had been on Monday night. The people who had got all dressed up went home, I suppose. The bridal couple had about nine hours of photographs, and all the people who had been camping on the street packed their spirit stoves into plastic bags and went off for lunch.

It was a superbly organised show, with all the actors playing their parts perfectly, timing and all. Everyone who had a role kept to it: the Duchess of Kent looked sweet and pure English girlhood, Princess Alexandra managed to give the odd vaguely tomboyish grin which she thinks is expected. The Duke of Edinburgh and Lord

Snowdon looked as self-effacing as Mark Phillips is beginning to look already.

The ushers saw us out, thrilled that we had been able to get there and hoping earnestly that we had a good view of everything. The evening papers were already on the streets with early photographs. 'The Snow White Princess!' screamed one headline, as if the readers had expected the bride to wear scarlet jodhpurs. It was a very well-produced show, no one could deny that, but then the actors are getting slightly above Equity rates.

This Practice Must Be Stopped

JOE MACANTHONY AND PAUL MURPHY (1974)

In the first half century of Irish independence, there was little journalistic scrutiny of corruption in public life. Local government in particular was a quiet backwater where, it was assumed, little of any significance occurred. As the pace of physical development accelerated dramatically in the late 1960s and early 1970s, the planning function of local authorities assumed an importance that was at first not widely recognized. Joe MacAnthony, who had graduated into journalism from public relations, was a pioneer of investigative journalism and long-form reporting in Irish weekly newspapers, notably the *Sunday Independent*, where the following piece was published; Paul Murphy was a local-government reporter with his ear to the ground. For reasons that now seem inexplicable, the scandalous practices they uncovered received little attention until 1997, when the Flood Tribunal was established. By that point, councillor Raphael P. Burke – better known as Ray – had been a government minister for twenty years.

After months of investigation, the *Sunday Independent* now believes there are grounds for a public inquiry into whether local authority representatives should declare their financial interest in matters coming before the Councils on which they sit as members. We believe also that there is need for examination of a system which legally allows councillors to profit at a later date from motions which they originally voted upon as public representatives.

Ironically, the piece of legislation which demanded that they do so was repealed in 1941. Apart from a public health ruling dating back to 1878, the only modern legislation which could demand a declaration of interest is Section 115 of the Housing Act, 1966. However, the Government Information Service says this section has not yet been brought into operation. Nor is there any pressure to create a register of business interests which would show publicly if councillors made a financial gain as a result of motions they voted on previously.

According to former Councillor Niall Andrews, a motion which he brought before the Council over a year ago to have representatives declare their business interest failed because he could not get a seconder from among his 24 fellow councillors. Mr Andrews, who stated he would raise the conflict of interest issue if he was re-elected to the Council, lost his seat in last week's election.

The absence of strict rules on the subject means that councillors who are auctioneers can freely vote to have land re-zoned with a steep rise in its value. Later, they can act as agents in selling the same land with a big increase in commission because of their earlier vote. We have examined certain land deals in the County Dublin area where councillors have been involved in precisely the manner described. None of these representatives acted illegally. Their business activities were entirely within the law.

One of the cases where this problem occurred was at Mountgorry, near Swords, Co. Dublin. In our inquiries into this transaction, we found that a member of Dublin County Council who seconded a motion to the Council on February 11th, 1971, which increased the value of a site there by almost 400,000 pounds, was allocated 15,000 pounds from the sale of the land under a contract registered last November (1973). The councillor involved is Raphael P. Burke, who has sat for the Swords area on the County Council since 1967. Mr Burke is also the Member for North County Dublin in Dáil Éireann. Under the terms of the contract, Mr Burke is named as being entitled to £15,000 or 5.85% of the net proceeds from the sale of 35 acres of industrial land at Mountgorry, near Swords, to Pagebar (Ireland) Ltd.

It is the same piece of land which Councillor Burke strongly urged should be newly zoned from agricultural to industrial use in February 1971 on the grounds that it would bring more jobs to the Swords area. The motion concerned was passed by 16 votes to 4 although the professional planning staff of Dublin County Council had strongly objected to development on the site. It was also passed at a time when the person who joined in setting up the company which was to eventually pay Mr Burke had options on the land involved.

We have spoken to Mr Burke about the Mountgorry transaction. According to him, the contract signed for the sale of the land and registered in the company's office has not now gone through.

He also made it clear that he regarded the zoning motion which he seconded and his later contracted payment from the sale of the land as entirely unrelated. He said he had no interest in the site when he urged its new zoning. Be that as it may, we found that Mr Burke had already shown an interest in negotiating the sale of a portion of the land to be newly zoned three months before his motion came before the Council.

We have also found that three weeks to the day after the resolution was passed, two men commercially associated with Mr Burke set up the company which was later to sell the newly zoned land to Pagebar Ltd. Their partner in the venture was the man who already held options on the Mountgorry land.

The site at Mountgorry lies about a half mile from Swords village on the main Swords/Malahide road. It has no services, it lies beneath the flight path to Dublin Airport and it forms part of the green belt around the growing village of Swords. These were some of the reasons why the planners zoned it as agricultural land when they drew up the County Draft Development plan in 1967. The distinction in zoning is important. Land designated for agricultural use holds the lowest value on the property developer's scale. Re-zoning it for industrial or housing use would increase its value by at least 300%.

In the case of Mountgorry, the planners expressed their belief that it should remain agricultural when they drew up the 1970 Draft Development Plan. However, at the same time as the experts were drawing up their zoning regulations, an auctioneer called Patrick Langan was also looking at Mountgorry. In 1970, Mr Langan believed that Mountgorry was a good bet for re-zoning. At that time he began picking up options at low prices, partly because the land's owners did not believe it would be re-zoned.

On October 8th of that year, the first attempt to change the zoning designation of Mountgorry came before Dublin County Council's Planning Committee. Councillor Jim Guinan proposed that 17 acres in the area owned by another Councillor, Joe Dignam, be newly zoned from agricultural to residential land. Mr Guinan, an auctioneer with considerable experience in land usage, found his views at variance with the professional planners. He had a seconder, however, in Mr Burke's father, P. J. Burke, and the motion was passed by 6 votes to 2.

Once the motion on the Dignam land was passed, Councillor John Boland proposed that the land adjacent to it on which Mr Langan had options be re-zoned. Mr Boland's motion was so all-embracing that it was deferred to set a boundary line on what was to be changed.

On October 20th, 1970, the Planning Committee again discussed the Mountgorry land. The Assistant County Manager made a strong argument against land other than the Dignam section being re-zoned and even asked that the decision relating to the Dignam land be reconsidered in view of his report. After discussion, the Dignam land was re-zoned industrial instead of residential and no decision was made on the adjoining land where Mr Langan had options. Despite this, Mr Langan remained optimistic and approached a building contractor to submit a planning application for an industrial estate on the site. The application was lodged on December 4th, 1970.

On February 3rd, 1971, the application was turned down for four reasons – the land was zoned agricultural, it was in a noise zone, there was no provision for sewage and to give permission would be contrary to good planning practice. Exactly eight days after this refusal, a fresh motion came before the Council to re-zone the land, making it eligible for industrial development. The motion, proposed by Councillor Guinan, was seconded by Raphael Burke, who made the argument for the change.

At the meeting, the Assistant County Manager left no doubts about the planning experts' view on the councillors' motion to change the zoning of the land. He stated that 'no professional officer on the Council's staff was prepared to recommend the adoption of the changes proposed'. Despite this, Mr Burke urged that the land be re-zoned. He said he wanted to bring more jobs to the Swords area. To illustrate the land he wished changed, according to those present, Mr Burke held up a map of the district and pointed out the site he was concerned with. It corresponded to the land which Mr Langan held options on. Although Mr Burke knew Mr Langan at the time, he said he was in no way connected with him when the motion was passed. In fact, he said he was not interested in the land as a business proposition at all.

If this was the case on February 11th, 1971, when the councillors overrode the planners and passed the re-zoning motion by 16 votes to 4, it had not been the case three months earlier.

According to one of those with a vested interest in the Mount-gorry land, he was approached in October 1970 by Mr Burke's father who told him that his son was in contact with two men who were prepared to buy a portion of his land. The offer was turned down.

At the time, Raphael Burke was associated with a firm of builders whose principals, Brennan and McGowan, hailed from Co. Mayo as did Mr Langan and the Burke family.

Three weeks after the council motion to re-zone the Mountgorry site as industrial was passed, the same Brennan and McGowan joined Patrick Langan in setting up a company called Dublin Airport Industrial Estates. This was the company which was later to contract to sell a large portion of the Mountgorry land to Pagebar (Ireland) Ltd and to pay Mr Burke 15,000 pounds under the heading of 'Planning'.

By early 1972, Dublin Airport Industrial Estates was making strong efforts to get full planning permission for an industrial estate at Mountgorry and Mr Burke was telling the *Drogheda Independent* that the company was preparing to build an industrial estate which would bring thousands of jobs to the Swords area. He did not mention that he was commercially involved with Messrs Brennan and McGowan, whose brainchild Dublin Airport Industrial Estates was. Nor did he mention the likelihood that the company was involved in what would turn out to be a classic piece of land speculation.

If readers of the *Drogheda Independent* were unaware of this, equally unknowing were the owners of the Mountgorry site, whose land was now being bought up by Dublin Airport Industrial Estates under Mr Langan's options. When they made the option deal with Mr Langan, the owners had little idea of the potential market value of their land.

Under the option, the owner of 20 acres, a man named James

Dickie of Seatown Castle, had to sell his land for around £110,000. Dublin Airport Industrial Estates later contracted with Pagebar Ltd to sell the same land for £335,675. A second owner, Stephen Larkin, had to sell his optioned land for £58,000. It was to be sold to Pagebar for £210,510.

The company thus stood to make around £388,000 profit out of the fateful re-zoning motion on February 11th, 1971. And the only outlay involved was in buying up Mr Langan's options, obtaining planning permission and, of course, getting the land re-zoned.

Mr Langan's options cost the company £10,000. Planning permission cost £4,000 in payment to the architect involved, Mr Desmond McCarthy. The most expensive professional involved in the deal would appear to have been Mr Burke. [. . .]

The Wet Summer of 1978

ANTHONY CRONIN (1978)

Magill magazine, founded in 1977 by Vincent Browne, afforded gifted writers like Anthony Cronin opportunities for long-form journalism that, to all intents and purposes, had not existed in Ireland up to then.

The Irish Derby is, indubitably, a Racing Occasion of some importance. It is also, supposedly, a Social Occasion. It owes its position as the first to the enterprise of the Sweep, who decided to put an enormous amount of money into it; as the second to the fact that we really haven't got social occasions like Cowes, Ascot, or Henley (the neighbouring island being of course the model in these things), and if you haven't got social occasions it is necessary to invent them.

About its quality as a racing occasion this year nobody could complain. Piggot, who has transformed so many Curragh occasions, was there, as was the legendary little American, Willie Shoemaker. The race itself, which had highly intriguing aspects, was won from an international field by the very game, genuine, and eye-filling Shirley Heights, a horse already sure of his place in history as the Epsom Derby winner.

Therefore it was, as often, a memorable day with a satisfying result. As a social occasion it looked to me, as it always has before, to be a bit of a flop, the product of an ad hoc society with few traditions and little sense of what it really wants or where it is going. The Curragh has no lawns or flower-beds or places to sit at dinky little garden tables and drink Veuve Clicquot under fringed umbrellas. It has boxes in the grandstand, but no reserved enclosures; and in so far as reserved enclosures would put us further away from the finish line the general public ('us') quite rightly wouldn't stand for their institution.

More important, perhaps, those who want it to be the sort of occasion which would gratify their own sense of social importance have no ultimate inner galaxies, circles, and stars to revolve around. In order to be a successful snob you have to have someone above you

as well as below. You have to have someone who can give the acco-
lade, a Queen Mum or a Queen Bee, and we have no one, with the
result that the bourgeoisie is left, at times like Derby day, milling
around looking at its own membership with a wild surmise. Their
backs may not exactly be, as Yeats said, 'aching for the lash', but they
are aching for the nod, the gracious inclination of the aristocratic
neck. Alas, there is no one to give it. The notion that there is an inner
circle of 'horsey' aristocratic people present on such occasions to
confer anything on anybody is largely a figment of their own imagination. The 'horsey' people are mostly, nowadays, our own. In racing
they are professionals with their eyes on the game itself; and the old
Protestant element has largely been reduced to the status of fellow
professionals who are interested in the results of professional endeavour. The king is dead; and long live the likes of you and me, however
much money they have, just will not do.

But if the Curragh is, to some extent, Ireland in search of a norm
then Galway is the norm from which we all more or less came, and
because it is the old norm it is, in its social aspects anyway, in process
of dissolution. On Hurdle and Plate days the racecourse itself was
packed to the gunwales and a place of the most extraordinary dis-
comfort. You would nearly believe, until you looked more closely,
the old story that all sorts of people came in large numbers from all
over to be there. A closer examination revealed that the attendance
was overwhelmingly rural; farmers and then more farmers, some
with wives and offspring, the wives carrying superfluous cardigans
and trailing a bit behind. The hobbledehoyness, the subtle wrong-
nesses of dress and make-up of those under thirty are still rather
extreme, and emphasised by the fact that the way they dress is now
much the same as the way people dress in the big city.

The popularity of Galway with the farming community is easily
explained. There is a lot of good mixed racing on a track made for
interest and drama and more important, it comes between hay and
harvest when as a general rule there is little to do. A man I met had a
farm in Westmeath, 'comfortable enough', he admitted. He brought
the family and they all stayed in a guest-house a couple of miles out.
They only came racing on one day but he came on them all. If he

won or lost twenty pounds on a day's racing 'it was as much as he wanted to win or lose'. He had seen a small dealer man from down his way, a cattle dealer, draw three hundred pounds after the last. 'He won't last long at that rate of going.' He himself could get into the car and go racing again at Mallow on the Saturday, but he wouldn't. He'd soon begin to neglect things that way and the twenty pounds he might win wouldn't keep them all for a day at home.

A sensible man he was and I suspect typical, giving the lie to the headlines which, screaming about a tote aggregate of over a quarter of a million, suggested that we were all gambling mad.

Galway, as I remember it, used to be one colossal booze-up for all sorts and conditions of male Irish humanity, but to say that it is all much, much soberer now might be slightly misleading. There are far less lugubrious or aggressive males jam-packed into the pubs seeking either oblivion or sudden death. The story of Kevin Barry in his lonely prison cell is scarcely to be heard (once only in Eyre Square). The man who brought his wife from Westmeath probably took her out each evening, and if the children were anywhere of an age they probably went out too. The drinking, in other words, is spread more evenly between the two sexes and the various age groups and it goes with other interests. In the comparative gloom of James Cullen's the banjos and the bodhrans continued to play even while the races were in progress and the place was evidently the same kind of glue pot for foreign girls as is O'Donoghue's of Merrion Row. The student bars, The Cellar and The Tavern, had much the same bedenimed, unisexual denizens as during term time. There were unlikely to have been women participants in any of the epic poker games taking place in the bedrooms of the Great Southern: but there were women in plenty in the bar of that establishment and, whether they were staying there or not, doubtless some of them wound up in the bedrooms too.

But the scene in Galway, race-week or not, is in Salthill, a mile-long stretch of bars, hotel bars, more bars, dance halls, and discos, which vibrate to the beat of several kinds of music throughout the summer. In the Lenabay Arms there was thunderous hard rock for an audience whose age precluded memories of the fifties but which greeted the announcement of any bit of fifties nostlagia with little squeals of delight. In the Hill Top a more eclectic local group was inducing a good deal of audience participation with a medley including country and western. This was a friendly group with a chatty leader who introduced some of his numbers with a nostalgia bit as well. There was no place to dance, but the audience was encouraged to get up, hold hands, and sway. Somewhat less than half were drunk enough, happy enough, or unselfconscious enough to do it. Of the others, some appeared to be wishing the thing was over or worried about what was going to happen afterwards. Some of the boys had nothing to say and were only pretending to join in the songs. Some of the girls looked embittered. Numbers of those present seemed to prefer to talk to a member of their own sex. The traumas of youth and adolescence are much as they ever were.

In Eyre Square (sorry, John F. Kennedy Square) on the Wednesday night John Joe McGirl and Councillor Frank Glynn were addressing a meeting about H Blocks. It was raining and the meeting was breaking up as I came along, so I asked John Joe if he had been getting any response. 'Fair bit,' he answered, but he seemed, for such a man, a bit dispirited.

On the Saturday a man I knew from Kevin Street Sinn Féin had set up a stall in the Square among the other market traders and was selling H Block pamphlets and other literature. He told me he had sold fifty pounds' worth, much of it to Northerners who, he said, wanted to find out what the Provisionals were really after and had no means of doing so up North. He had also sold a lot of songbooks. 'The country people are mad for songs,' he said.

Driving across the midlands we came up behind a security van escorted by two jeeploads of soldiers with automatic rifles. This was the summer when more precautions, and more armed men, were needed to convey money from place to place in Ireland than ever were necessary to ferry gold dust from camp to railroad in the American West. In Roscrea money from a bank was being transferred to a van while soldiers stood uneasily by with their weapons at the ready. This was the first summer since 1934 when soldiers were deployed in the streets of our country towns.

★

It was the summer of notices which asked, 'Are You Ready for RTÉ 2?' It was the summer of long flouncing skirts, banded round the hips, and of Afro hair-dos. And it was the summer when the country girls who came to town finally decided that 'east, west, home's best'.

Around where your correspondent lives is bed-sitter land, inhabited by myriads of working girls from the back of beyond. Once upon a time they all thought the city was the place to be. Latterly they have been about equally divided between the merits of town and country. Now at weekends they disappear from the laundrettes, the late-night grocers, and the Rathmines pubs. They take the bus, in a high state of excitement, and in the country towns the fellas meet the buses in cars. They say there is better crack down where they came from. They say the city is lonely, nasty, dirty, and dangerous. They say they wouldn't go to a disco or a dance hall in the city except with a chap they knew that had a car, and they don't know many that have that are interested in taking them. They say the fellas are nicer in the country and have more money. They are probably right.

In Connemara under torrential rain they are playing endless games of twenty-five in the pubs. The signs say 'Lóistín – 300 Metres'. At the Poitín Still the Swarbriggs are advertised and at other places simply 'Céilí Anocht'. Through Spiddal and beyond the neat little grant houses stand among the rocky fields, all of them in better taste than the Hispanophile and Georgian villas nearer Galway city, without architectural distinction. At Barna there is talk of a triumph over local authority: the new signposts are in Irish only. In a bar a few miles beyond, one English phrase, 'fifty-eight pound a week', is repeated over and over with varying emphasis.

Spiddal is a row of bars and supermarkets, what the whole area would be if it could, but beyond is dole country, though nearly every house has a car parked outside. Sudden flocks of city children in red and blue anoraks emerge from the Gaeltacht schools; and at Carraroe there are several couples, aged 13 at most, walking entwined, Dutch and German cars stream past westward with red and blue nylon gear flapping on the roofs beside yellow iceboxes. At Camas, the post-office has been picketed after mail deliveries were suspended because no postman could be found. (If you took the job you would forfeit the dole.) In another pub there is low-voiced talk of a fight outside a dance hall on the Saturday night. My friend, who knows the place, is told some of the story and a certain individual is condemned —*'fear scine,'* a man of the knife.

At Rosmuc, Pearse's cottage maintains a forlorn dignity beside the lake, but a sign between it and the road says that fishing rights are reserved and threatens prosecution for their infringement. There is a new police barracks, successor to the one burnt down not long ago – 'to give employment', a wag says; and a notice behind the bar tells (in English only) of 'EEC Direction No 225 Headage of Cattle in Disadvantaged Areas Benefits'. The proprietor says she hasn't seen so much English money in circulation for three or four years – other summers there it wasn't worthwhile separating it. Thirty thousand pounds will soon be spent on a community centre which can be used as a dance hall – this in a community of 200-and-odd households, 'half of them one old bachelor or two old bachelors living together'. There are supposed to be 219 houses in the locality but a guard doing a survey could only find 204. The others, presumably, were abandoned.

At Scoil na Bhfian Father Piarais O'Dúill is in charge. He wears an open-necked blue shirt and speaks with enthusiasm of recruitment of city children, 250 at a time throughout the summer. I refrain from asking him about their class background and perhaps raising an argument about the language becoming another middle-class advantage trick, but when I lived in Ringsend I never heard of any children going to the Gaeltacht in the summer holidays.

Driving away from the school we meet an endless stream of them on bicycles, a sudden kaleidoscope of coloured rain-proof clothing against the green and grey. In the pub at Screeb they are still playing twenty-five and talking about the price of cattle in the language the children have come to learn. On the Clifden Road the Dutch and German cars are still streaming west, the drivers wearing dark glasses under a dark sky.

In every town in Ireland a boutique: Tricia's Boutique, Joan's Boutique, even the homely Norah's. In the pubs of every town, Cabaret.

'Boutique' and 'Cabaret' are the great naturalised words of the seventies, but then to be sure, we naturalised 'garage' and 'restaurant' long ago.

Outside every town new 'Georgian' houses. In the old streets of many towns real Georgian houses moulder into decay. Georgian is one of the great words of the seventies. At the fine art auction in the Mansion House everything is Georgian: chairs, tables, hallstands, fire-irons, Victorian bed-steads. A people with no taste and hardly any visual sense is obsessed by the name and the faint whisper of a time when the oppressor knew what was what.

On every stretch of road, B and B signs. Supplying B and B is the great new industry.

Round the ring of Kerry, in sparkling sunshine which seems almost miraculous, go the Dutch and German cars, their drivers still wearing dark glasses. On the hill over the lake in Killarney, in full view of it and from it, perch the square, modern German chalets and the German Hotel. There was a row about planning permission but the Germans won. The hotel and chalets are owned by the concern which brought the huge new crane factory to the town. What, I ask, do they come for? One man tells me the tourists come for the past, for souterrains, cromlechs, and dolmens; about which they are very knowledgeable. Another that the executives come here because you'd want to be Baron Thyssen to have a life like they have at home. Here they have boating and shooting and fishing and maids in starched aprons.

In Ballybunion a middle-aged man with bushy eyebrows recites 'The Stag at Eve Had Drunk His Fill', a poem of considerable length by Sir Walter Scott. He is a local. His friends evidently know what to expect and prompt him when he falters. They are small-town cronies who drink together during the long winter months. They too are part of the past.

Motorcyclists gratuitously revving their engines, riding back and forward. Gangs of youths and girls. Why, having seen no evidence of any violence, do I think they are dangerous? We have been conditioned by the newspapers and the media to think each other dangerous. Perhaps they think I am. Humble people, couples and in-laws, in the hotel lounge singing 'I Did It My Way' with enormous intensity. But they didn't. They did it the way somebody else said they would.

At two o'clock in the morning the distant rock-beat merges with the sound of the sea. Below a sort of embankment a couple lies on the wet grass in the lightly falling rain. She appears to have taken her trousers off, he to have kept his on. It could be anywhere, but yet it's somehow unmistakeably Ireland. They are doing it their way.

Time was when we were all supposed to find illuminations of our common ancestral past at the big rural festivals. In the early days of the state there was an approved myth about such gatherings being the ultimate in Irishness and there was also the myth of class-lessness. The poets of the Free State were never done singing their praises. They spoke of the beauty of the lasses. They said it was of an order to induce dementia among strong young sheep farmers from the back of the hills and even in the poet himself, who was probably a civil servant desperately hoping for a transfer to Radio Éireann. The poeticism of the thimble-rigger, the trick o' the loop man, and the other pathetic operatives of the Irish fairground was a constant theme. Being born and brought up in rural parts themselves, the poets had probably once looked on such exotic strangers with wide-eyed wonder.

Puck Fair begins with the enthroning of the goat on a high plat-form in the square at Killorglin, supposedly at six o'clock on Thursday. At six thirty on a reasonably fine evening a subdued, not to say depresssed, crowd was still being informed about what was going to happen by a member of the committee with a hand micro-phone. He was coatless, had a slight though not pronounced Kerry accent, and was obviously a cut above some of us in the social scale recognised locally. He said he saw many Germans among us, and told us that in 1928 the German flag had been flown along with the Irish one from the top of the platform to celebrate the crossing of the Atlantic by a German aeroplane with an Irish crew member. 'So, well done, Germany.'

As the minutes passed he was driven to very remote expedients to fill in the time but he kept gallantly on. He said he had just been handed a poem by a certain Sigerson Clifford, a poet who had written something about Puck Fair, and he would like to read a bit of it out to us. Since I remembered the work of the said Sigerson from long ago, the lines read out held no surprises for me. Nor was I overly surprised when a few minutes later the young man said, 'I believe there is a whole book of poetry about Puck Fair written by this Sigerson Clifford, so if any of you have any interest in literature perhaps you'd like to try to get hold of it.'

At length he was able to announce that the parade was at hand, the Queen and King Puck were coming, and would we all move back a bit to let them into the square. There were two pipe bands, one of them a 'ladies' to which we were asked to give a big hand. After that came some bare-thighed Fenian warriors, one of them a female, on horseback. Then, just when a sensible man might be about to despair of the whole proceedings, to the complete astonishment of myself and some nearby Germans, there was carried into the square an indubitable, unmistakeable, ugly-as-sin phallus. It was about four feet high. It appeared to be made of some sort of grey paper material and it pointed unashamedly at the heavens. It had a platform of its own, also carried by Fenian warriors, and there may even have been a school of thought which said it was a round tower, but you can take it from your correspondent that it was a phallus and nothing else but. Round towers are prettier.

The commentator, who had been giving us a brief history of the ladies' pipe band and other matters, made no reference to it whatever; and so I shall never know what he or anybody else thought it was. True, a drunk near me did call out 'What's that yoke there?' and he and his friends evidently thought he had asked a funny question; but by that time the commentator was welcoming the queen herself, a wee mite not yet nubile perched on a dray and accompanied by her attendants (similar) and enthusing about the Billy Goat, who at last had come, tied down securely by all four feet and exuding that air of complete well-being which is the hallmark of a greyhound who has had his sufficiency of Valium. 'Isn't she beautiful?' he asked us about the little wench who was being towed after the phallus round the square; and 'Isn't he a splendid animal?' he queried of us about the beast itself, but neither by word nor sign did he illuminate for us what tradition told him about the thing made of grey paper.

And if it, whatever it was, seemed to promise totally uninhibited joys and disportings to come, I am afraid I saw no sign of them. The commentator told us about the ceilidhe, about the old-time waltz competition, about the dance for which the band known as Fish and Chips had been procured. He asked the prize winners in the egg and spoon race to come to the platform. He reminded us several times that *Confessions from a Holiday Camp* was to be seen at the town's cinema. He besought us to enjoy ourselves in whatever way we chose to celebrate the crowning of the Puck; but it soon became evident that Puck Fair was principally an event at which pints were consumed on a rather dull and repetitive, if admittedly somewhat gargantuan, scale. The pubs were open, that was what it amounted to; and they would stay open till three o'clock in the morning.

True there were the tatty little gambling tables so beloved by the Free State poets. There were the swings and roundabouts. There were the fortune tellers and the traders from afar (well, from Tralee anyway). True also that, as in the case of Eyre Square, the drinking was no longer the totally male, rancorous or lugubrious drinking of times gone by. There were young wans parading the streets and in and out of the pubs as well as young fellas. There was, let us even hope, some companioning and coupling before dawn lit the eastern slopes of Beenmore. But when I left at an advanced hour they had certainly not begun to tear the clothes off each other. There were doormen at a number of pubs to keep the tinkers out. The whole thing was patently sinking into booze.

Ten miles away in a rather smart hostelry of the middle-class persuasion the subject of Puck Fair came up next evening and it soon became evident that consensus held it to be an event which had little, if anything, to recommend it. Nobody quite went so far as to say it was for tinkers and bog trotters only, but that was the general impression. I had thought at first that a class thing had crept in recently; and in the streets and pubs of Killorglin I had wondered at the absence of all but townspeople, tourists, small farmers, and tinkers. Now I saw that the classlessness of it was a myth propagated by Radio Éireann poets. Puck Fair was an orgy for the lower orders and at best it was regarded by other Kerry people as a curiosity or with disdainful amusement. Judging from the phallus, there may, there must have been something which has degenerated, something in which a whole community, priests and princes included, perhaps once participated. Now it has degenerated beyond recall. A few days after the fair this year a newspaper suggested that there was a strong feeling among the more respectable citizens of the town itself that the whole thing should be abolished in spite of the money it brought in. It was, they said, a festival for tinkers only and the tinkers were a danger and a nusiance to other people. King Puck is dead. Long live John Travolta and Olivia Newton-John.

Was it or was it not the summer of the Boom? Mr Colley and Professor O'Donoghue were adamant that the Boom was coming, was under way, was here. Various bodies of experts saw, on the contrary, nothing but downturns in the entrails. One thing is certain: the Boom proves an illusion, Mr Colley and Professor O'Donoghue are merrily walking the plank.

It was undoubtedly the summer of the Breathalyser. Much of what your correspondent observed must be read in the light of that fact. It may just be that without the Breathalyser the Irish people en fete would have been drunker than they were. There might even have been more singing of 'Kevin Barry'.

On the night the Supreme Pontiff was laid to rest I went around the Leeson Street discos with a friend. They have appparently more than doubled their number in the last few months and there are now near a score of them within a very small radius of each other, 13 between the Adelaide Road and Hatch Street corners alone so, whatever other reasons there may be, there is certainly an obvious one for calling this stretch of Leeson Street the Strip, and for many people the summer now vanishing will have been the first summer of the discos and whatever happened after them.

What is supposed to happen to those who go there, male and female, seems in no doubt. In one of the first establishments we entered I was introduced to an affable fellow in light summer clothing who was said to be a big, big spender and who was entertaining several people to Steak Burgoyne. 'If you're looking for your Nat King Cole,' he said, 'you can't miss. There's plenty of it about tonight.' Of course your correspondent couldn't be sure until he tried, but from the looks of things there may actually well have been.

Make no mistake about it, however, the proprietors of these establishments mean to make a break with the old tradition in these islands which says that places devoted to the pursuit of your Nat King Cole must be rather sleazy and second-rate. These are classy places, so classy that they are turning business away; and before getting in anywhere you have to submit yourself to an examination through a peephole or grill. This is so that the doorman can get an idea of the general cut of your jib, including presumably your (money) spending power, but nearly all the places we visited had specific regulations about denims and the wearing of a tie. So much for the permissive-society aspect of it all.

The first place we went into occupied a hall floor as well as a basement, and it had a plush, richly furnished ante-chamber with old-fashioned leather sofas, like the drawing room of the sort of Edwardian establishment where the lady in charge preferred to establish a free-and-easy, brandy-and-soda atmosphere before enquiring about the client's tastes. This was followed by a quiet dining-room where couples and foursomes ate what seemed like good and not too expensive food in moderate comfort and discreet surroundings. The dancing, the foodless drinking, the jumping lights, the altogether hellish noise, and the casual-acquaintance-making were downstairs in a long room where the tables had telephones so that you could ring somebody at another table and ask them to dance or whatever. (Your correspondent's table was number 3 and nobody rang him up, but since the number was visible only to those at the table he didn't see how they could have. Incidentally Jack Buchanan visited an establishment where there were such table telephones in the movie *Goodnight Vienna,* circa 1931, so there's nothing new in the nightclub business.)

By the time we visited the second or third establishment my friend and I had, however, acquired a charming companion who is an habituée, and she told me things I would otherwise have had to discover by empirical methods. One place, for example, has a reputation for attracting married men and single ladies; another married dames and single gents. Some are places where you tend to bring your own date, wife or girlfriend, others where you have a fair good chance of finding a *companion de nuit* – or, let's face it, what's left either of the *nuit* or of your staying power after you have jumped and jived and guzzled Chambertin at five pounds a bottle until four in the morning. Pressed further she told us that the conjunctions made were not, for the most part, commercial. Many of the girls were working girls who paid their own whack and were not looking for anything from anybody except, perhaps, you know what. As to venues, she insisted she didn't know that much about it all! But she thought it was often as not the car.

And so there you have it. There may be two opinions about whether going down into the basements of Leeson Street and submitting yourself to the noise and the lights and the cheery, cheery converse for several hours is more like hard work than whatever you're going to get is worth. What would bother me a little more is the success orientation of which most of these places and people stink. There was one place which was a bit more democratic and bohemian in the old sense than others, and the girls were, many of them, human-seeming as well as personable enough, but the general impression was of success, conformity of a very intense degree, a conformity to which the sex bit was almost ancillary. As for spreading it around, what with peepholes and ties and the necessity for five-pound notes in every pocket they could almost be said to be restricting it.

The RDS: Stalls and compartments for both humans and horses, many private places of retreat. In a large empty, private tea room with white tablecloths three little girls are being served with tea, cakes and sandwiches by a maid in full uniform. Just next door, the wet general public is queueing up for soup and chips. Down at the end of the jumping arena, on a sort of Hill 16, young gurriers are clinging to the trees. When any member of the Irish team has a clear round the cheering is shrill and ecstatic. Later, in the main exhibition hall, a wave of excitement sweeps over us all. 'Ireland has won, Ireland has won!' somebody shouts. Why do I find this more offensive even than talk about 'Ireland' winning or losing other sorts of sporting events? Is it because I feel people have been conned by the democratic television into taking an interest in what is essentially somebody else's affair? A few minutes later I watch the middle classes filing down from the seats in the stand which they had booked many weeks in advance. For the most part quiet suburban people, now anxious about the rain and about getting home. Mothers and daughters. Yes, they have been conned. The horsey aristocrats, many of them English, were in the private stands.

Croke Park: Kerry overwhelming Roscommon in the pouring rain. In front of me are two country swains and two lasses. In the interval between the minor match and the senior one of the girls gets up to go somewhere. 'My arse is all wet,' she remarks cheerfully. A Roscommon man behind me, displeased by a member of the other team, shouts: 'G' long out a that ye dirty fuckery ye. Go home to Kerry ye dog ye.' He exhorts his own: 'Break his fuckin' leg.' When one of the Roscommon team is hurt he is concerned and indignant. While a Kerry player writhes on the ground in front of us he yells: 'Get up ye good for nothin'! Get up ye cunt ye!'

The Kerry girl beside me is with two Roscommon supporters, a boy and a girl. She tells me that she lives in a furnished room in Rathmines for which she pays ten pounds per week. 'But it's nice to have your own place.' She goes home by bus every third weekend. She doesn't go out much when she gets there. But then, she doesn't go out much in town either except when 'we all' go out.

There are no fights. In the long ago there would always be a fight somewhere nearby. While blows were struck and curses exchanged one would clutch one's father's hand in a mixture of terror and excitement.

Late at night in the Oscar Theatre in Ballsbridge, Mr Alan Amesby, otherwise Mr Pussy, entertains a mixed audience which is not camp, not overly queer: 'us' in fact. Some of it is sharp enough stuff, some of it old broad music hall, but we are in a relaxed mood and we seem prepared to take anything. 'I have a request here for Angela Dympna Joan and all the rest of the boys in Bartley Dunne's. If you are driving home tonight please be careful because 20 per cent of the population is due to accidents.'

There is a fire-eater, stripper, and, amongst other revue sketches, a genuinely outrageous take-off of the sort of young priest that used to appear on RTÉ's nauseating *Outlook* feature by a highly talented performer whose name I cannot catch. A general impression of some sort of bravery and defiance as well as of a native cabaret form struggling to be born. Good luck to all concerned.

On the 8th of August the London bookmaker William Hill laid odds of five to one against anybody predicting three dry spells of two consecutive days during the remainder of the month. A host of takers rushed in, the weekend of August 12th and 13th proving especially popular among the first punters. On Sunday August 13th, the day Kerry played Roscommon at Croke Park, it poured steadily and almost without cease over the islands. After that, although the offer remained open and some money was eventually won, business began to slacken off. Gamblers, like everybody else, have a sense of the inevitable. The summer was a wash-out and everybody knew it.

Seeing the Cordage Dance

CON HOULIHAN (1978)

Trained as a schoolmaster, Con Houlihan made his first appearance in print with a review of a Russian novel in the *Irish Press* in 1969, when he was in his mid forties. He went on to become one of the doyens of Irish sportswriting, writing also for the *Evening Press* and the *Sunday World*. This report on the 1978 All-Ireland football final, between Dublin and Houlihan's native Kerry, appeared in the *Evening Press*.

If a man who fishes for salmon with a stake net had seen his cordage dance as often as Paddy Cullen did in this astonishing All-Ireland final, he would have been very happy indeed with his day's work.

But there is an immensity of difference between bending to take out a salmon and stooping to pick up a ball that has got past you – and for long years to come Paddy will now and then rack his brains and try to find out what happened to him yesterday.

At about 20 minutes to four he had every reason to feel that his bowl of glory was about to flow over: Dublin were playing as if determined to get a patent for a new brand of Gaelic football – and Paddy himself was ruling his territory with a style and authority redolent of Bat Masterson.

And the many Kerry battalions in the crowd were as apprehensive as accused men waiting for the jury to return after the judge had given a most unfavourable summing-up against them.

And well they might – because in the first third of what was surely the most extraordinary final since Michael Cusack codified the rules of Gaelic football, their team seemed faced not only with defeat, but humiliation.

It looked every bit as one-sided as the meeting of Muhammad Ali and Leon Spinks – and the more it went on, the more the gap in ability was seen to widen.

In their glory-garnished odyssey since the early summer of '74, Dublin have never played better than in the opening third yesterday.

The symphony of classical football began with Paddy Cullen – he got no direct shot in that period, but his catching of a few swirling lofted balls, dropping almost onto his crossbar, was as composed and technically correct as if being done to illustrate a textbook. And his distribution was as cool and unerring as the dealing of a riverboat gambler.

So was that of his comrades in the rear three – Kerry's infrequent sallies towards the Canal End almost always ended up as launching-pads for a Dublin attack.

The drizzling rain seemed irrelevant as Dublin moved the ball with the confidence of a grandmaster playing chess against a novice. From foot and hand it travelled lucidly in swift triangular move-ments towards the Railway goal – Kerry were forced into fouls as desperate as the struggles of a drowning man. And Jimmy Keaveney was determined to show that crime did not pay: the ball took wing from his boot like a pigeon homing to an invisible loft strung above Kerry's crossbar.

The blue-and-navy favours danced in the wet grey air – the Hill revelled and licked its lips at the prospect of seeing Kerry butchered to make a Dublin holiday. They roared as the points sailed over – and one felt that they were only flexing their vocal muscles so that they might explode when Charlie Nelligan's net bulged. And such was Dublin's supremacy that a goal seemed inevitable – by the 25th min-ute it was less a match than a siege.

Dublin, as they have so often done, had brought forth a new ploy for the big occasion – this time the rabbit from the hat was the swift breakdown with hand or fist. It added to Kerry's multitude of wor-ries. And Kerry's not-so-secret weapons were misfiring: Jack O'Shea was not ruling the air in midfield and Kevin Moran was playing as if his namesake Denis had only come for a close-up view.

Kerry's map was in such tatters that Eoin Liston, their lofty target man, the pine tree in whose branches they hoped the long high ball would stick, was forced to forage so far down field that his marker, Sean Doherty, was operating within scoring distance of Kerry's goal.

After 25 minutes Dublin led by six points to one – it did not flatter them. It seemed less a lead than the foundation of a formidable total.

But perhaps it is true that whom the gods wish to destroy they first make mad – the ease with which Dublin were scaling the mountain seduced them into over-confidence.

They pushed too many troops forward and neglected their rear – and then a swift brace of passes from Jack O'Shea and Pat Spillane found a half-acre of green ground tenanted by only Paddy Cullen, and with Johnny Egan leading the race in its pursuit.

Paddy Cullen is a 'modern' 'keeper – he guards not only the goal but its forecourt. And it was one of the ironies of a game that might have been scripted by the king of the gremlins that now he was caught too far back.

He advanced desperately but Johnny Egan, scorer of that lethal first goal in the rainy final three years ago, held the big trump – and he coolly fisted the ball over the 'keeper and into the net.

That goal affected Kerry as a sudden day of May showers a languishing field of corn. Dublin were like climbers who had been driven back down the mountain by a rock fall – they had to set out again from a plateau not far above the base. Soon a few Kerry points had put them at the very foot – then Dublin went ahead with a point.

And now came the moment that will go into that department of sport's museum where abide such strange happenings as the Long Count and the goal that gave Cardiff their only English FA Cup and the fall of Devon Loch.

Its run-up began with a free from John O'Keeffe, deep in his own territory. Jack O'Shea made a flying catch and drove a long ball towards the middle of the 21-yard line.

Mikey Sheehy's fist put it behind the backs, breaking along the ground out towards Kerry's right. This time Paddy Cullen was better positioned and comfortably played the ball with his feet away from Sheehy.

He had an abundance of time and space in which to lift and clear, but his pick-up was a dubious one and the referee, Seamus Aldridge, decided against him. Or maybe he deemed his meeting with Ger Power illegal.

Whatever the reason, Paddy put on a show of righteous indignation that would get him a card from Equity, throwing up his hands to heaven as the referee kept pointing towards goal.

And while all this was going on, Mick Sheehy was running up to take the kick – and suddenly Paddy dashed back towards his goal like a woman who smells a cake burning.

The ball won the race and it curled inside the near post as Paddy crashed into the outside of the net and lay against it like a fireman who had returned to find his station ablaze.

Some time, Noel Pearson might make a musical of this amazing final and as the green flag goes up for that crazy goal he will have a banshee's voice crooning: 'And that was the end of poor Molly Malone.'

And so it was. A few minutes later came the tea-break. Kerry went in to a frenzy of green-and-gold and a tumult of acclaim. The champions looked like men who had worked hard and seen their savings plundered by bandits.

The great train robbers were first out onto the field for act two – an act that began almost as dramatically as the first had ended.

In their cave during the interval Dublin, no doubt, determined to send a posse in fierce pursuit – but within a minute of the restart, the bridge out of town had been broken down.

Eoin Liston was about to set out on a journey into folklore – and for the rest of the game it must have seemed to Sean Doherty that he had come face to face with the Incredible Hulk. Eoin proceeded to leave the kind of stamp on the second half that Mario Kempes left on the final of the World Cup.

People were still settling down for the second half when Jack O'Shea drove a long ball from midfield; Eoin, near the penalty spot and behind the backs, gathered, turned, and shot to the net.

Dublin's defence is justly famous for its covering, and the manner in which this score came indicated the level of their morale. Not everyone suspected it, but Dublin had conceded defeat. From then on only a few of them had their hearts in the battle.

Kevin Moran never surrendered and played magnificently all through that unreal second half. He had good lieutenants in Tommy

Drumm and Bernard Brogan. But they might as well have been trying to prove that George Davis was innocent, OK.

Every Kerry man seemed to have suddenly sprouted wings – they
seemed not members of a different county but of a different species.
And a cynic might have suspected that they had agents in the Dublin
camp – some of the men in blue sent the ball to their opponents with
unfailing accuracy.

Kerry's fourth goal was both a finisher and a symbol of their
immense superiority. A high ball dropped into the apron of Dublin's
goal. It seemed to be manned by a little man with spikes in his fore-
head who was shouting: 'Take me to your leader.'

The leader, of course, was Eoin Liston, who plucked it out of a
low flying cloud, gave an instant pass to Ger Power on his right and
moved onto an instant return. Eoin's right-footed shot was executed
with the panache of one who knew that he could do no wrong.

The remarkable aspect of what followed was that Kerry did not
score a dozen goals. They got only one more – when Eoin Liston
raced onto a fisted cross-goal pass from Johnny Egan on the right and
planted the ball in at the far post.

And so in the grey drizzle we saw the twilight of the gods.

The Hill watched, as lively as the Main Street of Knocknagoshel
on Good Friday. And it all seemed so unreal. The final score was no
reflection of Kerry's second-half superiority – neither did it tell the
truth about the difference between the teams.

For 25 minutes, Dublin were brilliant; for 45, Kerry were superb.
How come the change?

That wry prankster we call luck has the answer. [. . .]

Travelling the Desert with Warriors of Islam

CONOR O'CLERY (1980)

This article was published in August 1980, less than a year after the Soviet invasion of Afghanistan. Conor O'Clery was news editor at the *Irish Times*, and the journey described here was among his earliest foreign assigments. He was the only Irish staff journalist to report the beginnings of this war of attrition between the Soviet forces and the local militias, who were armed and aided by Pakistan and the United States.

They were two unlikely Afghan warriors. Jamal had a perpetual worried look on his dark, pitted face. He intoned 'Oh my God' in a gentle voice at every setback. Sherrifola was given, in quiet moments, to unwinding his cream-coloured, faintly scented turban, adjusting the embroidered cap underneath, and then scrutinising his handsome 21-year-old face in a pocket mirror.

Jamal and Sherrifola were Afghan rebel guides, assigned to take us through the tribal North West Frontier Province of Pakistan into a Moslem-held area of Soviet-occupied Afghanistan. They belonged to Hisbi-Islami, the largest and most fundamentally Islamic of the rebel troops fighting Russian and Afghan army troops in their beleaguered country.

Jamal had met us in the northern Pakistan city of Peshawar, near the Khyber Pass, and accompanied us by air to Rawalpindi and then to the remote 5,500-foot-high city of Quetta, capital of Baluchistan province in southern Pakistan. Camel trains ambled by the end of the Quetta runway as the Pakistan Air Boeing 747 touched down in blinding sunshine and huge ants darted from beneath passengers' feet on the hot tarmac. An old Morris Minor was waiting to take us to the Bloom Star Hotel for the night.

At six the next morning, Jamal, his face grey with illness brought on by forgetting to bring his blood-pressure tablets, took us through the early morning trickle of Pathan, Baluchi and Brahuis tribesmen in Quetta's streets to a courtyard off a side road. There, behind metal gates, several Afghans lay sleeping in the cool dawn air. On the yard wall hung a framed photograph of the black-bearded Hisbi-Islami leader, Gulbuddin Hekmatyar. Among these Afghans was Sherrifola, eager to leave his job as tractor driver in nearby Pishin town on any pretext to get back near the fighting. He was ready now to act as guide across the arid Baluchistan desert and the Toba Kakar mountains to the Afghanistan border, ten hours' drive away.

The men propped themselves up on elbows to watch, at first with curiosity, then with wide flashing grins, the sight of three foreigners shedding their western clothes to don Pathan costumes. Pakistan police stop traffic at road checks outside Quetta and at the Afghanistan border. Only tribesmen are allowed to move freely in the area and across the frontier.

Their amusement was derived not so much from the sight of myself and a Canadian freelance companion, Keith Leckie, dressing in baggy pyjama bottoms and turbans, but from the Othello-like dash cut by the third member of our group, Mark August, a tall reporter from *New Africa Magazine*, and one of the first black men many of the Afghan tribesmen had ever seen.

'Oh my God,' said Jamal, looking at the bespectacled black face topped by a magnificent white turban. 'How will we ever get you through the checkpoints?'

Jamal had arranged the transport across the desert, taking £150 the night before to secure a 'good car' and driver for the day-long trek. A covered blue Toyota jeep stood waiting for us outside the courtyard. Its windscreen was cracked. The radiator was also cracked and leaking, and the bearings were gone on the nearside front wheel, requiring a good splashing with water every twenty miles to cool it down, but we didn't discover this until well on the road out of town.

Mark was consigned to the gloom of the back of the jeep, with the jerry cans of water and petrol and packs of equipment prepared for the journey and for sleeping rough with the rebels in Afghanistan. Hot sunshine, lice, bed bugs, mosquitoes, scorpions and contaminated water have wreaked havoc with the health and comfort of journalists who have made the journey before (mostly to different areas of Afghanistan – Jamal told us we were among the first news-paper reporters to enter the country through the Baluchistan desert).

Our list of shopping purchased in Peshawar's cavernous pharma-cies and tiny bazaar shops included water filters, water bottles, water purifying tablets, antiseptic and antibiotic creams, Lomotil tablets for dysentery, tetracycline, bottles of aspirin, Lorexene cream for lice (this we applied in the pre-dawn hours in the Bloom Star Hotel to every inch of skin, even under the toe nails as instructed by the mak-ers), mosquito repellents, salt tablets, lavatory paper, bandages, gauze, chewing gum, cigarettes, presents for the rebel commander (a neces-sary ritual), boiled sweets, maps of Afghanistan and Jane's Pocket Book of Armoured Cars and Helicopters for identifying Soviet and rebel vehicles.

The police checkpoints outside Quetta were unmanned. We made good progress past walled mud villages and tall roadside sunflowers. After an hour, the road degenerated into a dusty track leading up into the Toba Kakar hills. The thin shoulder blankets of the Pathan dress proved invaluable as masks against the dust which swirled around the jeep, and as sun shades when we stopped by irrigation ditches to fill the radiator and splash water against the hissing metal of the front wheel. They also helped hide our faces from the inquisitive tribes-men who materialised when we stopped to examine the jeep. 'Do not let them know you are foreigners,' said Jamal, 'there are many Pakistan spies here. Just do not talk.'

By 10 o'clock, when it was already unbearably hot, the jeep had left behind the last villages, with their eerie roadside graves marked by tall poles with rams' horns fixed on top. For the rest of the long hot journey we encountered only shepherds slowly ushering flocks of sheep and black goats across the track. The road deteriorated stead-ily. As the jeep hit a boulder, half of the passenger windscreen fell into our laps. 'Oh my God,' said Jamal.

High in the deserted mountains, after endless hours of banging along dried-up river beds and wadis, we reached a wide yellow-coloured plateau, where half a dozen dust storms twisted in long lazy grey columns against the horizon. At the other side, visible for many miles, stood a square stone building, a former British fort now used by the Pakistani police. Beyond it was Afghanistan. When we reached the fort, a chain was stretched across the track. The driver sounded the horn and switched off his engine.

After five minutes a lone Pakistani policeman appeared. Mark covered his head in a white shawl. We closed our eyes and feigned sleep, as if that was possible on such a bone-jarring surface. 'Mujahideen' (fighters for Islam), the driver said, nodding towards us as the policeman inspected the passengers. 'Okay,' he replied in Pushtu. 'You can go ahead.'

On the other side came the first evidence to substantiate the rebels' claim to control the Afghanistan countryside. There were no Afghan Government or Soviet check posts. 'There were so many soldiers here last year,' said Jamal. 'Now they are all gone. We control all the border on this side.'

The jeep climbed for more than an hour through the jagged outcrops of the empty Shinkar mountains in Afghanistan's Zabul province. Around a bend in a gorge, at about 9,000 feet, a green Islamic flag hanging from a bamboo pole signalled the first outpost of the rebel camp. Beyond it, in a narrow valley, we came across four low tents and a volleyball net.

About twenty Afghan tribesmen in flowing shoulder blankets and turbans emerged to greet Jamal and Sherrifola with prolonged embraces. Afghan males do not hesitate to show their affection for their Islamic 'brothers'. Frequently we saw men walking hand-in-hand in the mountains. A few of those who greeted us carried Kalashnikov rifles and spoke in broken English. They giggled at the sight of Mark and ushered us into one of the tents.

Inside the floor was covered with blankets. Dozens of flies were brushed aside to make room for glasses of sugar, which were filled with black tea. According to Afghan custom, we were given the first glass for thirst, the second for hospitality, and the third for ostentation. The Mujahideen were friendly and pleasant. There was much handshaking (with both hands) all round from cross-legged positions under the low tent roof, much exchanging of the Moslem greeting 'Salaam aleikum' (peace be with you).

The tents here were to be our quarters for the night. The main camp, with its military equipment, was on the other side of the dry thorn-covered hills. On the craggy horizon above us, we caught occasional glimpses of Afghan fighters silhouetted with rifles in their hand, evocative of tales of nineteenth-century Afghan wars. They were on the lookout for Soviet MiG planes which had sorties against the camp, the most recent just before we arrived.

'You will see our commander and the real fighting forces of the Mujahideen soon,' said Jamal, as the cockroaches came out to clean up the crumbs after a meal of nan bread and greasy goat stew. 'When?' 'Tomorrow, inshalla' (God willing). Later, as a rebel with drooping moustache showed us to our thin mattresses in a nearby tent, a lizard peered up from the pillow by the sleeping space assigned to me. 'Don't worry,' said the fighter, shooing it away. 'It eats the mosquitoes.'

A Country of Exploiters

OLIVIA O'LEARY (1982)

The Falkland Islands were invaded and occupied by Argentine forces on 12 April 1982. Olivia O'Leary, a staff journalist with the *Irish Times* who was reporting daily from Argentina, published this piece in the *Spectator*.

'We must now throw the bathpipes at the British,' said the Air Force spokesman in Buenos Aires. He was somewhat distraught at British gains in the Falklands, otherwise he might have remembered that it is the kitchen sink one throws on those occasions. One felt a certain sympathy for him, as one can only feel for a people who get it so hopelessly wrong.

There are times in this city when one seems to be drowning in words. The melodramatic television announcers hardly stop to draw breath; the whining accents of Buenos Aires commentators nag on and on over the radio; with a sense of desperation one settles down to read vast acres of newsprint which may yield one salient comment. It is always either the long legal and historical arguments as to the legitimacy of claims of sovereignty based on the explorations of seventeenth-century adventurers; or the fulsome political denunciations of Britain's disproportionate reaction to the taking of the islands last month. The pre- and post-invasion periods are debated at length. 'But were we right to invade?' is a question which is somehow never answered, because it is never asked.

If you cannot get what is yours by negotiation, you grab it – that is the logic. But what if all countries adopted that attitude to territorial dispute? I asked a Peronist politician. What, for instance, if the Republic of Ireland were to invade the six counties of the North? 'Well, you would if you could, but you're not strong enough, or maybe you don't really believe your own claims,' he said contemptuously. *Machismo* is all so simple.

Las Malvinas have become a false god for the Argentinians. In the middle of economic chaos and political mutiny, the taking of the islands may well have been a handy distraction for the Galtieri government, but the ploy worked because a fatalistic people wanted some unifying cause, some release from the internal savagery of the last seven years.

'There are only two things we don't fight about,' a taxi-driver declared to me gloomily the other day. 'That's football and Las Malvinas. The last time I can remember being happy was in 1978.'

The Argentinians were naive enough to think they would get away with it. Only now are they beginning to realise there was always a price to be paid. 'We didn't think the British would react like this,' complained Nicanor Costa Mendes. 'We didn't think the United States would desert us,' moaned the Foreign Minister. 'We thought Europe would understand,' protested the battalions of European immigrants.

'Did we really think it was only a matter of overthrowing 80 marines and a funny man in a plumed hat?' asked an unusually brave columnist in last week's *La Prensa*. The popular paper *Clarin* put it more simply after the shock of last week's successful British landing on the Falklands. 'Since last Friday Argentina knows that war is not a game of football, that there are no goals without death and destruction. Therefore, amidst the din of battle we must think about an honourable peace.'

In Europe both these press comments would sound innocuous enough, but they express reservations that amount almost to high treason in the atmosphere of fervent nationalism created here over the last seven weeks. They also reflect a courage and a thoughtfulness that Argentina's own political and community leaders lack. The politicians have seized on the occasion to shake off the restrictions imposed on them by the military over the past seven years and they are organising actively again. Indeed, the Peronists are somewhat miffed that the Galtieri government has stolen the nationalist and anti-colonial platform that they consider belongs exclusively to the heirs of Juan Peron. They have been forced as nationalists to support the nationalist cause and they are ready to scream louder than any military hawk at the first sign of weakness on the sovereignty issue.

'If Galtieri loses these islands now, we'll hang him and the junta in the Plaza de Mayo,' said a wealthy son of Peron, smugly contemplating a return to power as he sliced open a thick and bloody fillet steak. The Peronists are never choosy about their opportunities.

The smaller Radical Party has tried to preach caution without getting into trouble, and as a result they say nothing. After an hour and a half of trying to crack the code to his oblique and meandering rhetoric, I asked a Radical politician for the hundredth time if he agreed with the principle of an armed intervention. 'Of course I don't, but they didn't exactly ask my opinion,' he snapped. 'It was the wrong way and the wrong time but I can't say that yet. Some day maybe I will, but right now it is suicidal. The thing is done and the public in retrospect has accepted it. The Government needs our support during the war and during the drawing-up of a peace settlement which is going to hurt more than any of my people realise. In return we, the politicians, may get some move towards a more democratic civilian-led government – and that is a deal we have to make.'

If the British re-take the islands this week, Galtieri must fall, they agreed. But obviously politicians would prefer the security of a negotiated deal on participation in a new government rather than another military coup which might prove to be even more right-wing. Outright humiliation, they feel, would produce the same consequences in Argentina as the Versailles treaty did in Germany.

This thoughtless nationalism, of course, is not helped by what the Argentinians see as the insufferable arrogance of the British. 'They've got to learn that they can't treat a major power like this,' British Ambassador Williams was overheard to remark as he prepared to leave his Buenos Aires embassy under the red and white Swiss flag. Just as the principle of opposing unacceptable use of force may have taken second place to Britain's need to defend her honour, the Argentinians for their part have damaged the prospect of world support for their quite respectable sovereignty claims in the euphoria of an armed intervention which was one in the eye for Britain. The British, they boasted, had no monopoly on teaching people lessons.

The Argentinians have all the prickly sensitivity of a former European colony which still apes the behaviour of the colonialists. 'The British think we're just Indians here,' they protest, trying to prove the sophistication of their own civilisation by pointing to the Paris-like parks of Buenos Aires and the shops full of Italian shoes. 'Don't you think we're very European?' they beg the stray visitor. 'We're no banana republic,' they argue.

They are an extraordinary mixture of bluster and insecurity. Why was it right for Britain to take the islands in 1833 and wrong for Argentina to take them back now? they complain with a fine disregard for the irritating requirements of international law. In the midst of condemning colonialism they admire the determination and even the arrogance which built up the great European empires. In a boys' school in the Buenos Aires suburb of Belgrano last week, at least five senior boys told me that what they admired about Britain after football and pop music was the grandeur of her imperial past, the great ambition and determination which had allowed her to impose her way of life on other people. They hate to be called a Third World or a small country and they dread pity. Though it suits them sometimes to represent themselves as David fighting off the British Goliath, they basically feel much more at home with Goliath.

'What we want more passionately than anything else,' said the editor of a Catholic review last week, 'is a state of order. Anarchy is the chronic disease from which we suffer and of which we are afraid. You must remember that our society is at the same stage of development as England in the seventeenth century and France in the eighteenth. Why did the British choose Charles II? Because they wanted order. Why do we put up with the military governments we grumble about all the time? Because we want a state of order.'

From his decidedly conservative political viewpoint an election automatically brings the Peronists back and Peronism, for him, means anarchy. He did not explain that the military establishment have continually undermined the stability of successive Peronist governments, and that instability has been increased by the Peronists' own neo-fascist streak. But the point really is that the conservatives' only path to power is with the military and by military coup. As one old lady explained sweetly to me the other day: 'I would so love elections, but the problem is that they [the Peronists] would get back in again!' It is the familiar logic. If you cannot get what you feel is yours peacefully, you grab it.

Argentina is a country of inhabitants, of residents, said my Catholic friend, paraphrasing the Argentinian writer Borges. It is not really a nation of citizens who contribute to the national good, he said. It has yet, despite the ubiquitous blue and white flags and the fervently sung national anthem, to find a sense of nationhood. It is a country of exploiters, he says, who have not yet left behind the immigrant mentality. Their exploitative nature has led them to cream off the easy pickings in their own economy and leave their potentially rich country underdeveloped and vulnerable. They undermine their own currency by playing the national game of currency speculation. 'The Church and the Army are the only two stable institutions here. Because we belong, we have to stay here. We cannot move on like immigrants when the going gets rough.' Indeed one could argue that the Galtieri government exploited the Falklands crisis for reasons of political survival. The politicians are exploiting the same crisis for the more justifiable reasons of making a deal which could see a return to civilian government. Argentinians themselves are exploiting it for the questionable short-term benefits of a unifying cause, a reason to celebrate, a wallow in self-congratulation.

For the sake of waving a flag over a set of forgotten islands they are risking their shaky economy, whatever political stability they had, their international relations, and the lives of those dark-eyed, slim-waisted young men of whom they are so proud. The only gain they can now make will be an improvement in the pre-2 April negotiating position on the islands – a gain they have dearly bought. They are paying for an unacceptable use of force. They are paying because they are wrong.

GUBU

CONOR CRUISE O'BRIEN (1982)

In the summer of 1982, it emerged that a murder suspect had been arrested while he was a house guest of the unwitting Patrick Connolly, Attorney-General in the government led by Charles Haughey. Connolly then left the country on holiday; he returned only after having been summoned by Haughey, and eventually resigned. Haughey's performance at a press conference regarding these events provoked this forensic analysis from Conor Cruise O'Brien, who had lost his Dáil seat – in the same constituency as that which returned Mr Haughey – five years earlier.

You've got to hand it to the man, you really have. He is grotesque, unbelievable, bizarre and unprecedented.

Those, remember, are the adjectives that sprang to his own lips, at that press conference of his last Tuesday, to characterise 'the situation which has arisen' in and around the flat of the Attorney-General.

No one, I think, would seriously challenge the applicability of these adjectives, emphatic though some of them are, to the situation on which they were bestowed.

'Unprecedented' is literally correct. There is indeed no precedent in the history of the State for the arrest of a man suspected of murder – even single murder – at the residence of the Attorney-General, host to the suspect.

So no one, not even Gustave Flaubert, could challenge this use of 'unprecedented'; it is unquestionably *le mot juste*.

'Grotesque', 'bizarre', are more subjective terms, but they hardly seem out of place in the context. The only one I reject is 'unbelievable'. As Aristotle so rightly observed in the *Poetics*: 'What has happened we know to be possible, because it has happened.' We know this thing to be possible because it has happened, though we have no excuse for not believing it, however improbable it may seem.

It was not the adjectives themselves that were remarkable, but the spirit in which they were introduced by this (here choose your own adjective) Taoiseach of ours, at his surreal press conference. The man poured these words on, exactly as if he were reading out rave reviews of some brilliant performance which he and his all-star cast had just turned in, to general acclaim.

At first, watching the man on television, I was disoriented by his unfamiliar use of words. How could 'grotesque', uttered in a tone of emphatic relish, have somehow turned into a term of self-approbation? For a moment, I felt as if I might be falling victim to some obscure lexical disorder that turns words inside out. After a while, however, I was able to enter into the spirit of the thing, and see how his mind was working. You see, the worse the situation that had arisen was, the better Mr Haughey looked, in his own estimation. If the situation was GUBU – that is to say, grotesque, unbelievable, bizarre and unprecedented – then the greater the credit due to Mr Haughey for dealing with it . . .

The more heads the hydra had, and the more fangs they bore, the more highly we think of Hercules. The more unprepossessing the Gorgon, and the more snaky her locks, the better Perseus. Those heroes handled the situation that had arisen, and they did so in a manner that has been generally admired. And so also it was with Mr Haughey, by his way of looking at it.

The GUBU had been a GUBU alright, no doubt about that, but Mr Haughey was there and the GUBU was taken care of . . .

'Quite satisfactory' is our hero's modest verdict on his recent exploits. Some of us, however, find the verdict not quite modest enough. For the fact is that the Taoiseach's handling of this matter, even on his own account of it, shows him to be lacking in elementary prudence and commonsense: alarming deficiencies in a Taoiseach. And the more he insists on how GUBU the situation was, in which he none-the-less permitted his Attorney-General to go on holiday, the more starkly Mr Haughey illuminates the folly of that permission.

Mr Haughey's contention that the Attorney-General, being 'a major constitutional officer', did not need his permission is pure sophistry. In the circumstances in which Mr Connolly found himself, he could not remain a major constitutional officer without the Taoiseach's acquiescence. The Taoiseach could have prevented Mr Connolly from leaving, by the exercise of that same authority by which he was able, when he woke up, to bring Mr Connolly back. Letting Mr Connolly go on his holiday was another Haughey misjudgement, not an inevitable result of arcane constitutional processes.

Under Mr Haughey, stunts have followed on happenings and happenings on stunts. The stunts have misfired and the happenings have been mishandled. The Taoiseach carries a large share of the responsibility for the fact that the State is now on the verge of financial ruin. He carries the entire responsibility for the gratuitous and damaging deterioration in our relations with our nearest neighbour. His offhand adoption of a collision course with the unions threatens to bring on what may be the most serious break-down in industrial relations that this country has ever known.

In these conditions many people – I believe most people – hope that the opposition will apply itself single-mindedly, when the Dáil resumes, to the urgent task of putting out a government which is unsafe at any speed.

Unfortunately, some members of the opposition seem to think differently. Mr John Kelly, for example, appears to hold the view that, since Mr Haughey is now (ostensibly at least) set on a course of financial rectitude, the Fine Gael party, being committed itself to financial rectitude, cannot put Mr Haughey out. Mr Haughey agrees with the view. It represents, at the moment, his best hope of political survival.

John Kelly is a good man, but there are times, as now, when he seems to be in the grip of an honourable death-wish, of positively Japanese proportions. Mr Kelly has himself, and recently, described the dominant section of the ruling party – the section that includes the Taoiseach and the Minister for Finance – as 'a foot-loose Mafia'. How can it possibly be in the interests of the country to allow people of whom you hold that opinion to remain in control of our government?

At a critical moment in the French Revolution, it became clear that, in the National Convention, there was a majority which had

had quite enough of Robespierre. Trouble was, they couldn't agree on exactly *why* they had enough, so they argued the toss about that, and seemed to be stuck. Then the Abbé Sieyes, that shrewd politician, suggested the solution. The Convention should just get rid of Robespierre without giving a reason. The Convention, he said, should pronounce 'death without phrases' – *la mort sans phrases* – and the Convention did just that.

In this case a plain motion of no confidence in Mr Haughey as Taoiseach, without anything else, ought to do the trick. *La mort sans phrases*.

The Moral Civil War

GENE KERRIGAN (1983)

The eighth amendment to the Irish Constitution, banning abortion, was passed by referendum on 7 September 1983. Six days earlier, *Magill* published Gene Kerrigan's account of the origins of the amendment, and the political and ideological battles it occasioned.

[...] Early evening, Friday February 8 1980, about two dozen people, mostly women, were picketing the British embassy. Several carried candles that flickered in the darkness. There's not much pedestrian traffic on Merrion Road at that time of day and the picketers didn't attract much attention. That day the Corrie Bill was up for voting in the British parliament. The Bill, proposed by John Corrie, aimed at restricting the 1967 Act which had introduced legalised abortion in Britain. There was a mass lobby of the House of Commons that evening and a handful of Irish feminists had mounted a picket on the embassy in sympathy with their British sisters. (The Corrie Bill, incidentally, was defeated.)

This was the first public pro-abortion-rights initiative in the current controversy. The issue had been discussed before, usually on an academic level in feminist and left-wing groups. In the Socialist Labour Party in 1978, for instance, there were three camps: those who supported the right to abortion, those who opposed it, and those who thought it political suicide to even mention the word.

The 'women's movement', once imagined to be a monolithic bloc, had become a diverse, informal network, its activists involved in dozens of campaigns, issues and projects. The most consistent coalition of interests was on the contraception issue, but that was flagging, bogged down in Haughey's Irish solution.

Inevitably, some of the women involved in the contraception campaign discussed initiatives on the abortion issue. Not because there is any predetermined contraception-abortion-euthanasia chain effect, but because we are a different society than existed twenty years ago. There is more sex around, more unwanted pregnancies; economic and social choices are not as narrow; abortion Irish style exists if you have the price of a boat ticket, which it did not before; above all, the women who discussed the issue had spent several years in the feminist movement, discussing problems, rights, theories and tactics. The fact that one half of the race bears the children is no small matter and no aspect of it would be left undiscussed. In the interminable but necessary discussions which the feminist movement had gone through it was not unnoticed that many of the problems and inequalities stemmed from that fact – including wages, working conditions, the right to work, financial dependence, health facilities and a host of others.

Fr Simon O'Byrne could tell *In Dublin* in July 1982 that Catholics should 'simply accept what the Holy Father says and what the bishop of the diocese teaches and do not allow yourselves to be confused by the opinions of others'. But that kind of thing didn't wash with people who knew you could lose a job or a flat if you became pregnant. Just as for those who adhere to the traditional values abortion is unthinkable, so for people who have escaped those values is it unthinkable that the authoritarianism of Fr O'Byrne's statement should prevail.

The discussion on how those who must bear the children can best control that biological fact and prevent it causing gross inequality inevitably involved discussion of abortion. Within the diverse feminist movement some agreed, some disagreed, some thought it pointless raising the issue.

In February 1980 a handful of women, including some of those who had been on the British Embassy picket, came together to form the Women's Right To Choose Group.

Two members of a British organisation, the Society for the Protection of the Unborn Child (SPUC), arrived in Dublin in July 1980 for discussions with like-minded people. Two months later an Irish SPUC was putting posters in shopping centres advertising meetings on 'The Case Against Abortion'. SPUC was facilitated by local Catholic priests, providing halls, announcing meetings, organising collections and in at least one case – Wexford – allowing SPUC members to speak from the pulpit. As yet, the Catholic bishops were not involved. SPUC's initial steps were taken on the periphery of media consciousness, but in the heartland of Catholicism – the parish halls, presbyteries and pulpits. It was a genuine grassroots movement. The section of the population which had held fast to the traditional values naturally contained a large number of priests, the foot soldiers of the old authoritarianism. The bishops, dealing with strategic and political matters, had to be more careful. Some might even have been compromised, recognising worthiness in some of the new values.

SPUC was distributing garish literature and within a few months had shown its equally garish film and slide show in about 250 schools. By then it had about 4,000 supporters, having quickly released the passions of the traditional forces long held in check. Its problem was that it was all dressed up, in its Sunday best, with nowhere to go. Abortion was already illegal.

One of the major strands in the development of the women's movement was its concern with health. Central to that were the particular problems deriving from pregnancy. Anne Connolly, who ran the Well Woman Centre in Dublin, became a key hate figure for the traditional forces. If a woman wanted an abortion, the centre, having discussed it with her and counselled her, would provide a referral to a British clinic. By January 1981 SPUC's campaign had permeated the grassroots political culture to such an extent that a routine Fianna Fáil meeting in Longford, where Albert Reynolds was stroking the troops, could include, in its calls for agricultural benefits, calls for the jailing of drug pushers, and for the removal of Kenny Everett from RTE, a demand that the abortion clinics in Dublin be shut down.

The law could do nothing. Abortion referral is not a crime. No government was prepared to contemplate the draconian laws necessary to close off the route that several thousand Irish women each year take to Britain. Early in 1981 there was a political force gathering without the traction to move in any particular direction. The traditional forces were fighting back, but they had no practical demands. When the Right To Choose Group had been formed in February 1980 there were expectations of an amplified version of the hysterical denunciation which had met the campaign on contraception.

However, there was little reaction. For the most part the media simply reported on developments, without carrying smears or admonishments. This was to continue for over a year. It was accepted that abortion could be argued as an issue like any other. The RTC people knew that SPUC was organising down among the grassroots but didn't respond. They didn't want that kind of confrontation and in any case were not equipped for that kind of campaign.

The RTC was always a group, never a campaign. It followed the traditional feminist road of internal discussion – a necessary process, but one often undertaken at the cost of a lack of public activity. They held meetings, but you had to have an eye and an ear tuned to the women's movement to know about them. One of the most successful meetings was held in the Junior Common Room of TCD on Friday, August 8 1980. Apart from the RTC speakers there was a speaker, Patricia McMahon, from the American group Catholics For a Free Choice, and Jan Parker from the National Abortion Campaign in Britain. About a hundred people attended.

The following month, on Tuesday September 9, the RTC Group held a press conference at 3 Belvedere Place, the old HQ of the Contraception Action Programme, and announced the setting up of the Irish Pregnancy Counselling Centre. This would provide counselling for women with unwanted pregnancies. The counselling would be non-directional, giving all the options including abortion, and helping the woman to follow whatever option she chose. If the woman wanted an abortion the IPCC referred her to a clinic in Britain and provided counselling after the abortion if she wanted it.

In strict political terms it could be argued that the Group's main achievement, the setting up of the IPCC, was a diversion, accommodating to the unwritten position of the state – which was to avoid controversy on abortion by exporting the problem to Britain. In practical terms there was little else they could do other than set up a service to support the decisions many women were already taking. They were a tiny group without resources or the political direction to launch a campaign. By the end of 1980 they had established their presence, found a niche within the feminist movement, and little more.

Less than three weeks after the setting up of the IPCC, two meetings were held in Dublin which would prove important in guiding
the traditional forces. About 200 doctors from various countries
staged a congress of the World Federation of Doctors Who Respect
Human Life. Dr David Nowlan of the *Irish Times*, who attended
the conference, described it as 'arrogant, paranoid and sex-obsessed',
with the issues of contraception and abortion being introduced
to almost all sessions, including those dealing with subjects such as
the care of the dying and doctors' responsibilities to prisoners. It
was organised by Professor John Bonnar, a promoter of natural contraception and a leading light of the Amendment campaign. Professor
Bonnar has links with both the Knights of Columbanus and Opus
Dei. In 1978 he lectured the Knights at their headquarters in Ely
Place. 'Ireland stands alone', he said, 'in her fight to defend the Judeo-
Christian moral code of sexual behaviour and the sanctity of life.'
His lecture was reproduced by Opus Dei in 1979 as part of their cov-
ert campaign against contraception legislation.

Some of the doctors from that conference organised a second
meeting at Carysfort College. This linked up the doctors with the
pressure groups which were preparing the grassroots campaign. Representatives from the British SPUC were there (the Irish SPUC was
just being formed), and members of The Responsible Society. This
group was set up in 1980 from a meeting on 'The Permissive Society'
organised by the Knights of Columbanus. This was the meeting at
which Professor John Bonnar made his 'Ireland stands alone' speech.
Fr Paul Marx, the energetic anti-abortion campaigner, famous for
careering around the world with foetuses in bottles, was also a par-
ticipant at the Carysfort meeting. Marx was a founder of the Doctors
Who Respect Human Life organisation.

Shortly after these two meetings, the strands of the Pro-Life
Amendment Campaign (PLAC) began to consolidate. The idea for
putting an Amendment in the Constitution had come from the
Catholic Doctors Guild a month or two earlier. This Guild, which
also has links with the Knights of Columbanus, was formed about
ten years earlier as a reaction to 'the decline in ethical values'.

The structural link between the doctors and the pressure groups was provided by the Council of Social Concern, an umbrella organisation for a number of groups (such as the League of Decency and the Family League) which had sprung up in the Sixties and Seventies to express the disagreement of the traditional forces with the changes that were taking place. The Christian Political Action Movement, which had canvassed against a number of politicians in 1977, was part of COSC.

In short, the organiser of the TCD conference which was the spark that began PLAC, Professor John Bonnar, had links with the Knights and Opus Dei. Dr Richard Wade, a key figure in the Catholic Doctors Guild, which first suggested a referendum, is a Knight. The Responsible Society was set up from a meeting organised by the Knights at their headquarters. The Council of Social Concern, which linked the doctors with the pressure groups, then operated from the headquarters of the Knights, 8 Ely Place. Professor Bonnar wasn't too happy about having the organisation fronted entirely by men, 'especially senior academic gynaecologists, who looked like a stuffy old bunch', he told *Magill* in June 1982. Dr Julia Vaughan became chairperson of the group.

From the beginning of 1981 PLAC, which was as yet just a small grouping of individuals with no public presence, began to seek the support of other traditional forces, such as the Catholic Nurses Guild and Muintir na Tíre. In April they pulled in the biggest and most effective force, SPUC. Previously, there had been some wariness about SPUC. Its supporters tend to shout abuse and make controversial statements about contraception and the like – not at all the image of responsible concern which PLAC was promoting. But if PLAC had its generals among the doctors, its colonels and captains among the pressure groups, it still needed its troops.

The original idea was to organise a national petition for a Constitutional referendum, but there was a possible short-cut through the nervous politicians. On March 30 1981 a vice-president of Fine Gael, Maria Stack, said that there were medical circumstances in which abortion might be permissible, in her opinion. Garret FitzGerald and Paddy Harte responded quickly and brutally and Stack was silenced.

There was an election coming up, the politicians were vulnerable.

On April 27 1981 PLAC held a press conference and announced its existence. Just three days later Garret FitzGerald and Charlie Haughey met its representatives.

Charlie Haughey immediately agreed in principle to a referendum and reported back three weeks later with agreement in detail. Frank Cluskey said Labour would consider it, and put it on the long finger.

Garret FitzGerald was in a tighter corner. If PLAC was to point the abortion finger during the forthcoming general election, Fine Gael would be particularly vulnerable because of the Stack incident. Also, there was a feeling amongst some of his advisers that Garret's perceived image with sections of the electorate was somewhat remote, insufficiently in tune with the traditional values of Catholicism. It was felt that some of the electorate didn't even know he was a Catholic. The PLAC demand was an opportunity to get into line.

FitzGerald met the PLAC delegation at his house on April 30, along with Gemma Hussey. The PLAC delegation comprised a doctor from the TCD conference, Julia Vaughan, Professor Éamon de Valera, Loretto Browne of SPUC, Frank Ryan (a lawyer), and Denis Barror of The Responsible Society. FitzGerald immediately agreed to their demand.

The wording which PLAC was pushing at the time was: 'The State recognises the absolute right to life of every unborn child from conception and accordingly guarantees to respect and protect such right by law.' There was no mention of the mother, and the commitment to an 'absolute right' placed the rights of the foetus above those of the mother. Such details didn't worry anyone in those days.

Last April a founder of PLAC told the *Sunday Tribune*, 'I'm sick to death of the whole Amendment business.' At least one other founder doubted the wisdom of continuing with the campaign.

It wasn't supposed to work out like this. The thing should have been slipped through as easily as a Finance Bill in the Dáil. Ireland, in the words of Julia Vaughan, would have 'once again become a beacon' which would 'turn the tide in the Western world'. In choosing such an emotive issue on which to fight, the traditional forces should have had a runaway victory by last March. People would be asked if they wanted to kill babies – answer, no, ergo triumph.

Instead, a moral civil war developed.

There were initial victories. Gay Byrne, who more than any other individual symbolised the openness of the new values and the willingness to discuss all issues and points of view, was successfully shouldered onto the sideline. [*The RTÉ Authority reacted strongly to a* Late Late Show *discussion of the topic and instituted pre-censorship of the programme on this topic. – Ed.*] A member of the Irish National Teachers Organisation running for the Senate this year was asked one question by his executive: not on education but on where he stood on the Amendment. When he said he opposed it he was refused his union's backing and withdrew from the election. On several RTE programmes, notably an interview with June Levine, there was censorship which precluded discussion of abortion. One producer was reprimanded and effectively barred from working on certain programmes after arranging an interview with Anne Connolly of the Well Woman Centre.

Such foretastes of the resurgence of traditional values culminated in the purging of the anti-Amendment elements from the Irish Farmers' Association. What wasn't expected was the size and strength of the opposition. The Right To Choose Group was supposed to be the devil at which the fingers would be pointed and all others would join in the finger-pointing or be revealed as 'anti-life'. Instead, the opposition emerged on a wide scale based on carefully thought-out grounds of respect for the mother's life and a general distaste at the moral superiority and authoritarianism which the traditional forces represent. [. . .]

At the time of Garret FitzGerald's assumption of the Fine Gael leadership, party activists believed that at least a quarter, perhaps more, of the National Executive of the party were Knights of Columbanus. Such a force, acting in concert while others acted individually, had a large influence. The demonstration of greater efficiency and the process of attrition through which FitzGerald's whiz kids assumed dominance in the party saw the quiet eviction of the Knights.

So nervous was FitzGerald of this power group that when he was forming his present Cabinet he extracted a declaration from each male Minister that he wasn't a Knight and a promise that if he should

join that organisation he would leave the Cabinet. Even so, the traditional forces were gathering within the party. In January 1982 the
Irish Catholic was able to report that a group of 'strenuously Catholic'
TDs and Senators was organising within the party. Significantly, this
group was aimed not alone at the Amendment but at 'the promoters
of marriage wrecking' – i.e. those who believed that the divorce laws
should reflect the reality of marital breakdown.

FitzGerald, belatedly convinced of the dangers of the Amendment, tried to straddle two camps, the traditional and modern, and
hold the party together. Surprisingly, Paddy Cooney was on his side
and argued strongly within the Cabinet that the wording was crazy.
(Cooney, however, like John Kelly, is unlikely to break with the traditional forces with which he normally sides.)

One bishop made it known to FitzGerald that there were reservations within the hierarchy about the Amendment but it was up to the
Government to stop it; the bishops were unable to stop it. Some were
totally committed to it – all recognised that the traditional forces
within the laity and the priests were making the running.

Fianna Fáil atrophied and then became so unstable because of personality battles that it dare not discuss a live political issue. The
hatches were battened down. Outside, the wolves were in the streets.

Last May a group of people held a meeting in Wexford to discuss
setting up a family-planning centre. About twenty members of
SPUC descended on the meeting, in White's Hotel, with such slogans as 'Instead of women controlling their fertility men should
control their virility'. A Fr Fortune, curate at Poulfur, criticised the
two Fine Gael deputies, Avril Doyle and Ivan Yates, who were present in support of the meeting. He said that he now knew that the
two TDs were not pro-life.

Fr Jack McCabe, Parish Administrator, subsequently apologised
to the TDs for the curate's remarks. There was no apology for Fr
McCabe's other remarks that he hoped that Catholic hospitals would
not be employing people who subscribed to these views. He also
made warning remarks about teachers. There were teachers on the
platform. There was some laughter amid the protests at the priest's
remarks.

Such remarks are not funny, neither are they idle threats. People keep files on people. On May 12 1980 the *Irish Times* printed a letter signed by Sally Keogh in her capacity as Information Officer of the National Social Service Council (NSSC). This was noted by the Council of Social Concern, a constituent part of PLAC and an organisation linked to the Knights. On June 6 John O'Reilly of COSC wrote a confidential letter to the Director of NSSC pointing out that a Sally Keogh had been secretary of the Irish Family Planning Association in 1978 and another Sally Keogh had been involved in the Contraception Action Programme.

'These latter two Sally Keoghs have their ideological colours nailed firmly to the mast', wrote O'Reilly. They and the NSSC Sally Keogh might be one and the same person. 'This is disturbing and I would be very grateful if you would confirm if it is true or assure us that it is false.' O'Reilly added: 'One could not help but worry that the post of Information Officer in your organisation afforded some good opportunity for the promotion of what we may call the ideology of the contraceptive clinics.'

O'Reilly is a former Knight, is vice-chairman of COSC and secretary of The Responsible Society – all organisations involved in the setting up of PLAC. Getting no response from the NSSC, he wrote to the director again on July 27 and warned, 'In the event of receiving no reply at all, reluctantly, I shall be compelled to circularise the members of the Council.' When this threat had no effect there were further measures to hound Sally Keogh.

On June 12 Nial Darragh, a Knight of Columbanus, member of COSC, veteran campaigner against contraception and for the Amendment, wrote a personal letter to Tomas Roseingrave, a member of the NSSC, enclosing a copy of O'Reilly's letter to the director. Darragh said, 'Need I say that there is absolutely no wish on my part to jeopardise the employment or career of the lady in question.' (Then why write?) 'However, as you know I am very concerned about the evil effects of contraception and the "contraception mentality" on our Christian Irish youth and teenagers.'

Darragh said that the letter previously sent to the director was to be sent to all members of the NSSC but instead he wished to 'seek less formal comment in confidence from a friend'. He closed with an ambiguous and confused remark: 'If what appears to be the situation is in fact so, there would appear to be a basis for reconsideration of the wisdom of appropriate action.'

Roseingrave appears to have been embarrassed by the approach and nothing transpired. A subsequent letter to Michael Woods, Minister for Health, brought the reply that if there were any specific allegations to be made against Sally Keogh they should be made to the director of the NSSC.

Sally Keogh kept her job. That time.

And the other trappings of Irish traditional values – the rabid accusations, the political speeches from the pulpit, the poison pen letters, the threatening phone calls, the attacks on the media, the bomb threats to RTE – have made their appearance. SPUC have announced that, whatever the vote, they are here to stay. Part of their plan is to monitor government activity and the law. The Knights and Opus Dei are more active than at any time in the past twenty years. On the other hand, the resurgence of traditional forces has forced a cohesion of progressive forces which had not existed before. Whatever the vote, the moral civil war has just begun.

A Woman in Gangland

JUNE LEVINE (1983)

Lyn Madden, born in Cork in 1944, spent much of her childhood in Catholic institutions in England. She began to work as a prostitute, and in 1966 she moved to Dublin. By the late 1970s, with Dolores Lynch, she was involved in activism on behalf of prostitutes, but she did not escape gangland, and she entered a relationship with John Cullen, a violent pimp. On 16 January 1983, Cullen started a fire at the house where Dolores Lynch, a former prostitute, lived with her mother and her aunt, while Lyn Madden waited in the garden. Cullen had waited seven years to exact his revenge on Dolores Lynch for going to the police about him. On 16 November 1983 Cullen was convicted on Madden's evidence. A fortnight later, *Magill* published June Levine's extensive account of Lyn Madden's life, which began with a detailed narrative of the events of 16 January.

Lyn had soaked in the bath for about an hour when she became aware that he was moving around the flat. She got into a state of panic. The man rarely moved from his horizontal position. He must be rooting for something to do a bondage job on her. Rope, scarves, tights, something to use as a whip. Maybe knives. She'd hidden everything. The kitchen knives were in the airing cupboard. That was since the time she woke up to find herself tied to the bed, spread-eagled.

Now she dried herself hurriedly, put on her nightdress and went into the bedroom. He was lying on the bed. She gave a quick glance around the room. No signs of any torturing equipment. The video-tape was still playing. It was a football match. He'd told her to put on a video and she'd picked football as the safest.

He lay there, a peculiar look on his face. She couldn't pinpoint it, but she knew she'd seen it before.

'John love, do you want a cup of tea and a sandwich?'

He stared thoughtfully at her. She got that cramped knot in her stomach, started sweating, the voice in her head said: 'Speak, will you, swine?'

'Yes,' said John.

She went into the kitchen and switched the kettle on.

Just what had he up his sleeve for tonight? She buttered bread, spread ham. She brought him the food. He didn't look at her, but said: 'OK Lyn.' Lyn sat down and picked up a book to read, but could not concentrate. Her mind insisted on debating what weirdo scene he was cooking up.

'Lyn, get dressed, we're going on a message.' It was 3.30 a.m. Jesus Christ, she thought.

'Where to, John?'

'Just do as you're told and get dressed.'

As they drove down Dorset Street, she asked: 'John, where are we going?'

'Mind your own business,' he replied matter of factly. She knew then that they were not going to the 24-hour shop. Tommy Carlysle's house? With 17 days to the court case she should have guessed why he was so quiet all evening. He was planning to give it to Tommy. How? She got even more scared. In a man-to-man fight Tommy Carlysle would tear John to pieces, so John must be planning something to catch Tommy unawares. Tommy would be within his rights if he beat the hell out of her for going to his house with John. 'I can't win no matter what I do,' she thought.

They were driving up Clanbrassil Street. Dolores! He turned left, then right, then drove slowly up a street lined with neat, semi-detached houses, counting out the number of each house as they passed on the right-hand side. Lyn's heartbeat slowed, she felt herself breathe normally. What had made her think of Dolores? Just because they turned down Clanbrassil Street? John had told her that Dolores lived in a terraced house like the ones in *Coronation Street*. This wasn't like *Coronation Street*. She couldn't figure what the hell he was doing. Perhaps he'd found another imaginary enemy. It had to be related to the trial. Now she realised it had been brewing for days.

John parked the car on a hill, took a pair of gloves off the dashboard and said: 'Get out.' Lyn followed him round to the boot of the car from which he was taking a large blue holdall bag. He was wearing the gloves.

[John Cullen entered the house in Drummond Street, off Clanbrassil Street, where Dolores Lynch lived with her mother and her aunt. As Lyn stood in the garden, Cullen set fire to the house.]

As they got near Lyn's flat in Ballymun, John suddenly laughed out loud. He was ecstatic. As soon as he got inside the flat he told Lyn to bring newspapers and spread them on the floor. He placed the holdall on the paper and stripped off every stitch of clothes onto the paper. He told her to take off her shoes and put them with the rest.

John was singing softly to himself. He stopped suddenly and asked: 'What are you lookin' at me like fuckin' that for? Do something. Make a cup of tea. Run the bath. Look out the window and see is the coast clear.' She did it all. As she was waiting for the kettle to boil, she heard the front door open and shut and heard the rubbish chute being slammed. He came back in and got into the bath, humming. 'I hope I got the right house,' he said and then carried on humming.

He lay on the bed and she handed him a cup of tea. She was afraid to look at him for fear he thought she was looking the wrong way. Lyn hadn't spoken a word since they had come back to the flat. She dared not speak for fear of setting him off. He pretended not to notice her silence. He told her to wash everything from the newspaper, put them into a plastic bag to be disposed of the next day. He stood by her at the kitchen sink as she washed the evidence. He got dressed, smiled and said: 'Have to go now, Lyn.' He said he'd be back around four the next afternoon. He was gone.

Lyn locked and bolted the door, took a few Valium and lay down on the bed. She didn't get between the sheets. She knew she wouldn't be sleeping. She squeezed her eyes against the screams in her head. It was 6 a.m., only two and a half hours since he had told her: 'Get dressed.'

She lay there, her mind racing. Even if she'd got out of the garden without the butcher's knife in her back, where would she run to? Even if she'd got away, he would have had to silence her. He had keys to her flat. Maybe he wouldn't get her right away, but one day she would walk into her flat and there he'd be, lying on her bed. Waiting.

John had always said that if he ever got locked up again he would kill Lyn before he went in. He had surely killed her tonight.

Full of Valium, Lyn debated the possibilities. She argued with herself until 5 p.m. the next day, Sunday. She avoided the radio all day. The police hadn't kicked in her door. She'd convinced herself whoever was in the house had escaped to safety. Cullen hadn't come back yet.

A good sign? John wasn't going to show up. Typical.

She switched on the television. Charles Mitchel's face flashed on the screen. A judge was shot in Belfast, blah, blah, blah. She let her breath out slowly. Charles Mitchel continued: 'Two women died in a fire in a house in Hammond Street early this morning and the daughter of one of them, Miss Dolores Lynch aged 34, died later in hospital.' A picture of the burned-out house flashed onto the screen. Lyn jumped up and switched off the set. Another fistful of Valium. It was hard to get the pills down because her hand shook so much that the water slopped out of the cup as she tried to hold it to her lips.

Then Lyn did something she had never done in her life.

She stood in the middle of the kitchen floor and screamed at the top of her voice. She didn't cry. She couldn't. She stood there and screamed and screamed. She screamed:

'You bastard John. You bastard. Bastard, bastard,' over and over. Then she lay down on the bed, closed her eyes and crossed her hands over her breast. Her heart beat so fast that she could feel her hands being lifted by the force. She lay there for two and a half hours, awake.

At 8.30 p.m. she opened the door to him. He walked past her, lay down on the bed, folded his hands under his head and said: 'Why haven't you got the telly on?'

'I had it on, did you hear the news?' she said. She didn't look at him. She knew if he saw the way she felt about him he would have to kill her. 'Yes,' he replied, 'I'm glad she's dead.' He didn't look at her as he said that. She went into the bathroom, locked the door and sat on the floor with her back to it. So he had watched the news. He'd heard about the Lynches. Had he spent the day as a normal family man with his wife and kids?

She splashed cold water on her own face and went back into the room. 'What are you standing there for,' he asked, 'come and lie down beside me.' She lay on the very edge of the bed. He leaned across and pulled her towards him. He was about to kiss her when she turned her head away from him: 'John, I can't, please don't kiss me.' 'Right,' he said, 'get all the gear together and we'll get rid of it.'

Sometimes when Lyn wakes out of a nightmare in her flat she goes and stands on her balcony. She looks around the flats in Ballymun. 'Did you know,' she asked me, 'that at night Ballymun looks like Manhattan? It's beautiful around 3 in the morning.' She stands there and thinks of all those people asleep in their beds, good people, bad people, working people, parasites. She thinks of the women, women struggling to make ends meet, a few prostitutes, shop-lifters, drug-pushers, cheque bouncers, but 'I know I am the only woman out there who has the guilt I have to live with.'

When they got rid of the gear they went back to the flat and he switched on the television and stretched out on the bed. He told her to make tea and sandwiches. He didn't speak until the television finished. Then he leaned over her, put his leg over her stomach and kissed her. 'John, I'm not looking for trouble, but please don't. I'm upset. It was bad enough last night but when I heard the 6 o'clock news I was shattered. I still am. I can't make love, I just can't.' She talked on, trying to placate him . . . 'I'll get over it in time but right now I just could not stand for you to make love to me.'

He studied her intently. She controlled the muscles in her face. She'd hoped she'd given the impression of love for him, but at the same time a stupid female revulsion of being tainted with death. At long last he spoke: 'Alright, love. I understand.' He kissed her very gently, then lay back on his own pillow: 'I suppose it's only natural you would feel upset. I suppose I should not have taken you with me but it's too late now. I won't try to make love to you until you feel ready. See Lyn, I can't think like you. I forget that something like that would probably hit you pretty hard. Lyn, I love you very much you know. If I didn't I wouldn't have taken you with me.'

'He took me with him – because he loved me?' Lyn asked herself. She dared ask him. In a whisper: 'John, how do you feel now?'

'I'm just glad she's dead,' he replied.

'John?'

'What?'

'What about her mother and her aunt?' He jumped off the bed: 'The fuckin' rat shouldn't have a mother and an aunt. I'm going home now, Lyn.' He left.

The next day was Monday and they bought all the newspapers to read about the fire. John was thrilled it had made the front page. It was also rent day and each week, after they'd paid it, they visited Lyn's friend, Grace Trimble. Grace was talking when she suddenly paused and said excitedly: 'Lyn, Dolores Lynch is dead. A taxi-driver told me last night.'

Lyn couldn't speak. She turned from the window towards Grace. Grace looked at Lyn, putting her cup back down on the table. She knew. She mimed the words: 'Was it John?' Lyn nodded. Grace mimed again: 'Were you with him?' Lyn nodded again. [...] Grace put her hand over Lyn's, squeezed, and pointed to the door and they both walked into the living room. 'John,' Lyn said, 'did you hear Dolores is dead?'

'I'm fuckin' delighted,' he said, not moving his eyes from the television screen. The women exchanged some eye talk. They went back into the bedroom. Lyn told her everything. She had to. She couldn't carry it alone.

John dropped Lyn back at her flat, saying he was going to see one of his prostitutes to collect his takings from her and he would be back later. Lyn felt the better for telling Grace. She knew Grace would not repeat it because she was absolutely terrified of John.

A couple of nights later, Lyn was stroking his feet the way he liked after his bath, when he said: 'Did I tell you, Lyn, that the women on the canal are making a collection for Dolores?' It was usual if one of the women was sick or a relative died or something, to make a collection.

'No, you didn't, how do you know?'

'Claire said it when I went up this morning. She said Betty was asking all the women for a fiver for Dolores's family. I told Claire that if I found out that she had given a penny to it I would break her neck. By the way, Lyn, Tommy has to be got rid of this weekend. I think I will burn his house.'

The holocaust, Lyn thought. She panicked: 'I know Tommy, his wife, his children. John, you will have to kill me. I will not stand again. I will not hear any more screams.' Tenderly, he replied that he'd do it alone this time. He didn't know why he'd taken her to the Lynch house: 'I had a feeling you were getting tired of me and wanted out, at least now I know you can't grass on me. You'd only be setting yourself up.' He went home then.

Even before the Lynch fire, there were several terrified families in Dublin. A member of each one of them had somehow crossed John Cullen. He had made a previous attempt to set fire to Dolores's house by putting fire-lighters through the letter-box. He'd burned a taxi because he'd found the young driver in bed with one of 'his' women, obviously not a paying customer. When it became obvious that the pair were in love with thoughts of permanency, John tried to burn down the man's father's house. They were respectable people and when the fire failed, they paid other penances at John Cullen's hands. John offered to sell the woman for £5,000 to the taxi-driver. The man said he didn't have that much money. John offered him a hire-purchase deal on the young woman.

After the fire, John went on a rampage on the canal. He raped several of the women, kidnapping them in his car. Women on the game for years were shocked and sickened by his sexual deviations. The degradation to which he submitted them went from horrific to impossible to describe.

John came to Lyn's flat on the day of Dolores's funeral. She was numb but alerted by his edginess. She managed to cook him dinner and was amazed that he ate it. He had a bath. It was a habit of Lyn's to sit on the toilet seat and talk to him in his bath. She called it her 'office' because in this situation she could always get him to talk.

'John, what's wrong?' she asked.

He did not answer for a long while. He always soaped and soaped his legs in slow firm movements. Rinsed and soaped and rinsed, over and over again. It was an obsessional ritual Lyn often wondered about. He kept soaping his body: 'Dolores,' he finally said, then fell silent again. Lyn thought the enormity of it all had finally hit him. She prompted: 'What about her?'

'I was down the canal last night. They are still colleccting for her. I will kill every whore down there. I fuckin' hate prostitutes. They know she is my enemy, they know she grassed on me, they know she's a rat,' he said, his face white with temper.

'John, for Christ's sake, the woman is dead. She was lowered into the ground today. Her mother and aunt were buried alongside her. The funeral was today. Can you not let her rest?'

John looked at her now with a sly crazy leer. 'Yes, I forgot, I hope the maggots are eating her,' he said. It hit Lyn that he was crazy. She'd always known he had psychopathic tendencies, but now he had flown over. Flipped. He was talking about Dolores as if she was still alive.

He kept on about Dolores, saying he'd kill every prostitute on the canal for sympathising with the family. He assured Lyn he wouldn't include her.

She said to him: 'I'm not talking about you killing the women. I'm talking about your obsession with Dolores.' He looked at the ceiling and then in the manner of an inquisitive child, asked: 'Do you reckon the maggots are eating her yet? She's been down there a day now.'

She was terrified. She tried to humour him: 'John baby, I don't know, I don't know how long it takes for maggots to eat through a coffin. You look so tense. Why don't you give your head a break and go up to Patsy and go for a drink?' The way he was looking at her was like a little child [. . .] She'd never seen it before. Eventually, he went, looking like a guilty boy for leaving Mammy on her own.

She bolted the door after him. She wouldn't let him in if he came back after the pub. She couldn't. She just could not stand to see John the boy, child, man, killer, headcase, that night.

At 10 the next morning there was a banging on her door. It was Anna's pimp: 'Is John here?'

'No,' said Lyn.

'Then can I bring Davy up?' She nodded and went to make coffee. The two pimps told her John Cullen had kidnapped her friend Grace off the canal the night before and she hadn't been seen since. Lyn sat down. John must have twigged she'd told Grace about the fire. Grace could be dead. Lyn asked Grace's pimp: 'Is she not in the flat?' He replied: 'Do you think I would walk into the flat and John Cullen be waiting for me with a knife. I came here to see if you knew anything. How will I find out if she's there?'

Lyn despised him at that moment. He had always been a 'gutless wonder' but now 'his own woman' could be lying dying and he was too scared to go into the flat. Lyn suggested they get Bella to go in and find out the score. 'He won't touch her. He knows she'll get him nicked.' Besides, Bella, a respectable neighbour, wasn't terrorised by anyone. She's a tiny woman with a ferocious temper who would confront anyone.

They found Grace in the flat. Bella and Lyn sat on Grace's bed in her flat until Grace poured out her nightmare during six hours with John Cullen. And he'd promised to return three nights a week to keep her company.

He said her pimp neglected her too much.

More women came to see Grace. Two of them had called to Grace's flat the night before in a taxi and honked the horn. They saw John looking out the window. He was naked. The next day another woman came forward to describe her ordeal with John Cullen, and then another and another. Mary, an unusually strong woman, had fought like a demon. She couldn't get John's car door open from the inside but she got the window open and made her getaway through it in spite of him trying to pull her back by the legs. She got free at Irishtown, flagged a taxi. John gave chase, driving up on the pavement, through red lights, but the taxi-driver managed to lose him. It was then John grabbed Grace, known to be the softest of the women, least able to defend herself.

Lyn attacked John about the rapes. He denied it. She described some of the details: 'Ring any bells, John? You tried to do the same to me. You asked me more than once to let you.'

There was a raging row. He said he was sick of brassers. He was going to exterminate every last one of the women on the canal.

Lyn stood with her hands on her hips: 'You are sick of brassers? You've caused a reign of terror down there. Every woman down that canal hates your guts, it was a sorry day for Dublin prostitutes the day you went into the pimping game. You won't find an Irish girl on the canal tonight. The word is out, they are scared out of their wits. None of those girls did you any harm and you have made a bloody good living from the canal. Supported your wife and three kids. Stay away from them. If you walk out of here now, I swear I'll be gone when you come back. I have to work alongside these women. I will not stand by and let you destroy them.'

He grabbed her by the hair: 'Lyn, baby, you're in no position to make threats. You are only reminding me that you are a danger to me over Dolores. You would want to be careful what you say to me.'

Lyn kept silent for some time. Then he said it was her fault if he screwed other women: 'If you let me make love to you I wouldn't have to go down the canal lookin' for it.'

It was only a week since the fire, John was a married man and had never had a very high sex drive. He left early that night.

January 23 was Lyn's birthday, thirty-nine years. [. . .] John came and insisted he take her for a birthday drink at the Swiss Cottage. She'd given up drink since the night of the first bondage session with him and she feared John on drink. He sat close and held her hand in the pub.

It left Lyn cold. He made her tell him she loved him. He kissed her. She had long since wearied of having to prove she loved him. For almost a year, he demanded proof: 'If you loved me you'd have my baby, but you can't because you insist on wearing that damn thing.' She'd fended it off as best she could. She didn't want to be pregnant. She'd three children and she felt she hadn't been able to do well by any of them. Besides, approaching forty, she didn't want to face all that again.

But John kept up the pressure. Every night. 'If you loved me . . .' or 'What's the use if we don't have a child of our own, it proves you're not going to stay.' Or the worst: 'Please, Lyn? Please?' That went on for the best part of a year. One night she agreed, when John was being especially loving, that yes, she would have a baby. He waited outside the clinic while she had her IUD removed.

She came out of the clinic in bits. She felt helpless, utterly vulnerable. All the way home in the car, tears stung her eyes and her hands shook when she tried to light a cigarette. It was as if she were watching some other woman do something crazy.

Within two months Lyn was pregnant. When she told John, he disappeared. Didn't turn up for weeks. Then he told her he'd decided, after all, that he would stay with her until she had the baby. A few more days: 'Lyn, it's a mistake, you'll have to have an abortion.' He kept on about the abortion and Lyn arranged to go to England with Grace to have an abortion. She didn't tell John. She knew now that she was going to do exactly as she wished, but she'd play him like a fish, let him think he ruled the roost. He changed his mind again. They would have the baby. Then, no it was out of the question. Then: 'Lyn, you have to make arrangements.' 'OK, John,' Lyn said wearily and kept her date in England. She was very ill after the abortion.

Tonight, a year later, he said: 'I think I know what the trouble is. I should never have made you get that abortion. We will have a baby. You can work for another two years, then pack it in and we'll have a baby.

She told him, gently, that all that was over now. There was no future for them. But he argued with her. He guaranteed her that in ten years' time they would have it made, have two houses set in flats, use the money from the rents to open a bookshop for Lyn. 'Our child would be about seven years old then. My own kids would be grown up and all this will be a bad dream.' He meant and believed every word.

'John, I don't know how you can talk about ten years from now. You are in cuckooland. You know we won't last ten years.'

He kissed her: 'Lyn, love, if I didn't believe in an afterlife I would leave my wife tomorrow and move in with you. I would divorce Judy and marry you.'

She asked him what an afterlife had to do with it.

He told her that he was scared that if he left his wife and God was waiting at the gates of heaven when he died he would never forgive him for leaving his wife. If he could know for sure that there was no afterlife, no heaven, he would move in with her and be happy. 'I wouldn't feel guilty about it.'

'John,' she said, 'you have burned three women to death. What the hell do you think your God thinks about that? If you leave your wife he won't forgive you? What about Dolores and her family? Do you think he will open the pearly gates for you after that?'

He withdrew his hand: 'We're back to that again. Look, God knows I'm in the right. He knows Dolores got me nicked. He understands.'

The evening went from bad to worse until Lyn blurted: 'I don't even think I love you anymore.' Now, she was skating on thin ice.

She began thinking of mad dogs. A dog you loved could savage a child. You'd love and miss the dog, she reasoned, but it had to be stopped. [. . .]

It was 7 a.m. He was back. Why hadn't she run last night?

Christ he'd knock the door off its hinges. But it wasn't him, she found, when she went to look. It was the police. About five of them: 'Who's in the flat with you?'

'Just my son,' she answered. The same guard said to her: 'Get dressed, I am arresting you under Section 30. Make your mother a cup of tea,' he said to the boy. As she was drinking the coffee (she doesn't like tea) the guard asked: 'You know what it's about, don't you?' She nodded.

When they were driving along, Lyn said: 'Have you got John?'

'Yes, you can relax, we have him.' She exhaled. 'What took you so long?' she asked. [. . .]

The Election of Gerry Adams

EMILY O'REILLY (1983)

In the early 1980s the political rise of Sinn Féin in Northern Ireland was largely unreported, and its significance underestimated, partly because of a hostile public and media consensus against the 'Armalite in one hand and ballot box in the other' strategy enunciated by Danny Morrison at the party's 1981 Ard Fheis. Two years later, that strategy had its first major success with the election of Gerry Adams as MP for West Belfast, unseating Gerry Fitt. Emily O'Reilly's portrait of Adams on the stump, and of the scene at the count, appeared in the *Sunday Tribune*.

The 'Voice of Principled Leadership' wore a red gansey for polling day. His wife wore a lemon skirt with toning beige shoes and followed her husband everywhere.

Even the Sinn Féin headquarters in Andytown were looking smart. The Republican mural on the outside wall had been tarted up and the James Connolly one up the road had been painted over with the picture of a young mother Ireland with streaming yellow hair.

James Connolly is coming back once they find a good wall.

Only the slogans hadn't changed: '13 gone but not forgotten, we got 13 and Mountbatten.'

The 'Voice of Principled Leadership' was concerned about personation. Six arrests had been made by half past ten. An hour later the number had risen to 22. By 2 p.m. over 60 had been taken in and all over the city bets were being made on the final tally. Sinn Féin were blaming the Sticks (Workers Party), then the SDLP. They made complaints to the RUC and wondered how much money anybody who'd been wrongfully arrested would get.

In the end, the Voice decided to hit the streets to sort things out. By eleven that morning he'd already toured every polling station in West Belfast. Now he was going to do it all over again.

Down in the Falls, Adams looked like the only candidate. Gerry

Fitt was nowhere in sight. No supporters, no personation agents, a handful of posters. Somebody had seen him hours ago, flying by in a car, but most reckoned he'd given up on the election anyway. He's away now to London, they jeered, getting his peerage, just you wait and see. He wasn't.

West Belfast's army of unemployed were at Gerry Adams' disposal for the day. Organisation was impressive. Outside every single polling station stood a Sinn Féin caravan, complete with sandwich makers and tally keepers. Sinn Féin voters were asked to report to the caravan after they'd voted. Their names were taken, just to help with the tally.

At every polling station the news was good despite horror stories of people being carted off in handcuffs by the RUC for alleged personation. In Castle Street, a woman with an American accent can tell Adams that out of 550 votes cast, 150 are theirs. Not a vote less, not a vote more.

Back in the car, Adams asks about events in Dublin; how was Nicky Kelly getting on? *[Nicky Kelly, a republican activist, had been sentenced to prison in 1978 for his alleged part in a mail-train robbery. After a lengthy campaign by sympathizers who maintained his innocence, he was released from prison in 1984 and was accorded a pardon – and substantial damages – in 1992. – Ed.]* He hasn't been in touch with all that for a while, he said, had a deal been done or what? He reckons that something had been arranged, despite the Irish Government denials, and that Kelly will be out soon.

The car stops every now and then and Adams chats to passersby. He breaks into Irish occasionally, self-consciously constructing halting, schoolboy sentences, waving 'Slán go deo' as he moves off. One of his leaflets talks about the party's efforts on behalf of Irish culture, the ceilis in the local halls, the Irish classes, the coaching for the Fáinne Nua. He will wear one himself for the count.

Driving through the streets again Adams breaks into song: 'Agus tabhair dom do lámh.'

His people reckon that Gerry should pull 20,000 votes. It might be more, but two recent events might have put the mockers on that, 'put the people off the party like'. Alice Purvis was shot dead in Derry, shielding her husband's body from a gunman's bullets, and that was 'nasty'. Another guy had his hands shattered by a couple of lads with concrete blocks. People didn't like that sort of thing, but maybe they were used to it by now and the party wouldn't suffer too much.

'Agus tabhair dom do lámh,' sings Gerry Adams.

The security presence is heavy. Up in Ballymurphy the army outnumber the voters. Adams drives up and gets out, grinning to his entourage: 'Watch me get rid of the Brits.' At a nod from Gerry, a photographer from *An Phoblacht* kneels, aims and shoots. The Brits melt away and Adams, the magician, laughs.

The next day at just about the same time, one of the soldiers will be dead, his head blown off in a booby-trap explosion. A dog will come and lick the blood on the footpath and the kids will laugh as another British soldier tries to pull the dog away. And tomorrow too Gerry Adams will say that the soldier shouldn't have been in the 'Murph' in the first place. [. . .]

The middle-aged women (the 'Bingo vote', as he calls them) bring him tea and stories. The young mothers bring him their kids, ordering the two-year-olds to shake hands with Mr Adams. Four-year-olds know him on sight, know his party. He kisses babies, he stands patiently while half a dozen toddlers take turns smoking his pipe. The democratic process.

His mates say that Adams isn't really into kissing babies. But the Voice doesn't seem to mind too much. Ten polling stations have still to be covered, but not before the man from the Pacemaker press photographic agency has taken all the time he needs to arrange a shot with Gerry, a two-year-old, and the two-year-old's mother. Later on the car gets a flat tyre and Gerry gets out to change it. This time the photographer from *An Phoblacht* gets the angles just right. Gerry Adams doing nice normal everyday things.

At lunchtime in Divis Flats, surrounded by dozens of adoring men, women and giggling children, he eats egg sandwiches out of a plastic Ormo bread wrapper and watches the skinhead kids in the yard set fire to the rubbish skips and throw stones at yelping dogs. He talks about housing to one woman while an aide discusses the problem of finding replacement glass for the bus that goes to Long Kesh every week. A few of the men tease him about his leaflets, 'Gerry Adams, the Voice of Principled Leadership'. He looks embarrassed.

The Adams family are told of two recent deaths in the area. Visits to the bereaved are woven into the itinerary. Lifts are arranged en route for the very old, the very ill, and the blind. Sinn Féin is getting the vote out. A coffin emerges from one house. 'I wonder who is using his vote today,' muses a passerby.

On Friday morning, the count begins in Belfast City Hall. At nine on the dot Adams is there. Six supporters stand vigil outside. Some of them are wearing ties. They spend their morning giggling and take photographs of each other outside the count. [. . .] Dozens more arrive and play cat and mouse with the RUC. Every time they move, so do the RUC. But there's no aggro.

At 9.25 the Brylcreemed, be-suited Gerry Fitt arrives, exuding cheer, making appointments for gin and tonics. He's told that one of his henchmen doesn't intend turning up until noon at least. The good humour dies; 'Get him,' grunts Fitt, entering the count.

A quick gander around the tables and he's out again. 'How's it going, Gerry?' asks a reporter. 'He's hacking it,' answers Fitt. Requests for a translation reveal that according to Gerry Fitt, Gerry Adams, one half hour into the count, is walking away with the seat.

The news spreads. At 9.30 Forbes McFaul [of RTÉ], in an empty lobby, to a silent camera, rehearses his 'Fitt is a goner' routine. One hour later Fitt is conceding defeat, publicly, to a word-perfect McFaul. So is the SDLP's Joe Hendron, but nobody is paying attention.

In the corridors reporters are looking for a new angle. They want somebody, anybody to say that not only is Fitt finished, but that he'll be doing well to finish second. Several people oblige.

Inside the count, there's hassle. The Unionists are complaining that Fitt has taken some of their vote. Fitt thinks it's because both sections of the community genuinely support his aims. Sinn Féin say not. Sinn Féin say that the Unionists will do anything to keep Adams out. Fitt goes away for another obituary interview. He stops to chat to three RUC men on the way out.

He hardly enters the count again, latching on to reporters instead, bringing them into quiet corners and explaining away the Gerry Adams vote. It takes his mind off his own.

At half past one the result is declared and for ten riotous minutes the Democratic Process is forgotten. Making his way to the main hall, Adams is cheered by the lads and heckled by women wearing big red Unionist rosettes.

The scrubbed Sinn Féiners in their ties scream support for the armed struggle, the red-faced women in their Sunday best tell Adams he is a murderer and that he'll roast in hell. The Voice remains impassive. A TV presenter talks about the scuffle over the air and almost has his knuckles rapped for doing so by a stick-wielding RUC man.

Inside the hall Adams is declared elected. The surprise, at long last surprise, is that his vote is lower than expected: 16,000 and odd as opposed to 20,000. Adams goes to the microphone.

'Ar dtús, caithfaidh me a rá cupla focail as Gailge, as ár dteanga . . .'

He tells the crowd that it's an historic election victory; that electoral politics will never be the same again; that he will represent all of the people. He talks about the morning's dead. The British soldier with his head blown off. He says that the responsibility lies with the British Government, that the British soldiers shouldn't have been in Ballymurphy. He tells his people that one day, 'Tiochfaidh ár lá.'

Adams leaves centre stage and the journalists, en masse, move with him. Fitt makes his speech to a less than attentive gathering. He reminds them that the promised landslide victory for Adams hasn't materialised. He recalls that half his own vote came from the Prods and half from the Catholic people. That factor, he says, has caused him to re-think his future.

Hendron thanks the people in the City Hall. He asks Adams to ask the IRA to call off their campaign. Adams isn't listening.

Ten minutes later, amid screams of abuse, he and his supporters make their getaway in black taxis. Red-faced women hammer on the windows and journalists beat each other back for vantage points. The three black taxis head away and fast, off up to Andytown with the Sinn Féin (Provisional) MP.

The Death of Ann Lovett

NELL MCCAFFERTY (1984)

Ann Lovett was a girl of fifteen who died after giving birth to a baby, on her own, at a Marian grotto in Granard, Co. Longford, in 1984. Nell McCafferty visited Granard, for *In Dublin* magazine, shortly after the tragedy.

As in her pregnancy, so it was in her death. The people of Granard say with one voice, 'Ask her family.' Ann Lovett's welfare was the inviolate responsibility of her parents. Had she, or they, asked outsiders for help it would have been forthcoming. So long as the family kept silent, the community honoured the unwritten code of non-interference with the basic unit of society.

'Even had I noticed she was pregnant,' says Canon Gilfillan, parish priest, 'I could hardly just come out and say, "You're pregnant."' A businessman who once worked with the St Vincent de Paul says, 'Why do you think I left St Vincent's? The days when you could intervene are long gone. If a family doesn't want you to acknowledge that you know, there's nothing you can do. We knew Ann Lovett was pregnant. The family said nothing. If a family is broke these days, you can't just offer them money. You can leave it secretly on the doorstep, but you can't go near them unless they ask.'

Diarmuid Lovett, father of nine and on the dole, is not broke in the sense of being entirely without standing. He has lived three years in Granard above his non-trading pub, the Copper Pot. He comes from a family of substance, the Lovetts who used to run a family building firm in nearby Kilnaleck. His brother John owns the Copper Kettle pub in Kilnaleck. Diarmuid Lovett is of sufficient standing in the area for his daughter's death to warrant a wreath from Kilnaleck Fianna Fáil Cumann, and the attendance at her funeral of Mr John Wilson, Fianna Fáil TD from neighbouring Mullaghoran. Diarmuid Lovett is, by general reckoning, an abrupt, independent man.

People could hardly just come out and offer help that might be misinterpreted as interference. It was assumed that the family knew and had made arrangements. Did the family know? 'Ask the family,' says the community, leaving the Lovetts to cope full-frontally with the disaster. The twenty-two-year-old sister of Ann Lovett, with whom Ann spent some time in Dublin before Christmas, says 'no comment'. The uncle of Ann Lovett says 'Ask the family,' adding that it is the business of no one but the parents.

The family sit behind the closed doors of the pub. Diarmuid and Patricia Lovett refuse to speak to reporters. The community will not, cannot, speak on their behalf. Canon Gilfillan says, 'I'd like to be able to help the family now but they've shut themselves away and seem to want to be alone. One's instinct is not to intrude.'

Ten days after Ann's death, the gardaí had not been able to secure an interview with her parents. Time is on their side, though, and they're playing a gentle waiting game. Soon, the guards know – as the townspeople know, as the public knows, as the church knows, as the Government which has instigated a private inquiry via the departments of Health and Education knows – the parents must supply at least part of the answer. The death, in a public place, of a teenage girl and her newborn baby demands an attempt at explanation.

It will not be other than an ordeal for the two people of whom it will be demanded, her parents, who are her family. The townspeople cannot or will not help them bear that ordeal. It will be up to the family to explain how it could be that their daughter died unaided and alone. The efforts of the townspeople are directed towards explaining how they, the townspeople, could not come to her aid, though her condition was common knowledge.

More effort has been expended in defending the social superstructure than in defending the basic unit. The Convent of Mercy School, for example, called in a solicitor who, over a period of several hours, helped them draft a statement to the effect that the staff 'did not know' that Ann Lovett was pregnant. Did they, however, 'suspect' that she was? A spokeswoman, trembling and refusing to give her name, told *In Dublin* that the school could not comment on whether or not they suspected. They certainly 'did not know'. Nor would the school comment on the allegation that a teacher who could not stomach the nice legal distinction between 'knowing' and 'suspecting' refused to stand with the staff when the school statement was read out to *Today Tonight*.

If the school, under the authority of headmistress Sister Maria, did not know or suspect anything, did the convent, a separate institution in the grounds, under the authority of Sister Immaculata, know or suspect that Ann Lovett was pregnant? (Convent sisters act as social workers in the town when they are not acting as teachers.) 'No comment.' Did the convent teachers, in their capacity as convent sisters, approach the parents? 'No comment.'

Eventually, with or without a solicitor's help, the School and Convent will make a comment to their employers, the Department of Education. In the meantime, 'Ask the family.'

While the family wait alone for the inquisitional noose to tighten, while they wait for us who are not family to tighten it, the gardaí pursue a duty which they describe as 'sickening'. A technical offence has been committed, that of carnal knowledge with an under-age girl. They must interview the boyfriend with whom she had been keeping company for two years, until the relationship ended one month before she gave birth. His father is dead and his mother went to England last year. The boyfriend – 'Buddy' – lives in the family house, but he was in England during the summer. Did this summer begin in May, just before the pregnancy began, or later? Certainly, the guards know, he gave the key of his house to another youth who has left town since Ann Lovett died. Ann used to be seen coming out of that house. It would be a mercy to establish the line of paternity from there, whether or not prosecution ensues, because that would eliminate a third line of inquiry in a town and country now bursting with outspoken rumour.

'Buddy' has been, since Ann Lovett's death, visiting the grotto wherein she gave birth on the moss-covered stone. By night he is to be found with other youths in the pool-halls, or pubs, for youth does not stay at home. On one such night, eleven nights after Ann Lovett's death, he stood in a pub with four of his pals, watching *The Late Late Show*. Gay Byrne was discussing pornography with an American woman of stout build. Her physical appearance drew the scorn of the youths.

Byrne ended the night by reviewing the early editions of the weekend papers. The camera closed in on the semi-naked front-page woman in the *Sunday World*. 'I wouldn't mind having her,' said one of Buddy's friends, and the others groaned assent. A studio guest criticised Mr Byrne for holding up the *Sunday World*. He replied that he was only reviewing the papers. She said the campaign against pornography was hopeless when such papers could be casually held up to view. 'She's right,' said one of the youths. They attempted a discussion on this point and couldn't sustain it. Gay Byrne had gone off the screen. The *Sunday World* couldn't be pornographic if it was a family paper. Buddy said nothing. The five boys went on to drink a little too much.

The conversation became raunchy. 'So I asked this girl to dance and held my cock right against her, like this' – the eldest boy demonstrated with body movements – 'and afterwards she looked me right in the eye, said thanks, and walked off the floor, the prick-teaser.' The boys admired her cool cheek and regretted his bad luck. The discussion moved on to drink and which pint was the best brand. It was typical Saturday night peer-group conversation among young males. The youths made no connection between sexual activity and family consequences. 'Family' means married people, females and their babies.

Next morning during the mass, Canon Gilfillan lashed out at the media for 'descending like locusts' to 'plague' and 'torment' the townspeople about a 'family matter'. His sermon veered from a plea that it should be treated as such, to a tirade against men committing adultery in their hearts when they lusted after women. And, he added, 'When divorce comes to the vote, as it surely will, we'll know where we stand. Against it, with the Church and with Christ.'

As for his teenage parishioners, a notice cut out of an *Irish Press* article on Ann Lovett's death has been tacked high up in a corner of the bulletin board in the church porch. 'Where to find help,' the newsprint reads. 'In pregnancy' has been pencilled in. They can find help anywhere but Granard, through Ally, Cherish and Cura in

Dublin, Kilkenny, Cork, Galway, Limerick, Waterford, and Sligo. No confidential telephone number in the town has been pencilled in.

Some of the services advertised use answering devices, which advise the caller to ring back. The services keep school hours. How often can you ring back from Granard's only public phone, in Main Street, when you should be in school, without attracting attention?

But then, Ann Lovett had attracted a lot of attention in her short lifetime.

'Wake up, Granard,' she used to shout down Main Street after nightfall. Her father used publicly to pull her home from the grocery store cum billiard-hall where she spent much of her time. The sight of him, and of her whom they knew to be pregnant, allayed concern as to who was taking responsibility for her welfare. 'He'd give her a cuff, many a father does. You don't call in the ISPCC, do you? If anything, you'd say he was doing his best, wouldn't you? And he'd be entitled to give you a cuff yourself if you stepped in. But why would we step in?'

The family looked all right. Ann Lovett looked properly fed and dressed and bright-eyed. The fact that she was pregnant besides was no reason for intervention. If there was a tension between her and her father, and there was, and it was known, which it was, that she spent a lot of her time in the house of her friends, what else could you expect in the circumstances? It was only natural, wasn't it?

That same Sunday night, in a pub in the town, a group of middle-aged men and women, married to each other, had a relaxing drink. The barman produced a leaflet which occasioned laughter. 'Prick of the Week' read the legend under a pen-and-ink reproduction of a tumescent penis, complete with scrotum. 'Prick of the Week, for having made a balls-up is . . .' read the mock certificate. It is up to the drinkers to fill in the name and the *faux pas* in question if they wish to engage in the pub joke.

A clear distinction was made between the joke and the tragedy of Ann Lovett, mention of whose name brought an angrily defensive response. That was serious. This was funny. References to men and their sexuality is a joke, isn't it? Not to be connected with women, for Christ's sake. Just like the joke on last night's *Late Late* about children in nappies and the connection with pornography. Naked little boys and girls aren't the same as naked big boys and girls. Can we not make jokes, for Christ's sake? Gay Byrne has a sense of humour. They identify more with Television than with Church.

On Monday, thirteen days after Ann Lovett's death, the spotlight swivelled on to another institution. The Guards were meeting in the station to co-ordinate procedure. Had a teenage boy been found dying from whatever cause, no one would have baulked at an inquiry. You don't walk away from a male youth, found dying in a grotto that celebrates the Virgin Birth. Nor can the Guards treat maternal death as an occurrence that is as natural or miraculous as conception, pregnancy and birth.

In the event, and in the panic, the other social units did. On the day of Ann Lovett's death nobody informed the Guards of the events in the grotto. One of them, coming on duty at six in the evening, remarked that there were rumours in the town of an abortion. It was eight o'clock, three and a half hours after Ann Lovett had been found, before the Guards established the facts, by dint of foot-slogging and telephone calls around the locality.

Dr Tom Donohoe, Deputy Coroner for the area, was a man well versed in the legal procedures that flow from the discovery of a dead body. It must not be moved. Dr Donohoe, who had treated Ann Lovett for shingles on her back shortly before Christmas, treated her as she lay dying in the grotto. She was then moved by ambulance to Meath, out of the jurisdiction of Longford. The baby, which was dead and should not have been moved, was taken with her. Dr Donohoe refused to comment on what was treated, in her circumstances, as a Family Affair.

Contrary to press reports, the grotto where Ann Lovett gave birth – where her baby died, where the priest gave her Extreme Unction and baptised her baby, where the doctor treated her, where her parents were brought to be with her – is not accessible to the public gaze. It is the most secluded spot in Granard town, which is why the young go there when they are mitching from school. It lies just beyond, but enough beyond, the church and the row of houses opposite the church which mark the end of the town proper.

Beyond the church and the houses, there is only a hill and beyond that, along the deserted country road, there is only the graveyard.

Unless you turned sharp left up a broad, leafy, walled lane and stepped through a gate into a lonely quarried dell enclosed by a tall thicket. High up the granite face of the dell is the Virgin Mary. She can be seen from the public road, through the evergreen trees. A person lying on the ground at her feet would not be seen. A girl giving birth at her feet would not be seen. A girl might give birth there and leave the baby behind. Other babies, in other places, have been left behind by young girls who then walked away.

A crazy idea in a small town, of course, but if no one knew for sure that she was pregnant, a young girl might persuade herself that she could get away with it.

Is that what happened?

Ask the Family. Journalists must ask the Family, after her death, what others would not ask the Family during her life.

Don't ask the State or the Church or the People. They did their duty last year, so amending the Constitution as to ensure that all pregnancies would be brought to full term. Nowhere in the amendment was provision made for life or lives beyond the point of birth.

Those are Family Matters.

Ann Lovett brought her pregnancy to full term.

On stony ground.

In winter.

Mother and child died.

Why? How?

Ask the Family.

We'll stand by them until they speak. Until they speak we'll stand by. You can't interfere with the Family, dead or alive.

At the Unionist Conference

FIONNUALA O CONNOR (1984)

A week before the 1984 conference of the Official Unionist party, at a press conference following an Anglo-Irish summit at Chequers, the British Prime Minister, Margaret Thatcher, explicitly rejected the initiatives developed by the New Ireland Forum as possible options to solve the Northern Ireland problem. This was the background to the air of triumphalism Fionnuala O Connor detected at the Unionist conference, and to Jim Molyneaux's reference to 'the abolition of initiatives'. The last line of O Connor's report was an allusion to *The Way Forward*, a party policy document produced in an attempt to create a clear distinction between the Official Unionists and Ian Paisley's Democratic Unionist Party.

It was surely not a decision with malice aforethought on the part of the Official Unionists to hold their conference this year in the splendour of the Slieve Donard Hotel in Newcastle where once, in their happier years, the SDLP held theirs. In the circumstances, however, the rubbing of noses in it seemed the likeliest explanation. The tone of the day set early, and set hard, and it was not the generosity Mr Robert McCartney, QC, had urged upon his never over-impressed colleagues earlier in the week which surfaced, but the triumphalism he warned against.

Not excited triumphalism, not a loud crude baying of delight, mind you. Simply a steady purr of pleasure at the performance of Mrs Thatcher and the discomfiture of the Republic and the SDLP. Official Unionists are not the kind of people who go in for strident street-stuff, generally. The rows of the well-heeled middle-aged and elderly, the sparkling of regimental ties, the cardigans and good tweeds, the occasional dapper young student, even the more rough-edged self-made men all saw their self-satisfaction reflected back to them very adequately, thank you, with no showiness, from 'Mr Leader', as the delegates called Jim Molyneaux – him of the grey pinstriped suit which matches Enoch Powell's. Jim came to tell the media in advance of his speech that there had been 'a bit of updating'. It remained for nine-tenths of its length a hymn of sober delight to 'our significant victory in securing the abolition of initiatives'. The freshly-added olive twiglet spoke of guarantees to majorities and minorities. That got a House of Commons type 'hear, hear', sedate and muted.

He wound up with another addition: 'Now Unionist attitudes must be positive and not defensive.' Hard to know whether to describe the tone of later debate as defensive or offensive. The anti-media current, a constant at Unionist conferences, grew stronger during the typically robust contribution from the deputy leader, Harold McCusker, which twinned a diatribe on Gerry Adams – man of blood and MP (drawing heavily with no apparent sense of irony, as did several other speakers, on last year's *World in Action* programme) – with a blast at media coverage of the IRA.

'We say to the media we're sick of you being used, with the way those ghouls are given time on television.' A chorus of hear, hear, a blast of glares towards the press table. By the time, multiple hostile references later, that the debate on 'Ulster culture' came along on a motion deploring 'the gradual erosion of the distinct Ulster ethos by the subtle introduction of a foreign culture via the press and visual media', the audience was ready for some unsubtle fun.

Which they got. In a half-empty hall, minus most of the big names (Molyneaux, Powell, Maginnis, McCartney) and all of the media but the BBC and the *Irish Times*, Councillor William Ward from Gilnahirk/Dundonald rose to second the motion and follow the lead of Alderman Samuel Semple, who had deplored among other things the extension of [the BBC television programme] *What the Papers Say* to cover the Dublin press, and warned: 'We are being Irishised right under our noses.'

Councillor Ward took it further. 'The other day I switched on my car radio and a voice said this was Radio Ulster. The next second a foreign language came over. I wondered if my radio had gone astray.' Laughter, applause. 'There is a deliberate attempt to introduce a foreign culture. How often I have been irritated as I'm sure you must be, by that dreadful pronunciation "Haitch".' Laughter. (Explanation for those unaccustomed to the fine points of Northern anthropology: the pronunciation is deemed to denote Catholicism, much as shifty eyes do, or coal in the bath.)

'Where did it come from? I hate the haitch,' beamed Councillor Ward, buoyant on a sea of happy chuckles, the best audience of his life. 'Give me the native Ulster "h".' [. . .]

He had them laughing and then produced something better. 'I'd like to point out some of the names that have crept into the BBC and I make no apology for reading them out': he read out eight or nine names, some lost in laughter, the first not a broadcaster but a spokesman for an anti-supergrass group, another formerly with the BBC but with other organisations for almost 10 years, winding up with the only ones it seems fair to print since their contributions are hardly local or sensitive: Frank Delaney and Terry Wogan. The names had one thing in common. They were all recognisably Irish, all identifiable locally if not in the wide, less aware world, as Catholic.

Mrs Hazel Bradford, chairwoman, rose laughingly to her feet after Terry Wogan and said: 'I must ask you to stop your list or we'll not have the benefit of the next speaker.' Councillor Ward concluded, unabashed: 'And all the rest of them. There's a silent revolution going on in the media.' All Unionists should organise to complain of same. He sat down to warm applause.

The motion was carried unanimously and left them laughing on their way to tea. A dozen delegates detoured by the way of the press table, however, to surround the BBC reporter. 'Why did you throw your pen down when that list was read?' asked a sharply dressed south Antrim delegate. 'I was amazed,' said the reporter, reasonably. 'The clear implication was that the BBC had biased employment policies and that the individuals named were biased because they had a certain kind of name.' The *Irish Times* reporter continued to make notes, did lose her temper and say it had been a display of naked sectarianism. Not at all, replied the south Antrim delegate, Councillor Ward had merely said there should be a fair proportion of employees.

The spotlight swung back to the British Broadcasting Corporation. 'It was a disgrace the way you reacted, why were you amazed?'

several people demanded at once. 'We feel alienated from our own media. It is a British agency, after all, isn't it? Surely we have enough native accents who could report fairly on Northern Ireland? How do we find so many Southern Irish accents on the radio?' The BBC tried reason: 'How many are there?' South Antrim: 'You're trying to badger me into saying something you can report.'

There was heat but little light. 'The sectarianism in the BBC is terrible. The percentage is terrible. Look how often you said that man shot in Newtownabbey was a Catholic.' (This from the south Antrim delegate. The dead man was a UVF victim.) 'We only see the representation of one culture. Look at Russell Harty the other night, all McPeakes and the Irish music, hijacked. If there is a second culture, our culture, where is it? UTV you could understand, and the *Belfast Telegraph*, they straddle the Border and have to appeal to the minority to make sales . . . surely I have the right to say to you my culture is never portrayed?'

But surely no one had the right to demand to know the BBC reporter's nationality – another of the North's coded ways of discovering religion – which several did together. In reply to questions the man from south Antrim began to insist that he did not support the reading out of names, but had simply been incensed by the reporter's reaction. We must not 'put him in along with that'.

It wasn't the worst row in the world. No one hit anyone. This was the OU conference after all, not the DUP's.

Tempers eventually cooled, some embarrassment became apparent from the party sophisticates on their way back from tea. OU general secretary and press officer, Frank Millar, junior, who had been on the platform for the list, came towards our squabbling group twice to call over to the BBC man: 'Are you OK?' Hazel Bradford stopped by the press table to deny that she had been amused by the list and to assure us she had simply been trying to be less than critical of an impromptu seconding speech. She was assured she had indeed been less than critical. Councillor Ward came to explain that he had not been given time to elaborate. 'I did not blame the people with those names for being there, I blamed others who don't take the opportunity to be there. I do want them there but I want balance.'

All our veneers were a shade scratched by this stage. When the conference closed with the singing of 'God Save the Queen', several reporters did not stand. Mr Robert McCartney, who had a short time previously repeated his 'Let's be generous' speech to a less than rapturous crowd, approached an English reporter, a non-stander who maintains this is his habitual policy, on the way out of the hall. 'Fuck off out of it, if you can't observe the niceties,' he told him. Then a slightly pink Mr Molyneaux came over to offer the media ritual thanks for their presence – thanks ritually withheld from the platform at Unionist conferences – and off we went, tired but happy at the end of the long way forward.

Haughey – The Interview

JOHN WATERS (1984)

While in opposition between his second and third terms as Taoiseach, Charles Haughey granted an interview to John Waters, for *Hot Press*. According to Waters' own subsequent account in *Jiving at the Crossroads*, Haughey did not understand that his interlocutor intended to publish a transcript of the interview. The Fianna Fáil leader's casual profanity was remarked upon when the interview was published, but, as the journalist Joe Joyce observed in a subsequent article in *In Dublin*, Haughey's 'initial horror that his interviewer had not cleaned up his language . . . subsided when the overall reaction was positive'.

When, after protracted negotiations, numerous disappointments and postponements, you finally get to interview Charles J. Haughey, it emerges that the procedure is slightly different than with other interviews. First of all, Charles J. Haughey interviews you. This, presumably, is so that he can reassure himself that you're not the kind of person who's going to come out with what is eloquently summed up by his colourful press secretary P. J. Mara as 'any of that Arms Trial shite'.

P.J. is very good on the subject of what happens when people do. Or when they confront The Boss with Sean Doherty, telephone tapping and tape-recorders. 'The shutters come down,' says P.J., illustrating graphically with both hands the downward motion of imaginary shutters descending to obscure Charles J. Haughey's face. 'The fuse starts to burn. And then you've had it.' [. . .]

'You look very MI5-ish,' says C. J. Haughey as he rises to greet the *Hot Press* reporter. His right hand is pressed against the left side of his midriff; either he's trying to look Napoleonic or the stomach is at him. 'What in the name of Jazus do you want to talk to me about?' Haughey's tone is one of wearied resignation, leavened with a sizable dollop of friendliness. P. J. Mara points out that all the details were in the letter he gave him a few weeks ago.

'What letter?' Haughey demands blankly. 'You gave me no letter. You never give me anything!' His gaze, mischievous but unflinching, meets P.J.'s head on. *He* knows that P.J. knows that he knows that in all probability P.J. did give him the letter. P.J. keeps his counsel.

It's explained to Haughey that rather than dealing with the nitty gritty of issues and policies – his views on which are already well documented – the interview will be personal in emphasis. We *would* like to talk to him about issues affecting young people in modern Ireland but with particular reference to his own experiences as an, ahem, young person.

A flicker of a smile breaks through Haughey's blank, quizzical expression. 'Sure I'd never be able to remember that far back! That's a long time ago.'

What kind of 'issues'?

Crime, vandalism . . .

'Well what could I say about that?' he thinks out loud. 'I don't think I could say that I approve of youngsters knocking off BMWs and so on,' he muses. 'Although, I must admit, I always had a hidden desire to do something like that! I don't suppose I could say anything like that, now could I?'

Hardly.

'What kind of other issues?'

The drug problem . . .

'Sex?' he asks and smiles sardonically. The reporter takes the opportunity to stress that the whole point of the interview is to portray the lighter, more personal side of Charles Haughey, which doesn't normally come across in the media. Most people see him as an austere individual.

'Oh but I *am* austere,' he responds, deadpan. 'Deep down I'm very austere.' There isn't the merest flicker of a smile. The reporter meets his stare, wondering if he's supposed to laugh. He does. So does Charles J. Haughey. The reporter, it appears, has passed the audition, and the interview is duly arranged for the following Monday, which as it happens is the day that Garret FitzGerald and Margaret Thatcher are due to have their now infamous summit meeting.

'What other people have you interviewed?' Haughey enquires.

The reporter does a quick mental check, in search of some respectable names to drop. For some odd reason he mentions Christy Moore. 'Ah, he's a bit of a rebel, isn't he?' remarks Charles J. Haughey. 'Christy wants to change the world!' He pauses. 'I gave up trying to change the world a long time ago.'

You were born in Castlebar. How much do you remember about it?

Well, I was only born in Castlebar. I left at a stage I don't even remember. As a child I lived in Dublin, to all intents and purposes. I also spent a lot of summer holidays in the North, in my grandmother's house. It was a small farm and I got a very good insight there of life on a small farm and of the social life and economics of small farming. And I also got a very clear impression of the community situation in Northern Ireland — how the Catholic small farmers viewed their Protestant neighbours and how they lived with them. But all my life, really, was spent in Dublin. I mean, I'm a *Dublin* person.

Were you very bright at school?

I'm afraid I was, yes. In those days there used to be a Dublin Corporation scholarship at primary school level, and I got first in Dublin.

You went to the Christian Brothers. They had quite a reputation in those days for violence towards pupils . . .

I would reject that. I liked school. By and large, the games at school made up for the less attractive side of it. If you did something particularly awful or outrageous, you got the leather, but it certainly left no lasting scars on me. It was just something of momentary importance. Tomorrow was a new day and the school would be playing Brunner — which was Brunswick Street — in the Phoenix Park, and you'd be off to that.

What other kind of pastimes did you have?

Well the main preoccupation in life was football and hurling — playing for the school and later for Vincent's and Parnell's. At a younger stage in my life I used to take up things like birdnesting —

collecting birds' eggs maybe. What else did we do? We went to the pictures once a week – if we had the money. Kids those days didn't have any money.

What kind of films did you like?

Well now . . . (*pauses*) They're all jumbled up in my mind. Cowboy films were the big deal. People like Gene Autry and things like that. Then, later on, I suppose, Humphrey Bogart and things like that. War films.

Do you go to the cinema nowadays?

No. (*Shakes head*) Very rarely.

Can you remember the last film you went to?

No. (*Laughs*) I don't know.

What was it like to be a teenager in your day?

When I was a teenager, the war was on, so the whole environment was totally different. Of course there were no motor cars. Everybody went on bikes. The whole country was down to subsistence level. You couldn't leave the country – there was no foreign travel. Young people today know absolutely nothing about it. (*Pauses*) But it wasn't all that *terrible*. Looking back on it now you'd think it must've been awful, but it wasn't really.

There wouldn't have been a lot of teenage crime in those days . . .

No. Almost certainly not. Literally, we only saw a policeman when he came to stop us playing football on the road! Of course we robbed orchards and things like that, but there was no great tension about it.

Do you think the advantages outweighed the disadvantages, that it was a better time to be growing up than today?

Ah, no. (*Pauses*) I wouldn't say it had any advantages, to be honest with you. I think teenagers today have a great time. I don't mean just now, in the middle of this terrible economic recession, but for a long period post-war, most of them had a great time – great opportunities, all sorts of new things: television, the exploration of space and all these things. And they had a thing that we never could have as teenagers, foreign travel. We just couldn't leave the country – unless you wanted to go off and join the British army, and fight in the war!

What are your recollections of the war?

The big thing was the number of one's friends that went off to join the British army. Because there was no work. You either joined the Irish army or the British army. And kids, if they were in a rebellious mood, and were, y'know, rowing with their teachers or parents, they'd go, 'Fuck you! I'll go off and join the British army if you don't appreciate me or treat me properly!'

Did you ever try that one?

No, I never said that. I was in the LDF and the FCA subsequently.

As a young man, did you have any inkling that one day you might end up as Taoiseach?

No. Not in the slightest.

You weren't aware of being different or special in any way?

Oh Jesus Christ, no! (*Laughs*)

What difference do you notice between young people nowadays and back then?

Well, the big difference is that young people today have far more confidence. Admittedly they're probably very depressed immediately now, about job prospects and so on. But apart from that, they have far more self-reliance and confidence than we ever had. They're a more sure generation. Our outlook, our scope, our dimensions were very limited. When I was young, you were very restricted in terms of careers. You dedicated yourself to the Civil Service or teaching, or whatever. It was all very regimented. It was very important to have what was known as a 'good job'. But young people today have none of those inhibitions. They couldn't give a damn about anything like that. And also, the way they dress: in our day it was very important to wear the right kind of clothes – you had to have a suit and tie and so on; nowadays kids are quite happy to go around in a pair of jeans and a jumper. I think young people today are fabulous. I *love* to be with young people. They make me feel good. I love their attitude to life.

[. . .]

You'd have been in your mid-thirties at the beginning of the '60s. Were you aware of the Beatles and all that stuff?

Oh very much. Well. Y'see, I experienced all through my children. I saw what they were doing and what they were interested in. So I was very aware of it. Not *part* of it, but very conscious of what was happening and what was affecting young people and what their interests were. And I could see the amazing changes in them, between them and me as a young fellow.

Did you go to dances as a teenager?

Oh yes. The local dances in the local halls. Much the same as they are now. There wasn't such a thing as a disco as far as I know. Just a band, y'know? Dance bands.

What kinds of music?

American music, largely. American jazz and American music. One of the big things that came in my lifetime was the swing back to traditional music and folk songs, the Dubliners and all that. When I was young, that sort of thing wasn't happening. The Clancy Brothers started all of that, I think.

What do you think of the current adulation of pop stars?

I think it's perfectly understandable. Kids always related to someone. We idolised somebody – I don't even remember who it was – some female film star. I can't even remember their names now! (*Laughs*) But we sort of related to them and idolised them and worshipped them. A big deal! And it's not any different now. No. I understand that completely.

It is, perhaps, slightly different insofar as the modern-day stars like Boy George and so on wear makeup and dresses and are openly bisexual.

Yeah, but there's also a tremendous following for people like the Dubliners. Ronnie Drew. And my friends The Fureys – they have their own following, and . . . Ah no, there's a sort of a healthy disparateness about the whole thing. I mean what was the last fellow in Croke Park there now? Or Slane Castle? Y'know? I totally appreciate and understand that. My kids go to that.

What do you think of Boy George?

I don't know anything about him. He seems a bit weird. But most of them, I think, are top-class musicians and professional artists.

You like the Fureys a lot?

I love the Fureys. I think they're great. My favourite piece of music is 'The Lonesome Boatman', as you know. But I also think the

Chieftains are fabulous. I'd go anywhere to hear the Chieftains and the Dubliners, and most of those.

What about the Wolfe Tones?

Yeah. I like them. They're a bit of the ould rabble-rousin', but sure they're alright! (*Laughs*) They've a very sort of limited medium, haven't they?

What about country and western? Do you like that at all?

No (*shakes head*), I don't. I never hear it. (*Laughs*) I don't know if I should say that, because Paschal Mooney is on the National Executive of Fianna Fáil!

Do you think that there should be some mechanism to allow young people a quicker access to politics?

Politics is not the Boy Scouts! It's a bit of a haul. And I think, per se it has to be; you've to sort of win your spurs and fight your way through. It's like anything: it's like what we were talking about — music and the entertainment world. It's a long, hard haul: most of the guys who are at the top have served out a pretty tough, demanding apprenticeship. And politics is the same. Experience counts a lot in politics. I don't mean that we all have to be like the Chinese: eighty years of age and very wise. But you have to find your way and get to know and handle people.

Young people are very cynical about politics and politicians.

But sure, *everybody* hates politicians! (*Laughs*) Old people are not any different. The ordinary guy in the pub thinks politicians are all useless and crooked and so on. That's not confined to young people. That's a healthy cynicism and distrust which most modern democracies — and certainly the Irish people — have always had, at all ages.

Do you think that the Irish are a particularly political race?

They're tremendous politicians, the Irish people. They're fascinated with politics. The ordinary guy in the pub can talk more intelligently and more wisely and with more depth about politics than anybody in any country in the world. Certainly he's about fifty times ahead of his bovine English counterpart, who knows about Margaret Thatcher and maybe one or two others — but that's all he knows.

You see, the Irish invented American politics. The whole American system is Irish founded and based. They made the Democratic Party. Brian Lenihan is very good on this – he's made a study of it. The Irish were trained here in local politics back in the nineteenth century, and when they went to the States they knew how to handle things, which most of their European counterparts didn't. The German and the French, for instance, knew nothing about democratic politics – they came from empire states.

One of the tendencies we've imported from America is the increasing emphasis on the personalities.

Yes. It's become increasingly so now, with the media. The individual politician or political leader becomes the focus, because the media haven't the interest or don't care about the issues. They're too tedious and take too much time to explain. They're much more interested in trying to hone in on A, B or C – on one person and what they're thinking and doing.

You see that as a negative development?

It's a bad thing, yeah.

But we Irish do seem to go for a strong personality.

Well, it's very tribal, you see. In rural Ireland, particularly, you have rural chieftains, like Blaney in Donegal and so on. I suppose it's a throwback to, a descendant from the Irish clan/chieftain system.

Yet politicians generally come across as fairly straight-laced, humourless, one-dimensional people.

I think politicians are hard done by, but then everybody thinks that about their own profession, I suppose. I don't think that the criticisms of politicians are very well balanced. Nobody ever sets out to try and describe a politician in the round, and say okay, maybe he's very wrong about this, but at least he's trying to do that. But then there's no point in complaining about that. That's part of the apparatus of political life – to be attacked and criticised. Very often, in one's own view, almost continually wrongly.

And there's another thing about this, which is that the ordinary . . . I hate using that word but it's hard to find another. There's no *such thing* as 'ordinary people': there's just *people* but, people are not fooled by all of this. I know that I have a perfectly good relationship with *my* people, my constituency. They know me, I know they trust me and I think they like me. They don't think I'm a bad person or am out to do anything detrimental to them or to their interests. And that's what matters. That is the compensation for when you read something in the paper that you know is unfair – grossly unfair – and wrong. And when that happens you're inclined to get outraged and angry about it, and upset about it. But that's only passing.

But, if the day ever comes when I'm driving through the city and the busman doesn't say 'Howya Charlie?' or the taxi fellow doesn't say 'Hello there, how's the goin'?' – if that day comes, then I'll be upset. All this stuff in the newspapers – it does upset, I can't deny that. You'd be a particularly insensitive and inhuman sort of individual if it didn't bother you, from time to time. But it's passing. The other thing is the reality. That's the sustaining reality.'

What aspect of Ireland or Irish society angers you the most?

Ah, there's nothing really. I couldn't live anywhere but in Ireland. I'm not perpetually angry about anything. I might suffer minor irritations, exasperations or anger about particular things, but . . . no, I like living in Ireland and in the Irish community. (*Here, he pauses at length and reflects, he looks me straight in the eye before continuing.*) I could instance a load of fuckers whose throats I'd cut and push over the nearest cliffs, but there's no percentage in that! (*Laughs*)

Smug people. I hate smug people. People who think they know it all. I know from my own experiences that nobody knows it all. Some of these commentators who purport to a smug knowallness, who pontificate . . . They'll say something today and they're totally wrong about it – completely wrong – and they're shown to be wrong about it. Then the next day they're back, pontificating the same as ever. That sort of smug, knowall commentator – I suppose if anything annoys me, that annoys me. But I don't have sleepless nights about it.

[. . .]*On the subject of the current contraception debate: isn't it true that the actual behaviour and practice of young people has long since made the question irrelevant?*

(*Pauses*) Ah yeah, I think that's probably true enough.

It's all very academic at this stage . . .

Yeah. (*Laughs*) I think so, yeah.

What about in your own day? Was it like that then?

Ah now! (*Laughs*) To my dying day, I'll regret that I was too late for the free society! We missed out on that! It came too late for my generation!

But yes, there was a very definite change. See, when I was young, too, authority was much more of a thing. Authority in society, in the community, in school, and of course the guards. You were afraid of the guards. Nowadays, kids aren't: they just call them 'pigs', y'know? But in my day, if a guard said to you 'fuck off', you fucked off as quick as you could! There was far more authority, and that was a big change. Kids nowadays have developed their own ethos and mores. And I think we've changed as parents too. I think we were much more understanding and sympathetic to our children than our parents were to us. My mother knew what was best for me, and told me what to do, and what not to do, and insisted that I did or didn't do it. I wasn't like that with my children. We certainly trusted them far more. We felt that what you had to do was just give them a home where they knew they were important, where they were loved and where they were trusted and where they could always come back to. If they made a fuck-up of things, they could always come back home and they would be welcomed and looked after and protected and helped. But our parents were different. So, not alone are young people different today, but we as parents were different to them.

So is there a dichotomy there between how you would find yourself respond-ing to issues, like contraception, as a parent, and the way you would feel obliged to respond to them as a politician?

'Well . . . no. (*Long pause*) You could exaggerate that. Y'see politics is concerned with more than just sexual morality and contraceptives and things like that. Now, mind you, these are the things that have a more or less fatal preoccupation for journalists. It's extraordinary that for one journalist who comes to me and asks me my views on economics, or the health services, or social welfare, or the North of Ireland, there's ten that want to know what I think about contra-ceptives. We in the political world are dealing with practical things. The social welfare system, for instance, looms very large in modern society – all the anomalies and the problems and the snarl-ups – that's

an enormous area, and it affects far more people than the contraceptives thing.

*What about the nuclear issue – how do you feel about that – on a personal
level?*

I'm increasingly angry about it, I think it's just lunacy itself – the
stockpiling of atomic weapons. Like, what's going to happen? What
are they there for? Ah, I don't, I suppose, basically believe that we're
all going to be wiped out tomorrow morning by a nuclear war. I suppose if any of us really believed that we'd just go and stick our heads
in a gas oven. It's too awful to contemplate. Even the most grotesque
film can only give you the vaguest impression of what the devasta-
tion is likely to be. So I don't suppose, basically, that I really think
that we're going to go up in a nuclear holocaust. But I do think that
it's a very real danger.

Is there anything that can be done about it?

Sometimes I like to think that you could get all the nuclear arms
into one, great big rocket – remember that rocket that went away
into outer space once? It was going to go around Mars once and then
go away into the infinite, never to be seen again. Well, if you could
put all the nuclear weapons into some sort of rocket like that. (*Pauses,
laughing*) But, sure, when the rocket would blast off, you'd probably
go up anyway! But it'd be a marvellous solution.

*Maybe it'd be safer if we all took off in the rocket and left the bombs
here . . .*

(*Laughs*) Yeah! You take your pick and I'll take mine! But what's
going to happen? I don't know. (*Pauses*) The question of nuclear
waste too, and the pollution of the seas and the atmosphere is something that worries me. Not paranoiac, or dramatically, or emotionally
disturbed about it, but I can understand people who are. I get increasingly angry at the failure of mankind to get to grips with it.

What do you do in your spare time?

Anything that comes up of interest, I'll have a go at it. Most
recently, I like to go down to my island, Inishvickillane. The main
attraction of the island, apart from its natural beauty, and the wild-
ness of it, is that we're more of a family down there. Fortunately, the
kids and the wife like it as much as I do. It's as much their place as

mine. I really got to know my kids better down there: in Dublin we're always coming and going. We meet tangently, coming and going out in the hall. But down there we're together, and we share experiences together. But I try and do as many things as possible. Like, for instance, my son Conor is an expert on scuba-diving, and I've got him to give me a little bit of instruction on that.

Do you read much?

I do and I don't. I certainly don't read anything like as much as I should. When I was younger, and at school and that, I read and read and read and read. I just read everything. But it's so difficult: you read a review of a book and you say, 'I must read that.' And then there's another one. There's so much going on in the world of literature that even if you had the time, it's very difficult to decide what to read. There's so much you want to read.

What would you read, if you had the time?

Well, let me see now . . . I like history type of books – historical novels, that sort of thing. And then I'm increasingly interested in wildlife, in nature, in the sea, and all that type of thing.

Do you watch much television?

No. Not very much. I think most television is tripe. Boring rubbish. To me, television is the news, or occasionally some very good documentary-type programmes. Very few. The news, some documentaries and sport.

Do you ever see Dallas *or any of those things?*

(*Laughs*) I see them because I have to confess that in my home there are those who look at *Dallas*. And well, I might go and do a bit of work, but sometimes I might sit through it. I really think it's shit. I think it's terrible shit. But then I know that's a minority view. (*Laughs*) I think most people think it's shit, like, but they look at it all the same.

Did you have any heroes growing up?

Well, I suppose Seán Lemass. He was the greatest human being that I ever met. Or could ever hope to meet.

What is the most important quality in a friend?

Well, there was a great word, d'ya see, that Seán Lemass in his whole life instanced but could never pronounce. Like most Dublin people, he could never pronounce 'loyalty' – he always pronounced it 'loylaty'. And I think that's the most important thing: loyalty. A Dublin man's loyalty. Not loyalty, because that's something different. But loylaty. I think that's the most important characteristic in friends.

Christmas is only a few weeks away now. Do you like Christmas?

Oh yeah! And I have to be at home for Christmas. To me, Christmas is a Dublin thing. I couldn't be anywhere else except home in Dublin for Christmas, meeting all my friends, having a drink with them, giving out presents, getting presents. I'm a sucker for Christmas!

Is there a day in your life that you remember as the happiest?

'Oh, FUCK OFF!! (*Laughs*) No!!! You're turning into a fuckin' woman's diary columnist now!'

Have you ever read George Orwell's Nineteen Eighty-Four?

Yes.

What would you find in Room 101? What, for Charles J. Haughey, is The Worst Thing in the World?

Ah, I'm not too introverted like that. (*Pauses*) Deep down, I'm a very shallow person. (*Laughs*)

Land of Hype and Glory

EAMON DUNPHY (1984)

The stereotypical narrative of a big sporting occasion like the
Olympics – triumph, humiliation, shattered hopes and all the rest –
usually defies demolition and re-assembly. It takes a fresh eye to
answer at least some of the questions you didn't know you wanted
to ask. Eamon Dunphy, who wrote this caustic account for *Magill*,
was also reporting for the *Sunday Tribune*.

There were thousands of journalists in Los Angeles. They were all
looking for The Story. The Grand Masters of the business – Hugh
McIlvanney, of *The Observer*, David Miller of *The Times*, Frank Keating of *The Guardian* and George Plimpton on an assignment for *Time*
magazine – looked as hard and long and desperately for The Story as
their humbler brethren whose task it was to send back news to people
who had received it hours before on television.

For the great and not so great of journalism these were to be the
Sorry But You Can't Go In There Olympics.

Ideally, a writer can lounge anonymously left of stage and watch
as the story unfolds. In Los Angeles anonymity was out of the question. On arrival you were taken to a room, photographed and given
a tag to wear around your neck.

This happens at all the great world events these days. Great events
like the Eurovision Song Contest, EEC Summits, United Nations
sessions and Arms Limitation talks. Your tag identifies you but more
importantly it determines that you cannot go into certain places.
Places where The Story is.

One of the more amusing side effects of the process occurs when
you meet someone whose face is familiar but whose name for the
moment escapes you. Depending on the light and the distance you
stood from old whatshisname it could take several minutes to distinguish the name on his tag.

Then it was Fred this and Fred that using his name (or he yours) 50 times a minute so that he knew that you knew his name. When two smart lads met, each knew that the other knew the er, nature of the problem.

Thus 7,000 men with notebooks began their quest for Olympic Gold.

Nothing, however inconsequential, would be overlooked. George Plimpton pointed out in *Time* magazine that when Carl Lewis won the 100 metres we knew that he wouldn't be speaking to the press afterwards. So when Lewis grabbed an outsize American flag on his lap of honour a group of desperate journalists swooped on the spectator whose flag it was. The next morning we learned his name (Tucker), where he was from (New Orleans), his age (50), and where he was sitting (Row 2 Section 27). It was further established that Lewis had returned the flag and that despite journalistic suspicions Mr Tucker and his flag were not planted as part of a Carl Lewis promotion. While the print journalist was being reduced to wearing dog tags and doing in-depth profiles of spectators, ABC television was controlling the Games.

After each gold-medal performance Carl Lewis granted an interview to television. Envious hacks turned up the volume in the press room and jotted down the great man's banalities.

The logistics of 'covering' the games means that writers fell further behind their better-off broadcasting cousins. There were 23 (I think) events going on at any one time. Once the writer had chosen his daily event that was it.

Roone Arledge, the executive director in charge of ABC coverage, sat in his control room in front of a montage of 23 pictures. On his command ABC could focus on the event of the moment. That Roone kept getting it wrong only added to the irritation felt by the dog-tagged hacks. For example, perhaps the most historic moment of the games was that in which Carl Lewis anchored the American 100 metres relay team to victory. This ensured that he had equalled Jesse Owens' achievement by winning his fourth gold medal.

Arriving breathless in the pressroom – where Lewis was to grant the long-awaited audience – we found to our astonishment that ABC were showing the preliminaries to the diving competition. Silly

Roone had not had the news sense to push the right button. It was 15 minutes after the historic moment before viewers saw Lewis win his fourth gold.

Roone earns over a million dollars a year and will be in charge of TV coverage for the 1988 Games. The long-awaited Lewis press conference was hardly worth hanging around for. But we did. After two minutes his relay team colleague, the 100-metre individual silver medallist Sam Graddy, walked out. He was sick of all the Carl Lewis hype.

Lewis spoke of God as if the ultimate gold medallist was a close relation and introduced his close relations (Mum and Dad) as if they were gods.

Lewis had taken some stick from the home press during the Games but the smarter American columnists kept well clear of press conferences. Here it was the Tell Us How It Feels school of journalism. It felt good. As Lewis is a student of communications at the University of Houston and as this seems odd given his barely concealed contempt for print journalists, your correspondent ventured a question, to wit: How would he define the role of the sportswriter? This was not so much a trick question as an attempt to discover if we were dealing with a serious man or a bible-thumping phoney with four gold medals.

It drew growls of anger from the assembled company but an appreciative wink from David Miller of the London *Times*, who was leaning at a sceptical angle on the fringe of the gathering. 'You won't print *my* answer,' Lewis chortled.

His answer was that the journalistic business was to 'sell newspapers'.

Note: Aspiring journalists should keep away from the University of Houston. *Evening Herald* please copy.

All roads led to the Main Press Centre (MPC) in downtown LA. While television stars enjoyed chauffeur-driven limos to and from events, the second-class citizens of the Global village were ferried in school buses.

While David Coleman, Jimmy Magee and Russell Harty flew down the fast lane in smoke-glassed chariots, the likes of Keating and McIlvanney rattled along in overcrowded buses, exchanging hard-luck stories. McIlvanney's problem was typical. He had planned to feature Neil Adams, England's lay-down bet for a judo gold medal.

Alas, Adams got dumped by a German and Hugh was up the creek without a story. He eventually settled for his first love, boxing. Jim Lawton, a former *Daily Express* man, now works for the *Vancouver Sun*. A superb writer. He is sitting on the school bus late one night. In walks the great Pat O'Callaghan of Irish Gold Medal legend.

'Hello,' says Pat. 'Hello,' says I. 'Who's that?' says Jim Lawton. 'Pat O'Callaghan,' says I, going on to tell the story of Pat's Gold Medal years. 'Move over,' says Jim. A problem solved for the *Vancouver Sun*.

I'm laughing. John Treacy has agreed to talk to me on the Thursday before his marathon run. John is, like all the major contenders, staying outside the Olympic Village – at a secret address.

In a moment of weakness after his 10,000-metre run he has agreed to talk to the *Sunday Tribune*. The *Sunday Tribune* has his secret phone number. Laughing.

On Thursday morning John decides that deep psychological probing by the *Sunday Tribune* is precisely what he doesn't want before his big race.

The *Sunday Tribune* understands and wishes this most delightful of athletes well. And begins to weep. Twenty-four hours to deadline.

Right. If George Plimpton can interview The Man Who Lent Carl Lewis His Flag, the *Trib* will go one better. The *Trib* determines to interview The Athlete Who Was Lapped In The 1500 Metres Heats. He is Brom from Gabon.

It takes two hours to run the man from Gabon to ground. He will, I know, be delighted to meet someone who is interested in his tale of woe, what it felt like to come all the way to be lapped. He will doubtless say that the Olympics are about Taking Part, and I will in a sense have got an interview that captures the Spirit of the Games. Who needs Carl Lewis?

'Excuse me,' I boldly approach the Spirit of the Games. 'I'm from Ireland [I hold my dog-tag up for inspection]. I'd like to talk to you about your experiences here.'

On the track The Spirit had looked pathetic. Up close he had the look of a smart cookie who, despite not being able to run very fast, had manoeuvred his way onto his country's Olympic team.

Was a man going to fall for the old Spirit of the Games ploy?
No.

'I'm sorry, but I have no time just now,' he replied. The accompanying look said, 'Piss off, man, find some other mug for your hard-luck story.'

So I went to the Biltmore. The Biltmore is the smart hotel in Los Angeles. The Irish were having a party – well, a reception actually. We were celebrating our gold medal triumph – of 50 years ago. Dr Pat O'Callaghan and Bob Tisdell were the honoured guests. These two wonderful old men (78 and 79 years old) will doubtless die of cocktail-sausage poisoning if we don't win another gold medal soon.

Ronnie Delaney was at the Biltmore. He is standing by to be launched on the cocktail circuit at future Olympics.

The reality of Los Angeles was that the Irish were inconsequential. In a world where Governments are increasingly aware of the benefits of making recreation available to the young, our leaders continue with their Four Green Fields policy. (The Fields are there so get out and play!) The Minister for Sport, Mr Donal Creed, was present, as indeed was his good lady Mrs Creed. It is usual at this point to castigate the Minister by alluding to the pittance allocated to sport and comparing that to the cost of bed and breakfast for two for three weeks at the Biltmore.

But really the people to castigate are those higher up the greasy political pole who replaced the dynamic former Minister Michael Keating with Mr Creed, who is nothing more or less than a genial political hack. Who needs a higher profile?

He will be disappointed by this characterisation because he did come over to talk to the *Sunday Tribune* and because this correspondent is a member of the same political party. There is no loyalty these days.

One man conspicuously absent from the Biltmore was Eamon Coghlan, our world 5,000 metres champion. Coghlan was last year's John Treacy. This year in LA mention of his name around Irish Olympic Committee haunts (like the Biltmore) was considered impolite. Coghlan was the leading figure in the Olympic fund-raising, The Hero pushed up front as a Good Example. Then he got injured. Then he agreed to work for RTE. Then he tried to hang on to his accreditation to the Olympic Village.

He said this was to enable him to keep in touch with athletics, to train a little, feel a part of the Olympics he had been so cruelly prevented from competing in.

They, those who told him he could not be accredited, claimed that what Yesterday's Hero was after was journalistic advantage. He was bitter. They stood firm. I spent a fair amount of time with Coghlan in LA. I admire him. He's a tough-minded man who has made it in the hard school of world athletics. The best athletes are businessmen whose principal asset, indeed only asset, is their ability to win races. There is absolutely nothing wrong with that. However, the world still hankers after the Sportsman as Gobshite – preferably Modest Gobshite. For world read Ireland in Coghlan's case. The Gobshite Sportsman doesn't ask for anything in return for being Hero. Coghlan did.

I had the pleasure of getting quietly drunk with him on our last night in LA. He is intent on carrying on in his sport. He will put the desperate disappointment of this year behind him. He will undoubtedly rise again and through long lonely months of training regain his place in world athletics. When he does he will not so readily play hero for the Irish Olympic Committee. And so one left Los Angeles convinced as never before that, as the great American sportswriter Damon Runyon had one of his creations Sam the Gonoph say: 'I long ago came to the conclusion that all life is six to five against.'

For the print journalist in LA you could make that thirty-three to one.

The odd man out was the freelance photographer who, denied a prime position at the finish line of the ladies' 3,000 metres, settled instead for an obscure vantage point 200 yards away. It was on this historic spot that Zola Budd and Mary Decker collided. Our man got the exclusive pictures. He sold them to UPI for 50,000 dollars. So at least one man got The Story . . . and The Gold.

Sean Quinn and the Thatcherite Blueprint

COLM TÓIBÍN (1987)

In 2007 *Forbes* magazine ranked Sean Quinn the 177th richest man in the world. By 2011 he was bankrupt, having made catastrophically large bets on the share price of Anglo Irish Bank. But a quarter of a century ago the name of Sean Quinn was hardly known outside counties Cavan and Fermanagh. In the course of a walk along the Irish border, Colm Tóibín came across Quinn, who was in the process of building his vast business empire.

I set off from Derrylin to walk to Ballyconnell. The rain came down in torrents. The road was narrow, and passing cars splashed water all over me. I was disconsolate, sorry I hadn't stayed with Basil and Joanne, oozing self-pity. Sometimes the rain would ease off and then start up again with immense ferocity, as though it was playing cat and mouse with the world. My shoes were now letting in the wet. Although it was only seven o'clock, signs of night were apparent. This was miserable.

At one point the road was blocked with floods, and I had to edge my way along the middle rung of a wooden fence, since the road was under at least a foot of water. There was a bridge over a narrow stream, which was now carrying tons of muddy water with immense speed. It was as though the winter had suddenly returned, or the great flood, and the road to Ballyconnell was endless. Up hill, down hill, bends in the road, straight stretches in the road, rain everywhere, soggy fields, rain running along the road as if the road was a river bed, cars splashing muck and muddy water all over. Me walking.

Eventually, I came to a cement factory, with lorries bearing the name 'Sean Quinn' parked in the yard. The factory, its offices, quarries and outhouses went on for about a mile. And after them was an army post, with a dry soldier wanting to know where I was coming from and where I was going.

If I expected to find Ballyconnell just beyond the army post, just over the border, I was wrong. It was another half an hour of sheer pain before I walked into the town and found myself a bed for the night. I put my clothes on a heater with my poor shoes beside them and got into bed. By the time I woke up they were almost dry, and it was time to venture out to explore the night life of Ballyconnell.

There was a young girl behind the bar of the Angler's Rest who talked to the couple and two young fellows who sat at the bar. She was emigrating, she said, there was nothing for her to do here. Everyone was going now. She was going to London. She'd never find a job in Ireland, she said. The other girl said she had been to New York to see her brother. He wanted to come home on holiday, but he couldn't, since, like a hundred thousand other young Irish people, he was an illegal immigrant in the United States; once he left, he wouldn't be able to go back. The two fellows at the bar talked about leaving as well. New York was the place to go; there was always work there, they said.

The recent census figures had shown that emigration, which had solved the unemployment problem of the 1940s and 1950s when people left the Republic to work in England and America, had returned. Between April 1985 and April 1986 the net emigration figure from the Republic was thirty-one thousand; most of these people had left Ireland to find work. Most of them were young, and many of them well educated. The newspapers carried reports of football teams in villages losing half their members in one year through emigration.

Yet Ballyconnell was lucky; Sean Quinn's quarry was just up the road and there was a plastics factory in the town. In other towns there was nothing. But even here there wasn't enough to keep young people from leaving.

There was a bigger crowd up the street that night in the Crow's Nest. When it came to closing time I discovered that the gardaí in Ballyconnell were not vigilant about drinking hours. I waited for the lights to be turned down and time to be called. Instead, more drink was poured. The man beside me owned a petrol station in the town. I offered him my sympathy; he told me that a roaring trade was being done by the petrol station which was north of the border, but on the southern side of the army checkpoint. He didn't do so badly,

however, he said. The gardaí, the Irish army and all the public servants used his station. We ordered our last drink at twelve-thirty, and
everyone was still drinking happily as I wandered home fifteen minutes later. The following morning I awoke from uneasy dreams and
turned on the radio. There was big news about the border. I thought
of going to the window and checking if it was all happening on the
streets of Ballyconnell, but when the headlines were repeated I knew
that I was miles away from the action.

The action had been caused by Peter Robinson, the deputy leader
of the Democratic Unionist Party, while his leader Ian Paisley was in
America. He had gathered together his followers, a chosen people,
and marched on the south, where they had scrawled slogans on the
walls of the village of Clontibret, beaten up two Gardai, and made
general nuisances of themselves. The purpose of this raid in the early
hours of the morning was to show that there was no border security,
that if a group of diehard Unionists could travel freely across the
border, then what could a small, stealthy band of IRA men do? Peter
Robinson was arrested.

When I got up, I rang Sean Quinn, the quarry owner whose name
was on most of the lorries in this locality, and he agreed to see me in
the afternoon. Several of his green lorries passed me as I walked back
towards the North. At the border the bloke from the army ascertained that I was walking. 'Rather you than me,' he said.

At the first office I was told that Sean Quinn was to be found in
another building up the road. I kept walking. It was another dark,
dreary day, but there was no rain.

Sean Quinn conformed, here in bandit country, where the UDR
foot patrols were afraid to venture, to a Thatcherite blueprint. When
I arrived at his office I had to wait. His assistant came in to fill me in
on the background. Sean Quinn had inherited a twenty-three-acre
farm in 1973; he was now a millionaire. He had begun to deliver
gravel, then diversified into concrete blocks and tiles. His enterprise
had grown every year. He had benefited enormously from the early
years of Thatcher, when there was a hundred per cent tax-free allowance on profits which were re-invested. There were no trade unions

in his business, nor was any employee paid a salary. Everyone was paid according to productivity.

His fame had spread far and wide, not just as an employer, a success story and a name over lorries, but as a man who hit a British soldier at a checkpoint, knocked him over and drove on. The soldier was black, according to some in the pub the previous night. Everyone agreed that there had been no retaliation. He was too important, Sean Quinn.

I asked Sean Quinn's assistant about relations with the army. 'There is generally no problem,' he said, 'just when a new regiment comes, it takes time to get used to them.' He didn't mention his boss hitting a soldier. Sixty per cent of the business was in the South, he continued, and there was a special agreement with the Northern customs people that the export documents were handed in at the Southern office and sent North, in one of those informal arrangements. Forty per cent of the staff of 140 came from the South. Certain things were cheaper in the South, he said, lorry tyres, for example, and road tax.

Eventually, the great Thatcherite himself came in. He was a dark, good-looking, gruff man in his late thirties, wearing an old grey pullover. He talked with an off-hand precision; the accent was straight Fermanagh. We were interrupted a few times by lorry drivers, who wanted to ask him something, and he seemed as at ease as they seemed diffident. He didn't act like the boss. And he certainly didn't look like a millionaire.

His father willed him this small farm, he told me. He had left school when he was young; he wasn't interested in it, unlike his brother and sisters. He was interested in making money and having a good time. He was known all over Fermanagh, Catholic Fermanagh, because he had been captain of the Gaelic football team in the early seventies, so when he advertised the gravel, undercutting other suppliers, people trusted him, liked him, wanted to do business with him. Things grew from there. Thatcher, he agreed, had improved the climate for business when she came to power, but in the past few years she had started to reduce incentives for investment.

Sean Quinn's big plan for expansion was being put into place down the road. He was spending twenty-five million pounds on a new cement factory, which would supply twenty-two per cent of the market, North and South. How did the present suppliers view his plans, I asked. 'They are not overjoyed,' he said.

The phone on his desk rang. He picked it up and began a long conversation with a man who had a strong British accent. He had a notebook on his desk and he began to write down figures, issuing instructions about buying and selling. I couldn't work out what he was doing. He was dour and casual, ringing off without any salutation, and trying to pick up the thread of what we were saying when the phone rang.

I interrupted him to ask what he was talking about on the phone. Stocks and shares, he said. He had started, six months before, to play the stock market. He showed me the list of items he dealt in – gold, oil, the Swiss franc against the dollar, aluminium. His broker, he said, phoned twice or three times a day and he told him what to do. A salesman brought him out the *Financial Times* from Enniskillen, so that he could read about his investments. It was interesting, he said, suggesting that playing the stock market was a form of amusement, implying somehow that it was a common pastime around Derrylin and Teemore.

He responded immediately when I asked him if he had floored a British soldier at the border. He did, he said. The British army post had been put up three years before. His lorries went through one hundred and fifty times a day, and each time they were delayed for an average of two minutes. I could, he looked at me sternly, calculate the cost myself. It was more or less the same as keeping one lorry full-time on the road, I said. He nodded. Why did he hit the soldier, I asked. He was going to a funeral, he said, and he was already late. They stopped him at the border, made him drive into the side and held him there, even though he passed up and down several times a day, even though his name was written on each of the 150 lorries which passed through the checkpoint. Time passed. They wouldn't let him go. After half an hour he told the soldier that he was going anyway, whether the soldier agreed or not. He knocked the soldier over and drove off.

I asked him about the IRA's threat to builders and suppliers who had dealings with the British army. He said that a friend of his had been shot dead by the IRA for doing business with the security forces, but that he himself didn't supply the security forces or deal with them, and never had; he was a nationalist. 'I didn't think it was prudent,' he said. He employed a few Protestants, he said, but there weren't very many in the area.

He lived just over the border in the South, on the road between Ballyconnell and Belturbet. He had bought land in the South, land his father had owned in the 1950s, land he remembered going to look at on an ass and cart, which he now drove to in his Mercedes. Land wasn't a good investment, he said, but he enjoyed going to look at stock two or three evenings a week. He was careful to avoid buying small pieces of land or pubs in the area and depriving local people of the chance to buy and make their sole living from them. Instead, he had bought the Cat and Cage pub in Drumcondra in Dublin for £640,000. He leased it out, but had recently enjoyed having a drink there after a football match in Dublin where he was following the fortunes of the Tyrone team.

He drove me to the border in his big car. He seemed genuinely puzzled by my walking. 'Can you not afford to buy a car?' he asked. He seemed to be expressing concern about my welfare. The soldier at the checkpoint waved him on. I told him what I had heard: that in the days following his assault on the soldier, they had carried truncheons, according to the people I spoke to in Ballyconnell. He chuckled to himself about this. We passed the filling station, still in the North, and it was doing thriving business. As we came to the line which separated the North from the South, County Fermanagh from County Cavan, he let me out, told me the story of the house which the border went right through like a slicer through a block of cheese, and drove off.

The house was a small, modest, old-fashioned cottage. When I knocked on the door a man in his sixties came out. His name was Felix Murray, I discovered, and the border ran through his house in which he and his two brothers lived. These days, he said, all three slept in the North, but there was a time when one of them had slept in the South. 'Only an odd time now,' he said, 'we sleep in the State.' There was a sofa in the kitchen, he pointed out through the window, where you could sit and let the border run through you.

They got their dog licence in the South, he said, it was cheaper, but their television licence, on the other hand, they bought in the North where it cost less. Their electricity was connected in the South, but their water in the North. They voted in the North. The grants were better in the North, he said. The border checkpoint was a nuisance, he said. Recently when he was crossing from the North to South on his bicycle he passed a red light, which called for the driver to stop, only to be told by the soldier that this applied to bicycles as well.

He changed the subject back to his predicament. He seemed to have it off by heart and it disturbed him that he had omitted a detail. Yes, he remembered, the postman came every day, one from the North and one from the South. The southern one came earlier.

I sympathised with him for the inconvenience of living in two states. He said it wasn't too bad; that wasn't the worst part of it at all. What was the worst part of it, I asked. He looked across the road to the ditch and the hill beyond the ditch. He left a dramatic silence. The interviewers, he said, the reporters, the television cameras; since he was a child they had come to tell the story of the Murrays cut in two by the border. There wasn't a single day went by but there wasn't a knock at the door. Yesterday a bus pulled up outside and he had 'seen them all leppin'' out and taking snaps'.

People had come 'from America and all over' to see the house. They never had any peace, himself or his brothers. That was the worst thing, he said, and looked at me frankly. I understood, I said. I took his point. He went back into the house and I walked back towards Ballyconnell.

As I made my way along, a huge car stopped and a man with a British accent offered me a lift. He said he was going to Belturbet, which was where I was going. I thought it would be churlish to refuse. The weather was still nasty-looking. I told him I had been talking to the big man himself, Sean Quinn. Yes, he said, he worked for Sean Quinn; he was in charge of getting the cement factory built in time and within budget. He had been a salesman, he said, and Quinn had spotted him and offered him the job.

We passed by Sean Quinn's house on the right-hand side of the road. It was much more modest than I had expected. We drove on to a side road and went along by a lake. The driver liked it around here, he said, it was beautiful; he liked Sean Quinn, liked the locals. He stopped at a junction and turned left. This was once the main Dublin to Enniskillen road, he said, now it was like a lane, leading nowhere; the bridge between the North and the South had been blown up.

There were still two houses on the southern side of the blown-up bridge. A few kids played in front of them as we got out of the car to look at the remains of the bridge. It had been a beautiful old stone bridge, we could still see bits of the stone, like innards, on the opposite side. It was hard not to feel an intense regret that it had not been spiked, or blocked; blowing it up, blowing away all the soft-coloured cut stone, seemed a travesty.

We drove into Belturbet and had several drinks in the Diamond Bar. The bar on the opposite side of the square was called the Railway Bar, but there was no railway here anywhere, just as there was no direct contact with the North. I went in search of a bed for the night as my driver went home for his dinner. I left my rucksack in a bed and breakfast, told the landlady that I wanted to be up early in the morning, found a bite to eat, and returned to the Diamond Bar. I sat up on a high stool and watched the first batch of lorries coming through the Diamond outside, travelling from the South with hay for the stricken farmers of the North, who had been ruined by the weather. For weeks now these lorries would be a constant presence on the roads.

They had opened the bridge one year, they told me in the bar; they had built a sort of temporary bridge at Christmas in 1972. And that was how the bombers made their way into Belturbet from the North and planted a bomb in the Diamond outside, just after Christmas in the same year. They pointed to the stool I was sitting on: the bomb had blown a man sitting on that stool over the counter, it had blown the door in. No one in the bar had died, but two people out in the Diamond had been killed, including a youth who was in the telephone box making a call. One of the Protestant paramilitary groups had carried out the bombing. The bridge hadn't been opened since.

The radio in the bar was tuned into a local illegal station, whose headquarters were a few miles down the road, which played country and western music all day and all night. It could be heard as far North as Strabane. It carried advertisements from almost every town within fifty miles. The American country and western stars joined in with their Irish counterparts in pulling the heartstrings of the locality where country and western music was big business. Johnny Cash sang 'O Lonesome Me' to be followed by a local singer, Big Tom, who sang 'Will I Ne'er See You More Gentle Mother?'

The Great Hunger Gathers Again

KEVIN MYERS (1987)

The catastrophic Ethiopian famine of 1983–5 provoked a high-profile international aid response, but continuing drought and civil war meant that famine returned, albeit on a smaller scale, in 1987. Kevin Myers's report in the *Irish Times* took up the challenge of breathing new life into a script that had become depressingly familiar.

Three years on, and the famine is back in Ethiopia. The famine never comes once to your door. Like a burglar who knows your address, it comes back and back. In the area of Tigre, east of Mekele in the northern part of the country, the drought during the growing season has been unparalleled and in that growing season, nothing grew; now catastrophe looms.

Already, thousands of Tigreans have fled their foodless homes and their scorched and cropless acres in search of food; for the time being they are getting it through the food distribution centres established by the Joint Relief Programme. The fear is that as the full catastrophe unfolds, these centres will not be able to cope, or the supply system will collapse; and then the true horror of a million starving to death en masse could come to pass.

The organisers of the Joint Relief Programme are determined that the food distribution centres will be no more than the name implies: that people will be given food and told to return to their villages, so that this time there will be no camps of starved, half-dead creatures lowing like cattle in the grey light of dawn, as there were three years ago.

'We tell the people it is better to die in the dignity of their homes, than it is to die in the camps,' said the Catholic primate of Tigre, Bishop Khedani. The whole thrust of the JRP campaign is that those terrible camps never again come into existence; so much so that the organiser of the smoothly-ticking machine which is distributing food throughout Tigre, Father Cesar Bullo, will not even discuss the possibility that the machine might break down.

This refusal to face the unpalatable is not confined to the JRP. Of the 54 different agencies now working in Ethiopia, only one has a medical team on standby to rush to that country in the event of the famine getting out of hand. That organisation is Concern, and its field director in Ethiopia, Jack Finucane, is extremely pessimistic about the prospects there.

'The whole relief programme is very fragile, very, very fragile, and it can easily break down. We have one million people in Tigre who are already affected by the famine and every indication is that the situation is worsening by the week. I don't want to see them back, but I see the camps as inevitable. Not as bad perhaps as 1984–1985, nor as many, but they'll be back.'

Each morning at daybreak, the first Lockheed Hercules transport plane touches down at Mekele military airport in Tigre. It carries 20 tons of food for the people of Mekele and the greater area around it: it will make four trips a day; there are three other such planes like it. No Hercules, and much of Tigre province lurches into starvation, according to the architect of the JRP, Cesar Bullo; the time-lag between a failure of road supply and the first widespread deaths is between four and five days.

The terrible truth is that though this famine has been long in the making, the entire Hercules operation is being run within excessively tight margins. Unacceptably high demands are being placed upon the four aircraft on the Mekele run. If a single bearing goes in one of a Hercules's four Allison engines, the JRP is short one plane. Four such bearings – let us look on the grim side: this is, after all, Ethiopia – and the camps of starving will start to form simultaneously at the distribution centres, with nothing to distribute.

As it stands, the relief programme is sometimes a miracle of improvisation and of astonishing hard work, for which the Ethiopians have received scant praise. One grain-carrying ship heading towards the Far East was diverted recently to the Ethiopian port of Masawa; when it arrived, 150 men clambered into each of the four holds and hand-filled, hand-stitched and uploaded 50-kilogram grain sacks which were loaded onto lorries and taken to Asmara, where they were stacked in the faithful Hercules and flown to Mekele.

The unloading at Mekele should be an obligatory sight for all those who say the Ethiopians do nothing to avert what befalls them; each Hercules is unloaded at a sprint, each man carrying a 50-kilogram bag from the Hercules hold, running to a lorry, heaving it into the back, and then sprinting back into the hold to get the next bag. By the time one Hercules is empty, another has lined up beside it for unloading. It is as if the men were under fire.

Which they might very well be soon, for one cannot escape the hammer and anvil effect of drought and war in Tigre and in Eritrea to the north. Bob Geldof, during his recent visit to Ethiopia, said the famine was 80 per cent due to the drought and 20 per cent to war. The rather more experienced Jack Finucane put the figures at 90 per cent and 10 per cent and the Bishop of Tigre, whose brother is a senior member of the Tigrean People's Liberation Front (TPLF), admits the war has considerably worsened the plight of the Tigrean people.

Bob Geldof blamed the fact that supplies cannot be safely trucked in Tigre and Eritrea equally upon the Eritrean People's Liberation Front and the TPLF and the Ethiopian government.

Ever so gently, Jack Finucane dissents: it is not the government which is landmining the roads; it is not the government which is ambushing the trucks. It is not within the government's power to make those roads passable. Its own troops, an increasingly demoralised and war-weary crowd, cannot safely travel those roads. If the people of Tigre and Eritrea go hungry because food cannot be trucked to them, then that is because the EPLF and the TPLF wish that to be so.

And if commonsense departs altogether – let us remind ourselves again: this is Ethiopia – then the JRP might discover there are more ways of stopping a Lockheed Hercules than with a worn-out bearing. Mekele, the capital of Tigre, and the garrison of Addis's pretension towards government there, is surrounded by a staunchly anti-government population. Equally to the point, it is overlooked virtually on all sides by mountains; it is as militarily indefensible and politically indispensible as Ypres or Dien Bien Phu. It has, indeed, already been taken by forces of the TPLF who opened the town's jail, killed a few poor government conscripts, and departed. It would be no great feat to down a Hercules from the foothills with a SAM-7 or a belt-fed Browning .5 inch, were the TPLF so inclined. Then, no more Hercules flight; five days later, the mass deaths start; and 53 of the 54 agencies are proved wrong. Ethiopia is that close to out-and-out disaster.

It would be a disaster long in the making. It takes more than a few successive droughts or a guerrilla war to fashion a calamity of such magnitude. Ethiopia's population is over 40 million, mostly crowded into highland regions where deforestation has stripped the country from 40 per cent tree-cover in 1900 to 4 per cent today. The result has been catastrophic land erosion, now running at a rate of 100 tons of topsoil per hectare a year – one ton per 120 square yards. Much of the soil of Northern Ethiopia is so degraded that it has the agricultural qualities of lunar dust.

One sees this soon after leaving Addis, heading northwards for Tigre: the terrain looks as if it has been the home of thermonuclear experiments. The soil is brown and scorched and broken, gouged by erosion and by the desperate attempts of the local population to entice food from it: there is almost no place, no matter how bleak, where somebody is not trying to survive.

This is so even in the Great Valley, that vast trench miles across and thousands of feet deep, formed by some terrible geological cataclysm. Towering columns of rock stand isolated within the valley, and upon their garden-sized summits will perch a field; and halfway up an almost vertical cliffside of shale and rubble one can see billiard-table fields lodged inaccessibly like eyries; a man working his microfield could fall to his death. In all of the places on this earth where men must live, this must be amongst the worst.

North of this abomination is Korem, film of which shocked the world in a way it had not been shocked since a gagging camera man turned his lens on the heaped bodies of Bergen-Belsen 40 years before.

Three years later, the camps are gone, and, it is hoped, they will never return. For miles and miles, roads into Korem teem with the

poor and hungry peasants trekking into the town: and like embur-
dened ants returning from a kill, they troop outwards again, but now
with enough food for a month for their families. When the system
works, it works well.

It works too at Wukru, a distribution centre and town north of
Mekele, deep in Tigrean territory, where the hungry have also been
gathering. Thousands of people congregate there daily, as they did
three years ago, then close to death, now the children play in the
dust, and their parents sit and patiently wait their turn for food.

'Seester, seester,' the children called at us when we arrived, reflecting the ubiquity of white nuns in this place. The children might be
peckish, miserable they were not. Their mothers, draped in shabby
sackcloth, sat in the sun, and ululated in approval at our visit, possibly thinking we were a television crew and knowing what was
expected of them.

Porters scuttled and swayed beneath 50-kilogram (1-cwt) sacks of
flour, which they deposited at the distribution point at the back of
the warehouse: scoops of flour, favours returned, are there exchanged.
Nearby is a large donkey park; donkeys for hire against the long journey home, which might be several days' walk. Each recipient is
registered, the name filed; there are no anonymous recipients. The
system works.

But there are signs that even now it is creaking at the outer seams.
Back at Mekele, just outside the town, we met two Irish nuns, Sister
Gabrielle Quirke and Sister Margaret Manley, who run the Latchi
clinic.

The clinic is a sort of seine net catching the smaller fry that elude
the JRP trawl. 'It very nearly got out of hand here last Monday,'
Margaret Manley reported. 'Hundreds of hungry people gathered
here and we had to close the gates. Some people had walked two
weeks to get here. I feel sure that a similar situation will recur in
January. All our figures show a steadily increasing number of famine
cases. You know them now because they're gesticulating to their
stomachs and making eating gestures. Oh, no doubt it will get very
much worse.'

Gabrielle Quirke showed us a young woman who had walked 200

kilometres with her sick child to get to the clinic; she is 16. Her two-year-old child weighs eight pounds. 'We've had children here who never have recovered from the last famine,' said Margaret Manley. 'They're at a consistent level of malnutrition; this makes it especially hard for them.'

Asked about cholera, she said, no, there wasn't any just yet; she spoke as if she would personally throttle it with her bare hands if it came near her clinic. Cholera, the great unspoken dread of: the famine disease that in that waterless domain confers a certain and excruciatingly terrible death.

But it was at the hospital outside Wukru that we saw the real progress of famine and death, though hospital is probably a grand name for the collection of huts where the bed-allocation is one to a family. 'We're getting one hundred new patients a day here,' said the young Dutch doctor in charge. 'Half of these are famine-related cases. Some of them are very close to death indeed. And the figures are going up all the time.'

Some children are so close to death that dramatic intervention alone will save them; dramatic intervention here means a direct injection of high-energy fluid through the stomach into the peritoneum. 'That is the only thing that can save them.'

It does not save them all. Half-a-dozen children a week are now dying of malnutrition in this clinic alone. 'Many of the mothers have no milk,' he added, echoing that chilling horror of three years ago, when countless babies died sucking at withered, milkless breasts.

The doctor moved to examine an 18-month-old girl he had earlier given a direct peritoneal injection to. This girl was four pounds in weight, as tiny and as silent as a toy; she seeped mucile diarrhoea onto the wrist of the nurse who lifted her. The doctor pinched her wizened thigh; the tissue hung loose on the bone. The child was dying. 'Maybe we can save her,' said the doctor; his nurse, saying nothing, leads him to another bed.

Here a mother lay with her son, a pale, ghostly little fellow, hunched and silent and desperately ill. Beside them, on the family's bed, sat the father, speechlessly showing a colour photograph of another son to all arrivals; that son had now died of malnutrition; his brother looked as if he might be joining him.

In a neighbouring ward, a 24-year-old man, the living image of the near-dying of Bergen-Belsen, lay in a bed, a collection of apparently disconnected bones. His eyes were uninterested, his flesh wasted. An African nurse explained that he had TB, never having recovered from the last famine. Sometimes it is not unlucky to die early.

Unless Ethiopia has a windfall of good fortune, these wretched creatures will be in the vanguard of what has become a commonplace – death at the hands of man's oldest and most implacable enemy, hunger, and on this, the third year of the famine. One visitor, after seeing such victims, reported that his hands trembled while he wrote of entering a native hut. Stretched in one corner, scarcely visible in the dark and in the rags that covered them, were three children huddled together, lying there because they were too weak to rise, their limbs emaciated, their eyes sunk, their voices gone and evidently in the last stages of actual starvation. Nearby was a shrivelled old woman, moaning piteously, begging for food; from her limbs, the folds of skin hung loose from the bones, as she pleaded in her native language for help.

The visitor was William Bennett, and the scene was Ireland in 1847, in the third year of the Famine.

Could Any of Us Have Shouted Stop?

MARY HOLLAND (1988)

On 16 March 1988, Michael Stone, a loyalist gunman, opened fire and lobbed grenades at the funeral of Provisional IRA members Mairéad Farrell, Daniel McCann and Seán Savage in Milltown Cemetery in Belfast, killing three and injuring sixty. Three days later, at the funeral of one of Stone's victims, two plainclothes British soldiers driving past the cortège were mistaken for loyalist paramilitaries. As reporters and cameramen watched, the soldiers were dragged out of their car, beaten, abducted and later shot dead by republicans. Mary Holland, who made her name as a journalist through her reporting on Northern Ireland for the *Observer*, later moved to the *Irish Times*, where this piece was published on 23 March.

They both wore the same shade of green, vivid as tropical birds against the grey of the Belfast sky and the dark clothes of the mourners. Daniel McCann's widow walked behind the coffin of her husband and later stood beside his grave, the gallant green of her coat contrasting with the red clay of the Milltown Cemetery. Grenades had just stopped exploding and youths were running towards where the sound of gunfire had come from, but she seemed oblivious to it.

She was trying to put a small bouquet of flowers on her husband's coffin in the grave, which had been dug to receive all three bodies, but it was too deep. Gerry Adams put his arm around her shoulders to steady her and helped her to place the flowers. Then the gravediggers started filling in the earth.

I saw the same jade green two [*recte* three] days later. It was the colour of the thick sweater the young soldier was wearing when they dragged him onto the pavement and into Casement Park. His face was covered with blood, red as the cemetery clay. A dark, handsome lad in a chain-store sweater, he could have passed for one of the crowd in the funeral procession. He might even have escaped if he and his companion had parked their car and simply joined the mourners.

How did we let it happen? He passed within a few feet of myself and dozens of other journalists. He didn't cry out, just looked at us with terrified eyes as though we were all enemies in a foreign country who wouldn't have understood what language he was speaking if he called out for help.

Later, it seemed like hours but was in fact minutes, I found myself in the bookmaker's shop phoning for an ambulance. Someone in the shop said to me: 'If anyone had tried to stop it, they'd have been killed too.'

Now, several days later, I wonder. Probably we couldn't have prevented their deaths but we might, if we'd made a concerted effort, have halted the frenzy of the crowd, given some of them the moments they needed to become individual human beings again, responsible for their own actions.

Nobody, at least as far as I could see, tried. Not the bystanders, nor the journalists who were at less serious risk. Not Gerry Adams who, two [*recte* three] days earlier, had cradled a widow's grief. There were priests in the crowd but not even they could stop a mob bent on lynching.

Heaven knows I'm not blaming them. Whenever in the future I see that green in a girl's dress on a summer beach, I will have to ask why I did not make some gesture to show the young man in the green sweater that he was not utterly alone in a hostile country.

We all let it happen. The people of west Belfast are not 'bestial', 'savage', 'barbaric', to repeat a few of the adjectives that have been applied to them. To suggest that they are is as offensive as some of the recent comments in the British press, to the effect that the Irish as a race are congenitally violent.

Last Saturday, west Belfast was a community in a state of nervous crisis unimaginable to most of us. All week, its people had walked to the cemetery behind the coffins of their dead or watched from the side of the road as the funerals passed. It was not a matter of their supporting the IRA, although undoubtedly many of them do just that. To many more, the young men and women who were buried were a part of their community. What filled the television screens were the paramilitary trappings of their funerals. But at the Requiem

Masses I attended, local priests spoke of more homely things –
membership of a football team, kindness to a handicapped child, religious devotion – the qualities any group of people recognises in its
neighbours' children.

On top of their communal grief last Saturday, they feared, as did
all who were present, that what was happening was another attack of
the kind that had killed three people and injured dozens of others
when Daniel McCann and his companions were buried.

Before the letter writers reach for their pens, I am not excusing the
killing of the soldiers and need no lectures on ambivalence from
people who condemn what happens in the North from the unam-
biguous comfort of an RTE studio at Montrose. I am suggesting that
the blame does not lie only on the crowd who ran amok last Saturday, but on many of the rest of us who have left this community
increasingly abandoned in recent years.

The sense of isolation in west Belfast and in similar Catholic ghet-
tos of the North has, if anything, increased since the Anglo-Irish
Agreement was signed three years ago. That may not have been
intended but it is the way it has turned out. These people have been
excluded from the reasonable, moderate consensus of the accord.
They vote Sinn Féin, elect a Sinn Féin MP and it has been made quite
clear to them that this expression of political views, albeit conducted
through the ballot box, puts them outside the pale as far as the body
politic in the Republic is concerned.

At least before the agreement was signed, the Irish Government
drew no distinction between good and bad members of the nationalist minority, welcoming those who voted for constitutional
nationalism and rejecting the others. They were all 'our people', and
if that description excluded the Unionists, it was a failure which politicians in the Republic tried to address in the Forum Report.

Now, instead of Unionists, we have categorised those who live in
west Belfast and places like it as political and sometimes even moral
lepers. In Dáil Éireann every political leader speaks of the need to
woo and reassure Unionists. I have done it myself in this column and
will do so again. It's a very long time indeed since any of us spoke of
wooing the people of west Belfast and drawing them back into the

mainstream of the nation. On the contrary, there are complaints that RTE devotes too much time to the North. A journalist is sacked because a feature on *Morning Ireland* allowed Martin McGuinness to speak perhaps 200 words about arrangements for Mairéad Farrell's funeral.

We now face the prospect of reaping the whirlwind.

The people of west Belfast showed us last weekend just how, if they are driven far enough, they will look after themselves. What happened on Saturday was not the work of the Provos, though many people would like to believe that relatively comforting theory. The IRA may in the end have shot the soldiers, but Sinn Féin was as powerless as anyone else in the crowd to control the lynching that led to their deaths.

Even if we would like to, we cannot write off Belfast as a place apart, isolate a community of 90,000 people as outlaws. We have to bring them and the political leaders who represent them in from the cold, give them some hope that progress is possible and that it will include them. It is a task of the greatest urgency for an Irish government, more important even than repairing the state of Anglo-Irish relations.

Out of the Dark

DEIRDRE PURCELL (1988)

Christopher Nolan, who was born with cerebral palsy, won the
Whitbread Book of the Year Award for his memoir *Under the Eye of the
Clock*, published when he was just twenty-one. Deirdre Purcell's *Sunday Tribune* profile gives a dramatic insight into Nolan's distinctive
methods of communication.

Crippled boy was easier. Easier to approach, to pet. Easier to return
with feel-good feelings. But crippled boy is now a crippled man and
crippled man shouts to be confronted. Crippled man is demanding.
He demands respect. He demands attention. Crippled man is ruthless. He uses his family without mercy because he has to – there is no
other way. He is singleminded and quite fearless.

Crippled man accepts awards only for work done. He (courteously) rejects those offered for 'courage' or 'bravery'. *You see*, he
writes, *I'm trying to bring about a new way of framing the crippled intelligent
man. I want folk to see him as an equal, not as someone who deserves an award
for struggling against the odds. Everyone struggles against individual odds, and
crippled man is no different in his struggle than his able-bodied brother.*

To the organisers of Britain's Man of the Year Awards: *Regretfully,
I have to decline your noble gesture. I have had to decline similar awards in
America, Chile, India, Belgium and Ireland. Please tell your committee how
sorry I feel at having to say 'no' to their kind and thoughtful salute to an Irish
writer.*

To an international organisation which asked him to allow his
name to front it: *You must continue with your rescue work all the time focussing on technology while I must continue rescue work all the time highlighting
the hidden consciousness within the tongue-tied disabled person.*

He writes to Lady Goulding of the Central Remedial Clinic
explaining why he turns down these awards and honours. *My life is
horrendous in its demands but then that is the ransom I must pay for the inheritance my disabled forefathers have entrusted to me.*

Twenty-three-year-old crippled man, who cannot speak nor walk nor chew, still dares to think like this. He engages the reporter's eyes to say he sees himself as 'a light as weak as matchflame in profound darkness but a light nonetheless'. He demands to be understood and will not let this subject drop until the reporter grasps the concept. He is in his Clontarf living room and here is how he does it:

He flicks his yes towards a lamp. *Light?*

Yes! (he flicks his eyes upwards)

He flicks his eyes towards an ashtray.

Cigarette?

No! (he jerks his head)

Match?

No!

Ashes?

No!

He flicks his eyes towards the lamp again.

Light? It is light?

– towards the ashtray –

Lighted matches?

Yes!

Small flames? Small light? Matchflame?

Yes! Yes! Yes!

The rest is simple logic, aided by flick-yeses and jerk-nos. It has been said that communication between himself and his family, particularly with his mother, is 'telepathic'. Although Christy writes: *my mother can reach my eyes in a fashion which no writer can convey*, this is a convenient 'out' for the fainthearted who would not try. 'Remember,' says Bernadette Nolan, 'that it is now a 23-year-old language, it started when he was six months old. Did he want something? I taught him to look upwards if he did, to shake his head if he didn't. And if he wanted to go to the toilet, he was to nod . . .' Christy took the language further. *I had to invent a new way of signing.*

(This interview was constructed partially in this manner, partially through the interpretations of Christy's mother, partially from observation of the author at rehearsals for his play *Torchlight and Laser Beams*, partially by direct correspondence.)

The effort to communicate a single concept, like the one above, results in heavy sweat and jerking, palsied spasms which stretch his body and snatch his hands and arms, feet and neck, until his teeth are loudly grinding. His deepening voice groans in counterpoint. His eyes are wild with trying.

These spasms are the heaviest cross to bear. They interfere, not only with his communication but with his urgent need to write. The more his wish to write is urgent the more the spasms hit. *When I'm writing, I'm at war with my body, I groan in frustration sometimes. My mind is like a spin-drier at full speed. Try then to imagine how frustrating it is to give expression to that avalanche in efforts of one great nod after another.* What rescues him from bathos is humour. Every so often he draws back to see himself objectively. When he does, he sees the image of 'a fellow with a stick on his head' as absurdly funny. *What else can I do but laugh at myself?*

Nevertheless, there is a tremendous effort of will and memory required: *I grab hold of the image I require and seal it in my mind then I select special adjectives with which to dress my image. When that is decided, I let go on my language – so my readers are really seeing joy typed in braille-like symbols on my typewritten page.*

Christy has not come to terms with these spasms. (When he is asked what it is he hates most in the world he flicks again towards the lamp. Then he glances at his inert hands, then downwards at his wheelchair. The concept is not light this time, but behind the light. *Electricity* – yes! – *body* – yes – *Spasms*!) He knows the damned spasms place dreadful walls between himself and TABs – those who are Temporarily Able-Bodied.

It takes a huge effort from me to make them look beyond my mainly open mouth (and the more I try to close it and look relaxed the more the mouth muscles spasm into a locked-open gape). Did you see me on the Late Late*? Well if you did you'll be better able now to appreciate the battle I was waging in order to get my spake in and my humour established. Never please, never see my efforts to speak as just involuntary vocalising, I always have a point of view but rescuing it from my dumbness takes a battle which no viewer can measure.*

At first, the cripple's joy was simply to communicate, to release the torrents of words and feelings he had stored for the first 11 years of his life. But now the task is tougher and more subtle. A publisher asks him to write a book for children. Christy begins to work but then discovers that the publisher requires a children's story about a child confined to a wheelchair.

Christy Nolan's life changed irrevocably on 19 January 1988, the day he won the Whitbread Award for Literature. *But when I calmed myself, I began to take note. Frantic joy was my first emotion. Great buckets of satisfaction deluged my crippled life and then I felt fresh humanity fleshing my harried body.* With calmness came the sight of opportunity. This 'fresh humanity' is now at the head of a crusade.

With the Whitbread also came a surging confidence. Now he faces the world, head up or down, mouth open or closed, and does not care how the world reacts to his appearance. Sometimes in communicating, he takes a short-cut to a concept – a piggy-back upon the words of others. He read an article about the gaoled Yorkshire Ripper, Peter Sutcliffe, in which the Ripper was quoted as saying: 'I don't give a fuck how people see me.' 'Christy showed me that and said that this was how he felt,' says Bernadette, his mother – 'that he doesn't give a fuck how people see him now. He said, "I don't care if I come out with my mouth open in a photograph or closed. I just don't care any more."'

Torchlight and Laserbeams is a step on this crusade and towards a wider audience. In St Catherine's Church in Thomas Street, where rehearsals are in progress, he flicks his eyes in wide arcs, looking first towards the upper air and then the floor. He is saying that he feels connected to the spirits of the dead buried in the vaults below his wheelchair, connected particularly to the shades of all the cripples who had gone before him and who had rotted as outcasts.

He now feels a responsibility to their memory . . . *Best thanks for coming to the cold damp church to see my play casting shadows on the floor of St Catherine's. As you join with me, will you help me to change the Millennium's history of deception and abuse of the human, damn rights of my disabled ancestors. New bygones are about to limp by as crippled man arrives on the drama-linked stage. Great causes need great slogans but mute man that I am, I cast my line far and wide looking for a bite from media folk in mulled brainland hoping my dreadful message will catch their breath.*

'Connections' are extremely important, connections to his disabled forbears, to his own deceased relatives, to linked names and
events. A central figure in the play is the Lady with the Lamp, the
figure of his grandmother. She died when Christy was still a child,
but one night before he had published anything, he dreamed she
came to him. She forecast that he would break free with writing and
would become famous. Her name was Catherine. He watches Eve
Watkinson rehearse Catherine's lines in St Catherine's Church and it
means more than coincidence. He is frantically worried at rumours
he has heard that the venerable church is due for demolition.

The play, like all his work so far, is autobiographical, relentlessly
so, gathering together all his work, published and unpublished, going
over and over the ground until the message dents the smooth shields
around the hearts of the TABs. It is a tough message, but some of the
language is soft, some funny, a lot of it is loving. His sense-memory
is extraordinary. Gifted with an IQ which gave him, all along the
line, comprehension equal with that of children twice his age, he sat
or lay in his farmhouse kitchen in Co. Westmeath, absorbing or stor-
ing smells, sights and sounds for later. He was arranging them, and
clothing them with words, always sure, he says, that some day he
would be able to communicate them.

*Loneliness gave me the silence necessary for trying to give expression to my
entrapped thoughts. I became aware of certain things very early in my childhood,
the taste of bread baking, pleasant clove smell from an apple pie, fresh milked
milk with the froth on the surface, the lustre off the bars of the cot as light glinted
from morning sunshine, the heat coming from the melon-coloured cooker, the day
the lamb came back to life when mam put his frozen body on the gentle heat of the
oven, the fright I got when he suddenly bleated, the feel of cold wet turf when I
was helped to stick my finger into its soft brown mush, the chirping of the day-old
chicks out in the motor shed.*

*He remembers the location of the clock on the sticking out shelf in the kitchen
in Rathgowan,* although the family left that particular house before
Christy was 15 months old. And he rebuts the notion that this sense-
memory might not be as vivid if he had been able-bodied all his life.
*Being crippled had next to nothing to do with it, it came through my being an
inquisitive child.*

On the other hand, he writes that his being crippled certainly has a lot to do with his being a writer. He may have become a writer anyway, had he been born a TAB, but *I might be a freedom-filled drop-out, a great bore, or, lastingly gifted, a painter. I have a love of colour youthfully garnered in the countryside.*

Some of the writing is, naturally, angry. Anger usually vents itself in blame. Who or what does Christy Nolan blame? His parents, his family, particularly his mother, are closest at hand.

Regardless of handicap all children blame their parents for something or other. They mention big noses, gappy teeth, straight or curly hair, long limbs or short ones, so in my case I just blamed my mother for everything. She was handy for my purpose and I looked on her as the creature to scorn. By sacrificing her, I got a scapegoat for my anger and for her to be confronted by an angry three-year-old son meant that she had to grow up quickly if she was going to be able to deal with my genius.

Nothing could have prepared me for my destiny but my mother, regardless of her gameness to stand by me, could not have been fairer as she dealt with my rebellion. Nowadays I look on my handicap as being but an inconvenience. I know my anger showed here and there in my books and poetry but then didn't joy find an outlet too.

He had the benefit of a very happy childhood surrounded by a large and loving extended family. *It's usually my parents and sister who figure in my publicity but they are nearest to hand. My family once included grandparents but now is narrowed to uncles and aunts and millions of great cousins. Their loyalty to me is fiercesome and heartwarming. I was wanted dearly, loved dearly, bullied fairly and treated normally. My folk never became too protective of me and most of all they accepted me just as though I was able-bodied.*

My father is game for long walks and creates adventure out of a day in Dublin's old streetways (a walk through the Liberties with Joe Nolan is Christy's favourite happiness). My mother never says 'no' when I want her support at my typing but her support can be as simple as greeting me with a smile to frantic sharing of voiceless communication. Most of all I freed myself from the historical stamp of helplessness by my being egged on by Yvonne.

Bernadette spent, still spends, long hours, up to 11 a day, standing behind her son, cradling his chin as he aims his 'unicorn stick' tied around his head, at one slow letter after another on the keyboard of his typewriter. (So does Yvonne, his sister, so do others.) Bernadette rejects completely any notion that she is anything other than a normal mother. 'I'm not doing anything for Christy that I haven't done for Yvonne, that any mother wouldn't do for her own child. The demands are more physical, that's the only difference.

Computer boffins from all over the world have written programmes to help her son towards independence, some of them ingenious. But none have yet been able to overcome the problem of Christy's spasms.

Independent operation of a chinswitch is fine for people who are merely paralysed, but when spasms strike the switch can inadvertently activate 'Delete' or 'Cancel'. But the day is drawing closer when computers can be harnessed directly to a cripple's brain, or at least his eyes. Already there are experimental military applications of this technology, where pilots can activate missiles with their eyes.

At present it is still one slow letter at a time. This laborious method is poignant in the area of drama. Drama means changes, drama means cutting and dropping all those tortuously produced words, but Christy has become hooked on drama, on the (however temporary) 'family' atmosphere in which rehearsals take place. For someone who has worked so long locked in isolation, the teamwork and collaboration is heady stuff. *I'm open to listen to everyone's opinion. The director and cast are patient with me and I too am patient with them. We have a lovely working atmosphere and the cast work extremely hard. I often giggle to myself as I watch the cast trying to read my eye signals – they usually have to draw on their imagination and sensitivity when I start TALKING! So far they have managed to understand me every single time. We're all in there together and we want the play to work.*

He is very religious (*heaven is my final destination but between ourselves I have the full of my jacket trying to make it down here!*) and there is a lot of religious imagery in the writing. He is musical too. When he first heard the score specially written for *Torchlight and Laser Beams* by the Belgian composer Wim Mertens, he was moved to tears. *I find it hauntingly beautiful and just hope that an audience would be similarly moved.*

When he finally gets off the media merry-go-round and gets back to work, where he has a novel *ready and waiting, it will surprise everyone!*, he admits that he will miss the stardom, with taxis pulling up at the door in Clontarf and international TV crews filming him day and night. He is very tolerant of media scrutiny – if very knowing: *masked behind their curiosity is the question 'what, can a cripple be clever, being crippled?' No, I'm never irritated by the questions of the media, I try to put myself in their shoes . . .*

The day when the doorbell and the telephone stop ringing cannot come soon enough for Bernadette and Joe, who have had little life of their own since the Whitbread, who have had no holiday this year and who have stayed with their son in the freezing conditions of St Catherine's Church, Thomas Street, until 11.00 at night and beyond – because he would not leave. 'All we want is to get back to what passes for normal life!' says Bernadette.

At the age of 12 Christy Nolan had already been flown to London on *beautiful EI 172* to receive the Spastics 'special' prize 'For Work Beyond Comparison' from the hands of Edna Healey. Edna had shown him around No. 11 Downing Street and had arranged a similar tour of Number 10. By 13, he had been photographed by Snowdon. By 22 he had won the Whitbread Prize. The difficulty is not, as might be expected, getting beyond his muteness and the spasms and his physical disability to approach his talent. The difficulty for TABs is getting beyond that again, to the Christy who is impatient, who laughs and cries and grumbles, who smokes cigars, loves vodka, gets cranky and is singleminded to the point of obsession. To the man whose unlikely all-time hero is the heavyweight boxing champion of the world, Mike Tyson.

To the little tyro who wrote, on 2 October 1977, when the dam of dreams had just burst: *The point about people being boring is that they put no interest into finding out what other people think. Regardless of a person's feelings they blow on and on, pointing their son's progress as purpose for vain glory. There are other people too, who love the sound of their own voices and rise my temper by ranting and raving. Then, there is the friendly one who loves petting you like a hairy dog.*

Despite all the ebullience and positive thinking, TABs (and media folk) worry about Christy's far future when Bernadette is gone.

Christy does not. ('He really doesn't,' says Bernadette, 'and that helps me too.') In his singleminded way, the question is seen first in terms of his continuing ability to write: *You may not believe me when I tell you that I don't fear the freedom which awaits me. I use my mother's voice but believe me, she's talking my own language and thoughts. I yes her to go on speaking out for me and mine but the truth is that the threshing [sic?], mumbled framework comes from me. My mother always challenged me not to be a milk-sop, nutty junior and I tried to justify her demand. When the day comes that I have to verify my very existence I'll do what's expected of me – after all in my life I have had a head start from my unique parents.*

The singlemindedness is perhaps not so surprising when so many avenues are closed off. No avenues towards 'normal' courtship or even lighthearted romance, for instance. There are some dreams which were washed away when the dam burst. *Deirdre, there is life in the old dog so he muses and mulls over romance and girls but the heart must heed the mind sometimes and you must guess what this mind tells this heart!*

Dev's People

FINTAN O'TOOLE (1989)

Thirteen and a half years after the death of Éamon de Valera, Fintan O'Toole visited the small village in Co. Clare where de Valera grew up. Emigration from Ireland rose to a level in 1989 that was not reached again until 2010.

The nun, Mrs Gorman remembers, knew what she wanted. Mrs Gorman keeps the keys to de Valera's Cottage, the neat little house at Knockmore, just outside Bruree, that is now a shrine to the memory of the patriarch. The roses that used to grow outside the door have been taken up and replaced with traditional paving stones. The cooker has been taken out from the grate and replaced with a traditional open hearth, the old iron kettle hanging from its hook. The lino has been taken from the floor and replaced with traditional flagstones. The bareness of the walls is broken by a holy trinity: a statue of the Blessed Virgin, a print of Daniel O'Connell and an embroidered American eagle in a frame.

The nun, though, was not much interested in these downstairs rooms. She climbed the steep, narrow stairs that led to what was once Éamon de Valera's bedroom. The bed, Mrs Gorman warned her, might be a bit dusty. She didn't mind. She climbed up on de Valera's old iron bed and lay there, her black habit spread out against the pink mattress. She looked up at the whitewashed sloping sides of the ceiling or, perhaps, out the tiny square window at the small patch of ground where, in his boyhood, as he later told the Dáil, young Éamon learned everything from 'the spancelling of a goat to the milking of a cow'. After a few minutes she got out of the bed, came down the stairs looking contented and left.

Up the road, in another of the neat villages that dot this gentle Limerick pastureland, there is a woman in her late thirties. 'I'm married,' she says, 'but we've been separated for eight years. He went off his own way and I've looked after our two daughters. One of them's still in school, but the other's in London. I have a man who comes in to me a few times a week, but he's afraid to move in with me. Not that the priests bother you any more. I had one nasty experience a while back, when a mother and daughter, who I can tell you were doing all they wanted to do themselves but liked to complain about other people, put the priest on to me. But that didn't last long – there's so much going on around here now that they just don't bother any more. Still, as soon as my youngest one is reared, I'm getting out.'

The young man who works in the garage in Bruree and is going home to Kilmallock and then, maybe, out to Madonna's Nite Club in Charleville, knows all about leaving. 'There used to be ten of us would go out together every Saturday night. After this week, I'm the only one left. There's a whole street in Elephant and Castle, it's more Kilmallock than Kilmallock, if you know what I mean. Sure, there's all that history around here, but what difference does it make? The young people just aren't interested in politics.'

Yet the past has its power around here, not least because the present keeps returning to it. At Knocklong, the railway station has closed and the bus comes just once a day. The maple-floored ballroom is closed up and the hotel no longer takes guests. There used to be traditional music a few years ago, played by an Australian couple and an Irishman, but the Australians went home. The Bord Fáilte traditional holiday cottages have been sold off. The days of turmoil when Bruree and Knocklong knew not one civil war but two – the big one when two thousand Republicans fought two thousand Free Staters for control of the Kilmallock Triangle, and the little one a year before when workers in both villages declared themselves Soviets and flew the red flag for a few days – are long gone.

What remains of those days is the de Valera museum in the old schoolhouse in Bruree. Here you can see the relics of a famous man's life: a headline copybook with the curling, punctilious handwriting – 'Queen Victoria was born 24 May 1819.' A jacket with a Fáinne worked in thread on the lapel. Prizes won at sports meetings and War of Independence medals. Rosary beads, prayer books, spectacles, a walking stick. The old school desk with the carved initials 'ED' that had to be deepened and enhanced before the museum was opened in 1972. And, more than these things, the words that de Valera spoke at an after-Mass meeting in Bruree in 1955 and that still remain in the hearts of many who live in and around the village: 'The Irish language is the bond that keeps our people together throughout the centuries, and enabled them to resist all the efforts to make them English. It would be useful to us that way today, when we have poured in upon us, from every direction, influences which are contrary to the traditional views and hopes of our people. It is on the character of our people that this nation will be built, and the character consists of very simple things: earnestness in our work, honesty and truthfulness.'

In the Deerpark Hotel in Charleville, they have their own little exhibition: a print of the scene in the GPO in 1916 beside a photograph of the shopping centre in Charleville, Australia.

The first time a helicopter ever landed at Bruree was on a Sunday evening in July, 1966. Not one but two of the great whirling machines descended from a clear blue sky on to Knockmore Hill, one carrying the President of the Republic the other containing his bodyguards. For Lorcan Ó Maonaigh, a local farmer and veteran member of the Éamon de Valera Cumann of Fianna Fáil, it was a day to remember. His daughter Máire was four at the time and he arranged for her to present the President with a bunch of flowers.

Dev, he says, was both pleased and amazed that a little girl from Bruree would be able to speak such good Irish as Máire could. The memory is a source of great pride to him, a part of his firm belief that 'apart from politics altogether, Dev was a great man, a wonderful type of person'. It is one of the things that has kept him loyal to Fianna Fáil through all the decades of change.

The other thing is the memory of an empty house. Lorcan was a young man when his uncle took him to see the house over the Cork border. It was in the house that a brother of Lorcan's mother was killed along with three other men during the Tan War. The men were having a meeting of the local IRA Brigade when the Tans attacked and shot them out of hand. One of those killed was a young man who had just built the house and was waiting to move into it with his bride-to-be. The house was never lived in again, and it stood there for decades, an admonition and a call-to-arms.

Lorcan isn't sure when he joined Fianna Fáil, since it seemed that he was always in the party. After the Civil War, you always knew which side you had been on, and his family's side was staunchly Republican. 'It wasn't that there was much bitterness or enmity round here, it was just that there was a different sort of relationship. The Fianna Fáil fellas knew each other very well, and the other crowd knew each other very well and there'd be a different sort of a hand-shake if you met on the road, that sort of a way.' A man who lived at the end of their boreen used to take Lorcan to Limerick every time that Dev was in town. 'I grew up with all those people, and I never changed.'

That loyalty, though, hasn't been easy. He watched the rise of the Men in Mohair Suits from the Sixties onwards with distinct unease. 'I wouldn't go along with 'em now. These men came from a different generation and they probably have a different education, but they'd want to look back to their roots, like. I don't see why they're yapping so much about republicanism if they're short of the whole picture. In the cities, people are different and they come more under outside pressures. You have writers and third-level students and intellectuals and those, and they mean great, but it doesn't all work out either. Charlie's had the divil's own luck – people have come to accept that they have to tighten their belts but you hear of the politicians then going on junkets. I do think that when people move into positions of power, they're often inclined to forget what put them there. I think de Valera was one of the few men who didn't ever forget his roots.

'When I was younger I would go canvassing, but now a lot of the things I thought were important, our people in the party don't bother with. Dev now, when he'd talk, the Irish language would have a pri-ority. He'd always begin his speeches in Irish and go along a good way, and then turn to English. But the people now, I don't know are they Irish or English. It isn't for me to say, I suppose, times are chang-ing.

'Until we get proud of ourselves again, I can't see us doing any-thing. I see ads on the television and they're advertising books on nature and they're saying "the Book of the British Countryside". That gets me. A lot of our TDs are decent enough people, but they don't seem to think about things. If we want independence we'll have to do something about it, and if not, we might as well sink back into the British world.'

He is not convinced that the party is as serious about a united Ireland as it was in Dev's time. 'I've a lot of regard for Charlie, but Charlie, too, is not altogether a disciple of de Valera's republicanism. A very, very able man, now, and a very human man, but I don't know has Charlie the right mix either. This Anglo-Irish Agreement, for instance, is so vague that both Charlie and Maggie can get something out of it. 'Tis just about better than nothing. A heap of words.' He feels that the violence of the Provisional IRA was inevitable because of the way the Catholics in the North were treated and he had a great deal of sympathy for the H-Block hunger strikers: 'There's a thing about it – you might not agree with these people, but they're your own people, no matter what.

'I think Dev would be fairly disappointed with the party now. But 'tis like Daniel O'Connell. He was regarded as the leader of the nationalist opinion, but the people who came after him didn't think that at all. I suppose you have to live in your own times. If you have a spade and a shovel and no tractor, you have to work with the spade and shovel.'

The image of a man on horseback riding into Bruree playing the fiddle is one that has stayed with Mainchin Seoighe from his childhood. Fiddling away furiously, the horse being led through the village, the whole thing lit by the light of candles in the windows. It was a victory parade, a celebration of Fianna Fáil's triumph in the 1932 election. He had seen de Valera for the first time a few months previously in Kilmallock. 'He came from Newcastle West. There was a great turnout, a torchlight procession and all the rest of it. I was too young to remember a word of what he said, of course, but the thing that struck me was I thought he spoke exactly as his uncle here in Bruree, Pat Coll, spoke. I would have sworn that it was Pat Coll speaking.'

Pat Coll and Mainchin's mother were neighbours, and later, after he had assumed power, Dev would call sometimes to see her. In 1965, Mainchin spent a day with Dev, taking him around all of the old places. They talked about schooldays, about the pitched battles that the boys from Ballynaught used to fight against the boys from Tankardstown on their way home, about Montecarlo Bergin who got his name from singing 'The Man Who Broke the Bank at Montecarlo' and used to travel the countryside for Foxy Pat Coll, selling tea from a pony and trap.

Mainchin remains devoted to Dev, is the curator of the de Valera Museum and has written poems in honour of his hero, poems like 'The Man From Bruree':

> When you honour in song and in story
> The men who at Easter uprose,
> Who struck for the freedom of Ireland,
> And faced the full might of their foes –
> Oh, remember the man from Bruree, boys,
> De Valera who answered the call,
> He fought in the thick of the battle,
> And was last to surrender of all.

Mainchin, too, thinks that Dev might be disappointed at the way both party politics and Irish society have gone. 'Dev was prepared to accept change all right, but I'd say he'd be disappointed at the same time. He'd be somewhat stronger nationally than political leaders are inclined to think now. I think he'd take a firmer stand with Britain than any one of our leaders would now. He would have been pleased at the standard of living and of education that we have now, but I don't know about social change and all these things that are being discussed now.

'Materialism, the consumer society, wouldn't be his ideal. You see when I was growing up, people round here wouldn't have thought anything strange about comely maidens and all that. It seems to the young people now that that doesn't make sense. But the older people would still believe in the moral order that Dev would have wanted. Society is so open now, with television and media and that, and young people are immature. There certainly seems to be a deviation from old standards. I grew up in the hungry Thirties and the isolation and, I suppose, insulation of the war years. Money was scarce, and we had none of the luxuries or amenities of modern life, but people were happier, certainly more contented than they are now. With advertising and everything now, young people's aims are set too high.'

Politics in Bruree is more about getting the vote out than it is about persuading people to vote the right way. Persuasion has little to do with a political landscape whose contours were set down nearly 70 years ago. Padraig Ó Liathain, another long-standing member of the Fianna Fáil cumann in Bruree, says that you can still point to each household in the area and say how they will vote in an election. 'Even to the present day, you'd know the families. Such a family is Fine Gael and such a family is Fianna Fáil. I have never known families to change their allegiance, even going back to their grandfathers. The families are still loyal to the parties that their ancestors and forebears fought for. You can estimate the vote, and in a general election, you wouldn't be out much. You wouldn't hit it head on, but you'd be within a couple of per cent anyway.'

Even getting the vote out isn't as much of a task as it used to be. 'In the early years, transport wasn't as plentiful and that was the problem. Up to the 1960s, there'd be two cars out in this area operating a shuttle service all day long. The Lemass era changed all that – now there's only one or two people who don't have their own transport.'

Padraig's mother's people were very active in the War of Independence, and when he was 16 and wandered into a Fianna Fáil cumann meeting by accident, he joined up on the spot. That was 30 years ago. 'Dev's first cousin, Mrs Maher, taught me at school, and we'd been hearing of Dev, little stories about him, old people that he knew. His name was a household word. There was fierce loyalty to Dev. No matter what Dev did or what he said, didn't matter. He was right, always right. It was never questioned. Now everything is questioned. Dev led and everyone followed. Nowadays, even if you're a party supporter, you question what the party are doing.'

His own period of questioning was when Fianna Fáil was led by

Jack Lynch. 'I have strong feelings on the North, and they'd be very traditionalist. I don't think unity will come overnight – it will be step by step, and I think the Anglo-Irish Agreement is only a tiny step on the road to unity, but come it must. I think the party did lose the nationalism for a while during the Sixties and early Seventies, they did stray a bit, but I think since Charlie became leader they have come back a little bit again.'

He is, he says, 'against violence and murder', but 'I wouldn't isolate the IRA and say that the IRA alone are committing those atrocities – the British Army is doing it too, along with the militant Unionists. There's no easy answer. I would like to see Sinn Fein brought back into the political process, and I wouldn't support Section 31 either. It's a crazy situation. I think that if they have something to say, let them say it, and let people decide.'

Like all of the Fianna Fáil cumann in Bruree, Padraig was against divorce, but he thinks it might come in a united Ireland. 'Maybe when talks are held on the unification of the country, maybe then that would be the time to make allowances.' But he doesn't believe social attitudes have changed around Bruree, anyway: 'Moral standards are the same as they have always been. We'd be leading a different kind of life from cities and towns. In a rural area, everyone knows everything about everyone else. You can't be a Jekyll-and-Hyde character. No matter what you do, it's common knowledge. That helps to keep people on the straight and narrow.'

Next Friday, as he has done for each of the past 25 years, Padraig will be heading for the Ard Fheis in Dublin, with at least one or two members of his family. 'At first, it was in the Mansion House, where the crowds were smaller and the atmosphere was more intimate. But even now you make a lot of friends there, you meet the same people year after year – it's more a social event than anything, with a lot of fringe happenings and functions. It's more a holiday weekend than a political event – I have an aunt in Blanchardstown and we stay there. I would go to some sessions of the Ard Fheis, but certainly not them all. I'd always go on a Saturday night for the leader's speech, of course. But most of the time would be spent going round in the vicinity of the RDS – the Burlington or Jury's or the social events in the hall itself.'

Whatever happens this year for Padraig it is unlikely to match the year in the mid-Sixties when he was up for the Ard Fheis. He called to Aras an Uachtaráin to ask if he could leave a photograph for Dev to sign. 'I just called to the gate of the Aras, no appointment or nothing. My mother was with me and my five-year-old son. I told the guard at the gate my business. He rang the house. Dev told the man to let us on in. We were ushered into the waiting room. Then we went into the study and sat opposite him. He spoke a lot about Bruree, families that he knew, trees and bushes that he remembered, the countryside and the simple life of the people.'

This year, at the Ard Fheis, Padraig will be near to the building site which he will not recognise. On it the most expensive group of houses to be built in Dublin this year – set to cost between £275,000 and £300,000 each – are being erected. The site is the former home at Cross Avenue of the Man from Bruree, Éamon de Valera.

The Coffin Was Our Passport

MAGGIE O'KANE (1992)

Maggie O'Kane served as the *Guardian's* correspondent in Sarajevo
between 1992 and 1996, when the city was besieged by Bosnian Serb
forces. This report captured the degree to which, once the siege had
begun, all inhabitants of the city were in grave danger from sniper
and mortar fire.

Jordi had his doubts on Sunday morning. He wanted to leave. At
12.10 on Sunday afternoon a mortar bomb dropped out of the sky
like a shot-put and killed him.

He was from Barcelona, 25 years old and wore his thick black shiny
hair in a pony tail. It was his first job and he told his friend, Santiago,
who had a bit job with Associated Press, that he wanted to be a war
photographer. His newspaper had put up $1,000 for the trip, $100 for
each picture. His last picture was a shot of a man fishing in the river
in the centre of Sarajevo with a burnt-out building rising above.

The mortar bomb came as mortar bombs do in Sarajevo, falling
out of the sky from no particular place with no particular logic except
terror. David Brauchli, the 27-year-old photographer, had a bullet-
proof vest. Jordi had none.

'Fuck, I've been hit,' he said. 'The blood is coming out of my
chest.'

David crawled into a doorway with shrapnel in his groin and leg.
'Help us,' he shouted. Jordi died quickly, losing consciousness on the
pavement. David was operated on immediately and survived.

On Monday they took Jordi's body to the mortuary and laid him
down beside a woman who had turned black. 'These days people just
can't get to the hospital to collect their dead,' his doctor said.

For the last month the siege of Sarajevo has been covered from the
outside, from the Bosnia Hotel six miles from the city. Last Thursday
it was hit by mortar bombs. The BBC were leaving, ITN telephoned
London – they were leaving too. The television teams left at five on

Friday morning and the rest, led by Tony Smith and David Brauchli of Associated Press, moved into town.

On Monday afternoon the Red Cross convoy winding along a small country road was hit by mortar bombs. Frederique Maurice, the Swiss leader of the convoy, died from wounds to his face and neck on Sunday night. His two companions were seriously injured and the medicines and food they brought went up in flames as a rocket sliced through their white lorry with its red cross.

Sarajevo is surrounded by hills, held by the Serbian militia and what remains of the Yugoslav federal army. Being in the city is like being in a doll's house that a giant has lifted the roof off of. Running past the Bristol Hotel had been the worst. The road is filled with holes that look like great splashes of ink where the mortar bombs have hit. We hear the bullets. Perhaps for us – perhaps not. At the crossroads a van had been hit by a rocket and as it burst into flames the men inside tried to crawl out. One had lost a part of his leg and as he dragged himself away from the van the snipers picked him off. One bullet, then another until he finally lay down on the pavement and died.

The Belvedere Hotel became our haven, hidden under the poplar trees in a side street. The owner, Druskic Suleyman, had played centre-forward for Udinese in northern Italy and earned $3 million. He had returned to Sarajevo, his home town, to get married and set up the Belvedere Hotel. 'I know this will all go up in smoke some day soon,' he said.

After Jordi Puyol died and David Brauchli was wounded we decided it was time to leave. On the road out we passed the burnt-out trams in Titova Street, where the corpses of nine soldiers had rotted for days, then passed the crossroads and the burnt-out electrical switching station.

On the road from the city the first of the women and children from the children's convoy trying to escape from the city were turning back. She was in her mid-thirties with two children walking back in the rain. She had two brown-paper bags and the children were carrying blankets that dripped on to the wet pavement. The children's convoy had been stopped at the Serbian militia checkpoint. No way out.

There were 3,500 women and children in the convoy. The mile-long queue would wait all day in the rain to be turned back as night fell. In the back of each car were children sitting amid bursting suitcases. Round the cars the Serbian militia in blue uniforms and green camouflage carried Kalashnikovs and strolled up and down past their little hostages.

It took 12 hours to get to the coast. Tony Smith of the AP in a smashed-up car led us through the checkpoint saying: 'We have one wounded and one dead.' The coffin was our passport. In the morning we woke in a hotel by the sea. Jordi's father was coming to take his son's body back to Barcelona. Eric wanted to buy clothes for the corpse. We thought about a suit but decided on a white T-shirt and denim trousers.

Stan Laurel and the Seven Dwarfs

JOSEPH O'CONNOR (1994)

Following Ireland's dramatic progress to the quarter-finals of the 1990 soccer World Cup, the 1994 World Cup, held in the United States, generated a torrent of coverage, much of it wildly patriotic and unreasonably optimistic. The supporters who travelled across the Atlantic were, at the end of the day, better material than the team.

Thursday 23 June. Orlando – the name of a city and not the name of an Irish soccer fan – is practically owned by the Disney Corporation. Hence today, against my better judgement, I trot along to Disney World's Magic Kingdom with a group of Irish supporters. Now, dear diary, I do not know if you have ever spent much time in the company of a large group of Irish men who are far away from home, in a hot climate, with only a large group of stuffed animals for company, but if you haven't, then take my advice. Don't. Ever.

And if you have, why, then you will know what a surreal experience it is.

The first bizarre thing about Disney World is that each of the car parks is named after one of the seven dwarfs. There is Bashful, Sleepy, Grumpy, Dopey and so on. Thus, when you get on the little commuter train that whisks you into the park, a grown adult has to call out, over the intercom, 'Now arriving at Happy, all passengers for Happy and Dopey, next stop Grumpy, hold tight now.' For some reason, I find this amazingly funny. We amuse ourselves by thinking up new dwarf names. Sleazy, Sarky, Horny and Crappy being my favourites.

Once into the park, we decide to go on the boat cruise through 'Small World'. There is a sign over the entrance to the tunnel. 'Welcome to the happiest little cruise in the world,' it says. Reading this, I feel like indulging in the almightiest little puke in the world, which phrase, conveniently enough, also describes the six-year-old child sitting beside me. He is humming to himself as he trails his little hand in the water. I utter a silent fervent prayer that alligators are native to this part of Florida.

Halfway through the tunnel, a party of Mexican fans are sighted in a neighbouring boat. The chant begins straight away. 'You'll Never Beat the Irish. You'll Never Beat the Irish.' The Mexicans chant back at us, waving their fists and cursing in Spanish. One of them holds out his right hand, pistol fashion, and begins roaring 'bangbang, bangbang'. While all this is going on, Mickey Mouse, Goofy, Pluto and Snow White are standing on the far bank of the pond, dancing up and down, blowing us kisses, waving their hands in the air, and singing 'Hi ho, hi ho, it's off to work we go.' The fans join in. 'With buckets and spades and hand grenades, hi ho, hi ho, hi ho, hi ho.'

Outside again, our tour guide, Wanda, is waiting for us. Wanda is a very nice young woman from Kissimmee. 'There's some rully good rides here at the Magic Kingdom,' she says, to a chorus of snuffles and titters. 'We have big rides, small rides, scary rides, happy rides, whatever kind of ride you like you can find here at the Magic Kingdom.' One fan is falling about the place now and another – Cocko by name – is laughing his bloody dentures out. Wanda must be wondering what it is she is saying that has all these grown men nearly widdling with laughter. But, true professional that she is, she continues.

'Er . . . some of the rides have been here for a long time, but other rides are new, and here at Disney we're constantly looking at ways to make rides more exciting.' The fans are slapping their thighs and guffawing at this stage. One usually quiet man from Laois is actually honking like a great big white-legged hysterical mallard duck. Honko, I'm going to call him from now on.

'What's so funny?' Wanda says.

'Nothing, Wanda,' Honko replies.

'No, c'mon,' she says. 'Am I like saying something funny?'

'Not at all, Wanda, you're grand, sweetheart. And c'mere, tell us, do you like the odd ride yourself, Wanda?'

'Oh yes, of course.'

'And how many rides would you have a day?'

'Oh, I dunno, three or four I guess. Depends how much spare time I get.'

Well, at this stage several of the fans have to go and sit down in the shade or pour water over themselves, so frantic are their cackles. Some are actually sobbing with laughter. Donald Duck wanders over to one of them and begins gently to peck him on the head with his enormous yellow beak. 'Go away, ye big feathery fairy,' the fan says. A hearty chant soon begins, the scheme of which is based on the considerable rhyming potential of the words Donald Duck. What a talent for poetry the Irish have! Seamus Heaney would have been proud.

Things are about to get even worse, however. An enormous structure depicting Mickey Mouse is pointed out on the horizon. Wanda tells us, her voice fairly brimming over with pride, 'And guys, you know what, that's the largest self-supporting Mickey in the whole of the United States.'

Well, I don't think I have to describe the communal reaction, really. It is as though the entire party has been blasted with laughing gas. Several of the supporters will need medical attention soon.

'Oh, there are other Mickeys,' Wanda sniffs, dismissively, 'there's a rully big Mickey in California of course, and there are some rully large Mickeys in some of the other states, and a big old Mickey over there in Eurodisney. But I gotta tell you, we're real proud of our superb superbig Mickey that we got down here in Florida.'

The sun is blazing hot now, and the white stone floor seems to be sucking the heat into itself. Tears of laughter are spilling down the faces of my companions. The seven dwarfs saunter past us, pursued by the Mad Hatter, the Wicked Witch of the West, the Queen of Hearts and various assorted fluffy tigers holding hands. The fans are chanting again now: 'You'll never beat the Irish. You'll never beat the Irish.' If Wanda smiles any harder, her eyebrows will disappear into her hairline. I close my eyes. I try to imagine just how much money you would have to spend on drugs to achieve this weird a feeling.

Friday 24 June. Match day is here at last! This is very good, because Orlando is the most boring place in the world, and if you did not have the football to go to, you'd end up trying to drown yourself in the swimming pool just to kill a bit of time.

The Orlando city authorities have made a bit of a hames of the traffic arrangements. We leave the hotel in a rattling little coach at 9.30 and arrive almost two hours later, sweaty, dejected and part-broiled, at the Citrus Bowl. There, we are invited to shell out thirty bucks for lurid baseball hats, forty or fifty for ghastly souvenir T-shirts that somehow you know you will wash just once before they shrink in your machine to the size of a J-cloth.

The roofless stadium is completely exposed to the midday sun, and is incredibly hot. The Mexican fans are a lot more in evidence today than the Italians were at the weekend. The teams troop out into the baking heat, the Mexicans in green, our boys in white. Jorge Campos, the Mexican goalie, is wearing a rather fetching cape-like number in orange, green, yellow and red. He looks like a part-time superhero, and, indeed, would not be out of place on one of the rides at Disneyland. 'Ye bleedin' Christmas tree, yeh,' shouts one of the fans behind me. 'You're only a feckin prettyboy.' Another one roars, 'Jorge Campos, the day-glo Dago.'

The match starts well for Ireland. Staunton attacks down the left-hand side. The Irish fans start humming the theme tune of the Laurel and Hardy films. This, I am told, is because Steve Staunton looks like Stan Laurel, which I really don't think he does. But anyway. In the 25th minute, Irwin is booked for wasting time. 'Referee, you're a tosser,' screams the Liverpool man behind me to Swiss Mr Roethlisburger, 'you're a bleedin' Barclays Banker, you are, you're a shaggin' hand-shandy merchant, ref.' Further imaginative opinions are widely expressed regarding auto-erotic activities chez Roethlisburger. Two minutes later Roy Keane narrowly avoids featuring in the little black book when he gamely puts the studs into one of the Mexicanos. I see a banner on the far side of the pitch.

TOMMY COYNE, SHARPER THAN JIMMY HILL'S CHIN

Just my luck, the man seated to my left turns out to be a statistics fiend. He tells me that Mexico scored 39 goals in their 12 qualifying games, and then he looks at me with a profound stare. 'You'll Never Beat the Irish,' we sing, 'You'll Never Beat the Irish.' Four minutes later, Luis Garcia rockets the ball from outside the area past Bonner's outstretched right hand. That shuts us all up, I can tell you.

The half-time break is depressing. Everyone around me is quiet. The statistics man takes a mint from his pocket, puts it in his mouth and sucks it. The thermometer on the stadium wall says that the pitch temperature is 110 degrees. Everyone else is losing gallons of body fluid every minute, but Mr Statistics looks like he has never sweated in his life.

We start the second half positively. Campos comes under severe pressure from Tommy Coyne. Mr Statistics is at it again. He leans over and breathes a mouthful of mint at me. Ireland have only ever scored 3 World Cup goals in 6 matches, he goes, with the air of a medieval mystic announcing the meaning of life. I wish he would stop talking. Every time he opens his beak Mexico get the ball and nearly score. 'Ah, we're finished,' he says, leaning back and folding his arms, 'I'm telling you, the goose is cooked now, my son. We'd be as well to go on home.'

Garcia slithers into a brilliant position and narrowly misses, his shot just curling away from the post. Mr Statistics seems almost pleased. 'What did I say?' he barks at me, 'I told you, didn't I? We're washed up.' He does have a point, I must say. We are 51 minutes into the game and bloody fortunate not to be two goals down.

Shortly after this, Campos is booked for time-wasting, which cheers us all up no end. Terrible slurs of a politically incorrect nature are cast on Campos, on Señor Campos senior, on his good lady wife, on all of Campos's female siblings, on the family pet mongrel, and, indeed, on the entire Mexican nation. Suggestions are made as to what a person could most usefully do with a sombrero, and, suffice it to say, they do not involve the Mexican hat dance. Unfortunately, Campos then saves a John Sheridan shot, which puts the mockers on us again.

It is getting even hotter now. Garcia jostles Roy Keane, who turns and growls and looks as though he's just about ready to batter seven shades of guacamole out of him. 'Go on Roy,' shouts the Liverpool man, 'give the little spic a good kicking for himself. Go on Roy, rip his greasy head off.'

A halt is called to our fun when, in the 65th minute, disaster strikes.

Garcia scores again, this time blasting it in from the edge of the box. 'That's it,' says Mr Statistics, 'I knew that was going to happen, I told you, didn't I?'

Down on the touchline a row seems to be brewing between John Aldridge, who wants to come on, and one of the FIFA officials, who is preventing him from doing so. Aldridge seems to be pushing the official and roaring at him. 'Put the shagging boot into him, John,' Mr Liverpool roars, 'Get stuck in there, son.' 'That's not the way at all,' says Mr Statistics. 'Send him home to Dagoland in a coffin,' suggests the Liverpool man, 'rip his lungs out.' Aldridge and McAteer come on, but things are falling apart for Ireland. Phelan gets booked. He and Irwin will both miss the Norway game. 'We may as well go home now,' sighs Mr Statistics, 'there's no point really, not without those two.'

Garcia continues to be absolutely tireless, lobbing in shots from all angles, while our players are beginning to look like sponges which have been squeezed too hard. Then, suddenly, in the 83rd minute, Aldridge bullets in a brilliant header, which bounces right on the line before ending up in the back of the net.

'WAAHHAAYYYYYYY' cries the man behind me. 'YESSSSSSSS' roar the rest of the crowd. We jump up and down and hug each other, '*YESSSSSSSSSS, YESSSSSSS, YESSSSS.*' 'You know?' says Mr Statistics, calmly unwrapping another Glacier mint, 'that's actually John Aldridge's fourteenth goal for Ireland.'

Everyone is standing up and roaring now. For some endearing cultural reason or another, Mr Liverpool is leading a chorus of 'Are You Watching, England?' (The answer, presumably, being 'Yes, and we're enjoying every minute of your crushing defeat, sad Scouse loser.') Even Mr Statistics shuffles to his feet and cries feebly, 'Come on, boys.' I say I think it's too late. There's only a few minutes to go; there's no way we can score. 'Actually, you're wrong there,' says Mr Statistics, 'you see, in 7 of the 17 games played so far in USA '94, crucial goals have been scored in the last 5 minutes.'

I make up my mind that if he opens his mouth just once more I will kill him myself, with my bare hands, and then happily skip to the electric chair feeling I've accomplished something useful in my life.

The game boils to a frantic climax. Ireland try to press forward, but the players are absolutely shagged out. The Liverpool man is chanting 'You'll Never Beat the Irish', which, at this stage, sounds profoundly optimistic. In the last minute, Campos stops a thunder-bolt of a shot from bleach-blond Andy Townsend. One minute of injury time. Then two. Mr Roethlisburger looks at his watch, blows his whistle and poops our party, big time. We've been hammered. We sink back into our seats, groaning and cursing. 'That was quite a lot of injury time, wasn't it?' says Mr Statistics. 'Third highest amount in the whole tournament so far actually. Quite remarkable.'

'Anyway, bye then, I'm off. Best to get out early if you want to get a bus, you know, cheerio.' He stands up and leaves his seat and climbs down the big steps towards the exits. Myself and the Liverpool man catch each other's eye. 'Tosser,' the Liverpool man says. I cannot help but agree.

An Interview with Mary McAleese

VINCENT BROWNE (1998)

On 1 September 1997, Vincent Browne recorded an interview with Mary McAleese, the Pro-Vice Chancellor of Queen's University Belfast, for an RTÉ series entitled *Conversations With . . .* Shortly after the interview was taped, and before it could be broadcast, McAleese became the Fianna Fáil candidate for the Presidency in the election that autumn. The interview could not be broadcast after she became a candidate, and by the time she had been elected the series had concluded. Browne published a transcript of the interview in *Magill* in February 1998, under the heading 'What Have We Done? The Real Mary McAleese'.

Vincent Browne: *In 1984, you represented the Catholic hierarchy at the Forum for a New Ireland. It's therefore all the more surprising to read an article by you in the* Tablet *[15 March 1997] in which your critique of the Catholic Church and the Catholic hierarchy is in many ways as vehement a critique as you'd expect from Free Presbyterians. Why is that?*

Mary McAleese: Well, the difference between the two events you are referring to, an event in 1984 and an event in, I think, 1997 — there's been quite a trajectory of development and thinking in the meantime, both on my own part, I suppose, and on the part of the Church as well. It will come as no surprise to anybody to know that the hierarchy have been under quite an amount of critiquing for quite some time now, coming at them from a variety of sources.

But I think perhaps the strongest source of ongoing criticism or critiquing has come from within Christian feminism, and I count myself among that happy band of people who would regard themselves as Christian feminists. I think that it certainly shouldn't shock anybody that there's an impatience among women in the Church, who are committed to the Church, at what they perceive as a certain unwillingness, even at this late stage, to enter into the kind of dialogue one might have expected to have been entered into by now.

If you look back at the kind of things we were hearing after Vatican II, and in particular some of the comments of Pope Paul VI, who talked about the need to engage women in dialogue and who talked very openly about the fact that women's talents and giftedness within the Church had not been fully utilised and who looked forward to the day when they might be, I think that people are entitled to feel, perhaps, some sense of impatience that we've just never, we've never opened up that debate – and if anything we've watched the closing down of that debate.

You're almost contemptuously dismissive of the present pope in his efforts to apologise on behalf of the Church for the wrongs done to women by the Church.

I hope that's not true. I hope that that isn't the tone in which it was written. I don't regard the present pope contemptuously at all. I have an enormous admiration for him, but also, apart from the great impatience at his failure to engage in a dialogue that he, I think, as an intelligent man, must know is coming at him from, you know, from all areas and all parts.

You wrote in the Tablet *in March 1997, 'The very fact that this pope has felt it necessary to return frequently in the past few years to the subject of women tells its own story. His words are not those of a man who believes he is on the comfortable side of a debate. Far from it; they are the words of a man who is slowly realising that the citadel's defences have been breached and its once staunch defenders are a declining population.'*

I hope that doesn't carry with it a hint of contempt, I wouldn't like that . . .

Almost a hint of hypocrisy . . .

On the part of the pope?

Yes.

Well, I think that what I'm saying there is that the evidence is all around him of a very, very, very loud and vocal and unhappy debate from within the Church. A widespread debate on the issue of the lack of openness that the Church is offering to women and, indeed, to laity generally, but particularly to women. And I think there is a genuine sense of impatience. People have responded, perhaps with some degree of concern, to the way in which over the last year, two years, instead of opening up the debate, we've had the declaration, for example in relation to women and ordination, a declaration that purports to be an infallible doctrine. Now, I could see where a doctrine like that might happen, though I hope it wouldn't happen, but I could see where it might happen after a very long and detailed look at 2,000 years of sexism and the damage that has done to the Church. Particularly when this pope and his predecessor, Pope Paul VI, and indeed John XXIII, all acknowledged that there was a problem, if you like, at the heart of the Church, of sexism.

It seems to me once you acknowledge that, it's very important that you then explore it and you ask yourself the question, 'Well, what damage has that done, and before we make any decision about how we would go forward, let's understand where we've come from.' I mean, it's not a question of just doing damage in the Church. It's also done damage to the wider society and done damage particularly to women.

That's correct.

You've characterised the absorption of women in that sexist culture [. . .] What's surprising, perhaps, is that you could remain so staunchly with an institution that is so flawed fundamentally.

Of course it's flawed. It's always been flawed. But fundamentally, the Church has been flawed from the very earliest days. I mean, I love the Church. I love it with a tremendous fondness and a determination that I'm going to remain as fond of it as I've always been.

Why do you remain fond of an institution that has done such damage?

Well, because I look at, you know, at the founding stone on which the Church was first based, the first great apostle, Peter, and you know, he was no great shakes. The man was a coward and a liar according to the gospel, someone who denied Christ . . .

He was a misogynist as well.

Well, and very likely. Certainly, that probably is true. But I also look at what the Church, what is it a repository [of] at the end of the day, and at the end of the day it's also my spiritual home. I look at the history of the Church. There have been many, many worse epochs than this. There's been far worse hypocrisy in the Church than this. I see it growing as an institution. I see it having enormous influence globally if it can be brought off the learning curve. And there's plenty of evidence that it will eventually be dragged, screaming, up, you know, up the equal-opportunities learning curve.

And for me that's very important, because the reach of the Church globally is such that if it once made that option for women, if it once was able to admit in humility that it has been wrong, that it has played its own part and, indeed, it has not been the only agency – it certainly has not monopolised sexism. I mean, it has been a cultural feature right across the globe of many, many cultures, many religions, many. Indeed, many cultures that don't even have an apparent relationship with a strong religious ethos or ethic. And so, I would take that view, that I can patiently wait – well, maybe impatiently wait – for the Church to come up that learning curve, precisely because its reach is so global. And I think the transformative effect once it makes that option for women could be quite stunning.

You write in this article in the Tablet, *'Women have observed the enormous drain of heterosexual males from the priesthood and the growing phenomenon of gay priests. They are quietly asking what is happening at the core of the call to priesthood that attracts homosexuals in much greater numbers than their popu-lation distribution would explain.' In society at large, I assume.*

You have to read the next bit of that to make sure that you make it clear that I was not being homophobic.

All right . . .

Because I'm a very strong . . .

You deny being homophobic, but . . .

I am and have been a very strong defender of gay rights.

Maybe I will read the next bit: 'These questions are not being raised in any homophobic way but are among the raft of questions bubbling to the surface as we struggle to come to terms with the manifest demise of the model of the priest-hood on which the priest–mother alliance was once founded and is now floundering.'

Yes.

I don't see how that detracts from the core of the criticism that you make, that it is becoming a priesthood dominated by gay priests.

I didn't say that it was dominated by gay priests. Now, I think what's important to say is that the core . . . The call to the priesthood that attracts homosexuals in such greater numbers. I think it is impor-tant. I'm bearing in mind you've only read this article five minutes before we started this conversation, and it took me a very long time to put that article together, and every word is balanced and measured. What I'm trying to get across is the changed demography of priesthood in a very, very short space of time. All of us who lived through the 1970s and the 1980s will know of the enormous drain away and the impact that the debate on celibacy has had on that drain. We also know that – and I suppose it's a matter of public record – the concerns that have been expressed, particularly, for example, in American seminaries about the increased phenomenon of large numbers of young gay men being attracted to the priesthood. Now, I have no difficulty with young gay men being attracted to the priesthood, but that was what I was at pains to point out there. What I am concerned about is what's wrong with priesthood that we are not also able to attract a similar number, in proportion to their . . . That there is something about the priesthood that is particularly attractive to homosexuals. I don't know, you see. And I pose the question there. I'm not sure what the answer to this perplexing issue is. I'm saying that it's an issue that people have observed, and they are quietly – and I said it there – they are quietly pondering these things and saying, 'Well, what direction, down what vortex is the priesthood being taken?'

Does it matter whether the priesthood is gay or not?

Well, it would matter to this extent, that I would like to see a priesthood that is a healthy priesthood in the sense of being able to attract a wide variety and across the spectrum, the human spectrum, of men and women, of all genders and all sexual orientations. I would be concerned if it was unable to do that.

Insofar as it attracts heterosexuals to the priesthood, you could argue with some justification that the people who are attracted are in a large measure dysfunctional.

Well, I don't know that to be true. And I would . . .

Do you suspect that? Is that not part of the point you are making?

No, I don't think so. I don't think that is part of the point that I'm making. What I'm saying is that the nature . . . I think it is very important that it's not seen . . . this is not really seen as an article about . . . in fact that was a small part of an overall article about priesthood. What I'm saying is that the priesthood as we have known it and as I grew up with it has changed so phenomenally and over a very short space of time. People are only beginning to acclimatise to those changes. I mean, frankly, many people are not even sure of what those changes mean – in what direction this priesthood is going. The only questions that I'm raising there really are sort of speaking out of my own heart and of my own experience, saying what is happening at the core of priesthood. Manifestly, there is something wrong with the model of priesthood as we have experienced it.

Sounds very anti-clerical.

Well, it might, it might. I think the kind of clericalism that, the kind of clerical Church that we have come from is nowadays perceived widely as in fairly radical need of reform.

I raise that point because in April 1984, at the Lenten talk in the Pro-Cathedral, you said that the division between northern nationalists and loyalists was no more bitter and no more real than the gulf between Catholic and anti-clerical in Dublin. The gulf between you and the Catholic Church would appear to be at least as large.

Well, I hope that's not true. As I say, I am a very committed and loving member of the Church. I think the world has moved on very considerably since 1984 . . .

Do you have any sense of embarrassment at your identification with a hierarchy that you castigate so seriously?

Absolutely not. Absolutely not. Absolutely not. I have tremendous admiration for many of our hierarchy. I think that they operate, you know, within a system that of its nature is really very confining, and they find themselves in a kind of situation quite different now from 1984. I mean, the world has moved on very considerably, put them under enormous pressure, not least through the kind of scandals that they've endured, not least because of the growing, if you like, the mainstreaming of issues like Christian feminism. Twenty years ago, 15 years ago, many of these issues were regarded, if you like, as outside the Church rather than within the mainstream of the Church. They've now come firmly inside the mainstream, and I think the world has moved on; particularly the world of the Church has moved on quite phenomenally in the period of 14 years since then.

In Fionnuala O Connor's book In Search of a State: Catholics in Northern Ireland, *you're quoted as saying, as uttering another criticism of the Church:* 'You never hear that from the bishops, the voice of forgiveness. The person we associate most strongly with forgiveness was not a churchman at all but the father of a girl who died in Enniskillen.' *Gordon Wilson.* 'Are they afraid to say it? I think possibly they are. I am quite happy to say this because I said it to the cardinal.' *That's Cardinal Daly, I assume.* 'Face to face, told the bishops it.' *This is in relation to the Church's teaching on the Provos. What did you have in mind then?*

It's a while back, but I think what I was saying, and I think it is probably as valid today as it was then, is that the . . . As I look back on Northern Ireland and as I look back on, you know, the absolutely appalling things that have happened, every atrocity produced a litany of condemnation and righteous condemnation, but the voice that said, you know, 'Father forgive them, for they know not what they do,' the voice of the gospel, was a very muted, a very, very muted voice, and it always struck me as very strange that when Gordon Wilson spoke those words, you know, it was almost as if he was speaking them for the first time, or as if they were being spoken for the first time, because they seemed to almost stop the moment. I'm sure people know that Gordon Wilson, God rest him, had no easy ride after he uttered those words. There were many people who were offended by what he said and, you know, who sent him hate mail and who told him he had no business forgiving and how dare he forgive. Literally as if he were saying these words for the very first time. And, unfortunately, I think it has been the case that the churches in Northern Ireland have been seen more as part of the problem, in the sense that there's a perception, rightly or wrongly, that they have tended to bleed more when their own side bled – that they have been more concerned with the language of politics than to really preach the gospel emphatically, and I think that is generally true.

You were born in Belfast, of course, and brought up in the Ardoyne and experienced a lot of the troubles there in the early 1970s. And then you came to live in the South, and particularly while you worked in RTÉ you were regarded as a 'Provo' very often.

I hope that's not true. Where on earth did you get that from?

From interviews that you gave yourself. You said that you were treated as though you were a Provo.

Ah well, we are talking about a very small coterie of people who might have regarded ... who might have used that epithet and, indeed, whom I eventually took to court and sued successfully. That would not have been generally or universally true. But I think you and I both know that in RTÉ at that time [in the early 1980s] it was a very, very unhealthy place in which to work. It was deeply conspiratorial, and it was an extraordinary place to work, and I must say I was probably quite an innocent abroad. I am not now, never have been and, please God, never will be a supporter of IRA violence. Indeed, unlike most of my colleagues in RTÉ, if in fact not all of them, I had endured that violence, my parents had been victims of it. We had a business that was fire-bombed by the IRA, so why would I have any particular brief for them? But when I came to work in RTÉ, I was surprised by the level to which, as an institution, it had come to be, effectively, in the grip of people who had very, very, very strong political views and who to some extent appeared to use their power within the media to give voice to those views – and who were very, I think perhaps tragically, dismissive of other people's views. I suppose what I'm saying really, something that I think is generally true of Ireland as a whole, is that it was not a very good listening environment. That when people said something with which you disagreed, instead of listening and trying to understand where that person was coming from, it was always so much easier to label them – and once you've put the label on, you didn't have to deal with what they were saying, you were able to stereotype them, to dismiss it.

In this Fionnuala O Connor book that I mentioned earlier, you're quoted as saying, 'I'd a dreadful time' – this was when you were with RTÉ – 'I'd a dreadful time with the Workers' Party, people who now [1993] hold very important positions in RTÉ, people whose idea of coming to the North was to talk to Unionist politicians whom they cultivated in a really obsequious way, to talk to other Workers' Party people and then to come back to Dublin and tell what was happening in the North.' Was this something that you experienced frequently?

It wasn't all of the time, but it was certainly a significant part of

Great Irish Reportage

the time. It wasn't just my experience, it was the experience, I think, of many of us who worked there. I think it is fairly well documented. I think, actually, you might be one of the people who also documented it very well during that time. It was very unhealthy. Very unhealthy and a very unhappy, personally very unhappy, time for me.

I have no problem with cultivating unionist politicians. I think that we should all be cultivated, and I think that part of what we urgently need in Ireland – have needed for some very long time – has been this ability to listen to each other with respect, even if we are hearing things that deeply burn us and hurt us. But in those days that was not what was happening. That was not what was happening.

You also said that RTÉ was a deeply sexist institution.

It was dreadfully so. Does that come as a surprise to you?

Could you explain why you thought that?

Well, I felt it. I felt it to be so.

How did it manifest itself?

Well, I used to look around at the very talented women, and [RTÉ] wasn't a place that celebrated the gifts of women to any significant extent at that time. It wasn't very affirmative of women, and particularly now, as I look over the last ten or eleven or twelve years – and have done quite a bit of work in the field of equal opportunities – I realise that it badly needed a dose of equal-opportunities training. There was just a very poor consciousness, really, about the extent to which women were stereotyped, and their skills and their giftedness were kept corralled effectively. I don't think all that is generally any longer true. I think that there are some marvellous women who have made great contributions now in RTÉ, but at that time I have to say that it was a very highly sexist environment. It wasn't a very particularly pleasant environment generally, though. By its nature, I think television tends to produce prima donnas, and it also tends to produce a level of, let's say, everyday social intercourse, you know, that can sometimes get quite shrill as an environment. And you need to have a fairly thick skin to endure it.

Were you a prima donna?

Well now, the awful thing about prima donnas is that they totally, utterly lack any personal insight, so I think you'd have to ask other people about that. I, of course, would tell you no, never. It wouldn't be in my nature.

It wasn't a particularly successful period for you career-wise, was it? And therefore I wonder whether your criticisms of RTÉ now are somewhat coloured by the lack of success.

Do you think so? I've never heard that said before. I always thought that I was reasonably successful; I made my own career choices, but I'd be interested to hear what you have to say about it. It's the first time it's ever been put to me in that way.

In a passage of the interview [with Fionnuala O Connor] where you spoke about Dublin being a very shocking experience, you went on as saying, 'But I went there first when Conor Cruise O'Brien was in the ascendant, and if ever anyone was a culture shock, Conor Cruise O'Brien was to me. Here was this extraordinarily arrogant man in the process of revising everything that I had known to be a given and a truth about Irish history, and he set in motion a way of looking at Northern Ireland that we are only now beginning to grow up and grow out of.'

So I think it is important to say that that shock, if you like, was, and what I was referring to in the book was the culture shock of coming down from the North in 1975 and coming away from an environment that I really did want to escape, because we had just been through so much personal family pain, and I wanted to make a fresh start.

What was that personal family pain?

We endured a lot as a family. We had our home several times attacked in sectarian attacks. My brother, who is profoundly deaf, was very badly assaulted, a murderous attack on him. We had two gentlemen come to our door with sub-machine guns, which they emptied through our windows, and it's only God's mercy that we weren't killed. My father's two businesses were, one of them blown up, the other one fire-bombed.

Two pubs.

Yes. A young girl killed, a young mother killed in the second explosion. On the morning I was married, two of my very dear friends were murdered on the morning of my wedding. And many,

many of my friends – because I lived in Ardoyne – were murdered in sectarian murders, so there would have been a litany of things. Any one of them happening over a lifetime would produce trauma and would produce stress. At that time, they were happening to so many people, and we came out of an environment, I think, which is inherently stoical, which teaches you to take things on the chin, not to articulate your pain – and particularly when other people around you were suffering and enduring much, much worse than we had endured. I don't think that we dealt with it terribly well. I still don't think that as a community we have dealt with these things terribly well.

So that was the background. I was coming away from that, my parents had just left Belfast. They had uprooted after a lifetime there, they had uprooted a family of nine children to move to a small village to find peace and tranquillity somewhere. And I then moved on to Dublin, and I came with a great hope and expectation that – and I've said this before – that I thought I was coming, in a sense, to a spiritual and, if you like, political homeland. Now, if that was naivety on my part – and I now look on reflection, I had no right to expect that, I had no right to expect that of Dublin – and I suppose when I came and found this extraordinary man, Conor Cruise [O'Brien], who, at the time when he spoke, I used to say to people, 'He sounds like a unionist,' and they'd say, 'Oh no, he's an Irish nationalist.' And then, thankfully, in later life he obliged me by joining the United Kingdom Unionist Party, which helped enormously, but didn't give me much comfort in those days.

But wasn't the journalism of Conor Cruise O'Brien a very important antidote to the unquestioning nationalist assumptions that we lived with here for so many years?

Well, I think it's important to question and challenge, you're quite right to critique, and I don't in any shape or form say that what we lived through was a healthy analysis of Irish nationalism. I think it was very important that we did open it up, explore it, look at its mythologies, look at its language, look at the way in which, you know, it cultivated the cult of martyr, particularly the blood sacrifice. All of that which we've lived with the dreadful legacy of. So yes.

On the other hand, I'm not so sure that what was being held up as, if you like, the opposing version was any nearer, if you like, a truth or the truth. But I think that we have kind of stumbled our way to a variety of versions of the truth in the meantime, and I also think about that period that it was a harsh, very harsh period. People roared at each other, you know, across barricades. It wasn't a seemly debate, it wasn't a courteous debate. It was a very contemptuous debate. I don't think ultimately it conduced to the good of the community, that kind of shrill debate.

But you are right to say, yes it is very important, and it still remains important, not to accept the myths and mythologies and the givens of the past. I mean, I think that one of the things that I've become most conscious of in the intervening years has been this need to unlearn so many of the things that we went to an awful lot of bother either to be taught or to learn.

What is the main element of what you've unlearnt?

I don't think it comes down to one element. I think it comes down to a lot of things, to many, many things – the first process of unlearning is to try and develop an ear for listening to those people who in the past one has been trained really to listen to in a very curious kind of way, because [those] who one is politically opposed to are speaking. Even if you are not actually talking back, you are firing back almost verbal Exocets in your head as they speak, you see. Now, I think one of the things that I've tried, successfully or unsuccessfully, to do over the last number of years is to train myself to listen, to understand where they are coming from, precisely because I would like that same understanding and, if you like, that kind of same respectful listening for where I'm coming from.

Given what you and your family experienced when you were in your child-hood and early adulthood, were you ever attracted to the republican movement?

No. No, I could have been [but] I wasn't, and thanks be to God I wasn't. I think perhaps that's also why the stereotyping of one's political views was so hurtful, because from a very early stage in the troubles, right from the very beginning – I mean, I was born and reared in Ardoyne, lived right through the worst of the times, right through the B Specials, the burning down of homes of people who lived beside me, so there was a lot to be provoked by, there was a lot to be hurt by. And when you're 17 or 18, the passions run high. Naturally, it is attractive to be drawn into that, if you like that vortex of violence. And I'm always very grateful that I wasn't, though a number of people whom I knew and knew well were, but I wasn't.

I think one of the reasons for that was that I always had – first of all, I came from a very prayerful home, I came from a home where, you know, religion, and not religiosity but religion, actually did play a part and where the gospel meant something. And so that side of me was fairly well developed, if you like. The spiritual side of me was fairly well developed, and that's the side that I think kept me, that acted as a kind of cantilever to the, you know, the pull of violence.

Are you still a nationalist, or has that process of unlearning led you away from nationalism?

No, I wouldn't say it's led me away from nationalism, but what it has done, though, is revise the rather crude early perspective that I would have had on nationalism. I would still regard myself and would define myself as an Irish nationalist, yes. And then, beyond that, though, when I talk about or when I would talk about, for example, the ambition that is at the heart of Irish nationalism, is for an Ireland that is united. Now, when I was growing up that was a very crude kind of term, and when I realised that the one and a half million unionists who live in Northern Ireland identified that simply as meaning that they would be totally overwhelmed; that their viewpoint would simply be subsumed, would be ignored, it would be, you know, wiped away – I think the process of unlearning and the process of redefining nationalism for me has meant that I now come to the issue of where we're up to, for example, in Northern Ireland as we approach talks, which we hope will lead to consensus, that I have a very open view now about what shape Ireland might take for the future. I'd be very open about the kind of consensus that might come out of a dialogue between nationalists and unionists in Ireland and Britain as to the future of this island.

The old, if you like that old image, that old and rather crude concept of a united Ireland, the words, the concept that is raised by that image, I think, no longer fits the profile of where a modern Ireland would like to go to. I think that we have to be open to the possibility that what we're looking at is quite a complex set of arrangements.

That complex set of arrangements would inevitably involve a respect for other values and of other ideals. Have you in political positions you've taken on issues, such as divorce and abortion, been sensitive to those considerations?

I'm not too sure to what extent they play into the issue of Catholic versus Protestant or nationalism versus unionism. Funnily enough, I don't regard those, fundamentally, as two issues that touch on the issue of nationalism and unionism. I know they can be perceived as such, because of what is perceived as being the confessional nature of the Irish state, but, for example, even in Northern Ireland I was deeply conscious of the fact that in relation to divorce we never followed the British. The law that applied in Great Britain was always aeons further down the line than in Northern Ireland, because there was a spectrum of thought. By and large, Northern Ireland tended to be much more conservative and still, indeed, is much more conservative on both those issues than would be Great Britain generally, and on those issues was much closer to the spectrum of thought that existed in the Republic. I think these are issues that are global; every community, every society faces them and deals with them and deliberates upon them with the same passion, and exactly the same argument and the same shift of focus as we have experienced here.

Except that on the issue of divorce, for instance, the rhetoric of the Catholic Church during the divorce referendum, of the Catholic hierarchy during the divorce referendum, was very much to the effect that their version or their view of the common good is something that ought to be embraced by society as a whole, irrespective of minority views and what might be termed pluralities.

Well, I think you'd have to address them on that. I didn't write their scripts for them and, thankfully, that's not a position that I would have ever taken myself; so I think that's a matter that you'd really want to address to them.

You flirted with Fianna Fáil for quite a long time. Indeed, you were a candidate for Fianna Fáil.

You call that flirting; now, you must have confused this expression 'flirting'.

How would you describe it?

I joined Fianna Fáil.

Held hands . . .

Held hands?

You ran for the party in 1987 in Dublin, and in the run-up to that you described Éamon de Valera as the greatest visionary Ireland has had.

Mmmmm.

That was very far-fetched.

Was it? Sure, we all say those sorts of things in a moment . . .

When we're looking for a nomination . . .

. . . In a moment. May I say, I do have great admiration for Éamon de Valera. Enormous admiration for him.

Is it still your view that he was the greatest visionary Ireland ever had?

I think he was a tremendous visionary, yes. But Ireland . . . I mean, it depends on your time scale, you know, it really does depend on the time scale. There are new visionaries will have emerged, but I wouldn't take from him. No, I would not take from him what he achieved, and leaving it back I think one of the difficulties – isn't it, you know, ipso facto – looking back over history we're a very cynical lot, and we've an awful habit of looking back over people's, you know, even the most gifted of people and looking straight for the clay feet. I think, taken in the round, yes, he was a visionary and, yes, he made an enormous contribution . . .

You also said around that time about Charles Haughey, 'Yes, I do admire the man, and my husband, Martin, is a relentless Charlie fan. I admire in him predominantly his staying power and ability not to cave in in the face of the relentless pursuit of him by the media and, indeed, from within his own party. I also have a very deep admiration for anyone whom the British government fears, and I'm sure they fear Charlie.'

Mmmm.

Do you now have the same opinion of him?

Well, now. We're all an awful lot older and an awful lot wiser, Vincent, you and I both, and I wouldn't take from him his innovative skills in those days when I first came to Dublin. And one of the things that I found interesting about him was the fact that many of the things which were innovative in terms of legislation had his stamp on them somewhere, and that was intriguing and interesting and I wouldn't take that from him. But we all know now what the story was, a story that I certainly didn't know anything about until the McCracken tribunal, any more than you or anybody else.

You didn't know in 1984 that his lifestyle was such as not to be conceivably affordable by the income he was getting as a public representative?

Well, how would I have known that? How would I particularly have known that?

Everyone in the country had known that.

Did they? And what did you do about it as well? You were working in the field of journalism, like myself, at that time. You know, some of these things are tediously silly, really, Vincent. I mean, a lot of people asked questions at that time and, with the greatest respect to those people who now look back, I mean I would have to say to you about that time, there were a lot of questions around at that time, and my view as a lawyer would be very, very simple. If people have allegations to make, let them make the allegations and let them stand over them.

There were hundreds of people at that time who made those allegations who never at the end of the day saw them through to the end of the line. And it seems to me extraordinary looking back on those days now, now that we know the story, the story's actually beyond credulity, it is so dreadful, and it shows, if you like, such a contempt on his part for people like me, actually, and for other people who did have a faith in him and who did believe that when he talked about his vision for Ireland and that when he did defend the nation and when he was essentially one of Ireland's first citizens, and, when you think about, one should have and would be entitled to have both a respect and pride in one's politicians – and that when I look back on that and see how people like me were essentially duped.

Yes, one does feel very foolish, not surprised, not shocked, but one feels very, very foolish. But I'd have to say that it wasn't my function then as a very small underling in a party. I didn't know the man hardly at all, I'd barely met him, maybe I saw him once or twice, maybe, in my entire life. There were people who were around him who were very, very close to him, there were institutions of the state, there were tax collectors, tax inspectors, all sorts of people who would have a role to ask the very questions – I think you're, you know, you're posing now – and more importantly to take those tracks and to track right down to the very end, and they did not do that, and I think those questions still remain open. It just strikes me as extraordinary that we only now have this appalling insight into this man and to the, I suppose, to the strange nature of this man, this very twisted nature, and we only have that because of a private family dispute that went awry. Not one single organ of the state, not one single journalist, not one single politician, not one single person who was in a position to alter the course of history actually did it in relation to Charlie Haughey. It was only almost by, you know, by happenstance, by accident or coincidence, that he managed to be found out before eventually death got him.

Mary McAleese, thank you.

'Glasses Needed for 977'

MARY RAFTERY AND EOIN O'SULLIVAN (1999)

The incarceration and abuse of young children in mainly religious-run Irish institutions, with the collusion of the state and society, finally became an unavoidable crisis of the national conscience in the 1990s. The journalist who spearheaded this reckoning was Mary Raftery, whose 1999 RTÉ television documentary *States of Fear* forced a laggardly state to begin to accept its share of responsibility. In their book *Suffer the Little Children: The Inside Story of Ireland's Industrial Schools*, extracted here, Raftery and the sociologist Eoin O'Sullivan developed the reporting and research first brought to the attention of the public in *States of Fear*.

One of the most enduring legacies of the industrial schools was the sense of shame they instilled in the minds of many who grew up there. It has dogged the survivors of the system, often for their entire lives. Even some of those now in their eighties continue to feel that society looks down on them because of their upbringing. There are still many, particularly those living in small rural areas, who while they were happy to have their stories told in this book, felt that to fully reveal their own identities would expose them to hostility within their communities.

This reveals two important aspects of the industrial schools system. Firstly, the general popular view of these children was that they were mainly either criminals or born out of wedlock. Consequently, they quickly learnt to hide their origins, and there are those even today who feel unable to tell their partners or their children about where they themselves grew up.

Secondly, there was the fact that as children, they were constantly told that they were no good, that they had been rejected, and that it was their own fault that they had ended up in industrial schools. This was such a persistent aspect of the schools that many of those who emerged from them actually believed it, and tragically in some cases continue to suffer today from an enormous lack of self-confidence.

Occasionally in their adult lives, many attempted to reveal to those around them some limited aspects of what had happened to them as children. That they were universally not believed served to reinforce their isolation and the sense that they were themselves in some way responsible for the way in which they had been abused by their carers – nuns and brothers who were held by society in the highest esteem.

It was not only society at large that had such a disastrously inaccurate understanding of the nature of industrial schools and those detained within them. The victims of this system themselves equally had no clear view of how it operated. Most of them believed all their lives that they were objects of the charity of religious orders. This is what they had been told by the nuns and brothers who raised them, and they were instructed that they should be grateful to them and to God for this. Many survivors speak of guilt they experienced when feeling anger, rather than gratitude, towards the nuns and brothers, and even towards God. Had they been aware that it was in fact the State, and not the Catholic Church, who paid to maintain them in the schools – that they as children were funded as of right and not out of charity – they might well have been able to develop a very different view of their undoubted worth and value within society.

The charity myth was so pervasive that many well-meaning local people believed it their duty to assist the industrial schools, or 'orphanages', as they were more euphemistically called, in their area. Former inmates speak with great gratitude of local communities organising summer outings or parties at Christmas. Both the buildings and the children always looked their best on these occasions. The premises were spotlessly clean, and the children well-dressed and happy looking. From the point of view of those who had contact with the industrial schools in this way, nothing appeared amiss. They were not to know that it was the children themselves who had slaved to polish every corner of the building until it shone, that any fruit or flowers on display would be immediately removed after the event, that the children only ever wore those nice clothes when visitors were around, and that any presents the youngsters were given, at Christmas or Easter for instance, were very often taken away from them as soon as their benefactors had left.

It was partly this two-faced nature of the institutions which allowed them to exist unchallenged for so many decades. While people clearly pitied the unfortunate children, they preferred to believe the superficial evidence presented to them that things were perhaps not so bad for the inmates after all.

Many people, however, do have memories of the 'orphanage' children which did disturb them. The people of Galway noticed that the children from St Joseph's Industrial School in Salthill, run by the Christian Brothers, used to go swimming on one of the poorest beaches in the area, that which was closest to a sewage outlet. They rarely appeared near any of the better swimming spots. People living close to the school also vividly remember hearing the screams of children at night, and simply not knowing what to do about it. This is also reported for Daingean, the tiny village in Co. Offaly which housed the country's only reformatory for boys. People there talk about the same sense of paralysis as to what, if any, action they could take.

The people of Dun Laoghaire have vivid memories of the children from Carraiglea Park Industrial School, also run by the Christian Brothers, being taken for their weekly walks. They describe being able to hear them before they saw them – the sound of 100 pairs of hobnail boots hitting the pavement in unison as they were marched around military style. A well-known comedian who often entertained school groups has said that the hardest audience he ever played was the children from Glin Industrial School in County Limerick, another Christian Brothers institution. They never once even smiled, and watched the entertainment nervously as black-clad Brothers patrolled the hall.

There is also the indelible memory of the boys of Artane Industrial School brought to the occasional GAA match in Croke Park, carefully policed by Christian Brothers, and confined in what people describe as a cage-like area. Spectators used to sometimes throw them sweets or cigarettes – almost like feeding the animals in the zoo. The boys, however, were delighted to get out and grateful for anything thrown to them.

The publicity surrounding the 1963 incident in Bundoran involving the shaving of girls' heads in the local industrial school also had a deep impact on the local community. The phrase 'a Bundoran haircut' entered the local vocabulary, and children all along the border counties were threatened with this if they misbehaved.

The practice in industrial schools of bringing the children out for a walk, usually on a Sunday, is one which has often been remarked on. In towns the length and breadth of the country, they were highly visible on these occasions, marching two-by-two in a long file, with a nun or a Brother at either end. Many people remember the children looking different from the norm, being abnormally subdued and docile.

People in the general community would also have been aware of the industrial school children in many of the local primary schools. In several towns, these schools were run by the Sisters of Mercy and were part of the complex which also housed an industrial school. In class, the local town children mixed with what were often referred to as the 'house' children. In very many cases, the industrial school inmates received considerably harsher treatment than did the children from the outside community, and this would generally have been well-known.

Another point of contact with the general population was the fact that many families took in industrial school children for a holiday during the summer. This was usually for only a week or two, but the children were often visibly miserable on having to return to their industrial school. With a few notable exceptions where they were abused by these families, most inmates speak of these holidays as being the happiest times of their young lives. They were often amazed by the quantity of food served to them – what would have been considered normal meals by these families. RTE television carried an extraordinary interview with one such young boy in the early 1960s who had spent time with a family in the Kilkenny area – he listed at great length, and in palpable awe, all the different types of food he had been given to eat during his stay. He remarked with pride that he was even provided with a knife and fork to eat his meals with, something he clearly had never experienced before.

There was one town where the community was brought into close contact with its industrial school in the most tragic way. This was in Cavan, in 1943, when St Joseph's Industrial School, run by the Order of the Poor Clares, burnt to the ground, killing thirty-five children and one elderly woman.

It is also revealing to examine the Department of Education's files on the Cavan fire. For such an enormously tragic event, they are remarkably scant. The bulk of the documents deal with how likely the Department was to be sued as a result of the disaster. The inquiry team's report had strongly indicated that the Department should have been much more rigorous in its inspection of the fire safety precautions. However, Department files show that they concluded that as there were no known parental addresses for ten of the dead children, and most of the others had been committed at a very young age, the State was unlikely to face compensation claims. There is no record in the Department's files if it ever did.

It is interesting to note that in the Department's file on the Cavan fire, the dead children are referred to by their numbers. The practice of assigning a number to each child in an industrial school was universal. In several schools, the children were called only by their numbers, with their names never being used. This practice died out in the 1960s.

Official documentation also commonly used the numbering system. Lists of numbers appear in Department of Education files under the heading 'the following for dental treatment' – often names are not mentioned. An entry in one file, for instance, refers to 'glasses needed for 977'. While the numbering system might have had certain practical uses in dealing with such large groups of children, former inmates testify strongly to its dehumanising effect on them. Many believe the use of numbers served to reinforce the view that they were inferior and consequently made it easier for nuns and Brothers to beat and abuse them.

Even in death, industrial school children were treated differently to others. The victims of the Cavan fire were buried in a mass grave

in the town graveyard, marked only by a small metal cross. No dates
or names were marked on the cross, only an inscription which read
'In Memoriam to the Orphans who died in St Joseph's Industrial
School, Cavan. May They Rest in Peace. Amen'. The impression was
clear – these children did not exist as individuals, but only as a group
to be prayed for. During the 1980s, this cross was replaced with a
headstone. All reference to the industrial school or the fire was
removed. It merely said 'In Loving Memory of the Little Ones of St
Clare. R.I.P. Children pray for us'.

There was one constant theme that continuously informed the
way in which industrial school children were treated. That was the
clear perception from the religious that they were in some way less
valuable and less worthy than other children. Much of this view was
shared by society in general, and gives a unique insight into the
nuances of the very rigid class system which operated in Ireland during this century. The fact that the children themselves were in no
way responsible for their condition in life did not appear to mitigate
the view that they were less deserving than children from better-off
backgrounds, and were consequently treated accordingly. Nowhere
was this more true than in the harshness reserved for the many so-
called illegitimate children within the system.

It is not possible to give accurate figures for the numbers of such
children in industrial schools. Statistics were never properly com-
piled by the system, although the schools' admission forms for each
child did have a heading marked 'illegitimate'. However, it is clear
that they were always in a minority within the industrial schools.

Across the board these children were singled out for particularly
severe treatment, and were invariably those who were confined to
menial cleaning and washing duties, particularly in the girls' schools.
The Department of Education's discovery in 1952 that many nuns
actually believed that illegitimate children were barred from employment in the civil service gives some indication of the extraordinary
depth of prejudice against these children that existed in the minds of
the religious. The Department hastened to disabuse them of this false
notion.

One such group spread across the schools was that of black or 'coloured' children, as they were called. A number of them have spoken out prominently in recent years about their experiences in industrial schools – Christine Buckley in St Vincent's, Goldenbridge, Sharon Murphy in St Joseph's, Clifden, and Kevin Sharkey in St Joseph's, Salthill. During Sharon's time in Clifden in the 1960s and 1970s, there were a total of eleven other black children there. She describes how they generally did not experience racism within the school, but rather they were singled out for comment by the locals whenever they went into the town.

The Department of Education commented on these children in 1966, saying that:

... their future especially in the case of the girls presented a problem difficult of any satisfactory solution. Their prospects of marriage especially in this country are practically nil and their future happiness and welfare can only be assured in a country with a fair multi-racial population, since they are not well received by either 'black or white' ... It was quite apparent the nuns give special attention to these unfortunate children who are frequently found hot tempered and difficult to control. The coloured boys do not present quite the same problem. It would seem that they also got special attention and that they were popular with the other boys.

Not only were these remarks racist, they were also inaccurate. Many of these so-called 'coloured' children now testify that they received no such 'special attention' – they say that they received the same beatings and abuse as most of the other children within the system.

It does seem that, in general, girls (whether black or white) born to single parents were more harshly treated in this regard than boys. While all the orders of nuns who ran industrial schools were guilty of this, several accounts point to the Good Shepherd Sisters as being especially hard on the so-called illegitimate children in their care.

Many single mothers who gave birth in Mother and Baby homes gave up their babies to the religious orders running these institutions. While some were informally adopted, a high proportion ended up in industrial schools. They had been given up so young that contact with their mothers was very often permanently lost.

However, there was a significant number of single mothers who did try to keep their children with them. This was no easy task, and a combination of pressure from their families and communities, and a genuine belief that the child might be better off, often resulted in committal to industrial schools for the infant. In many of these cases, the mothers did manage to maintain some contact with their children through visits, which usually were allowed only once a month.

However, the industrial schools made no attempt to facilitate these visits. The mothers were often treated disdainfully by the nuns, and this was usually in front of their children. Many former inmates report that their mothers were not even allowed inside the building for visits, which had to take place outdoors regardless of the weather.

This was particularly hard, especially as in many cases the mother was herself paying for the upkeep of her child or children. These 'parental monies', as they were known, are one of the more mysterious aspects of the system. In Dublin, there was a specific official of the Department of Education assigned to this task, known as the 'Parental Money Collector'. Elsewhere in the country, the money was collected by the local Gardaí.

The Parental Monies scheme illustrated a particular attitude to the parents of children in industrial schools – namely that they should be in some way penalised for being unable to bring up their own children. This was very much part of the rationale of the times – that people who were either single parents or who were simply poor were the architects of their own misfortune. Amounts extorted in this way by the State from parents varied during the 1950s from 2/6 to 10 shillings a week per child, a substantial sum for many who could ill afford it. Many young single mothers, especially those in domestic service, would have been fortunate to have been earning over £1 a week at this time. A most unsavoury aspect of the scheme was the implicit threat to expose anyone who was not paying up regularly. While there is no documented case of this ever having happened, the fear of exposure and consequent public humiliation (especially for single mothers) was clearly sufficient to ensure compliance.

This was entirely a State-run scheme, with no connections to any other body. While the money was collected by the Department of Education, there is no record as to how it was spent. It is probable that it went into central exchequer funds; there is certainly no record of it ever having been used directly to improve conditions for the children concerned. The amounts collected were by today's standards not large – an average of £9,600 a year during the 1950s and 1960s. When calculated as a comparison with average wage levels at the time, this amount is equivalent to about £500,000 today. It must, however, be remembered that it was in all cases collected from the very poorest members of society.

It was not only single mothers who were badly treated by nuns and Brothers while attempting to visit their own children. Widows, widowers and those fallen on hard times were also dismissed as being unworthy of even the most basic facilities in which to talk to their children. Former inmates report children seen huddling in doorways or under trees with a parent, trying to shelter from the rain. In some cases, parents were unable to continue to accept the humiliation, and stopped visiting their children.

This attitude to the children's families was starkly at odds with the frequent public utterances of the Church and State concerning the fundamental importance of family and family values to a Christian Irish society. It is clear that the families of a particular class of people, those who lived in poverty, were of less value and less importance in this context. Consequently, not only was no effort made to keep industrial schools children in contact with their families, in fact the direct reverse was the case – those families were often actually broken up and torn apart.

While the bulk of this hostile attitude to family came from the religious orders, there is no doubt that the State colluded in it. Many children were deliberately committed by the courts to industrial schools hundreds of miles from their homes. This was a highly effective means of cutting off all contact with their families, as the expense of travelling to visit was an effective barrier for many of their parents.

When, as often occurred, large families of children were committed to industrial school at the same time, sisters and brothers were invariably split up. But, often, even a group of sisters from the same families would be spread across a number of different schools, and would lose all contact with each other. There are endless stories of people only discovering in middle age the identities of siblings they never knew they had. Geraldine, whose story appears in these pages and who grew up in the Sisters of Mercy industrial school in Tralee, had a total of seven brothers and sisters, spread across no fewer than seven different industrial schools.

Even when sisters (or brothers) were within the same industrial school, they were not encouraged to view themselves as family. There are numerous cases from girls' schools of sisters being forbidden to have any contact with each other. Some of the saddest cases are those of brothers having been placed when very young into different junior boys' industrial schools, and ending up in the enormous Artane school from the age of ten, never knowing of each other's existence. The Christian Brothers apparently felt no need to inform them that they had family members in the same school.

All this served even more to isolate the children, to make it clear to them that they were completely alone, and that no one either would or could help them. It was one of the arsenal of tactics used, particularly by nuns, to break the children's spirit and so shape them for their place in life – namely as docile servants in the houses of the middle classes, a large number of whose female members had of course been given a full and complete education by the very same nuns.

In cases where this had not worked, and a girl managed to maintain a sense of individuality, frequently expressed as defiance of the nuns, she was very often perceived by them as being either unreformable or insane. For those who refused to conform to the draconian discipline of the industrial schools, there was always another institution used as a threat – a place even worse than where they were already. Boys were threatened with Letterfrack or Daingean, girls with being sent to Magdalen laundries run by the Good Shepherds.

The girls knew that if they ended up in this type of laundry, it could be a life sentence for them. Children from a very early age had an enormous fear of such places instilled in them. They knew less about psychiatric hospitals, but there is testimony from a number of women who were sent as children to be detained in these facilities because they were considered by the nuns to be uncontrollable.

It is interesting to note that while Magdalen laundries or psychiatric hospitals were used as threats for those in industrial schools, children in the often paying orphanages had a great fear of being sent to those same industrial schools. Girls in St Joseph's Orphanage on Tivoli Road in Dun Laoghaire, run by the Daughters of the Heart of Mary, remember being told they would be sent to Goldenbridge Industrial School in Inchicore if they misbehaved. Children in St Vincent's Orphanage in Glasnevin, which was for middle-class orphaned boys, were threatened with Artane Industrial School. It seems clear from this that everyone within the child-care system at the time was aware of a hierarchy of institutions.

For the more general society, the threat of incarceration of errant children was also a reality. The primary factor here was one of geography. Each locality was acutely aware of its own facility for locking up children. Boys in Cork feared being sent to Upton, for girls it was the Good Shepherds. Boys in the Midlands were terrified of Daingean, in Limerick it was Glin and in Galway it was Letterfrack. In Dublin, Artane was used as the local demon to frighten children. These threats had teeth – the places were known to be unpleasant, and were considered useful in this context. However, it is likely that people did not draw any precise connection between making the threat and a detailed awareness of just how terrible conditions were for the children in these institutions.

What all of this paints is a picture of a society which was vaguely aware of the iniquities of the industrial schools – one which simultaneously both knew and did not know just how badly treated the children were. Even if the unthinkable were true, and revered nuns, priests and Brothers were treating the child inmates with cruelty, the population lacked any mechanism for dealing with this. All attempts to denigrate the Catholic Church were viewed with extreme hostility, and those few individuals who did so often paid a heavy price. Irish society in this regard had certain similarities with Germany during and after the Second World War and the question of what ordinary Germans knew about the Nazi concentration camps.

Much has been written about the culpability or otherwise of the German people for the Holocaust. There has always been considerable dissension within that country as to the exact level of general awareness of the death camps. The only reasonable answer lies, as in Ireland, in the peculiar phenomenon of people both knowing and not knowing at the same time, or perhaps more precisely, knowing enough not to probe any further. [. . .]

Somewhat the same analogy can be made with any number of countries where gross injustices have been perpetrated against the vulnerable minorities within them. What Ireland shares with many societies around the world is a dangerous reality: once a group of people is isolated as being in some way inferior, the general population becomes less concerned with how they are treated, even in the face of evidence of cruelty and abuse. In Ireland's case, the thousands of victims of industrial schools bear witness to a society unwilling to question its own comfortable certainties out of a fear that those beliefs might turn out to have been built on sand.

'For $200,000 You Can Have Ali'

PAUL KIMMAGE (2000)

Muhammad Ali's visit to Dublin in 1972 could still cause ripples almost three decades later. Paul Kimmage reconstructed the great man's visit for the *Sunday Independent*.

A cold December afternoon in the Dublin suburb of Terenure. Sean 'Dutch' Brereton lays down his tools and descends from the attic he is converting on Greenlea Road and greets you with a smile at the door. Short and stocky with a pleasantly rounded face, you could pass this 67-year-old Offaly man one hundred times on the street and never figure the glorious secret of his past, but appearances can be deceptive.

Leading you inside to a seat at the kitchen table, he casts his mind back to the summer of '72 and the day it all began. A 40-year-old father of eight sons, he had just finished a job for Bord Na Móna when the invitation came to build the ring at Croke Park. Setting out that morning from his home in Edenderry, Dutch never imagined he would get close to Muhammad Ali, but from the moment they shook hands he was smitten.

'I've wanted to meet you since you won the Olympic Games. This is a great day in my life,' he told the former world champion.

'I hear you're into boxing yourself,' Ali replied.

'I am,' Dutch laughed. 'In fact if I'd been born in America, I'd have been a pro like you.'

'Well, we'll see,' Ali smiled, 'I hope you do a good job for me.'

The love story had begun.

Entrusted with the construction of the ring and the supervision of the training facilities in the build-up to the fight, Dutch followed Ali's every movement for the next week and was soon on first-name terms with Angelo Dundee and the rest of his entourage. On the third day, when the session had just ended, Dutch asked Ali if he might spar with him: 'I just want to be able to say I fought the great

Muhammad Ali.' Ali flicked his wrist and invited him through the ropes but couldn't take him seriously: 'Grow, Sean, grow,' he laughed.

Best of all, however, was the moment after training when he was invited by Dundee to give Ali a massage. Sometimes, when he closes his eyes, he can still see that magnificent frame and feel the flesh between his fingers. Sometimes, he gazes at his hands and wonders if it really happened. It was all over so fast, it all passed so quickly. One minute, he was rubbing the shoulders of the most famous athlete in the world and the next he was a builder from Offaly again, trying to earn an honest crust.

'I nearly went back with them. They were setting up a training camp at Deer Lake and Angelo [Dundee] was twisting my arm to go. I was ready to abandon everything and jump on the first plane but Yul Brynner's son called me to one side and said, "Don't be mad, Sean, when Ali stops boxing this circus will be over. You have everything going for you here."'

He produces a small framed photograph from his pocket and shakes his head. There are so many things he would have done that week given the chance to live it again. 'If only I had a tape recording of some of the things we said that week and the times we spent together.

'Look at him smiling,' he says, pointing to the photo. 'You know I used to make him laugh. It was the best July there ever was.'

Aficionados of Duffy's Circus in the fifties often recall an act featuring a strong man and a musician called Michael Doyle. The act began each evening with the sound of music as Doyle entered the spotlight with his accordion, suspended high above the stage in a chair, clasped between the teeth of Ireland's Strongest Man. The strong man, it has to be said, was no ordinary beefcake. Butty Sugrue believed in doing things with style.

Sugrue was one of three tough brothers, born and raised near Killorglin. Typically cute in the South Kerry way, he was a man of no profession who built his fortune and fame with feats of immense power and strength – he would tow a double-decker bus with a rope clenched between his teeth – at carnivals and fairs all over the country. In 1953, he defeated the former boxing legend Jack Doyle in a wrestling match at Puck Fair and began to dabble as an entrepreneur.

In the early 1960s he left Ireland for London and bought a pub, The Wellington, in Shepherds Bush but continued to return home regularly. In 1964, he organised a series of variety shows at the Mansion House in Dublin featuring the voice of Jack Doyle, followed by an exhibition of boxing between the British heavyweight champion Henry Cooper and his brother George. When Nelson's pillar was blown up in 1966, the head (though it may have been a plaster cast) was sighted on the counter of The Wellington the following evening.

Butty began to enjoy the high life. When he wasn't dining with Marlon Brando on the set of *A Countess of Hong Kong*, he was busy paving the way for the visit of the boxing legend Joe Louis to Dublin. The success of that venture whetted his appetite for bigger, better, more. In March of 1971, his attention was drawn to an event being staged at Madison Square Garden in New York.

Six months after returning to the ring after the four-year exile imposed on him for refusing to join the US armed forces in Vietnam, Muhammad Ali had been granted a tilt at Joe Frazier for the heavyweight championship of the world. Over the next four and a half years Ali and Frazier would meet three times in fights that would become the pyramids of boxing. It was as great a rivalry as sport has ever seen and captured the imagination of the world.

The first fight would set the tone. It was the classic match between boxer and slugger. For the first time in history, two undefeated heavyweights, each with a legitimate claim to the title, would meet for the undisputed championship of the world. Seven hundred and sixty press credentials were granted, requests were refused for five hundred more. Each fighter was paid the previously unheard of sum of $2,500,000 and when the fifteen rounds had ended, everyone agreed it had been worth every dime.

Ali's loss was a stunning blow to everyone who believed in him, but if the night belonged to Frazier, Ali emerged with great credit in defeat. On the morning after the fight, the lobby of his New York hotel was dangerously crowded by fans drawn to the magnet. A police officer raised his hand and tried to restore order. 'You're creating a fire hazard,' he warned, 'you'll have to move back. Somebody could get killed.' When nobody moved he turned away hopelessly: 'And all this for a beaten fighter.'

Beaten for the first time as a professional, Ali began to chart his comeback. Four months after the defeat by Frazier, he returned to winning ways with a twelfth-round knockout of his childhood friend Jimmy Ellis. In November, the defeat of Buster Mathis was followed six weeks later in Switzerland by another facile win over a German fighter called Jurgen Blin. In April of '72, he beat Mac Foster over fifteen rounds in Tokyo and followed it in May and June with encores against George Chuvalo and Jerry Quarry.

Butty Sugrue followed his progress from the other side of the Atlantic. What would it take, he wondered, to bring the world's most famous athlete to Ireland? He began making some calls. Harold Conrad was the promoter closest to Ali, following his return from exile. In the book *Muhammad Ali: His Life and Times* by Thomas Hauser, Conrad recounts a visit one day from a small, barrel-chested Irishman.

Harold Conrad: 'It was always my dream to do a big heavyweight fight in Ireland. I'm not Irish, it's nothing like that, but Ireland is where fights started. You ever been there? They fight; they argue all the time. If you don't argue with them, they get mad at you in Ireland. And this guy, his name was Butty Sugrue, owned a pub in Dublin. He wanted to promote a fight, so I told him, for two hundred thousand dollars, you can have Ali.'

When he stepped from the plane at Dublin Airport, shortly after ten on the morning of the second Tuesday in July, Muhammad Ali was thirty years old. Less than two months had passed since his defeat of Jerry Quarry. He had fought six times on three continents in the fourteen months since Frazier and the constant travelling was wearing him down. When he picked up a cold before his departure to Dublin, he briefly considered postponing the fight.

His opponent, Al 'Blue' Lewis, wasn't much to get excited about and the money wasn't spectacular. Ali had never been to Ireland and wasn't overly enamoured by what he had seen of it on TV. Thirteen people had been shot dead at a civil rights march in Derry and an IRA ceasefire had just broken down. Northern Ireland was entering one of its bloodiest and most terrible phases. There were many good reasons for Muhammad to stay at home.

But he was nothing if not professional, nothing if not the greatest showman ever born, and from the moment he stepped from the plane in Dublin he was value for money. Greeted on arrival by the Emerald Girl Pipers and presented with a shillelagh by Chub O'Connor, the Kerry TD, he was led inside to the first press conference of the week and was soon in full flow.

He was asked about his most recent fight with Jerry Quarry.

'You gotta remember that some guys lose heart when I beat them, but it's no disgrace – I'm the greatest . . . It's hard to be modest when you're as good as I am.'

He was asked about the situation in Northern Ireland.

'I do not know the reason why there are shootings and killings up there and when you do not know the reason it is not wise to comment.'

He was asked if it was true he had Irish blood in his veins?

'You never can tell, there was a lot of sneaking around in those [slave plantation] days.'

He was asked how the return fight with Frazier would go?

'I'll whup him easy now,' he smiled, brandishing a shillelagh.

The 'largest gathering of reporters and cameramen ever seen' loved every moment of Ali's 40-minute recital. 'WHAT A PERFORMANCE BY MUHAMMAD,' the *Irish Independent* announced. 'EX-CHAMP IS A BIG HIT WITH NEWSMEN AT DUBLIN AIRPORT,' trumpeted the *Herald*. A crowd of six hundred autograph hunters had gathered in the arrivals hall. Ali was whisked into a black Mercedes and driven to his hotel at the foot of the Dublin mountains.

Harold Conrad: 'When Ali stepped off the plane onto Irish soil at the airport, the people went wild. He told them his great-grandfather was named Grady and had come from Ireland and they loved it. Then, the next day, he called me up and asked, 'Where are all the niggers in this town?' That's Ali talking, not me. I told him, 'Ali, there aren't any' and he said, 'Oh.'

Ali was up early next morning for his first 'official' day in the week-long prologue to the fight. After a lung-opening jog, he break-fasted on coffee before retiring to his room for a nap. In the afternoon he was driven to Croke Park for his first training session of the week, where he sparred with Bunny Sterling, John Conteh and Joe Bugner. And then it was off to Dáil Éireann for a meeting with the Taoiseach, Jack Lynch.

Raymond Smith covered the event for the *Irish Independent*. 'Muhammad took Leinster House by storm. Not since President Kennedy addressed both houses of the Oireachtas has the visit of one celebrity engendered such spontaneous excitement. Protocol was forgotten more than once during this whirlwind visit – and it seemed to me that Muhammad must have shaken the hand of every member of the Cabinet as he made his way down the corridor to the Taoise-ach's office and later the hand of every leading member of the Opposition.'

Ben Briscoe and John Bruton were two who had their hands shaken.

Ben Briscoe: 'I'd done a bit of boxing myself and had the pleasure of meeting him in Jack Lynch's office. He said to Jack, "Is there any chance you can come along and see the fight?" And Jack said, "Well I don't know if I can make it or not but I'll try." And Ali said, "Well let me know if you are coming and I'll try to make it last a bit longer." He then started telling us how he used to turn it on for the media. He was brilliant, such a sweet guy.'

John Bruton: 'I remember it was at the beginning of my career when I was either the Fine Gael spokesman on agriculture or the assistant whip. I was introduced to him in the corridor outside the Dáil bar by Dr Hugh Byrne, who had boxed during his college days and was a great fan. The thing that struck me about him, apart from his size, was his tremendous wit. He was tremendously witty and very eloquent. I think he would have got on very well in politics.'

After signing the visitor's book and observing the Dáil proceed-ings for a while from the Distinguished Visitors Gallery, Ali was escorted to the restaurant at Leinster House, where his first Irish meal was two sirloin steaks and veg, washed down with a Coke. At the table, he signed autographs and engaged with the excited restaurant staff. When one worker decided he would have to tell his wife, Ali reached out and grabbed the phone. 'Your husband is with the greatest boxer in the world. Now you just don't go whuppin him tonight, cause he's with the champion . . .'

Raymond Smith recalls how the evening ended. 'There was 12 of us sitting with him around the table and when he had finished eating, he looked at me and said: "What were the last words the Lord uttered at the last supper?" And I thought about it. "Ali, it's very hard to say exactly what his last words were." And he smiled, "Let every man pick up his own cheque."'

There's a story told about the fight between Muhammad Ali and Joe Bugner in Kuala Lumpur in 1975. Champion again after his legendary defeat of George Foreman in Zaire, Ali's subsequent victories over Chuck Wepner and Ron Lyle were pretty dull and uninspired and the fight against Bugner was proving a difficult sell. No one gave Bugner a chance.

Aware of the general indifference, the promoters convened a week before the fight to try and find a way to generate some interest. When they had reached agreement, Bobby Goodman was dispatched to break the idea to Ali. 'This is the idea,' he said, 'but you are going to have to sound serious. In fact, you have to be close to tears for this to be believable and help the fight.' Ali, as ever, had no objections. He rehearsed his lines and was calm and controlled when the press conference was called.

'The reason I called you guys together is to say that this is my last fight,' he announced. 'All the years I've been on the road, all the training camps and time away from my wife and children; it's just too much. I miss my family. My life with them is more important than boxing. I want to retire while I'm still at the top.' His eyes began to get watery as he reminisced about his career and the splendours of his life in boxing. There was a stunned silence as the newspapermen allowed the news to sink in. 'But what about Joe Frazier?' a reporter asked. 'Aren't you going to fight Frazier again?'

Ali tried to bite his lip but it was no use. His eyes lit up. His mouth began to ignite. Words began to explode like rockets off his tongue. 'Joe Frazier! I want him bad. How much money do you think I can get if I go and whup Joe Frazier?' The scam was exposed. He just couldn't help it.

For the week he spent in Ireland in the build-up to the fight with Lewis, Ali stayed with his sixty-strong entourage at the recently opened Oppermann Country Club in Kilternan. The view from Ali's bedroom might have been different to other places he had been around the world, but the mission for the week remained the same. He would sell this fight to the best of his ability. He would try his damnedest to put bums on seats.

Sean Brereton: 'There was one day, I remember, when he came into the handball alley where the crowd had gathered to watch him training and he started breaking up the seats. The arrangement was that Lewis would train for two hours before Ali, but when Ali arrived and Lewis was still there he went berserk and started breaking up seats. "What's wrong, what's wrong?" we asked. "GET THAT BUM OUT OF MY DRESSING ROOM," he roared. He was pointing at Lewis, really losing the head and it was a good ten minutes before he calmed down. And then he looks at me and winks, "Do you think that will sell a few tickets?"'

Eddie Keher was also roped into the publicity machine. 'I was working in the AIB in Capel Street at the time and they were doing a bit of pre-publicity for the fight and asked me if I would take out a couple of hurleys and a sliotar to Kilternan. We hit a few balls and I got him to rise a few balls and he started sparring with me, trying to get as much hype going as possible: "Come on," he said, "keep it going." He wasn't that co-ordinated as a hurler but I don't think it would have taken him too long. I'm sure we could have found a place for him on the Kilkenny team.'

Cathal O'Shannon from RTE was another visitor to the Oppermann hotel that week. He was researching an interview to be broadcast on the night before the fight before a live studio audience. 'The way we did it was John Condon, who directed it, and I went over to the BBC to have a look at the thing he had done with

Parkinson. We talked to the producers there and they told us they had paid him £14,000 and brought over his entourage of 20 people. Now when we heard this, we thought we had no chance but John did a deal with Angelo Dundee for £100 to be paid in £1 notes.

'When he came into the studio on the night before the fight he had a cold and seemed in very bad form. He said, "I hate this f★★★kin place!" I said, "What do you mean, RTE?" "No," he said, "that place I'm staying in. I should have stayed in that place [the Gresham] I went into last night." And I thought, "This is going to be great, he has a cold, he's in bad humour," but once he got out there he was magnificent, really great. It was at a stage of his career when he was very much into the black brotherhood and was making almost a religion of being anti-white, but the impression I got was that he didn't really hate white people . . .'

Muhammad Ali v Cathal O'Shannon (edited highlight)

O'Shannon: 'How was it, Muhammad, to be a Negro boy in the south?'

Ali: 'We say black now.'

O'Shannon: 'All right, black.'

(*Ali grumbles.*)

O'Shannon: 'Is it not the same thing?'

Ali: 'No Negro is . . . we're talking about . . . all people are named after a country. The Chinese are named after China, the Cubans are named after Cuba, Irish people are named after Ireland, Indonesians named after Indonesia, Japanese are named after Japan, Australians are named after Australia but there's no country named Negro!'

O'Shannon: 'All right, let me . . .'

Ali: 'Do you understand?'

O'Shannon: 'I understand.'

Ali: 'You're not as dumb as you look.'

O'Shannon: 'Do I look dumb?'

Ali: 'Naah, only kiddin.'

O'Shannon: 'What I really mean is did you feel that you were deprived, that you and your family and other blacks were second-class citizens?'

Ali: 'Did we feel it? We knew it! Add up all of the nationalities you have on earth – they come first. Right now, you can come to my home town and you're more freer in America than I am.'

O'Shannon: 'This is something you feel strongly about?'

Ali: 'Strongly? I know it's the truth, I live right there every day. We see Jesus, he's white with blond hair and blue eyes . . . We see the Lord's Supper, all white people . . . We see the angels in heaven, all white people. We look at Miss Universe, a white woman . . . Miss America, a white woman . . . Miss World, a white woman . . . Even Tarzan, the King of the Jungle in Africa, he was white.' (*The audience laughs. He cups his hands to his mouth and does an imitation of Tarzan's roar.*)

'You see a white man swinging around Africa, Ahhhhhyaaaayaaa, with a diaper on, Ahhhyaaayaaaa . . . he beats up all the Africans and makes the law in the jungle and the Africans been in Africa for centuries but can't yet talk to the animals! But Tarzan, all of the sudden some goat raised him up and he can talk to the animals. So I'm just showing you how the black man in America has been whitewashed. And then we look at the good cowboys, they rode the white horses . . . And the President lives in a white house. They got TV commercials: "White House Cigars" White Swan Soap. White cloth tissue paper. White Tornado Floor Wax. White plus toothpaste . . . the angel food cake was the white cake but the devil food cake was the chocolate cake. Everything good is white!'

Almost thirty years on, the interview remains a classic. O'Shannon reflects modestly on his achievement. 'It was a great challenge and a great pleasure to do but ahh . . . he had done it a million times before and I was basically just another gobshite. There was nothing I was going to throw at him that he wasn't going to be able to deal with, not that it was my intention to do that. It's hard to think back now of the way people thought of him. It was almost like Jack Kennedy coming here – this was the most famous American in the world.'

A week can be a long time in Dublin when your name is Muhammad Ali. After a week of shaking hands and signing his name for the Irish people, Ali seemed almost deflated as he stepped onto the scales for the official weigh-in at the Gresham Hotel on the morning of the fight. He smiled and nodded politely at reporters but there was none of the theatrics he had shown in the past. Al 'Blue' Lewis was no Sonny Liston, just another day at the office.

A copy of the *Irish Independent* cost 4p on the morning of Wednesday July 19, 1972. A lb of butter, a pack of twin toilet rolls and a bottle of Johnnie Walker cost 24p, 6p and £2.55 respectively in Quinnsworth. The Indians were playing at the National Ballroom, *Ryan's Daughter* was playing in the Green or, if you fancied following the 'leaders of Church and State' to the big fight, there were tickets to be had at the gate for £15, £10, £5 and £2. Seventeen thousand people formed a queue. Butty Sugrue needed 'twenty' to break even.

Jack Lynch, no stranger it has to be said to the venue, kept his promise to Ali and was escorted to a seat in the second row beside Bishop Eamon Casey and a little too close for comfort to Neil Blaney. Luke Kelly, John Huston, Eamonn Andrews, Peter O'Toole, Bernadette Devlin, Paddy Devlin, Pat Quinn, Siobhán McKenna, Billy Conn, Terry Downes and Freddy Gilroy were among the celebrities in the audience. Micheál O'Hehir was Master of Ceremonies. At 8.45 it was time for the main event.

Draped in a white satin robe and wearing matching white boots and trunks, the people's champion began the walk from his dressing room beneath the Cusack Stand to the ring.

Mick Dowling: 'I was with the national squad, preparing for the '72 Olympics at the time of the fight. I had a reasonably decent seat in the Hogan Stand. He totally outclassed Lewis but the thing I remember most about the evening was this smart alec in the crowd before the main bout when John Conteh was fighting. "Go on, Conteh, punch him," he said, "you have the wind behind you now."'

Harold Conrad: 'The night before the fight I was in a pub talking with some guy who said he was going to see the fight. I asked, "Did you get tickets already?" And he said, "Tickets? It's an insult for an Irishman to pay to see a fight." I should have made a note of that, because the next day seven thousand people crashed the main gate, tore it down. Seven thousand got in for free. But it was a good fight. Ali had a little cold and Lewis was there to win. He bloodied Ali's nose, but Ali chopped him down towards the end and stopped him in the eleventh round.'

Raymond Smith: 'Because of the late start, Vinny Doyle [editor of the *Irish Independent*] had asked me to find out from Ali when the fight might end so he could plan for the various editions. So I put it to Muhammad on the eve of the fight and he said, "You can go and tell your boss that this guy will last no more than five rounds, two minutes because that's all television will take of this bum." And he moved in exactly after two minutes of the fifth round and knocked Lewis down. The fight would have ended but Ali went to the wrong corner, he didn't go to a neutral corner and the referee was late starting the count. Lewis got back on his feet at nine and Ali finished him off in the 11th.'

Peter Byrne was ringside for the *Irish Times*: 'The fight itself was so-so. Ali boxed well but nothing like he could and the one abiding memory I have was the pandemonium that started when he got out of the ring and was trying to make his way back to his dressing room. He was stranded for about twenty minutes with his heavies all around him, trying to make a path through the crowd but it was a case of one step forward, two steps back. So with that, this little Dublin fellow jumped up onto the apron and started addressing the crowd.

"'Lads," he said, "we've had a great night. Muhammad has given us all a night to remember, now Jaysus be fair to the man and give him a bit of room. Muhammad wants to go to his dressing room." And with that there was a pregnant pause before someone shouted from the crowd: "Let the dressing room come to Muhammad."'

Nell McCafferty described the ensuing chaos in a front-page piece in the *Irish Times*. 'Muhammad Ali came into the ring looking sad-eyed and disinterested and left the ring looking scarcely more enlivened. The Gardaí took more punishment than he did in their efforts afterwards to give him safe passage through Croke Park, back to his dressing room. A total lack of stewarding or ropes to emphasise passageways between the blocks of seats ensured riotous access of young Dubliners to their hero.

'It was charmingly Irish, an Englishman said, as he picked himself up off the ground. We made our way to the dressing room and got caught up in a jam in the pitch dark alley under the stand. Peter O'Toole managed to get his friends through and a tall Negro said to a policeman, "Whaddya mean am I in Clay's team! Look at my face, will ya?" He lit a match and the crowd opened before him.

'A very nice police inspector took me through, all the way into the dressing room, where Angelo Dundee became apoplectic. "He's naked, he's naked, we can't have a lady in here." His loins were in fact covered with a towel, but modesty dictated that I leave at once.'

Sean Brereton: 'One of the most striking things about Ali when he was stripped was the size of his . . . Jaysus, I'm not joking, I'd never seen a weapon like it in all of my life. There was one day I was talking to him and I said, "Ali, tell me this, what would you think of sex before a fight?" "Oh," he said, "not before a fight, Dutch, definitely not before a fight – three days before perhaps, but definitely not before a fight."'

Nell McCafferty: 'His equipment was bigger than anything ever seen in Ireland? Such things were far from my mind, I can tell you. All I remember about it was that I went into the dressing room afterwards to interview him and he had a towel across his legs, talking to all of the fellows. They told me to leave. I was very disappointed. I had followed him all the way through university and just wanted to hear him talk and laugh but I never actually got to speak to him. I didn't get to meet my hero.'

Butty Sugrue spoke to Tom Myler of the *Evening Herald* after the fight: 'I achieved one ambition with the Croke Park fight. I succeeded in putting Ireland on the fighting map. I feel I did something good for the country in a time when the tourist trade has hit a slump because of the troubles in Northern Ireland. If the fight is remembered for this alone it will have been worthwhile.'

Al 'Blue' Lewis was stopped by Muhammad Ali after a minute and 15 seconds of the eleventh round. When it was over, the celebrities adjourned to a celebration out at the Oppermann hotel which lasted into the early hours, but Ali wasn't interested and after speaking to a few reporters, slipped off to bed. He was gone next morning on the first flight to Heathrow. He said he'd be back to holiday in the West with his family, but Foreman and Frazier and the fights that would make him the greatest athlete of the century were just around the corner. In more ways than one, Muhammad Ali never came back.

A Dublin Journal

ANDREW O'HAGAN (2002)

The Scottish novelist Andrew O'Hagan taught at Trinity College Dublin in the autumn of 2002. His diary of that time, published in the *Dublin Review*, caught the city's atmospheres, old and new.

6 October 2002. 'Let your senses guide you,' says a large ad for Bailey's Irish Cream in Dublin Airport. For some reason, Irish advertisements don't only tell you what to buy, they tell you how to live. 'Don't give out if you don't,' says an advert telling people to vote in the referendum.

Trinity College is the kind of campus that Columbia could never hope to be: beautiful grey stone, trees a hundred years older than their planters, lamps that stand over the cobbled stones like a thought maintained. My rooms overlook the greens on either side; the large Georgian windows catch the shadows of the trees at night, and in the morning everything is clear, the Irish light, the leaves falling onto the stones.

The students arrived today in their thousands. Looking at them, I think of my old granny and her thoughts of the Ireland her family barely remembered, and her telling me constantly that it was all in front of me. It's all in front of them, I say to myself at the window, watching their smiles, their free-floating embarrassments, but the statues are there too, and the old buildings, and I realize how much it's all behind us as well. [. . .]

8 October 2002. The rain is coming down so hard it is making the car alarms go off. Under my window, running long-armed over the cobbles, are a couple of giant gorillas, each clutching a sheaf of white leaflets in its rubbery paw. Hmmph. Rag week. Looking onto the green, I realize that no one except university lecturers and rock promoters ever sees this number of young people together.

Here they all come, the youth of today, so self-conscious with their cigarettes and haircuts. Taking in the statues, I remember the words of J. P. Mahaffy, Trinity's former provost, who hated *Ulysses* with a vengeance. 'It was a mistake,' he said, 'to establish a separate university for the aborigines of this island, for the cornerboys who spit into the Liffey.'

In the evening, Colm Tóibín meets me at the front gate. We go to the launch of a book at Liberty Hall; the book is about the brilliant Argentinean journalist Rodolfo Walsh. The man who wrote the book comes into the room wearing a red PLO-style scarf – one of those items one used to wear to annoy the priesthood. He passes a sign that says 'Yes, we want bread, but we want roses too.' I realize all of a sudden that I'm enjoying an evening with the Irish Left. The author, Michael McCaughan, is also wearing a too-small, velvet, pinstripe suit with baseball boots coming out the bottom; the suit is like something from the closet of the late Bunny Roger.

Tóibín: 'He's just wearing that scarf to annoy me, now.'

McCaughan: 'Hello, Colm.'

The author starts, quite unwittingly, unconsciously, without a word, and very slowly, to draw the scarf off his neck and stuff it into his pocket.

Tóibín: 'Mmmm. The suit.'

McCaughan: 'Would you believe it? Second hand.'

Tóibín: 'Yes. The nouveaux poor.'

Outside, for the first time, I see the autumn nights arriving. The glass towers over in the financial district are cold-looking, and the cranes around them are still busy, moving against the sky. The evening's props tell you everything you need to know about the party's personnel: South American drinking cups abound, as do knapsacks, Fair Isle jumpers, moustaches, children in full school uniform, and the pleasingly Leftish spectacle of every other person wearing small spectacles. 'Buenas noches!' shouts Mr McCaughan.

One of the schoolchildren sits on his father's knee drinking from a glass of red wine. Colm Tóibín has the task of introducing the book. He starts by saying it would be foolish to think, as people once did, of Argentina as a paradise, a European city in South America. He looks straight at the Lefties in their baseball boots, and speaks, in the context of the disintegration of Rodolfo Walsh's work, of 'the solitude, distance, and separateness that a writer needs'. I don't think the gathering quite understands him; they don't appear to believe in separateness, and distance is not what they care about. They don't want to be alone; they want togetherness, like this, the kind of togetherness that celebrates itself.

Out on the street I meet Ciarán Cuffe, the Green TD for Dún Laoghaire. 'Jeezo, that was a right '70s flashback that!' he says. When I tell him I'm working at Trinity, he starts talking about the College's unecological ambitions into Pearse Street, and asks if I could stop them buying up buildings and putting up walls and destroying the city. 'I just talk to young postgraduates about verbs and adjectives,' I wanted to say, but he was gone in a flash of environmental-friendliness.

A new play at the Peacock, *Done Up Like a Kipper* by Mark Harmon. As soon as I see the set – a suburban living-room – I begin to wonder if there will ever be a Scottish or Irish play not set in a living-room, a kitchen, or a pub. The theatre needs a new world of interiors: whatever happened to workplaces, where people spend most of their days, or bedrooms, where they lie all night? Orange-faced, working-class women talking over the kitchen table, things going badly, husbands-wise, things looking better, vodka-wise, and the production splutters almost as soon as it starts. Truth is the play is about six to ten drafts short of being ready, and the Abbey should know better than to expose a young writer to this kind of chaos. [. . .]

12 October 2002. At 9.25 this morning, a strange, intergalactic noise was coming from Government Buildings on Merrion Street. Five clear notes, like those understood by the aliens in *Close Encounters of the Third Kind*. Nobody about the place, so I poked my face through the railings and thought: 'We are your friends.' A couple of Canadian tourists came past. 'What the hell is that?' said one of them.

'It's the Irish parliament,' I said. 'They bring a message from another world.' [. . .]

In the Gaiety for the last night of Tom Murphy's *Conversations on a Homecoming*. Sitting there, looking up the tiers, you can see, even now, that Irish theatre bears a deep and traditional relation to the political landscape and plays a part in the creation of a national consciousness. It is not in any way like the London theatre: here, and the other night too, at *Sive*, John B. Keane's play, you feel the audience is engaged in a conversation with some aspect of their own conscience, and that the words and events onstage pour over the people and through them into their own past, or perhaps into the past of the country itself. London theatregoers watch what is happening onstage as if it were happening behind glass. Maybe that is why television stars are currently so popular in the West End.

Evidence for the social interestingness of the Dublin theatre audience can be gleaned from watching them watching one another; there is drama in the stalls, opera in the dress circle, as people wave down to each other, whispering, gesturing, walking quickly down the aisles to say hello. Never in the London theatre does anyone wave to anyone, or recognize the events, onstage or off, as things that are happening in a social way. Maybe that's tourism, but I think it's more than tourism: it's culture, and the lack of it. If that's good news for Ireland, it's the last of such for tonight: Murphy's play tells as many difficult truths as you can tell in two hours.

In the green room afterwards, Tom Murphy stood with a pint. He had only just come back from New York, where *Bailegangaire* is being produced, and he seemed relieved to be among people he could talk to. Murphy stands something like a man who is standing his ground. He is quite compact, and he spreads his weight pretty evenly between his feet; he's proud of his chest in that way that some men are, and proud of his arms too, and he looks to me like he wouldn't go down in a hurry.

We talk about the origin of a line in the play, where the main character looks over the audience and says 'ugliness, ugliness, ugliness'.

Murphy: 'It was a West of Ireland politician. He was to give a speech to the great and the good. He'd had a drink. A few drinks. He stood like that. [Murphy crosses his legs like someone desperate for a pee.] He looked over the audience and said "ugliness, ugliness,

ugliness" and that was all he said. He was going on later that he felt humiliated and I said I thought it was just the greatest eloquence.' [. . .]

22 October 2002. The high-rise flats at Inchicore are due to be pulled down, and something will be lost to the people there. 'You're going to have a special treat,' says Cathleen O'Neill. 'It's about the threat to an entire culture and it's about displacement in Dublin.' When I asked her to show me the condemned flats in St Michael's Estate, Cathleen had seemed pleased to make it happen, and drove me there in her car.

'Will You Go, Lassie, Go' is playing on the tape deck. Cathleen explains that Keogh Square had been an army barracks before the British left, and was later turned into housing for those Dublin-dwellers who had trouble paying their rent. Then in the 1960s the old barracks were torn down and the new high-rises were put up. Like many in Glasgow or Manchester, the tower blocks quickly went bad, and people living on St Michael's Estate were surrounded by poverty. 'It became the place where many of the women we have worked with would have come to get their drugs,' said Cathleen.

Cathleen believes in progressive feminism, in 'empowering women', and she has a strong community development ethos, which would appear to grow out of her own experience and her sense of a commitment to working-class life in Ireland. 'Robert Emmet was hung, drawn and quartered there,' she says as we pass a church in Thomas Street. 'His memorial is on the ground for the dogs to pee on.' When we reach the high flats you see a long cloth hanging down the length of one of the blocks; it features the mostly-smiling faces of everybody who's ever lived on the estate.

Rita Fagan comes fizzing towards us. She's famous for a show called *Once Is Too Much*, about domestic violence. 'Hello hello,' she says, 'come in here. You be nice to him now, he's an illuminary.' She takes us into one of the ground-floor flats – most of the people had already gone from their homes – and Rita had turned the flat into an art gallery, a mini-Hayward, where work made by the St Michael's residents stood in pristine rooms. 'The exhibition is about memory,' said Rita. 'It's the hidden Ireland.' She pointed to a painting. 'And unlike the estate, this painting will last,' she said.

The most striking things to be found in the rooms are the 'Memory Chairs', where women have used photographs of their loved ones (some of them dead from cancer, asthma, and drugs) and fashioned patterns out of them around a chair, using bits of mirror and net curtain and domestic bric-à-brac. 'Love labour is what women do all the time in their lives,' says Cathleen, 'and it is not counted in the gross domestic product.' We stop in front of a wall of photographs, mainly young people going from the estate on summer bus trips years ago, and Rita begins pointing out young faces.

'Dead,' she says. 'Dead. Dead. Dead.'

'But it's about giving people their story back,' says Cathleen.

'Exactly,' says Rita. 'I can see my story in this, is what many of the women who come here say to me.'

I spoke to some of the old-age pensioners who had gathered that afternoon for a writing class. The elderly ladies spoke and laughed among themselves and someone pointed out that the ladies have the old Dublin way of speaking. 'I'm not very artistic, by any means,' says the first one.

'Where are you going to live now?' I asked.

'I'm getting a bungalow,' she said, 'if I'm not in St James's first. First I'd one bad leg and now it's two.'

'I know your face,' said a second old lady to Cathleen. 'Were you on the telly?'

'I was.'

'That was it, Joan. She was on the telly.'

'I'm still embarrassed by it,' said Cathleen.

'Why should you be?' said the second lady, hobbling over to the table and picking up a writing pad. 'It's your gift. You've got it.' [. . .]

25 *October 2002*. Walking over O'Connell Bridge I'm stopped by a woman holding a baby. 'Please give,' she says.

'Where are you from?'

'Please give me,' she says.

Beggars are much keener to be ignored or humiliated than they are to be questioned. I found this out years ago when I spent several months hanging around with beggars. I remember a night-shelter next to the Tropical Diseases Hospital in Camden Town, where many of the men were Irish or Scottish, waiting out the night over their vast bowls of pea soup. All the intricacies of coins collected and drink procured could be discussed, but when you asked a person where he came from, how he got here, a sad, protective cloud of silence would gather about him, and he'd only shake his head.

'Are you Romanian?' I said to the woman on O'Connell Bridge.

'Little money for baby,' she said.

'I will give you money,' I replied. 'I will certainly give you this' – I took out a note – 'but can I only ask you about yourself?'

'This,' she said.

'Here it is,' I said. 'Will you speak with me for one minute? Did you come here from Romania?'

'The baby needs food,' she said. 'From Romania, yes.'

'Where do you live now?'

'We are living out here with family.'

'Your own family?'

'With family, yes. Here with family.'

'Do you live in a house?'

'In a house.'

Then she took the note, made a gesture with her hand, and made quickly off. I guess the woman was nervous about discussing her circumstances because they were quite possibly illegal. The Liffey looked dull as it flowed and when I turned round the woman had disappeared into the crowd, once again among the unknowables. [. . .]

13 November 2002. Up early to go in a car to *Kenny Live*. It must be one of the chief advantages of small-nationhood: you can feel everyone is listening to the same radio show in the morning, and Britain has no national equivalent to *Kenny Live*. Next to it the *Today* programme on Radio 4 can seem sepulchral.

Pat Kenny is Ireland's Tom Brokaw – so handsome he's almost ugly, and similarly tuned in to the average appetites and pieties of his own people. I was interviewed by him once before, a few years ago on the television, and even there his technique seemed odd: what he says with his mouth is quite intimate and cosy, but his eyes are elsewhere, nowhere near yours, and if you fail to trust his speech you can feel harried by his attentiveness to the clock. What I most remember from our last encounter was him asking me to explain something about Western culture's fascination with serial killers, then, as the camera came to me, combing his hair repeatedly and very daintily with his fingers.

I only really want to say one thing about Scotland. That is that it can not be the modern country it wants to be until it stops blaming England for everything; it is not courageous, not manly, not intelligent, not faithful, not progressive, to rely on an ancient narrative of injury to explain your current woes. It is the behaviour of a small culture, and Scotland is not a small culture, just a small country in which the national will is enslaved by its negative options. Fools among the Irish intelligentsia lean back in their pews to tell us that we should have followed their example and ditched England in 1920; that is a dense-minded view that little understands Scotland's experience within the British Union, its experience as an imperialist force, a colonizer, a world warrior, and a commercial entity *par excellence*. It is not the occupied territory the Scots Nats call it, nor has it, as a Protestant country, ever had (despite all our good songs) anything other than a footnote-able amount of the Home Rule spirit so pleasant to the Irish mind and heart, and liked by the Scottish ear alone.

Pat Kenny is tolerant enough of all this. Then he asks me what I think of the idea of a super-league that would include the English and Scottish football teams. Now, this allows me to tell you exactly what it means to be Scottish. Despite everything I've said, and despite not even liking football, at the sound of this question the Dr Jekyll of small patriotism rises unrestrained in my breast: I don't want a super-league, I want small divisional teams like Forfar and Brechin and Queen of the South not to fall by the wayside; I want equal rights for small towns in the Highlands; I want recognition for the small man; I want equality. I want our Scottish rights! I want FREEDOM!

By the time I reach the car my face has taken on the obligatory Mel Gibson aspect, imaginary blue wode and non-imaginary nationalistic fury blazing defiantly in the eyes of reason.

'That was good craic,' says the driver.

14 November 2002. Dublin doesn't really work, you know, as a city. If you want to be far-fetched it's like Calcutta – full of nice British buildings, with too many people for its size, too many cars, and a rather steep inner-city distinction between the newly rich and the old-fashioned poor. For what the tourist brochures like to call a twenty-first-century city, it has a mad shortage of cash machines, taxis, and wine shops, though no shortage of Ryanair Generation winos out on stag nights. The food in the restaurants isn't nice and it costs too much. There are queues everywhere, for cash, for drinks, for Marks & Spencer.

The glory is the Georgian squares, the talk of books, the neon signs, the poetic force of the drama, the jokes, the soda bread, and a general fair-play attitude that makes everybody seem accountable and nobody secluded from what is best and worst in the Irish day. Unlike Edinburgh, whose present-day middle class is unintellectual, the Dublin middle class are old-fashionedly attentive to their own political and literary culture: they read the *Irish Times* and fill the Abbey; the novelists appear on the radio discussing moral crises; the work of abstract painters goes on sale, and, in any event, the artists are given money and shelter by the government from the roughs of the marketplace. I'm too short to start arguing with the likes of James Joyce, so it may be true that Irish art is a cracked mirror held up by a servant, yet a mirror is at least a mirror, and not a pitiless void, and an outsider in Dublin may feel that all is not entirely lost when it comes to workaday relations between money and thoughts.

The artists this week were scared the government was about to remove their tax exemption, but it didn't happen. What's the point in pissing off the nation's premier big-mouths in order to accrue an extra two or three million euro a year? A London literary agent tells me all his Irish clients were phoning last week in a tremendous panic.

After the deluge, comes the deluge: rain is general all over Ireland. I walk to Lower Abbey Street in a treacly downpour to be interviewed on Eamon Dunphy's radio show. The neon is picking out the puddles at four o'clock in the afternoon.

I like Dunphy. He has the face he deserves at fifty-two. Into the room he comes like a punch-drunk Glasgow boxer – three parts Jimmy Breslin, two parts Ken Buchanan – and he's busy in the way good journalists ought always to be busy, keeping the spinning plates of the news diary and his lifelong obsessions turning on high sticks. Sitting in front of the microphone Dunphy is one of the last of the valiant smokers. He makes good points and he likes conversation; it's noticeable that he doesn't waste any of his famous ire on a friendly target. He's a populist, I suppose, but before long we're talking about Patrick Kavanagh and Brendan Behan, and he smirks when I say it's a myth about people not reading the way they used to. 'I know,' he says, 'I've sold over 500,000 copies of the Roy Keane book in hardback.' [. . .]

18 November 2002. I was telling a journalist in Neary's pub about my day on Saturday, and he put me in my place by telling me about Bono's day on Saturday. 'First thing. Breakfast in his house with the US Secretary of Health and his three aides. Then he goes to a gallery at lunchtime to paint a big frieze for charity, works all the way to nine o'clock at night with hardly a break. Then he has his dinner and talks about another big project with a guy. Walks home and writes a song before going to bed at one o'clock. Then he gets up first thing to catch a flight to New York.'

1 December 2002. You wonder how much of Dublin has been lost to the renovations. I walk past Sweny's chemist, the one that features in *Ulysses*, and notice they have heritage-style lemon soap in the window, to tickle the literary tourists no doubt, but everything around the shop and beyond suggests Dublin is a city much fiddled with and hammered, as if certain modern uglinesses have moral precedence over guilty old beauty every time.

Walking over the squares you see that nearly every one of the spectacular houses is now an office. Looking at the upper floors, I wonder what single people do now to live, and if they are still hanging in there and paying the exorbitant rents. [. . .]

Barrier Methods

HARRY BROWNE (2002)

With the onset of economic prosperity, Ireland went from being a country of net emigration to a country of net immigration – a shift with which the state never wholly came to terms. In a piece for the *Dublin Review*, Harry Browne investigated reports that the Garda Síochána were employing discriminatory immigration-control methods.

At Dundalk's railway station, in a gully overlooked by a brewery, the prettifiers have been in. Clarke Station, as it is officially called after the 1916 rebel leader Thomas Clarke, has a distinctly Tidy Towns feel to it: a dozen or so flower pots hang along each platform; clean yellow bricks gleam in 'heritage' splendour; historical railway knick-knacks are on display in a museum that doubles as a waiting room between the tracks; poems and fragments of poems about train travel are stencilled or stuck on what seems like every available surface.

Over a white-painted portico, partly obscured by the overhanging brilliance of yellow daisies and red poppies, are these words: 'You'll never see the man again who sat across from you.' Then, around the corner, on a shorter cornice: 'Better to look away.' Sometimes, here, there have been four or five police officers waiting on the platform when the train coming from Belfast, en route to Dublin, pulls into the station. Wearing bright yellow tops with 'Garda' on them, but with no individual identification visible (it is not required outside Dublin), they walk along or through the carriages performing their duty for the state as 'Immigration Officers'.

'It would only take two or three minutes, though it might be a little longer if it was crowded, with a lot of people getting on a morning train,' says an Iarnród Éireann employee at the station. 'They were very efficient the way they did it.' The process appears to have been at its peak last winter, when virtually every train was checked and 'maybe once a day people were taken off', according to this regular if casual observer of the operation, a man whose main interest is seeing that the trains run on time.

Such efficiency – carrying out immigration checks on a couple of hundred metres of train in two or three minutes – demands selectivity. According to Superintendent M. P. Staunton from the Dundalk Garda station, in a letter to Belfast solicitor Maura Hutchinson, the police 'carry out such checks on persons whom they suspected to be in breach of the relevant legal [sic] provisions'. He denied that officers 'select people on the basis of the colour of their skin', and added: 'our record clearly shows that a very high proportion of those persons stopped and checked are in fact found to be in breach of those provisions'.

Maura Hutchinson is one of several people who have complained about events they witnessed in Clarke Station from their seats aboard the Belfast-to-Dublin train. On 7 February she was travelling to attend a meeting about immigration law when she saw such law in action. 'We were in Dundalk and there was a prolonged stop. I heard raised voices behind me, and mentions of "Ireland" and "Southern Ireland". I thought perhaps there were tourists who were a bit lost.

'When we were pulling off, there was an announcement apologizing for the delay and saying it was due to immigration control. I looked out the window and saw three or four officers leading two men away. I hadn't seen the officers previously – they didn't even walk up and down the length of the train. They certainly asked no one in our carriage if they had correct immigration clearance to enter the Republic of Ireland.'

Hutchinson took her complaint about the incident directly to the Garda Síochána. She wrote to the Garda station in Dundalk: 'I am deeply concerned at the way in which this is taking place; these men were indentified purely due to the colour of their skin, which is clearly discriminatory and would appear to be an arbitrary abuse of your powers.'

Brendan Fanning, a dentist from Ashford, Co. Wicklow, was returning from a conference in Belfast on the morning of 4 May.

'Two big guys came in, one of them with that psychedelic yellow pull-over, and roared something about passports and identification papers. They asked one group of guys where they came from – "Belfast, right." Then they got into a conversation with another passenger. I heard him say, "I have it in my bag." Then I heard one of the guards say, "Well, if you have, you can get the next train." As we pulled away from the station I saw five black guys left huddled in a corner of the platform. I tell you, at that point the conversation in the carriage went instantly from nil to "Ireland of the Welcomes". Mind you, if you were white and an illegal immigrant you'd have no problem on that train.'

Seamus Dooley, Irish Secretary for the National Union of Journalists, travelled south on the same day. In his carriage there was plenty of conversation before they reached Dundalk: young, obviously foreign, white-skinned tourists sat across from him, chatting about queueing for the Queen Mother's funeral. A few seats away, six or seven young black students also appeared to be in 'lively, chatty' form, Dooley says.

'One garda boarded the carriage at Dundalk, and passed us without a glance.' He went straight to the black students and commenced what Dooley calls a 'hostile grilling'. 'The men said they had been in Belfast for the day. The garda said: "You're entering a foreign country, and when you move from one country to another you should have passports." He asked them for identification, but at no stage did he present identification. There was no explanation as to what the checks are, no "We're carrying out routine inspections." He never explained: "This is what we're looking for."' The men were allowed to remain on the train and, in contrast to Brendan Fanning's carriage, 'silence descended'. 'What do you do? What do you say? "Sorry for your troubles"?' The young white American tourist sitting opposite Dooley was 'genuinely shocked and disturbed', Dooley says, not least because he himself had been entirely overlooked by the inspection.

'Such checks fly in the face of the Good Friday Agreement – passports to travel to Northern Ireland, security checks at Dundalk,' Seamus Dooley says. If immigration controls are to be carried out at the Irish border, says Dooley, they need to be done fairly, without the strong whiff of 'racial profiling' that has hung over them. 'If it is official state policy that those travelling by rail should carry identification, we should be told and it should apply to everyone. It's not enough to leave it to a garda's hunch.'

Selective immigration checks at the border have not been confined to rail passengers. 'Sue', a white New Zealander living in Ireland who prefers to remain anonymous, is a frequent cross-border bus passenger. On one occasion last year she was travelling south, with a great pile of belongings and without a passport. She said as much to a garda who was doing a 'cursory' document check. 'He said, "We'll see about that," then he went to the back of the bus to join a colleague who was questioning a black passenger.' The black man was removed; Sue faced no further questions.

There is a place just up the road, outside Newry, that was the scene of border controls truly worthy of the name until a few years ago. Each car that came along the road was forced into a narrow, heavily fortified side lane, and nervous-looking British squaddies aimed their automatic weapons in every direction. When you passed through the Newry checkpoint during tense times, it was always possible to spot at least one weapon pointed at you.

Today the checkpoint is a faint memory on the landscape, blocked off by crumbling bollards, overgrown with grass and wildflowers, easily missed entirely, but also virtually the only landmark to remind an observant, historically minded visitor that somewhere along this stretch of road there is a change of jurisdiction.

In both jurisdictions, 'cracking down' on immigrants, be they dark-skinned or of eastern European origin, is regarded as smart politics – with a potential only partly masked by an all-party 'anti-racism protocol' that essentially kept immigration off the short-term agenda during the last general election in the Republic. Once the election was out of the way, the new Minister for Justice, Michael McDowell, put 'illegal immigration' at the forefront of publicity and of policy. The most dramatic expression of this was Operation Hyphen: on 16 and 23 July a total of five hundred gardaí, under the direction of the Garda National Immigration Bureau, carried out raids around the country. What were they looking for? The bureau cited a figure of 2,600 people 'evading deportation orders', and most media were happy to repeat it. As a count of the number of cases still on the books, it was doubtless accurate; as an estimate of the true number of such would-be deportees in the country, it was a large exaggeration, as a Garda spokesman was happy to admit to me. Immigration lawyer Derek Stewart told me that, at a conservative estimate, at least half that number had already 'abandoned the jurisdiction'.

Operation Hyphen resulted in the arrest of only fifteen people who were subject to deportation orders. A further 125 people were taken into custody, in many cases for upwards of a week, because of problems with documentation. As a means of communicating aggressively to immigrants and would-be immigrants that the state was getting tougher, this may have been effective. As a media exercise, in which an image emerged of impenetrable warrens of illegals (Garda spokesmen always referred to 'premises' being raided rather than 'homes'), it certainly made a powerful point, with the help of loose talk about the phantom 2,600.

McDowell's own role was more explicit on other immigration matters. He announced in July that he was preparing to amend, if necessary, the state's citizenship laws 'to make it clear that persons who are born in Ireland, and acquire Irish citizenship rights as a consequence, don't confer on their parents a semi-formal right of residence'. Even while a case along these lines was before the Supreme Court, the Minister was using the summer media lull to boost his get-tough image, and the *Sunday Independent* duly reported that he was moving to end the 'loophole' and 'scam' whereby a group of Irish citizens – Irish-born children of foreign parents – are allowed to remain in the country with those parents. (So much for 'cherishing all the children of the nation equally', words from the Proclamation of the Irish Republic on which Thomas Clarke's is the first name.) It is in this crackdown context that over the past five years a border that was meant to be fading away, and a rail line that carried campaigning condom-smugglers three decades ago, have become the setting for a new, highly selective, rather haphazard 'barrier method' of immigration control.

★

When Garda Superintendent M. P. Staunton wrote to Maura Hutchinson from Dundalk in April, he told her: 'It is now an established fact that the vast majority of foreign nationals who enter / attempt to enter this part of Ireland illegally do so by crossing the Border from Northern Ireland into the South.' Unless by 'this part of Ireland' he was referring to County Louth – and it's highly unlikely – he was making a claim about the predominant route of 'illegal immigration' into the Republic that is by no means simple to establish as fact.

Attempting to do so, the obvious place to look is the recently published first annual report of the Office of the Refugee Applications Commissioner (ORAC). This eight-page glossy could pass as bumf from your bank – except that behind the dreadful bureaucracy-meets-PR prose, the friendly logo and the photos of happy, white-skinned officials among the potted plants of their open plan office, the reader encounters titbits about deportation, fingerprinting, and even X-ray exams on asylum-seekers who claim to be 'unaccompanied minors' to see if they really are as young as they say. At the back are the statistics, among them this one: from the time of the establishment of ORAC in November 2000 to the end of 2001, some 75.4 per cent of the 11,357 asylum applications were made at ORAC, rather than at Dublin Airport (18.7 per cent) or 'Other' (5.9 per cent).

Asylum applications remain the only reliable way of getting a handle on what we might call 'informal' immigration (i.e. not involving Irish or EU nationals or others with work permits). The Minister for Justice acknowledges that a large majority of such immigrants are legally and correctly engaged in the system of application, appeal, etc. At least some of Operation Hyphen's 'illegals' turned out to be people whose status was confused, not-yet-updated or caught between phases, rather than clandestine. However, with the ORAC report showing that the office's refusals of asylum applications outnumber its grants by about ten to one, it wouldn't be entirely surprising if many immigrants, especially those without an Irish-born child or the prospect of one, simply tried to evade the system completely. A source close to the application process told me that the official prospects for Nigerians and Romanians (who together made

up nearly half of applications to ORAC in its first thirteen months)
are especially dismal: the state has deportation arrangements with
their home countries, and not only do most of their asylum applications fail, but the last-gasp post-rejection procedure, application for
temporary humanitarian leave to remain, is virtually certain to fail
for applicants from these countries.

So are 'the vast majority' of informal immigrants coming via
Northern Ireland? Extrapolating from such numbers as exist isn't
entirely straightforward. In a 2000 'Blue Paper' on the Common
Travel Area between the UK and Ireland, published by the Policy
Institute in association with the Department of Justice, researcher
Elizabeth Meehan interpreted earlier place-of-asylum-application
statistics as follows: 'By inference, it would seem . . . that the majority of applicants for asylum must have evaded detection at the first
point of clearance in Great Britain, becoming able to enter Ireland
from the North – or possibly, landing at Dublin airport without
announcing themselves or being noticed. It is, however, not impossible that they may have arrived undetected via the "outer perimeter",
either having been smuggled through Rosslare, or having travelled
openly with false documents, and proceeded inland.'

That's an awful lot of 'inference', 'possibly', 'not impossible' and
'either/or', and not a lot of established fact. There is anecdotal evidence that some North–South 'smuggling' does take place – most
notably among Chinese immigrants – but given the abundance of
unsecured roads across the border, this is much more likely to involve
hiring a car or taxi than boarding the train.

Though it seems an odd use of state resources to place up to five
gardaí virtually full-time at Dundalk's train station to prevent perhaps one person a day from entering the Republic, immigration
checks along the border are not entirely eccentric. An informed
guess, according to one immigrant, is that something less than half
but more than a third of asylum-seekers have entered from the North.
He says the estimate is complicated by a further twist: some people
use Northern Ireland and the Republic as transit points into Britain,
by flying from a third country into Belfast – regarded as a relatively
'easy' airport for immigrants – and then crossing the border, finally

ferrying or even flying to Britain, where boats and flights originating in Ireland receive little immigration scrutiny.

Prior to 1997, travellers entering the Republic from any part of the UK did not encounter immigration controls, owing to the special arrangement between the two states known as the Common Travel Area. In June of that year, with an election approaching, the Minister for Justice, Nora Owen, secured an amendment to the Aliens Order that gave 'Immigration Officers' the power to carry out checks on such travellers and to 'refuse such persons leave to land on the same grounds as apply to persons arriving from outside the Common Travel Area', according to a Department of Justice leaflet. This arose, the Department says, 'from growing evidence that the Common Travel Area was being abused by persons who were not entitled to avail of it'. In relation to the Belfast train, there were initially spot checks at Connolly Station in Dublin; these subsequently gave way, for obvious reasons of geography – and perhaps, less obviously, because checks at a busy Dublin commuter station could become a focus for political opposition – to the activity up the line at Clarke Station.

When the Illegal Immigration (Trafficking) Act (2000) was being framed and debated, there was a proposal that carriers should face 'strict liability' – that is, they could be fined or punished for carrying 'illegals' whether or not they knew they were doing so. Much of the debate focused on lorry drivers who might unwittingly carry a human cargo, but airlines, shipping companies and, of course, Iarnród Éireann and Northern Ireland Rail might also have been affected. Strict liability was dropped from the legislation, but Michael McDowell has indicated that a new immigration bill will return to the issue and place the onus on carriers: 'They should not carry [people] into Ireland for profit and/or reward unless they have checked that it's legal for them to come here,' he told the *Sunday Independent*.

But wouldn't this mean that railway officials would face the same dilemma that immigration officers do now: either engage in racial profiling or carry out document checks on every intending passenger? They would probably be on questionable ground under the

Equal Status Act (1999) if they did the former, and would certainly incur significant costs in time and effort if they tried the latter.

According to Niall Crowley, chief executive of the Equality Authority, it is not yet clear whether Garda behaviour like that witnessed in Dundalk can be viewed as illegally discriminatory under the Equal Status Act. The state is subject to the provisions of the Act in relation to the provision of 'services', but not to the exercise of 'functions'. On the face of it, immigration control would appear to be a function rather than a service, but 'we still need to see what contribution the legislation has to offer', Crowley says. He would like to see the legislation amended to cover 'functions' – as happened in England and Wales following the enquiry into the London Metropolitan Police investigation of the racially motivated killing of Stephen Lawrence.

Back in Dundalk, something has changed. When I visited Clarke Station in late July, I was told by an employee that 'there haven't been any checks here in two or three months'. 'I think they're doing it on the roads now,' another man said.

A Garda spokesman was not prepared to comment on the specific reasons for any change – demurring with the standard references to 'operational matters' – but denied that the practice of checking rail passengers had been abandoned. He suggested, instead, that the force was keeping up with the changing transit tactics of potential illegal immigrants: 'Operationally, the position would be changing all the time, and we have to tailor our policies to suit.' What about the apparent coincidence between a small flurry of negative publicity about the Dundalk checks in the late spring of this year and their apparent cessation? 'Oh yes, we take our policies directly from the letters page of the *Irish Times*,' the Garda spokesman said.

The Garda Síochána is not covered by the Freedom of Information Act, so it is difficult to gain further insight into the force's policies and practices in this area. 'It says something about the approach to security of the state that the Army is covered but the Garda are not,' says Seamus Dooley. Iarnród Éireann and the other CIÉ companies are also not covered.

The Department of Justice, Equality and Law Reform, largely responsible for immigration policy, *is* covered by the Freedom of Information Act, but the wholeheartedness of its commitment is less clear. The story is told that when the Act came in five years ago, the then junior minister in the Department of the Taoiseach, Eithne Fitzgerald – responsible, in the main, for the legislation – raised her glass at the celebrations 'to absent friends in the Department of Justice'.

In early June, I made a request to the Department's freedom of information officer for access to records relating to the policy, procedures and practice of immigration controls on the Belfast–Dublin rail service and at train stations in the Republic, as well as records of the deliberations leading to Nora Owen's amendment to the Aliens Order, including but not limited to assessments of the abuse of the Common Travel Area by aliens travelling by rail.

The legislation requires that I receive a response within four weeks. Just over a month had passed when I received a mildly apologetic phone call admitting that the Department had failed to comply and that I was now entitled to seek an internal review into that failure, but really if I hung on a few more days they would have a proper reply for me. I was given to understand, intriguingly, that the delay was due to a 'third-party consultation' with 'British authorities'. After another week's wait, I was told that, in fact, the 'third party' – they were no longer declaring this to be the British authorities – had until the end of July to reply to the 'consultation'. Well, surely there were records that didn't involve the third party? Indeed, it seemed there probably were, and they'd scare those up for me within another few days.

Another few days passed. By this stage I was doing all the phoning, and promised replies never came. On 26 July there was still nothing, and the relevant officer in the immigration division was apparently on leave, so I would have to wait a few more days.

Eight weeks on from the request, on 2 August, I was sent a brown envelope containing twenty-six pages of 'records', seven of which were a photocopy of passages from the British Immigration Act (1971) and subsequent statutory instruments relating to travel from the Republic of Ireland to the UK. The paucity of documentation was surprising enough; what was really astonishing, though, was the cover letter. You see, the Freedom of Information Act took effect, for the Department of Justice, on 21 April 1998; I had specifically requested documents reaching back prior to that date, on the grounds, laid out in the Act, that they would be necessary to understand records created later. However, the civil servant's letter said: 'As all the records held by this Department in respect of this matter were created prior to the commencement of the Act, the right of access, under the Act, does not exist.' That's right: the Department responsible for the state's immigration policy and procedures says it has no records, no letters, no documents, no emails, no notes of telephone calls, relating to immigration controls on the Belfast–Dublin train or at railway stations dating from the past four and a half years.

Suddenly, the yarns one hears about civil servants being warned, since 1998, to 'write nothing down' gained a measure of credibility. As a small consolation prize, the Department utilized Section 6(8) of the Act to release information not otherwise covered by the Act, a series of pre-1998 letters and notes relating to the 1997 amendment to the Aliens Order. None of these make any reference to rail travel or, indeed, any specific reference to movement of migrants from North to South. It's clear that the emphasis of the Department's thinking at the time was on passengers arriving from Great Britain. An October 1996 letter from a British immigration official to an Irish counterpart, Noel Waters, spelled out how the UK law worked in relation to passengers from Ireland: the British Act enables officers to check 'any persons who have arrived in the United Kingdom by ship or aircraft', though 'it is not normally our practice to examine persons arriving from Ireland'.

Four months later, in a February 1997 submission to colleagues and the Minister, Noel Waters wrote (and I quote verbatim): 'The UK side of the CTA [Common Travel Area] have long since a legislative provision in place of the type now being contemplated by us . . . Obviously the whole area of illegal immigration and large numbers of asylum seekers which is only coming to the fore here now, has been a thorn in the side of the UK for many years . . .' As evidence of the need for controls, Waters cited a week-long Garda operation at Dún Laoghaire and North Wall ports, in which 'a total of 29 persons comprising Kenyan, Zairian, Nigerian, Angolan and Romanian nationals were turned back'. Again, there was no mention of overland transport. By 20 June 1997, with a general election fast approaching, a Department official was writing to the Attorney General's office to request 'the urgent drafting of a suitable amending order' to the Aliens Order. And urgent it was, with Nora Owen signing the order on 25 June. From then on, though there were to be no formal immigration controls at places of entry, 'an immigration officer may examine an alien arriving in the state from Great Britain or Northern Ireland'. A 'briefing note' of November 1997 states that 'since the Order was introduced, over 940 persons have been detected seeking to enter the state illegally from Britain or Northern Ireland'.

And that's it, a short history of the Aliens (Amendment) (No. 3) Order, 1997. We are presumably meant to believe that after this flurry of bureaucratic activity in 1996 and 1997, the operation of the Order was left solely in the hands of the Garda Síochána, with no further thought given to it by the Department. Is that really all the state has to tell us about how, why, and at whose direction black people have been taken off trains at Dundalk?

Stranger Here Myself

GLENN PATTERSON (2005)

> The novelist Glenn Patterson has produced an impressive body of
> journalism and essays, devoted largely to his distinctive take on life in
> his native Belfast. This piece appeared in the *Guardian*.

My friend Andy is in town. My friend Liz has rung to tell me to ring
her back when he's rung me. We have been complicating arrangements like this for fifteen years. Then, I had just returned from
Manchester to write my second novel. Andy was in a flat off the
Lisburn Road making his fourth album, *Out There*. He had a song on
it called 'Waiting for the 38' after the bus down the Lisburn Road
into town. Now Andy is in Australia, back on tour twice a year.

He rings. 'Half nine,' I say, as I always do, and then, thinking I'm
saying something new, 'Bar Bacca.' Bar Bacca is just behind our old
meeting place, the Crown Bar. Just behind and a million miles from.
The theme is Eastern — candles, cushions, sunken sofas, great big
Buddha — though the east it mostly recalls is Berlin's when I first
visited at the end of the Eighties. In fact, if Bar Bacca has a draw-
back, that's it: when you walk out the door you're not actually in
Prenzlauer Berg.

At half nine plus five, Andy appears. 'They've changed the 39 to
the 9A,' he says. It's the new Metrolink system. At half nine plus ten
he says, 'So where will we go when Liz gets here?' It seems I wasn't
saying anything new when I said Bar Bacca. It seems I have been saying Bar Bacca for the last five years and that for five years Bar Bacca is
too loud for the catching-up chat we want to have.

'It's usually Ten Square after this,' Andy says, and I remember, just
after the hotel opened at the back of the City Hall, a couple of nights
when we were the only customers in its ground floor bar. That was
before *Cosmopolitan* voted Ten Square as one of its six sexiest weekend retreats.

'It'll be packed,' I say.

'So what about these new places?' Andy asks.

It's got to that even in Belfast. Five years is old.

Liz arrives. 'Help me,' I say the second after she says it's a bit loud. 'Andy wants to go somewhere really new.'

We have a drink to think.

'I know,' I say. 'Malmaison.'

Malmaison was recently named as one of the world's Hot New Hotels by Condé Nast. Belfast is suddenly coming down with interesting hotel facts, at least more interesting than the Europa being the most bombed hotel in the world, though even in 1990 when the three of us started going out for drinks together that had grown a bit hoary. That was part of what the novel I was writing was about; part of the background to *Out There*.

Malmaison is just up the street from the enormous hole in the ground that will soon be the Victoria Centre, Belfast's largest retail development. It is the makeover of a previous hot new place to go, the McCausland, which was itself the renovation of a nineteenth century seed warehouse. A pretty spectacular seed warehouse, it has to be said. Andy, Liz and I fetch up there a little after eleven. (Make that two drinks to think in Bar Bacca.) The door from the street into the bar is locked, but undeterred we breeze in by the lobby entrance. Lots of purples and reds, chairs that look like the churches we have deserted for Sainsbury's on a Sunday. The barman asks us are we residents. By coincidence – happy, we think – Andy is going to be a resident in a couple of nights' time, after this Belfast gig.

'But, not at the moment?' the barman says.

No, not at the moment.

'Then, I'm afraid . . .' The barman spreads his hands.

We are staggered. You have to understand, late-night drinking in Belfast has been an established fact for close on two decades: a long story, but a desire to draw support away from paramilitary drinking clubs is involved.

Maybe the lure of drinking clubs is as past-tense as the Europa's most-bombed gong. Maybe we just caught Malmaison on a bad night. The website invites you to come into the bar any night of the week between eleven in the morning and midnight. Mind you, the website also tells you that they have nicknamed the hotel 'Mal Bellefast' and promises guests 'more than a drop of the blarney'. That'll be Blarney as in County Cork. That'll be the cliché predating the 'Bad but beautiful', which itself predates the one I may be peddling of Belfast, the butterfly emerging from its chrysalis.

It's not the fact of change that is new in Belfast, it's the speed. I always fancied I knew the city pretty well, and not just as a writer. Even in the very worst times, Belfast never lacked tourists. What it lacked was a tourist infrastructure. Like most people with a spare room (or floor) and a car, I have been a hotelier and a tour guide, though I confess I once drove the American novelist – and Van Morrison fan – Rick Moody around east Belfast for an hour failing to find Cyprus Avenue.

(You can come back now, Rick. I drove up it every day on my way home, and the music journalist Stuart Bailie does a tour of Van-related sites: Cyprus Avenue, Hyndford Street, Beechie river, Davey's chipper . . .)

The Malmaison's leap into the limelight took me by surprise. I used to worry when I didn't recognise band names on bills posted outside bars. These days I don't even recognise the bars. Like the Potthouse. You would think you couldn't miss the Potthouse. In an area – the slow-to-the-tongue 'Cathedral Quarter' – where blending in with the old commercial architecture is the norm, it jumps out: three floors of solid glass all lit up in yellow. Yet the first I knew of it opening was reading a review of it in the *Observer*.

The Potthouse is the first place we see on stepping out the Malmaison's doors. This part of town, the streets around High Street and the landmark Albert Clock, is where Belfast began and is the new nightlife centre, a mile or so removed from the Shaftesbury Square/ university area that was, all through my teens and 20s, the one place where you felt free of the baleful influence of the balaclava brigades. Shaftesbury Square and the university area are still teeming at the weekends. If you've seen documentaries about binge drinking in your part of the world, you've been there already.

So down to the Potthouse we go. There has been a fashion show earlier in the evening. Liz was on the catwalk. The bar is full of fashion-show people. Very beautiful, very inclined to talk very loudly very close to one another's faces (and Liz's, those who know her). We leave again. It's now half eleven. The Metrolink, like City-bus which it replaced, has stopped running. But this is not a problem. Belfast always was a very walkable city. The problem was most often you felt like running. There is, even ten years after the ceasefires, and even with the paramilitaries' occasionally liberal interpretation of the term, something thrilling to someone of my age, bumping around these streets late on a summer's night. Temple Bar in Dublin is sup-posed to be the model, but Temple Bar is more like Shaftesbury Square these days.

This reminds me more of Canal Street when I lived in Manchester, before Canal Street became Temple Bar too. And we are not stuck for choice. A couple of hundred yards away there is the guaranteed welcome of the John Hewitt. Closer, but less predictably congenial, is the Northern Whig, named for the newspaper once published in the building, and displaying an ironic take on barroom politics in the shape of cast-off statues from Soviet-era Prague. But this is a night for somewhere we've never been before. Ali, my wife, just moved offices down this end of town. She has told me of another place. We cut back across High Street and up the narrow Church Lane and find it: Nicholl Bar Brasserie. I remember this under another name when it advertised itself as, at seven feet wide, the smallest bar in Belfast. (I tried to go in once, but someone else was already in it.) Nicholl isn't a whole lot wider. There are maybe ten customers downstairs when we arrive and it's pretty full. Ten customers and no two of them appearing in the same film; a few of them aren't even in colour. Despite the 'brasserie', Nicholl at this time of the night is all bar, and none the worse for that. It's exactly what we've been looking for. It's what Belfast lost and may be finding again. When we leave, loose of limb, before the new chucking out time of one o'clock, it doesn't matter that it's not Prenzlauer Berg out there.

I mention this, a couple of Sundays later, to a German journalist who has just flown in on one of the new direct flights from Berlin. I take her on a tour. We drive into town behind the 9A along the Lisburn Road. I tell her about the Northern Ireland Tourist Board initiative, 'Be a Tourist at Home'. I tell her I would have to start at the Lisburn Road. I once rented a house here, but in the decade since I decamped to east Belfast, I have often felt like a stranger coming back. There has been no Condé Nast or *Cosmopolitan* poll, but I would defy anyone to show me a more chic mile and a half in Ireland.

We wind up in the Cathedral Quarter. I am talking up Belfast's radical heritage when I suddenly blurt, 'I love this city.' And standing on Donegall Street on a sunny Sunday morning, I am in no doubt I do. Whether despite or due to the attempts to market it, something really distinctive has taken root in this part of town in recent years.

But then . . . Directly across the street from us is the shuttered entrance to the North Street Arcade, which until it caught fire in May 2004 – at both ends simultaneously – was one of the finest examples of 1930s architecture in the city and home to some of Belfast's most individual businesses and organisations: the Cathedral Quarter Arts festival; Factotum, publishers of the *Vacuum* free newspaper; the latest in a long line of record shops belonging to Terri Hooley, who twenty-five years ago took the Undertones into a studio down an entry off Donegall Street to record 'Teenage Kicks'. Terri's hand might not have been too far from the aerosol that has written across the shutters, what many people believe, 'they burnt us out'.

There are rumours of a multi-storey car park in the vicinity; more-than rumours of a retail development to eclipse the Victoria Centre; fears that the Cathedral Quarter was all along a cover for the developers' long-term ambitions.

I hope these fears are unfounded. I hope that in pursuit of Urban Outfitters the developers don't make strangers of a whole lot more of Belfast's citizens.

A Series of Accidents

ANN MARIE HOURIHANE (2006)

Ann Marie Hourihane's essay on two historical pageants staged in
Dublin in April 2006 – the official observances of the ninetieth anni-
versary of the Easter Rising, and Michael Flatley's dance extravaganza
Celtic Tiger – begins with a survey of the history of Rising commem-
orations, which reached a peak on the fiftieth anniversary in 1966.
Forty years later the perils of excess were better understood – by the
Irish state, if not by Mr Flatley.

On Monday, 24 April 1916, the Inland Revenue wrote to an obscure
Dublin schoolmaster, Patrick Pearse, threatening to confiscate his
property for non-payment of tax. Pearse, a polite and respectable
man, was beset by money worries. The previous evening, Easter Sunday, he had left a letter to the headmistress of the girls' school that he
had founded. Wages for his teaching staff were hard for him to find:
'I enclose you [*sic*] chq. £5 as a further instalment. Wishing you a
very happy Easter.' Pearse then cycled into the city with his brother.
With a handful of disparate comrades, representing a dissident minority of the Irish Volunteers, they seized a number of substantial
buildings in the centre of town, making the General Post Office their
headquarters, and waited for the British army to attack. Nobody
asked Pearse, or anyone else, to do it. On Monday also Pearse stood
in front of the GPO and read out a proclamation from 'the provisional government of the Irish Republic', a document of which he
was probably the main author, to onlookers in O'Connell Street.
One of Pearse's supporters later recalled: 'The response was chilling;
a few thin, perfunctory cheers, no direct hostility just then; but no
enthusiasm whatever.' On Saturday Pearse gave the British his unconditional surrender. He was placed in solitary confinement. His
comrades were jeered by their fellow citizens as they were led away
to prison.

On Wednesday, 3 May 1916, at 3.30 in the morning, Pearse was executed by firing squad. His comrades Thomas Clarke, a veteran of the Irish Republican Brotherhood, and Thomas MacDonagh, a university lecturer who had once taught at Pearse's school, were shot with him. On the night after Pearse's trial one of the three military judges, General Blackader, dined with Elizabeth, Countess of Fingal. In her memoirs she reports the General as having been depressed because 'I have had to condemn to death one of the finest characters I have ever come across. There must be something very wrong in the state of things that makes a man like that a Rebel. I don't wonder that his pupils adored him.'

The rebels and the British army had more in common than either side would admit. Áine Ceannt remembered that when they were told that her husband, Eamon, had been executed, 'My sister in law suggested that we go and purchase some mourning. As the War was raging at that time and there were many young widows, it was easy to procure an outfit.'

For an Irish person any examination of the Easter Rising of 1916 is like looking too closely at the circumstances of one's own conception. At first they tell you that you were lovingly planned, and just what Mummy and Daddy had been hoping for. Then you begin to suspect that there are facts which are being withheld from you. As time passes you become convinced that you have been lied to. Eventually you realize that, far from being a carefully nurtured project, your existence is the result of a series of accidents and the actions of a small minority who were interested only in fulfilling their own desires and had only the vaguest idea of the consequences. All the leaders of the Easter Rising except two, Éamon de Valera and Constance Markievicz, were executed. It was a grave mistake, turning a group of unsupported extremists into martyrs. The advanced nationalist party Sinn Féin, which had no involvement in the Rising, won a landslide victory over the moderate nationalists at the 1918 election. And so, we have always been told, modern Ireland was born.

Monty Python used to have a joke, the tag line of which was

'Nobody expects the Spanish Inquistion.' This joke involved actors dressed as members of the Spanish Inquisition bursting in to contemporary scenes – an ordinary modern living room, for example – and shouting in a very serious way, 'Nobody expects the Spanish Inquisition!' The incongruity was the joke. The Easter Rising is a bit like that in modern Ireland: it explodes into our lives at the strangest moments. And, of course, no one ever did expect the Easter Rising. Not even in 1916.

The writer James Stephens, in his eyewitness account of the Rising, had this to say about Dublin crowds: 'Almost everyone was smiling and attentive, and a democratic feeling was abroad, to which our City is very much a stranger; for while in private we are a sociable and talkative people we have no street manners or public ease whatever.'

At the time of the Rising Stephens was trying to learn to read music, in preparation for learning to play the dulcimer. He was reading a theosophist book by Madame Blavatsky. He was working at the National Gallery on Merrion Square. When the rebellion started he spent his time on the streets, cataloguing astonishment. He saw an innocent man shot down by the Volunteers in Stephen's Green because he had tried to remove his wagon from one of their barricades – barricades were made from bicycles, from clocks, from the rolls of newsprint taken from the *Irish Times*. 'One does not know how ugly blood can look until it has been seen clotted in hair,' Stephens wrote.

At night Stephens paced the floor. He was very fond of normality. 'This morning also there has been no bread, no milk, no meat, no newspapers, but the sun is shining. It is astonishing that, thus early in the Spring, the weather should be so beautiful.' Stephens missed the newspapers particularly. He went about gathering snippets of his own: 'There is not a cat or a dog left alive in Camden Street.' He was alive to rumour, and the lunacy of rumour: 'There were one hundred German submarines lying in Stephen's Green pond.' Above all he saw the madness of warfare in an ordinary city: 'An officer in this part [of the city] had his brains blown into the roadway. A young girl ran into the road, picked up his cap and scraped the brains into it. She

covered this poor debris with a little straw, and carried the hat piously
to the nearest hospital in order that the brains might be buried with
their owner.'

Stephens cast a shrewd eye on the looting. On the Saturday of
Easter week, 'Another young boy was standing near embracing a
large ham. He had been trying for three days to convey his ham to a
house near the Gresham Hotel where his sister lived. He had almost
given up hope, and he hearkened intelligently to the idea that he
should himself eat the ham and so get rid of it.' Most looters were
not so strategically minded. 'The shops attacked were mainly haber-
dashers, shoe shops and sweet shops. Very many sweet shops were
raided, and until the end of the rising sweet shops were the favourite
mark of looters.'

For a contemporary Irish person it is rather heartening to learn
that the sense of bewilderment engendered by 1916 was there from
the very beginning. On the Sunday after the Rising, when the surrender was complete, Stephens wrote: 'All we know in Dublin is that
our city burst into a kind of spontaneous war; that we lived through
it during one singular week, and that it faded away and disappeared
almost as swiftly as it had come.'

Pearse became a secular saint. It was understood that he did not
smoke or drink alcohol. He had ploughed the profits from his father's
substantial business into his schools. His picture hangs in the office of
the Taoiseach, Bertie Ahern, a talisman of Irish purity, of Gaelic
Ireland – the Irish language was Pearse's first love – and of men who
did not want to have fun. Anything further from the Ireland of today
is hard to imagine.

Streets, schools, railway stations and blocks of council flats were
named after the leaders of the Easter Rising, and in one way it
seemed, growing up in Ireland, that there was no escape from their
unsmiling faces. And yet I do not remember being taught one thing
about the Rising at primary or secondary school. Teachers seemed to
assume that we knew all about it already. Or perhaps they were
embarrassed. There was no sense that 1916 was relevant to our lives,
or even interesting. Our nun told us that Wolfe Tone, an eighteenth-
century rebel who became a hero to later nationalists like Pearse, had

not really attempted suicide and that this was a slanderous rumour spread by the British authorities. This startling news got short shrift when I brought it home.

The annual commemoration had always been a fragile flower, sometimes forgotten and sometimes forced to bloom. In 1926 the Rising was commemorated with a Mass in Whitefriar Street and a visit to the Republican Plot at Glasnevin cemetery. The most extravagant gesture that year was the renaming of Dublin's Great Brunswick Street, where Pearse had lived as a boy, as Pearse Street. In 1929, on the fiftieth anniversary of Pearse's birth, celebrations were low-key. In 1932, with the first Fianna Fáil government in office, the Rising was celebrated with unprecedented ceremony. In 1935 the leader of Fine Gael, William Cosgrave, who had fought in 1916 himself, said, 'The time is not right for an adequate commemoration of 1916, which would be accompanied by that generous national enthusiasm indispensable to success.'

In 1941, on the twenty-fifth anniversary of the Rising, a large parade took place, although it was not as elaborate as some enthusiasts at the Department of Defence had proposed. In December 1940 a memorandum headed 'Victory Parade Past the GPO' had been returned to the Department of Defence from the Department of the Taoiseach with the word 'victory' corralled between brackets. The Taoiseach was Éamon de Valera, the first man to receive the newly minted 1916 medals.

In 1946 the *Irish Times* radio critic was already complaining about the predictability and pedestrian nature of the Rising commemorations. By the late 1940s the Old IRA Men's Association was complaining that no municipal buildings flew the tricolour during Easter Week. The government replied that flags would be flown on all buildings 'equipped with permanent flagpoles'. In 1962 there were several parades at different venues, and in June of that year the Federation of IRA 1916–1921 wrote to the Taoiseach, Seán Lemass: 'This multiplication of parades has not been for the best. The citizens of Dublin have become so used to seeing handfuls of old men marching behind the national flag that they no longer turn their heads to look at them, while the drivers of buses and cars hoot them

out of the way and break their ranks with indifference, if not contempt.'

Coming up to 1966, the fiftieth anniversary of the Rising, things
became more heated. Tom Clarke's widow, Kathleen, wrote to
Lemass in fury at the way her husband's role in 1916 had steadily been
eclipsed by that of Pearse. She said she would speak out if anyone
claimed that Pearse, and not her husband, had been President of the
Republic. 'Surely Pearse should have been satisfied with the honour
of Commander-in-Chief,' she wrote, 'when he knew as much about
commanding as my dog.' Kathleen Clarke's anger notwithstanding,
the 1966 observances were elaborate. I remember the commemorative stamps. My father told me that one stamp depicted a flame,
although in retrospect I think that it was a lily (still a republican symbol today).

The annual 1916 parade was discontinued in 1971, shortly after
the onset of the Troubles in Northern Ireland, when the Provisional IRA's campaign seemed to change the contemporary
significance of the Rising. The state observances on the seventy-
fifth anniversary of the Rising, in 1991, were strikingly muted. To
those outside the Irish republic a ninetieth anniversary may seem a
strange one to celebrate, but in October 2005, at Fianna Fáil's Ard
Fheis, Bertie Ahern announced that the anniversary would be
marked with a military parade. It was said that Fianna Fáil had
noted remarks by Gerry Adams about the need for Sinn Féin to
start preparing for the hundredth anniversary of the Rising, in
2016, and that they were furious over a historical pageant staged by
Sinn Féin, to celebrate the hundredth anniversary of the founding
of the party, in which its youth wing donned the uniforms of the
rebellion period. Now Bertie Ahern wished to reclaim the legacy
of 1916 from a party that poses an ever-growing electoral threat to
the government.

I phoned the Department of the Taoiseach a couple of times in February with queries about the Easter arrangements, and no one
returned my calls. The office of the Taoiseach issued a form for press
accreditation which had the wrong mobile phone number on it. In

April the Department of Defence website only gave details for the day of the parade itself, yet the newspapers carried reports of other events taking place well in advance of it. The press was not notified that the Minister of Defence would be unveiling a commemorative stone at the Irish army's headquarters in the Curragh, County Kildare. 'We didn't know ourselves,' said the very nice civil servant. 'It's only a road sign.'

'I don't care,' I said rudely. 'I would have gone if I'd known about it.'

In fact the unveiled stone is not a road sign, though it is sited near the car park at the entrance to the Curragh. According to the defence forces' press office – the most efficient press office by far – the seven barracks at the Curragh were re-named after the seven signatories of the Proclamation in 1929. The stone unveiled commemorates that fact, and gives directions to the individual barracks.

On Sunday 9 April the Taoiseach swept in to Collins Barracks Museum on his usual wave of charm to open an exhibition called 'Understanding 1916: The Easter Rising'. He gave a speech entitled 'Remembrance, Reconciliation, Renewal' in which, amongst other things, he called on us to do voluntary work in our communities. The exhibition stretched from the 1913 Lockout – a time of industrial warfare in which the trade unions squared up to the bosses, and lost – through to 1923 and the end of the Civil War: 'The whole revolutionary moment,' as the civil servant in the Department of the Taoiseach called it.

At a dinner five days before the parade another civil servant cheerfully told me that the arrangements were 'Chaos. The invitations haven't gone out. The booklets aren't even printed.'

In Marlborough Street, opposite the Pro-Cathedral, the private coaches were waiting. The limousine drivers were waiting inside the fence of the Department of Education, and were not inclined to talk to people with notebooks. In Cathal Brugha Street my handbag got its one search of the day. In 1916 Cathal Brugha was taken out of the South Dublin Union (a workhouse, now St James's Hospital) with twenty-five wounds which left him permanently crippled. He was eventually killed fighting in O'Connell Street during the Civil War. He had attended Belvedere College, and been educated there by the Jesuits. Like so many of the 1916 leaders, he was a nice middle-class boy.

When the journalists got off the bus we were a respectable, middle-aged lot with the exception of one young man who had recently shaved his head. 'He's representing the looters,' said one of his colleagues. Dublin looters are a live issue today, after a demonstration against a loyalist parade down O'Connell Street in February turned into a riot. The looters targeted a fashionable shoe shop and were scorned for their stupidity when they were reported to have run off with a lot of single shoes.

Two viewing stands were placed in front of the GPO, on either side of the northbound traffic lane, with the government and other dignitaries on the GPO side and journalists and relatives of 1916 veterans on the broad traffic island, with our backs to the Ann Summers sex shop. We had a clear view of the government. There is a tendency in Fianna Fáil to wear coats too long. Bertie's coat was too long, Willie O'Dea's coat was too long. Willie O'Dea, who is Minister for Defence, was swamped by a loose coat that flapped off him like a dressing gown as the troops looked at Willie, as Willie looked at the troops. This is what military parades are about, this looking at each other.

The President, Mary McAleese, was wearing a sage green coat and high boots. 'That's because she has terrible legs,' says the journalist beside me. 'Great highlights.' The previous president always looked as though she had been called from her study, and was on her way back to it. Mary McAleese, on the other hand, gives the impression that there is nothing she would rather be doing than standing in O'Connell Street on a Sunday morning, looking at soldiers who are looking back at her.

The obsequies that preceded the parade were moving, in parts. When the Honour Guard lowered its collective head. When the lament was played. When the band played 'Mise Éire'. When Captain Tom Ryan read the Proclamation, which is beautiful.

From where we sat, very comfortably, the crowd seemed quite

large, but it was hard to tell; the canopy circumscribed our view. Once the obsequies were over there seemed little point in staying in the stand. It took a little bit of manoeuvring to get away from so much privilege. When I got down to ground level I could see that the wide pavements of O'Connell Street were not thronged with spectators, that the crowd at the barriers was only three people deep. There were a lot of grey heads. I saw a neighbour of mine, who calls himself the Weather Man, pushed up against the barrier outside Clery's. He is a handsome man, and he was wearing a green shirt. I have not seen him since, to ask him what he thought.

Of course the parade was boring. Our army is so small, and seen so rarely, that we are not really used to it. I think we feel affection for it, but it's hard to tell. The upper windows of O'Connell Street's numerous burger palaces were filled with parents and children, watching. At the O'Connell statue near the bridge mothers and fathers sat with their children amongst the four angels at Daniel's feet.

Two young men stood and sat, respectively, on one angel, and the standing young man became the wag. In Dublin there is always a wag. The applause was polite as the army's modest hardware drove past. Some kind of space suit, uninhabited, appeared on the back of a vehicle belonging to the bomb disposal unit. No one seemed to find this sight strange, or to consider that the bloodiest bombers produced by Ireland have claimed to be the rightful heirs of the men of 1916. The tanks were applauded. A bizarre vehicle called the Aardvark Flail – which turned out to be for mine-removal – rolled past. A band played 'Eileen Óg'. The standing young man was on his mobile. 'Look, a hot chick,' he shouted as a female soldier drove past on a tank. Three helicopters flew up O'Connell Street. 'I like that big gun, Mister.'

It seemed to come down to the fact that the bigger the gun that was driven past us, the bigger the cheer it received. The RBS 70, for example, which is a rocket launcher, was very warmly received. But the biggest cheer by far came for the UN Peacekeepers' float. It featured a rather fragile, branched sign, pointing variously to Lebanon, Afghanistan, Kosovo, Ireland. 'Ah, that's excellent,' said an older woman to what looked like her grandchild.

The gardaí marched past. I could not see them, but the young man standing on the angel shouted, 'Boo! Boo! Bastards.' I thought of the looter who was brought to Pearse in the GPO. An order had gone out that all looters would be shot. Pearse, who knew little about the people he had decided to save, said, 'Ah, poor man. Put him with the others.'

At the foot of the statue a young father wearing corduroy trousers watched his Asian daughter toddling slowly on the traffic island. The crowd would be estimated at 100,000. It did not look that big to me. Nineteen-sixteen has never been about numbers. But now it is as if we cannot afford to admit that even our commemorations are anything but an unqualified success.

Immediately after the parade there was a reception in the basement of the Gresham Hotel for the relatives of those who had fought in 1916, along with most of the Cabinet and quite a few journalists. Well, there was food. On the circular tables were squares of pizza, and ham sandwiches. There were also sandwiches of tuna and sweet corn. There were small vessels of brown sauce and red sauce. There were Cornish pasties, which had been sliced into manageable portions. There was breaded chicken fillet. And also on each table was a square glass vase, like a small aquarium, in which floated the head of an orange gerbera, which is, I think, a desert flower. The water in the vases was getting a bit murky.

Everyone was hungry. We'd been outdoors since well before noon, and there was a sense of relief that we were warm again at last. Over at the far wall a group of thirteen adults was having a photograph taken. 'All relatives of Thomas MacDonagh,' someone said, as they smiled for several cameras. As the Rising wore on MacDonagh showed signs of what the historian Charles Townshend calls 'intense strain'; Peadar Kearney described him as 'careworn and dishevelled'. He was commanding officer at Jacob's biscuit factory in Bishop Street.

Síle de Valera and Éamon Ó Cuiv, who are first cousins and TDs, were in demand, as a sort of matching pair, for photographs. The family of William Barrett was there. 'He was in Jacob's with Thomas

MacDonagh. He died on the twenty-fifth anniversary of the Rising, funnily enough.'

Someone walked up to a middle-aged man and said, 'You're Patrick Pearse, are you?' and the middle-aged man said, 'Yes.' He was Patrick Pearse O'Hanrahan. There is a bridge in New Ross named after Michael O'Hanrahan, who also fought at Jacob's, and was subsequently executed. There is a working men's club in Carlow called after him, there is a football team with his name.

Later that night, at the State Reception at Dublin Castle, the rooms were full of judges and clergymen and Capuchin monks – spiritual descendants of the Capuchins who were the confessors to the revolutionaries before their executions. I was shown the room where the wounded James Connolly spent the night before his execution. 'They were going to make Margaret Thatcher sleep in there when she was over on a visit,' someone said. The Taoiseach arrived, looking determined. He has taken 1916 back from Sinn Féin, his new electoral rivals. He is lying upon it, fighting the other boys off.

The parade was on Easter Sunday. The following Thursday a crowd that seemed much larger than Sunday's caused traffic chaos in its eagerness to see Michael Flatley's latest dance extravaganza, *Celtic Tiger*, at the Point Theatre, a mile or so down the Liffey quays from O'Connell Street.

Michael Flatley is not confused by Irish history; his view of it is crystal clear. From the moment *Celtic Tiger* opens with a video projection of a mouth whispering 'There's no place like home . . . There's no place like home . . . There's no place like home', you know that you are in the hands of a confident man. Not for Flatley the complications of economics, the rivalries of widows or the untidiness of the truth. To him, Irish history is a children's story, just like *The Wizard of Oz*. In a daring move, Flatley, who is pushing fifty, inserts himself within it, as Dorothy.

This was a paying crowd. Our tickets cost €85 each, and we were lucky to get them. We sat in the wrong seats by mistake and were displaced some way into the show by a party that included the aviation tycoon Tony Ryan.

Michael Flatley became famous as the male lead in *Riverdance*, which made pioneering use of girls in short skirts performing Irish dances for unconscionable periods of time, and there is no good reason for him to stray from this formula. In the first number Flatley wore a short skirt himself, although, disappointingly, he also wore tracksuit bottoms underneath. His skirt and his leather breastplates led me to believe he was a Roman on the brink of invading, which would have sent the whole evening clattering into hypothesis. But then one of my companions pointed out the dolmen projected on the screen: we were in the presence of Celts.

It takes a brave man, it takes a happy man, to rescue the dolmen from the satiric grip of *Spinal Tap*. Flatley strode around the stage a good bit, directing the rows of dancers. *Riverdance* was intensely martial, and although Michael Flatley has recently said that his great hero is his fellow Irish-American Jimmy Cagney, his choreography seems to owe its greatest debt to Busby Berkeley, of whom it was once said that he had a great talent for turning people into things. The sheer number of pretty girls on stage overwhelmed the smaller and much less attractive corps of male dancers – except for Flatley, of course. The shortness of the skirts and the sheer monotony of the Irish dancing movements invited the thought that at any moment the whole spectacle could tip into orgy.

In the second number girls in red leotards rolled around the stage, seemingly in some distress. A snake writhed on the screen, showing a bit too much fang. Electronic chanting came from the taped soundtrack. In one of the more shocking moments of the evening, eight male dancers rolled onstage like Cossacks, dressed in ecclesiastical robes, and suppressed the right of Irish women to wear red leotards for the foreseeable future.

Then a humble farmer came on stage and sang, 'A sleeping tiger waits . . . a thousand years or more of war, struggle and strife. The destiny of a nation, finally coming to life . . . Just look how far we've come with our true colours unfurled, the envy of the world.' This was but a brief foretaste of the ecstatic present, before *Celtic Tiger* returned to the nightmare of our Irish past. The Vikings came on and danced with some native Irish girls. The horns on the Viking helmets looked a bit dodgy – 'Like steers,' as my friend said.

Redcoats jigged out for the next number and performed a horn-pipe to a few bars from 'Rule Britannia'. A thatched cottage was projected onto the backdrop and flames began to lick its thatch as the redcoats evicted an enormous number of scantily clad Irish peasants, all of whom had had time to wash their hair. At the climax of the eviction scene Michael Flatley appeared dressed in a soutane and car-rying rosary beads. He just had time to intone 'Forgive those who trespass against us' before he was surrounded by pesky redcoats and the stage was plunged into darkness. The humble farmer came out again and sang 'Four Green Fields', in front of helicopter shots of Irish scenery. 'I have Four Green Fields, but one of them is in bond-age . . .' There was warm applause.

As a lone male footballer entered, a tank appeared on the back-drop and lowered its gun straight at the footballer, and straight at the audience. It shot him, and us. And then we were straight into a street scene in front of the GPO, with stout Irish lads challenging the red-coats to a dancing competition. Michael was wearing a tweed cap and high-waisted trousers and the music was 'The Wearing of the Green'. The redcoats' uniforms looked a bit antique for 1916, and their tracer bullets seemed a bit advanced. Our lads fought the red-coats, wrist to wrist. There were no looters, or dead horses, or brains being scraped into hats. Instead a very pretty girl wearing a white gown and wings flew high over the stage, mouthing a wordless song. This was Peace.

Then the humble farmer came out and sang 'A Nation Once Again'. A tricolour fluttered on the backdrop. There was tumultu-ous applause. Two women in our section stood up to applaud. Flatley came out punching the air, shaking his head and shouting 'Yeah!'

During the interval everyone was slightly breathless at having been whisked so quickly through so much history. What would Michael do in the second half? The planning tribunals? Clerical child abuse? We settled on the Pope's visit and the assassination of JFK.

What happened next showed Michael Flatley's genius as a show-man and his ability to sashay through any cultural minefield. The second half opened on a naughty Aer Lingus hostess, complete with white gloves. As Flatley strode on to the stage in a pilot's uniform and large sunglasses a cheer of anticipation went up from the crowd. Flatley gave a self-deprecatory smile – in this, as in so many things, he is reminiscent of that other great entertainer, Liberace.

An army of airline pilots then entered and the naughty air hostess, looking increasingly nervous, stretched her arms out like an aeroplane and all the pilots carried her past the Statue of Liberty to America. There she performed a striptease, right down to a stars-and-stripes bikini (the top was starred, the bottom was striped). The audience fell back, exhausted.

Then we had the melting-pot number – Irish people happily dancing with other ethnic groups. Then we had the reflective number, in which Michael came out in a white satin tuxedo and played the flute. As he did this a young couple in medieval costume danced in front of an impressionist landscape which was projected onto the backdrop complete with its frame. I still don't understand what this was about, and could not find anybody who did.

Then Flatley came on in a gangster's pinstripe suit, and a girl came on in another stars-and-stripes bikini and handed him a machine gun. Here we saw Flatley at his cleverest. By transporting the whole second half to America Michael lost none of the violence, but merely shifted it to Hollywood. *Celtic Tiger* had no time for 'the whole revolutionary moment', or for the remainder of the twentieth century on the island of Ireland, or even for the present-day Ireland to which the show's title would seem to refer. All we got was a guitar solo of the Irish national anthem, and the projection of famous Irish icons on the screen: Jack Lynch, Westlife, James Joyce, JFK (twice), Colin Farrell and a pint of Guinness (three times).

Finally, the girls in bikinis and boys dressed as officers in the US navy danced to the tune of 'Yankee Doodle'. I thought that they were going to invade Iraq. Flatley wore a heavily braided hat.

It was the end. Michael had to rouse us to even stronger applause. He roused the audience on our side of the stage, which was the one place where there was no camera recording the show, and thus the one place where he could do his rousing unobserved by posterity.

Afterwards we decided that Tony Ryan was very good at laughing silently. We had laughed so loud that the woman behind us, my friend said, had hit her deliberately with a handbag, several times.

For God & St Patrick

EOIN BUTLER (2007)

The annual July pilgrimage to Croagh Patrick, Co. Mayo, is – take your pick – either a commemoration of the time St Patrick spent forty days on the mountain, disposing of various evil spirits and banishing snakes as he did so, or a late-flowering Catholic baptism of a pre-Christian summer solstice festival. Some of the accompanying manifestations appear to belong to neither tradition. Eoin Butler's account of the 2007 pilgrimage, and of the Catholic Youth Festival at Knock, was published in *Mongrel*.

'Take my hand,' croons the singer on Midwest Radio. 'Lord Jesus, take my hand.' It's 9 a.m. on the last Sunday in July, and the crowd outside Campbell's pub, at the foot of Croagh Patrick, are basking in the early-morning sunshine. They wear county jerseys, and clutch pints of Guinness and bottles of Bulmers. An old man plays the box accordion, while the jukebox inside blasts 'Sean South from Garry-owen'. Some appear weary from their morning's exertions. But the mood is one of festive celebration. We're at the bottom of a mountain, but at the very apex of a summer.

Approach roads from Westport are clogged, with cars parked bumper to bumper on either side. Pathways leading up to the Reek are lined with traders selling religious souvenirs, walking sticks, sweets and chocolate. The resourcefulness of these men, most of them Travellers, has got to be admired. One is selling mirrors inscribed with the words of the poem 'Don't Quit' – with a picture of St Patrick crudely superimposed in the top corner. Another man, in a three-piece suit, is extolling, through a loud speaker, the benefits of the grapes his son is selling.

On the car radio, *Faith Alive* presenter Fr Brendan Hoban dedicates a song to all of those making the annual pilgrimage up Mayo's holy mountain today. The hardiest of these set out at 4 a.m. for mass on the summit at dawn. By lunchtime, 30,000 pilgrims will have completed the 2,510-foot ascent, some in their bare feet. The high turnout comes despite dire safety warnings from the Gardaí, from meteorologists and even the Catholic Church. Standing by on the mountainside this morning are 150 Mayo Mountain Rescue, 150 Order of Malta and 25 Civil Defence volunteers, supported by helicopters from the Air Corps.

The ascendancy of the US religious right, in the last decade, has fuelled a European fascination with the overt religiosity of the American heartland. From tub-thumping televangelists, to roadside billboards proclaiming the imminence of judgment day, the iconography of the Bible belt is instantly recognizable. But what can be overlooked is that Christian fervour is not unique to the red states of middle America. Religious devotion in my native Co. Mayo, for example, though less overt, is no less deeply ingrained. And it manifests itself in ways that, to outside eyes, could appear equally bizarre.

For evangelicals, Christianity is defined in black and white terms like heaven or hell; sin or salvation; God or mammon. In Catholic Ireland, the picture is a little more complex. Religious beliefs and practices in Mayo are informed by ancient tradition, galvanized by history and shot through always with the strangest, and most profound, ambiguity. Nowhere is this better illustrated than on the stony slopes of Croagh Patrick.

The annual pilgrimage here nominally commemorates St Patrick, who is said to have built the first church at the summit. Setting out from Aghagower, Patrick prayed and fasted for 40 days and nights at what is now called Leaba Phadraig (or Patrick's Bed). There he was tormented by demons, in the form of great black birds that swooped about him. Finally, he rang his bell, and the demons fled, perishing in the sea beyond Achill Island. He descended from the mountain on Holy Saturday in the year 441.

In truth, however, the mountain has been a pilgrimage site for over 5,000 years. It was originally the location for the harvest festival of Lughnasa, held in honour of the Celtic sun god Lugh. And although it was given a cursory Christian makeover after Patrick's arrival in Mayo, those pagan overtones never fully disappeared. When William Makepeace Thackeray came by in 1842, he found fifty tents erected at the foot of the mountain, where, once the formalities were out of the way, a great orgy of 'drinking, dancing and lovemaking' commenced. Only the Great Famine of 1845–50 would usher in an era of more pious religious devotion.

The famine hit few places harder than Mayo. In the space of a few years, at least a third of its pre-famine population (of circa 400,000) vanished from the land. And the trauma of that loss was felt for generations. Those who survived turned to their Catholic faith for protection against a repeat of the catastrophe. But local famines continued to hit the county for decades after. My late father remembered, as a boy in the 1950s, being made by his grandmother to eat stale bread and drink sour milk. She was raised to believe that famines were a punishment from God against those who wasted food.

One of the most horrific episodes of the Great Famine occurred not far from Croagh Patrick. In March of 1849, hundreds of starving people from the nearby parish of Louisburgh walked 15 miles to Delphi Lodge, where they were told relief aid would be distributed. When they arrived, the Board of Guardians refused to see them (according to local lore, because they had just sat down to eat dinner). On the return journey through the hauntingly beautiful valley of Doolough, dozens of these human skeletons were blown into Doolough lake. Others perished on the roadside, where their bodies were ravaged by dogs. A memorial, unveiled by Desmond Tutu in 1993, prompted renewed interest in Doolough nationally. Around here though, people had never forgotten.

Back on the mountainside, the sun is now higher in the sky, and hundreds of climbers have abandoned their jackets on fences along the way. A small, respectably dressed lady is asking passers-by if they are Catholic. Most ignore her. The few who answer in the affirmative are advised to steer clear of the people handing out flyers up ahead. They're Protestants, she warns. What's most surreal is that the woman's manner is not that of a wild-eyed zealot. It's more like that of a thoughtful motorist flashing their headlights to warn others that there are, well, Protestants lurking in the vicinity.

Fifteen to twenty Evangelical Christians from Northern Ireland have been making the annual trip to Croagh Patrick for a number of years now. As well as the (pretty innocuous) leaflets they hand out, they also distribute cold drinks to thirsty climbers. They don't, however, talk to journalists. 'We just do this as a service for people,' one of them tells me. 'We just do it as a weekend away – we're not looking for any publicity.' The reception from most climbers – crazy lady notwithstanding – is grateful.

It reminds me of an expression an old teacher of mine once used. Ronnie Flanagan had just been made Chief Constable of the RUC and our teacher told us Flanagan's people had obviously 'taken the soup'. She never explained what she meant by that, but we understood her well enough. She was implying that, as a Protestant with a Catholic-sounding name, Flanagan must be descended from apostates, who abandoned their religion in return for aid during the famine. I smile as I imagine what she would say if she were here today. *The Protestants are back, baby. This time they've got MiWadi orange – and it's going down a treat!*

At the first station, Leacht Benain, pilgrims walk around a mound of rocks seven times, reciting seven Our Fathers, seven Hail Marys and one Creed. In stones on the hillside behind them, someone has written I (HEART) KATHLEEN in enormous letters. Two first-time climbers regard the ritual a little dubiously. 'Do we have to do that?' asks one. 'Ach, I don't think so,' replies the other. In truth, the vast majority of pilgrims don't bother with it. I meet my neighbour, Billy Phillips from Ballyhaunis, whose son Adrian is climbing for the first time. Billy isn't entirely happy about the good weather. 'I don't think this fella is getting the real experience,' he smirks. We admire the view for a moment.

On the summit, a priest is saying mass from within a sort of Perspex glass box at the side of the chapel. The loudspeakers aren't working, so the congregation, standing only a few feet away outside, can decipher almost none of what he says. 'If they just opened the fucking window,' mutters one man. At the door to the left of the altar, pilgrims are queuing up to have their confessions heard inside. Inside the door on the right, the Archbishop of Tuam, in a fetching Adidas tracksuit, is handing out communion.

Tucking into my sandwiches, I get chatting to a sprightly old lady in mountaineering gear. It's beautiful up here, I say. She agrees. The first time she was here was in 1960, when she was 18. 'I had to decide whether to get married or enter the religious life,' she remembers. 'It's so tranquil here.' I take it she opted for the latter then. The man next to us is being interviewed for Midlands Radio. Is it religious devotion, the interviewer wonders, that brings people from the midlands back to Croagh Patrick year after year? Or do they only come along for the crack? The man weighs it up for a moment. 'A bit of both,' he answers. 'I wouldn't say there's too many is all of one, and none of the other.'

It's the night before my sister's wedding. Maureen, our neighbour, lifts the Child of Prague down from the mantelpiece in her kitchen. She tucks it under her arm, walks out into the garden and stashes it under a bush. The Child of Prague statue is commonly found in homes in rural Ireland. And tradition has it that leaving it outside overnight will guarantee fine weather the next day. When the rain holds off for Una's wedding (give or take the odd thundershower), Maureen is quick to remind us where the credit is due. Traditions like this one, though not taken hugely seriously, nonetheless persist.

'There is a huge underbelly of localized religious customs here alright,' agrees Liamy McNally, a journalist with Midwest Radio. 'There are countless mass rocks, holy wells and pilgrimage routes across the county.' He mentions two pilgrimage routes in particular, both of which I walked as a teenager. The first, Tochar Phadraig (Patrick's Way), starts at Ballintubber Abbey, where mass has been said for 800 years unbroken. ('Not even Cromwell and his boys could shut it down,' says McNally.) It runs for 22 miles to the summit of Croagh Patrick and it predates Christianity.

The second begins at various locations around east Mayo and Roscommon and finishes with mass at dawn at the Marian shrine in

Knock. It takes place on August 15th, the Feast of the Assumption. I grew up only a few miles from Knock, and participation in the walk was popular among my friends when we were in our early teens. To be honest, it was just an excuse to get up to all of the sorts of unholy things teenagers tend to get up to. And I felt a tiny bit guilty about that at the time. A few years later, my grandmother described to me the things that had gone on when she did the same pilgrimage in the early 1930s. Very little had changed.

'Forget about Oxegen,' gloats Catholic newspaper *Alive*. 'Knock is where it's at!' The headline refers to Knock's Catholic Youth Festival, a depressing jamboree of maladjusted teens and twentysomethings. Comparisons to Ireland's largest music festival would be much more aptly applied, however, to the annual Knock Novena, an enormous event, which kicks off on the eve of the Feast of the Assumption. For nine days, name speakers address near-capacity crowds twice daily at the 10,000-seat Basilica. Each ceremony concludes with a statue of the Virgin Mary being wheeled around the car park. It is, by any standards, an absurd spectacle.

Late on the opening night, an usher in a green sash offers to help find me a seat. I decline, opting instead to observe proceedings from the ramp that runs around the building. A man I know quite well walks by me with scarcely a nod. He's saying the Rosary, and his rich baritone echoes after him as he disappears down the gangway: 'Hail Holy Queen, mother of mercy. Hail our life, our sweetness and our hope. To you we cry, poor banished children of Eve. To you we send up our sighs, mourning and weeping in this valley of tears . . .'

Groups of Traveller men congregate at the doorways, right the way around the Basilica, laughing and cursing. They're upholding that proud Irish male tradition of turning up to mass, but not actually going in. Inside, a sea of mostly grey heads listens to Fr Fintan Brennan-Whitmore deliver a sermon entitled 'Following Christ in Hospitality and Outreach'. It's not the most scintillating topic, whatever way you spin it. The row of pews directly opposite me is marked 'Priests Only'. I allow myself a small chuckle. The makers of *Father Ted* have a lot to answer for.

The strip of souvenir shops outside is deserted. By day, the tackiness of this place is merely amusing. By night, the shop fronts become weirdly mesmerizing, the gaudy merchandise luminous in the fading light. I hunt about for my all-time favourite item of Knock tat: a photo-quality holographic image of a blow-dried, TV movie Jesus on the cross. When you move it, his eyes open and close: Alive. Dead. Alive. Dead. It isn't here, but there are hundreds of equally deranged gift options in its place. Behind a row of religious-themed snow shakers, a notice warns shoplifters that CCTV cameras are in operation. The mind boggles. What a wonderful world.

Back at the Basilica, as the men in green sashes distribute communion, a priest announces the cancellation of the procession outside, due to inclement weather. The disappointment is palpable. Instead, the statue of the Virgin Mary is wheeled around the altar a couple of times. Five old men march behind it carrying the flags of Ireland's four provinces and the Holy See. They're followed by a group of nuns in white dresses, who are in turn followed by more old men carrying the flags of Ireland's seventeen dioceses and four archdioceses. I can imagine that, in the days before television and wireless broadband, this sort of spectacle could have been very impressive. Nowadays, though, it looks just a little bit silly.

The next day is the Feast of the Assumption, the date on which Travellers traditionally descend on Knock for a week of devotion and trade. There are almost 50 caravans in the immediate vicinity of the shrine alone when I arrive in the morning. By the following Sunday, after what the *Western People* describes as a 'week of mayhem' in the village, tensions with the settled community will have boiled over into an ugly confrontation. For now though, things are more or less peaceful. Only the older Traveller women and children appear to attend services in the Basilica. They sit in the pews to the rear, some attracting reproachful glares for the commotion they tend to bring in their wake.

The men remain outside admiring the talent. And what talent. The Feast of the Assumption is the Travellers' traditional date for matchmaking, and there's high excitement among the girls parading outside. They sport short skirts, high heels, bare midriffs and lots of cleavage. It's quite a spectacle: many of these outfits would be deemed OTT for Eurovision. Aggie and her husband Cha, Travellers themselves, are not impressed. 'A woman with her legs or shoulders showing has no right to be doing the Stations of the Cross,' tuts Aggie. I ask for her surname. She cheerfully declines. 'Get away from me,' she cackles. 'You won't incriminate me!' [. . .]

The End of the Party

FRANK MCDONALD AND KATHY SHERIDAN (2008)

Just as the Irish housing bubble was starting to burst, *Irish Times* journalists Frank McDonald and Kathy Sheridan produced a series of articles on Ireland's leading developers, who had not hitherto received much scrutiny. In the epilogue to their book *The Builders*, they captured a moment when the froth of the boom tipped over into a queasy anticipation of a crash and painted a vivid portrait of a young developer whose luck was on the turn.

There was an end-of-empire feel about Donal Caulfield's party on a Monday night in April 2007 to launch Belmayne, the developer's 2,200-unit scheme on the Malahide Road, in north Dublin. Rival developers turned out in numbers at Belmayne's futuristic marketing suite, where TV garden designer Diarmuid Gavin, flouncy interiors consultant Laurence Llewelyn-Bowen and a slew of scantily clad young women rubbed shoulders with property journalists and gossip columnists. Former Liverpool footballer Jamie Redknapp and his wife Louise provided the minor celebrity glitz, champagne flowed late into the night and many pondered Caulfield's full-colour, full-on, racy marketing strategy in a – whisper it – shaky market.

The highly provocative media campaign created by multinational advertising agency McCann Erickson had become a major talking point, involving such steamy antics as a couple lying astride one another on top of a kitchen island unit, and another with two young ones lounging on a bed, minimally clad, with a male hoving into view behind them. Truly, the days of the tastefully drawn artist's impression to sell property were over. Then again, so were the nights when panicky young couples had to queue in their sleeping bags and throw themselves at the mercy of smug young agents for the privilege of chaining themselves to a property bubble.

Now a property developer had to do what a property developer had to do: try harder. And Caulfield, a likeable, UCD-educated civil engineer and former captain of the under-21 Wexford Gaelic football team, was doing just that. In his diamanté-studded Roberto Cavalli beanie, Versace jeans, *Matrix*-style coat and shades – worn indoors and out – he was bling incarnate, light years from the traditional country developer. So, naturally, there would be no Portakabins masquerading as marketing suites at Belmayne. The 'information centre' alone cost €2 million to build, the ten olive trees planted around it contributing €60,000 to the bill. The coffee dock, smart sofas and *Star Trek*-style computer-generated images were an invitation to linger and sample a 'lifestyle' for sale, one graced with the interior designs of Llewelyn-Bowen, gardens by Gavin and a flashy chauffeur-driven Chrysler Voyager to ferry viewers the short distance to the show apartment.

It would be easy to dismiss Caulfield – a former European kick-boxing champion with a former Miss-Universe-entrant-turned-civil-engineer for a fiancée, who drives a red Ferrari and paid many millions for the Belmayne site while still in his thirties – as a flash git. In fact, he is one of the most straight-talking men in the business, his wild oats well and truly sown. In conversation, he returns repeatedly to the importance of 'first principles' – strong design, sustainable developments, schools and parks – and regards more experienced developers such as Joe O'Reilly, Gerry Gannon and Garrett Kelleher very highly. 'But they're in a different league. They have 15 years on our company, the guys who bought the land in 1998/99 when I was kick-boxing. The older developers have hundreds of millions of liquidity as a result of their developments. Our generation is going to have a harder time. Now we will really have to work first principles to survive.'

He has tried to spread his risk, with developments in Poland, the Canaries, London, Madrid and Ibiza. 'In terms of GDV [Gross Development Value, or total sales value] I'm about half here and half abroad. On GDV, you're always aiming to make 10 to 20 per cent margins. Some would have been on 30 to 60 per cent of GDV. We have to be more realistic now. You have to work at it . . .'

So the big glitzy marketing push at Belmayne was not a bit over the top, then? 'To shift 330 units in this market will take two to two and a half years and you'd spend €2 million in advertising, marketing and show-off costs. That half-million-euro hoarding is our main medium of advertising. The fact is that most people buy in their own area. If you're a northsider, you'll usually stay a northsider, and 90 per cent of first-time buyers here actually live within a five-kilometre radius of us. So for two years, they won't be able to avoid seeing that hoarding in front of them.'

Meanwhile, Caulfield admits, he is sitting on several hundred million euro in loans and didn't see the slump coming. 'Development is not a business for the faint-hearted. When I bought the Belmayne site, I thought I'd sell to first-time buyers, that there would be inward investment and continuous growth and the east European immigrants would keep coming. We thought the €330,000 buyers would always be there because it's affordable. What we're looking at now is 10 to 12 per cent less in sale prices and a probable 30–35 per cent drop in projected profits. I would probably have paid less for the site if I'd foreseen this.'

In the information centre, the bizarre mélange of new and traditional is illustrated by one of his 'gorgeous girls' wall posters framed by curtains on either side. The purpose of the curtains becomes evident on alternative Sundays, when they are closed over the steamy poster and become the backdrop to a Mass altar, for the new Belmayne inhabitants.

While the first batch of apartments booked are closing now and helping to alleviate that massive debt, he anticipates a crunch in about 18 months' time, when the absence of first-time buyers in early to mid-2008 will expose the more vulnerable developers. 'That's when the banks will start looking for interest. So we have to keep selling and that means 80 per cent of our sales are to investors now.' So these are worrying times? 'It gets you out of bed in the morning. Definitely. It's not just about having a legacy to show your children,' he said, speaking at a time when his financée, Louise Doheny, was expecting their first child. 'It's your own pride.'

Caulfield is a classic developer, never content to pull off a spectacularly lucrative deal and become a lotus-eater. After an undistinguished start as an engineer, and a few years of kick-boxing his way around the world, mainly making money by betting on himself, he went to work with Michael Cotter's Park Developments, where he managed the set-up of the industrial-commercial division. At 28, he was driving a Porsche – 'I was getting well paid' – and was buying and selling units for himself.

He left Park because he didn't want to be an employee any more and went into business with Leo Meenagh, the owner of a construction company, LM Developments Ltd, on a 50–50 profit-share basis. Their first major project together was the development and construction of 900 units and a shopping centre in Cityside in north Finglas. At the height of the boom, the company employed up to 1,200 people. That first foray into development for Caulfield was achieved with the cooperation of a patient landowner, a silent partner who was prepared to wait four years for the development to materialize before he took his gains. 'So a million quid was all I needed to start. Once I had the contracts signed, and with my Cotter background, the banks gave us the go-ahead for finance. We were very lucky. We all made a good return on our money, up to 50 per cent cash return.'

Four years after leaving Park, he was able to buy a jet for the business. 'It's not so much about owning the jet. It's about having the money to give you the freedom to do what you want, to say what you want. The more money people have, the more free they are, if they have the right psyche. Having a jet means you're not queueing up for an hour in Dublin or London airports. Money is pure and utter freedom. If you want to wear shades inside, which I often do, I don't care what people say about me. My da, Joseph, used to say that money was freedom. But he had five kids, he was a great goer, a great small builder, but he couldn't risk it because he had five kids.'

In those hedonistic early days, Caulfield's taste for luxury was impressive. 'I'm happy to admit that when I first started seeing returns, I might have got carried away. I was into clothes, holidays, cars. I was a Versace fan, a shopaholic,' he said wryly. 'Every second weekend, I was in Marbella, Paris, Rome. I lived in the penthouse of the Conrad Hotel for eight months when I was refurbishing my home. I loved it.' Even with a parking place for his Aston Martin thrown in at the Conrad, accommodation alone must have run to a high five-figure bill every month.

'I've always been a car fanatic. I used to have seven or eight cars – Ferraris, Porsches, Lamborghinis. I still have the Ferrari, two Porsches, a Lamborghini and a Range Rover jeep. One of the biggest kicks I got was taking my sisters and girlfriend shopping. You'd get a buzz off that. When Louise and I were going out, we would have been away five weekends out of six. Now I've happily swapped the weekends away for walking the Weimaraner dogs in the park with Louise. I'm saturated with the travel and shopping, although I can say that I never went into the drink or drugs. I was too into health and fitness.

'I'm a country guy and I've managed to keep my friends from 15 to 20 years ago. I don't talk about money and that's why I don't spend a huge amount of time with other developers. I don't go to race meetings or balls – I think that whole scene is not real. What's real to me are my friends and family.' But surely all that spending and extravagance simply confirms suspicions that developers were making obscene profits on the backs of struggling homebuyers? 'They deserve every single euro they make – though the exception I'd make are the ones who were doing poor design, defacing the public landscape. That particular type of 10-year boom will never happen again because, for most of it, the rewards were in no way proportionate to the efforts or brilliance of many developers. You could be the worst builder/developer with no sense of design or landscaping yet everything they built, they sold. So many poor builders made so much money that they didn't deserve.

'But most of them are honourable, good, solid people. And the point is that if you put your balls on the table, you get the reward or you get the kick. It can go one way or the other. Guys are now feeling the squeeze and if it goes on, a lot of them are in trouble. I was lucky. If you'd asked me a year and a half ago, I'd have said the market would still be flying now.' Of course, he would not have been the only one. In the words of Warren Buffett, investors should 'be fearful when others are greedy and greedy when others are fearful'. The trouble was that those who were fearful – or urging caution – were apt to be accused of 'talking' the country into a recession.

Bertie's Long Goodbye

PAT LEAHY (2009)

Shortly after the general election of May 2007, in which Bertie Ahern was elected as Taoiseach for the third time, the planning tribunal's scrutiny of his unorthodox financial affairs reached a new pitch of intensity. Within a year of the election, the political damage imposed by his tribunal performances led him to announce his resignation. In his book *Showtime: The Inside Story of Fianna Fáil in Power*, *Sunday Business Post* political editor Pat Leahy gave an account of Ahern's downfall that drew upon the insights of his network of well-placed – and unnamed – sources.

For hundreds of years, Dublin Castle has loomed large in the psyche of the Irish people. The seat of British power, it was also the policing and security hub of the ruling administration, and its cells and dungeons had seen many a gruesome interrogation. The hangar-like room where the tribunal's hearings took place was more comfortable than the dungeons, but it must have aroused similar feelings in some of the witnesses.

On Thursday 13 September [2007], Ahern followed [his former partner, Celia] Larkin and [one of his donors, Michael] Wall into the witness box. It was a gala day at Dublin Castle. Crowds awaited Ahern's arrival and thronged the large hall where the hearings were conducted. They hung around afterwards to cheer and jeer him on the way out; the tribunal team was also cheered and applauded. The press benches overflowed, and journalists vied with one another to point out the significance of various statements.

Ahern insisted that he was glad that the day had finally arrived when he could face in public the accusations against him. 'It's the first opportunity in seven and a half years of being tormented about these issues that I have had the chance to come before the justices,' he declared. This was a courageous claim, as the tribunal would establish quickly. After a few hours in the box, Ahern acknowledged that he had not supplied the tribunal with the information it had sought – to the extent that in March 2006, it had threatened him with a summons to a public sitting of the tribunal. In other words, they were saying it was Ahern who had been responsible for the delay. The tribunal seemed at least as concerned with this affront to its dignity and authority as it was with the import of Ahern's evidence. On that Thursday, he conceded that his earlier evidence might have been incorrect. The tribunal was also anxious to point out that Ahern's earlier, incomplete accounts effectively left a 'hole' in the money trail.

Ahern's spin doctors and aides briefed assiduously while simultaneously complaining that the event had turned into a media circus. His press secretary, Eoghan Ó Neachtain, complained to RTÉ that he had counted nineteen staff from the national broadcaster in the press section, not counting technical people. Will ye get a grip, he advised. He was right – it was a media circus. It was a media circus because the tribunal was destroying Ahern in full public view.

Ahern spent four days in the witness box in late September, and the tribunal indicated that several more sessions would be required. The day after he left the box, the Dáil resumed after its summer break. The Ceann Comhairle, John O'Donoghue, who had been dropped by Ahern from the cabinet after the election, set the tone for the forthcoming term when he told deputies that they must realize that the Dáil had effectively delegated its function to hold the Taoiseach accountable for certain matters to the tribunal. 'However, we must be realistic. I understand that in the political domain there may be a wish by the party leaders to question the Taoiseach on the Mahon Tribunal. Therefore, it would be nonsensical of me to refuse that political imperative.'

Ahern had answered questions in the house before, of course, but O'Donoghue was almost sanctioning the opening of another front on Ahern. In doing so, he may have been affording a neat payback for his demotion: but he was also quite properly fulfilling his constitutional responsibilities, which are to the entire Dáil, not to the leader of his party. It was a new and dangerous development for Ahern; the judgements of politics are sometimes rougher and readier than those of law. They are certainly less governed by the rules of logic and evidence.

That evening, Fine Gael gave concrete parliamentary form to its new aggressiveness on tribunal matters, forcing a debate on a motion of no confidence in the Taoiseach. Often a government welcomes a motion of no confidence as a means of rallying support among its own waverers. Not this time. Ahern gave a lengthy speech. 'To many my affairs are unorthodox. That is because my lifestyle in that dark period was unorthodox. Many who have gone through the trauma of marital separation and legal proceedings will feel empathy with me. Mine was not a perfect life, nor a perfect family and matrimonial environment, but as I emerged from that period I was assisted by friends and my affairs were regularized over a short period.

'I have always been consistent in this one, fundamental matter. I did not receive any payments from Mr O'Callaghan,' he said. This was true. But there were other parts of his story that hadn't been consistent, and this was becoming plain, too. In response, the Fine Gael leader was blunt in his assessment of Ahern's account. 'Most of the events we were discussing never happened. In my view, they are fictitious. They are complicated stories, part of a web of complicated stories designed to mask hard facts, and constructed stories to fit known facts ... We became besotted with stories about whip-arounds, after-dinner presentations and, more recently, a bag of sterling to refurbish a virtually new house.'

The Fianna Fáil speeches were combative, but awkward: they dwelt on Ahern's achievements and the need for due process to take its course. They steered away from the detail of the explanations offered by Ahern, though a new note was introduced by Cowen. 'I believe political loyalty is a virtue and that loyalty will be maintained by the government for the Taoiseach on the basis of his achievements and what he has to offer which is far greater than anything that Deputy Kenny could even contemplate.' There was no endorsement of the Taoiseach's evidence. It was a deeply uncomfortable episode for many ministers.

There were several contradictions and admissions of strangeness by Ahern and friendly witnesses during those fevered days of autumn 2008. Often, entering Dublin Castle required almost a suspension of disbelief in two areas. One required the listener to enter the odd world of Bertie Ahern's personal relationships and finances in the early to mid-1990s, a world in which the man who regularly proclaimed his lack of interest in money and possessions was in receipt of large sums from a variety of sources. The second strange presumption was to accept it was necessary and appropriate and fitting that the Taoiseach should be brought through his financial dealings in such minute detail on the hearsay suggestion of Tom Gilmartin, an unreliable witness.

The process ground grimly onwards. The close friends who had lent him money followed him into the witness box, when it transpired that some of them were neither close nor friends of his at the time. But with the exception of stockbroker Padraic O'Connor – whose account of matters differed substantially from Ahern's and revealed the important role that Des Richardson had played in the affair – they largely supported Ahern's account of the dig-outs and the Christmas donations. In the days before Christmas, Ahern returned to the witness box. He was no longer the battling figure intent on clearing his name; now he was a hunted figure, trying to stay ahead of the pursuing pack. In further cross-examination about the fundraising on his behalf in 1993 and 1994, he sustained more damage to the credibility of his story. He publicly railed against the inquiry now, accusing it from the witness box of trying to 'stitch me up'; but it proceeded with its relentless work, detailing another £5,000 lodgement that it was inquiring about in the minutes before it rose for the Christmas holidays. In his office on the Saturday before Christmas, while his staff detailed the list of Christmas presents that they had purchased on his behalf, he complained that the tribunal was managing the news cycles, bringing up issues just before adjournments so that they would be featured prominently in reports.

The new year dawned with the government facing the same two pressing problems that it had when it had taken office the previous June: the rapidly deteriorating economy and the question of its leader's future. Neither issue had been productively or conclusively addressed – in fact, the uncertainty over the leadership was actively militating against action on the economy. Heads had been in the sand for six months now, but neither issue would go away.

Full-year exchequer figures published in January confirmed the slide in many areas of revenue, with tax revenues coming in at nearly €2 billion below what was expected. Department of Finance officials began to worry that the deterioration had been accelerating in the last part of the previous year, as the contagion in property and construction fed into the rest of the economy. In February, ministers received a briefing about the declining state of the exchequer finances. One minister recalls it being especially stark. It was clear to many of them that the situation was likely to deteriorate further and that measures to restrict spending could be necessary before the end of the year. Nothing was done. 'Look,' says one aide, 'there was very little being done in government by the Bert – apart from the elephant in the room.'

'The government was paralysed at the centre,' says one official who held a number of urgent and increasingly pessimistic conversations with his colleagues, who despaired of getting decisions taken and the normal work of government processed. 'Some of his advisers were concentrating wholly on the tribunal; there were rows internally when Ó Neachtain couldn't get them to go out and defend him.' Another insider concurs. 'A huge amount of time and effort and political capital was going in to defending him,' he told me. Even one of his most loyal staffers acknowledged that it was becoming impossible for the government to function properly. 'We couldn't get anything else done. It just sucked up all the oxygen.' Senior figures across government have all attested to this fact that dominated Ahern's final months. [. . .]

At an Ogra–Fianna Fáil conference in Tullamore, [Finance Minister Brian] Cowen sought to focus the message on the Lisbon Treaty. One aide remembers that Cowen did three interviews; in every one of them, Bertie Ahern's finances were the principal topic. Reflecting afterwards, the aide thought, This just can't go on.

The definitively final phase began when Ahern returned to the witness box on 21 February [2008]. Amid fractious exchanges between Ahern's legal team and a defensive and agitated tribunal,

Ahern was grilled about lodgements from accounts in the Irish Permanent that he had not originally disclosed to the tribunal. Some of the money may have come from his late father's estate, he thought; he wasn't sure. Some of it may have come from 'personal donations for my personal use'; we had now gone well beyond innocent dig-outs and surprise whip-arounds. Now we were in the Ray Burke territory of 'walking-around money' for buying raffle tickets and suchlike. He was bleeding now, but there was worse, much worse, to come.

One of the accounts showed a withdrawal of £30,000. This, Ahern explained, was for a staff member in St Luke's, whose elderly relatives faced a difficulty when their landlord died. The money went towards the purchase of the house, which was now owned by the staff member. The following day, after some hours of re-examination, tribunal counsel, with the air of a poker player who knows he has a winning hand and is enjoying the wait to reveal it, asked: who was the staff member? Ahern, hunched and defensive, answered quietly but clearly: 'Celia Larkin.'

There was an intake of breath in the public gallery. The press benches paused, then scribbled and typed furiously. Radio reporters jumped out of their seats and left the hall to phone in the bombshell to their newsrooms. It was clear that the revelation that Celia Larkin had bought a house with money which came from an account that the Taoiseach was saying was a Fianna Fáil account was dynamite, whatever way you looked at it. The explanation that the money was a loan and had been repaid didn't make it look any better – it had only been repaid a few weeks previously when the tribunal had started asking questions about the account. It changed the context of the entire encounter. Few people had the time or the inclination to fol-low the detail of the tribunal inquiries, but here was something they could easily understand. It was simple and it was devastating. For Fianna Fáil people up and down the country, who stood on church gate collections and dipped into their wallets and purses for raffle tickets, a Rubicon had been crossed. As Miriam Lord concluded the following day in one of her riveting accounts of days at the tribunal, 'This is not good. Not good at all.'

It was unclear what it had to do with the tribunal's legally proper inquiries into the allegation that Ahern had received bribes from Owen O'Callaghan. If the tribunal believed that some O'Callaghan money had been channelled to Ahern through a labyrinthine web that implicated virtually his entire network of friends and contacts, they had yet to produce the evidence for this suspicion. But they had shown that many of Ahern's explanations of his finances were inconsistent. The official explanation was that the tribunal had to ascertain that the considerable sums in Ahern's accounts did not come from O'Callaghan. Ahern was perhaps entitled to feel that there was no necessity to prove that their inquiries were not relevant to their terms of reference by means of extended public hearings that revealed facts about his finances that could only be politically ruinous. The legal consequences of all this were unclear, and would be the subject of much future wrangling. But the political consequences were quickly taking shape.

Ahern's lack of credibility on the tribunal's inquiries had severely undermined him among the public. In early March, a *Sunday Business Post*/Red C tracking poll only underlined the widespread disbelief of his story, though support for Fianna Fáil was holding up. [. . .] More than half of all voters said they didn't believe his evidence to the tribunal, while exactly half of all voters said they no longer trusted him to run the country following his appearances at Dublin Castle. Almost 70 per cent of voters said he should resign if he was found to have misled the tribunal.

If the revelations about Larkin's gift/loan diminished Ahern amongst his own, the evidence of Gráinne Carruth would belittle him further among ordinary people, and particularly women. Carruth had been a secretary in St Luke's from 1987 to 1999, and had lodged money on Ahern's behalf to an account in the Irish Permanent branch across the road. She had previously given evidence that she had not made particular lodgements and never dealt in sterling. That story was now coming apart, and Carruth appeared terrified by that realization. Over two days, Carruth endured an uncomfortable cross-examination from Des O'Neill, the tribunal counsel, during which she was forced to admit that her earlier evidence was incorrect. She was warned that the consequences of lying to the tribunal could include massive fines and jail. Accepting 'as a matter of probability' that she had lodged sterling to Ahern's account, she repeatedly broke down in tears and told the tribunal at one stage, 'I just want to go home.'

The reaction was savage – not towards the witness who had revised her evidence, not towards the tribunal counsel who had leaned on her, but towards the man many believed had sent her down to the tribunal to cover for him. Ahern was incensed at her treatment, but he could hardly escape the implications of it: in any case, the *Irish Independent* spelled them out for him the following day on page one: 'Taoiseach Bertie Ahern's entire credibility as a tribunal witness was in tatters last night after his former secretary flatly contradicted his explanation of the latest tranche of cash to appear in his accounts.'

The Fianna Fáil organization was hardly immune to the constant drip-drip of revelations. One of the failings of the Irish political system is that TDs are so close to their electorates; but one of its strengths is also that they are so close to them. TDs were hearing the grass-roots' rumblings, and they were bringing them back to Dublin. One person with a valid claim to know the mind of ordinary members is blunt: 'He had lost the confidence of the organization . . . After Celia and Gráinne Carruth, it was all over.' The same sentiment that was spreading throughout the Fianna Fáil organization was also feeding into a media climate that was increasingly hostile. It was given regular outings to Dublin Castle to exercise its feelings.

The twin forces of the media – some of which pursued Ahern with an almost feral bloodlust – and the organization's growing unease were prompting a round of what-are-we-going-to-do, something-has-to-be-done phone conversations between ministers. Ministerial responses to the effect that Ahern's finances, albeit messy, had nothing whatsoever to do with the tribunal's Quarryvale investigations, and that all questions should be answered at the tribunal, were growing thin, even to their ears. The Larkin house revelation and the Carruth evidence had blown that sort of response out of the water. A fear of going out to defend him was developing, not just because they didn't believe him, but because they didn't know if what he was going to say next might make them look stupid. Cowen and Micheál Martin were fire-fighting, telling people to back off, warning them not to do anything rash. They all knew Cowen would succeed him, and nobody wanted to be in a new Taoiseach's black books. But politicians can be impulsive sorts, and it wouldn't hold for ever.

In the last week of March, a Green councillor, Niall Ó Brolcháin, surfaced and said that Ahern should resign. Ó Brolcháin wasn't just some obscure county councillor: he was a former mayor of Galway and had been tipped for a Dáil seat the previous year. He was working for the party leadership in Dublin, though his comments were a solo run. More tellingly, though, he indicated that the issue was likely to be discussed at the party's conference, due a fortnight later. Most people in the Green Party thought the Taoiseach should resign, he added.

A day later, another wound. Fiona O'Malley, who was in the midst of a leadership election in the Progressive Democrats, earned herself a front-page story in the *Irish Times* with a call on Ahern to clarify contradictions on his evidence. He was, she said, bringing the profession of politics into disrepute. The following day, asked by reporters to respond to O'Malley's concerns, [PD leader Mary] Harney came out and conceded there was 'considerable public disquiet' about the Taoiseach's evidence.

Momentum was building now. The laws of coalition politics dictated that if the Progressive Democrats were concerned, the Greens had to be even more concerned. John Gormley was attending a meeting in Lucan when his press officer, Liam Reid, joined him, holding a copy of the morning paper. 'Take a look at this,' he told him. 'What? What is it?' Gormley replied. 'That's the break,' Reid said. 'There's no way you can't come out and match that.' Soon, their phones started to ring with news of Harney's comments. Reporters wanted to know where Gormley would be later. He would have to have a line by the time they reached him. The arrangements were duly made and when Gormley later found himself in front of a TV3 microphone, he conceded there was a 'growing public interest in this issue and there are concerns'. It was in Ahern's 'best interest and that of his party and the country that a clarifying statement is made'.

A day later, a Fianna Fáil TD, Bobby Aylward, told reporters that the Taoiseach should clarify his evidence in the light of Carruth's testimony. Batt O'Keeffe, a junior minister and close friend of Cowen, merely reflected that Ahern 'knows best what to do'. But he added, 'and will know the appropriate time'. This was a new type of pressure, and Ahern knew it wouldn't go away.

When Cowen returned from an official St Patrick's Day visit to Malaysia and a short family holiday in Vietnam, he went to St Luke's on Thursday 27 March to meet Ahern. The fact of the meeting itself was a sign. According to someone with knowledge of the encounter, there was no ultimatum from Cowen, but both men acknowledged the reality of the situation.

The following Wednesday, 2 April, Ahern was due to attend yet another Dáil session to answer opposition questions, the latest of a series of encounters he had already stumbled through. It made sense to go before then. Cowen and Ahern spoke by phone again a few times in the intervening days. Ahern was concerned that Cowen understood that he was actually going to go through with his resignation, at one stage calling him to say, 'You do know what I said?' By Saturday, he began to think about making the arrangements. Early on Sunday morning, he called his special adviser and principal speech-writer, Brian Murphy, and asked him to come to St Luke's. They chatted aimlessly about a few things while Murphy wondered what it was all about. Ahern disappeared upstairs and returned with a notepad, and suddenly said: 'It's like this – I'm going to jack it in!' 'What?!' Murphy was dumbfounded. 'I'm going to jack it in,' Ahern repeated.

Murphy was stunned, and tried to talk him out of it. Hang on, even until the summer. Go in your own time. Ahern advanced his reasons; there were several. Eventually, he said, 'Listen, let's do the speech and talk about what we'll say, and then we can come back and talk about it.' He produced some notes he had scribbled on a pad. Murphy understood: that was it. There would be no going back. This was one Bertie Ahern decision that wasn't open to revision.

Later that evening, agriculture minister Mary Coughlan appeared on RTÉ's *The Week in Politics* programme. Repeatedly asked by presenter Sean O'Rourke, she declined to say that she personally believed the Taoiseach's version of events. Five times she dodged the question. 'It's not a matter for me to believe or otherwise,' she insisted. Her evasions prompted a flurry of late-night calls and texts among ministers and advisers. Was there a push on? Coughlan was very close to Cowen. If not, should there be? And what was Ahern going to do? They didn't know that the decision had already been made.

With utmost secrecy, the arrangements were put together over the following two days in St Luke's. Mandy Johnston had been among those Ahern had consulted and informed over the weekend and she planned the choreography of the final days. Cowen came in on Tuesday and Rory Brady, who remained close to Ahern although he was no longer attorney general, reviewed his speech and recommended the inclusion of the line 'I have done no wrong and wronged no one.' That evening a small group including Brady, Johnston, Cyprian Brady, Sandra Cullough, Murphy and Dermot Carew gathered to make the final arrangements. In sombre mood, they adjourned across the road to Fagan's for a few drinks. They watched Manchester United defeat Roma 2–0 in a Champions League game. Business as usual. But not for Ahern. 'It'll be bedlam in here tomorrow night,' he told them.

Gormley received a message that Ahern wanted to speak to him. 'I have a way out of all this,' the Taoiseach told him. 'And I think you'll be happy with it.' They arranged to meet earlier than usual before cabinet the following day. Gormley didn't know what Ahern intended to do. What do you think? he asked his staff. No idea, they replied.

The same evening, Harney was in l'Ecrivain, the Michelin-starred restaurant on Baggot Street, when her phone rang. Normally in such circumstances, she wouldn't take the call but would return it later. However, when she saw the number flashing, she immediately excused herself and went outside to take the call. It was Ahern. The two spoke briefly. Harney had become very fond of Ahern since she had joined him in government in 1997, and she was immensely saddened by the way he was leaving. But she knew there was no choice.

On Wednesday morning, 2 April, ministers assembled for the weekly cabinet meeting. Mobile phones began to beep. Journalists had been summoned to an unscheduled and immediate press conference, and press officers and advisers were being asked: what's going on? Is he really – ?

He was.

When I get back from the US, he told ministers, I will resign. Now I'd like if you would come down with me to make the announcement. His advisers milled around outside; they recorded that several members of the cabinet were emotional. Moving downstairs for the announcement, ministers saw the journalists around the marble steps of the entrance hall in Government Buildings in a state of nervous excitement. Some were quieter, absorbing the historic nature of what they were about to witness. Staff crowded around the balcony overlooking the hall. As Ahern spoke, many were in tears.

He had never, he said, put his own interests before the interests of the Irish people. He had done no wrong, and wronged no one. But the time had come. He would tender his resignation on 6 May, but in the meantime, he would continue to 'work hard'.

The Bertie Ahern era was over.

The Archbishop and the Abusers

CATRIONA CROWE (2011)

As part of a long survey for the *Dublin Review* of the clerical sex-abuse scandals, the various responses to them, and their implications, Catriona Crowe profiled Diarmuid Martin, who was appointed Catholic Archbishop of Dublin in 2004, having spent much of his career outside of Ireland.

In July of last year, I was present at the ordination of Conleth Meehan, a 45-year-old who had worked as a butcher in Co. Tyrone before entering the seminary at Maynooth in 2004. The ceremony took place in the Pro-Cathedral in Marlborough Street in central Dublin, and was accompanied by the commissioning of nine lay pastoral workers, most of them women, who were to take up positions in parishes in the diocese, having undergone a year of intensive training. Meehan was the only Catholic priest to be ordained for the Archdiocese of Dublin, Ireland's biggest archdiocese, in 2010, and the Pro-Cathedral was full of prominent notices proclaiming the urgent need for more priests. In the 1980s, an average of 150 men began training for the priesthood in Ireland every year. Last year, only sixteen enrolled.

The ordination ceremony was long and complex, accompanied by glorious music chosen and conducted by the justly famous Father Pat O'Donoghue, Diocesan Director of Music. Conleth Meehan's family was present, and participated in the ceremony, obviously full of pride. Diarmuid Martin, the Archbishop of Dublin, presided. He was flanked on the altar by Auxiliary Bishops Eamonn Walsh and Raymond Field, both of whom have been the focus of calls for resignation by victims of clerical sexual abuse who believe they did nothing to challenge the culture in the Church that made abuse and its concealment possible. Archbishop Martin moved speedily around the altar and seemed to be on bad terms with his mitre, the long ribbons of which he kept sweeping back. His address focused on the necessity for the Church to respond creatively to a changing society: 'Catholicism in Ireland and Irish Catholicism are changing. There is no point in thinking that things have not changed radically and, in many cases, I believe we are not addressing all the dimensions of that change. The church lives within a particular society and in a particular culture . . . The church must also in its own unique way influence and shape that culture.'

Martin had by this time delivered several hard-hitting speeches on the subject of clerical sexual abuse and the damage it had caused to victims. In April 2009, anticipating the findings of the major investigation into clerical abuse in the archdiocese headed by Judge Yvonne Murphy, he said: 'It is likely that thousands of children or young people across Ireland were abused by priests in the period under investigation and the horror of that abuse was not recognized for what it is. The report will make each of us and the entire church in Dublin a humbler church.' In March 2010, when John Magee, the Bishop of Cloyne, reluctantly stepped down in the face of allegations of negligence with regard to clerical sexual abuse in his diocese, Martin said: 'The indications are that thousands of children may have been victims of child sexual abuse by church personnel over the past thirty to forty years. Survivors live with their suffering day by day. Children have been let down. Lives have been devastated. People are rightly angry at what has been done to victims, to their families and indeed to good priests who go about their ministry daily.'

Martin's emphasis in his public speeches on the damage done by clerical child sexual abuse is striking for being so unusual. Most of his colleagues in the Irish hierarchy, including Cardinal Seán Brady, head of the Catholic Church in Ireland, have either not spoken on the subject or have done so only in response to events like the Pope's letter to the Irish faithful of March 2010, and then in much less trenchant terms than Martin. Martin's willingness to meet victims of clerical abuse also stands in contrast to his colleagues.

Diarmuid Martin is a complex and interesting individual. Ordained in 1969, his only experience of pastoral work was as a curate in Cabinteely, Co. Dublin, and as one of the participants in the Irish pilgrimage to Rome in the Holy Year of 1975. His career for the next quarter-century was that of a Vatican diplomat: he entered the service of the Holy See in 1976, as a member of the Pontifical Council for the Family. In 1986 he was appointed Under-Secretary of the Pontifical Council for Justice and Peace, and in 1994 Secretary of that Council. In that capacity, Martin represented the Vatican at the World Bank and the International Monetary Fund, focusing especially on the themes of international debt and poverty reduction. He also represented the Holy See at the major United Nations conferences on social questions. In 2003, *Irish Times* columnist Fintan O'Toole reviewed his interventions at two key UN conferences, on Population and Development, in Cairo, in 1994, and on Women, in Beijing, in 1995. He wrote of Martin's key involvement in 'the Vatican delegations that pushed a medieval line: condoms cause AIDS; women who had been raped in war should not be allowed to use emergency contraception; women in developing countries have no interest in individual rights, but only want to serve the community; adolescents have no right to confidential education on sexuality; homosexuality should not be recognized.'

In 2001 Martin continued his ascent as a Vatican diplomat when he was created Archbishop and Apostolic Nuncio and undertook responsibilities as Permanent Observer of the Holy See in Geneva, at the United Nations Office and Specialized Agencies and at the World Trade Organization. In 2003 he was appointed Coadjutor Archbishop of Dublin, and the following year he succeeded Cardinal Desmond Connell as Archbishop of Dublin. In the early days of his new office, Martin was criticized, mainly by his priests, on two grounds: his lack of pastoral experience, which was seen as having left him with a limited understanding of the realities of parish life; and his frequent absences from the country, often to accompany Pope John Paul II on his trips abroad. He was sometimes referred to as Martin of Tours, an in-joke properly understood only by Catholics of a certain age. It was assumed that he was serving his time in Dublin with a view to eventually returning to Rome in a more elevated position at the Holy See.

It has been suggested that Martin was chosen for the Dublin post with a particular task in mind: dealing with the burgeoning scandal of child abuse by Catholic priests in the archdiocese. The fact that he had few personal ties to the Irish hierarchy or to the priests in Dublin, and that he had been absent from Ireland throughout the years when the abuse was endemic and was being covered up, might have been seen as helpful in this regard. On Martin's own account, however, the abuse scandal in Dublin, far from being at the front of the Vatican's mind when he was sent to the archdiocese in 2003, seems barely to have been discussed. Mandate or no mandate, he found himself in the middle of a rapidly developing crisis, and began to speak about it immediately. On his appointment as Coadjutor Bishop in May 2003, after a speech by Archbishop Connell that did not mention the child abuse scandals, Martin said: 'There are also many who are estranged from the Church. I am aware that there are those for whom meaning and hope were lost in their lives through the actions of Church personnel. Their hurt is all the greater if they feel betrayed by someone they had turned to in trust.'

Martin is said by his friends to be very good company, funny, interesting and interested in many things not Church-related. He is also theologically conservative, refusing to even discuss celibacy or women priests. His espousal of the appointment of paid lay pastoral workers in his diocese, most of them women, may be a clever way of involving women at a higher level in Church organization without having to bite the bullet of female ordination. [. . .]

In 2004, the Oireachtas passed legislation that enabled the establishment, in March 2006, of a Commission of Investigation to examine complaints relating to sexual abuse of children by Catholic clergy in the archdiocese of Dublin between 1 January 1975 and 1 May 2004, and to investigate the response of Church authorities to these complaints. The commission was headed by Judge Yvonne Murphy of the Circuit Court, assisted by barrister Ita Mangan and solicitor Hugh O'Neill.

The commission received information about complaints, suspicions or knowledge of child sexual abuse in respect of 183 priests. After a preliminary examination, the commission concluded that 102 of these priests came within the remit of their investigation. This number was reduced to a representative sample of 46 priests, and the commission examined complaints by over 300 children against the 46. A substantial majority of the complaints related to boys: the ratio was 2.3 boys to 1 girl. Of the 46 priests examined, 11 pleaded guilty to or were convicted in the criminal courts of sexual assaults on children.

In the course of its activities, the commission held 145 formal hearings. Those interviewed included Archbishop Martin, former bishops and archbishops of the Dublin Archdiocese, a number of other diocesan authorities, members of thirty-eight religious orders operating within the Dublin archdiocese, employees of the Health Service Executive and of An Garda Síochána, the Director of Public Prosecutions, staff at Our Lady's Hospital for Sick Children, Crumlin, and Children's University Hospital, Temple Street, civil servants from the Department of Education and the Department of Health, and a number of other individuals whom the commission considered might have information relevant to its work. The commission examined over 70,000 documents.

The commission's report, known as the Murphy report, published in November 2009, stated that the commission had no doubt that clerical child abuse was covered up by the Archdiocese of Dublin and other church authorities, and that the structures and rules of the Church facilitated that cover-up. It also found that state authorities facilitated the cover-up by allowing the Church to be beyond the reach of the law, and that the welfare of children, which should have been everyone's first priority, was not even considered until the early 1980s by state or Church authorities; the preservation of the good name, status and assets of Church institutions was the paramount consideration.

Have we learned the necessary lessons of over a decade of discussion of child sexual abuse, or is there another scandalous situation in the making?

Archbishop Martin is widely seen by victims as having championed their cause and genuinely empathized with their suffering and their struggle to be heard. After his homily in March 2009 anticipating the terrible contents of the Murphy report, Maeve Lewis, executive director of One in Four, an organization that campaigns for the victims of clerical sex abuse, said, 'For the first time, a member of the hierarchy has accepted the depth of the abuse that took place over the years.' In April of this year, Marie Collins, a clerical abuse survivor, said of Martin: 'He's the only bishop who has the support of the people.'

Martin continues to speak out against forces in the Church that resist change. On 5 May 2010 he said: 'Why am I discouraged? The most obvious reason is the drip-by-drip never-ending revelation about child sexual abuse and the disastrous way it was handled. There are still strong forces which would prefer that the truth did not emerge. The truth will make us free, even when that truth is uncomfortable. There are signs of subconscious denial on the part of many about the extent of the abuse which occurred within the Church of Jesus Christ in Ireland and how it was covered up. There are other signs of rejection of a sense of responsibility for what had happened. There are worrying signs that despite solid regulations and norms these are not being followed with the rigour required.'

The current pope, Benedict XVI, has proved difficult and obtuse in his responses to the Irish church scandals. The visit of Irish bishops to Rome, at his invitation, in February 2010 resulted in a PR disaster, with emphasis by the media on photographs and broadcasts of 24 Irish bishops queueing up to kiss the Pope's ring, and on the fact that he refused to meet survivors' groups. His letter to Irish Catholics of March 2010 was full of vague platitudes, but failed, significantly, to endorse the document prepared by the Irish bishops in 1996 on how to deal with clerical sexual abuse, generally regarded as a long-overdue and appropriate template for such issues. The Pope's failure to enforce the resignations of auxiliary bishops found wanting by the Murphy report, and to whom Archbishop Martin has refused his endorsement, increased survivors' and general public anger at a man seen to be completely out of touch with ordinary Catholics.

Allegations of sexual abuse against Catholic clergy in Ireland continue to be made. The National Board for Safeguarding Children, the watchdog body set up by the hierarchy in 2006, has revealed that it received very poor co-operation from clergy and bishops in relation to allegations of clerical abuse during 2010. The organization's annual report reveals that more than two hundred new allegations of clerical child abuse made to Church authorities were withheld from the board until very recently, even though Church authorities have committed themselves to contacting the board as soon as such allegations are made.

This state of affairs can only cause grave disquiet to Diarmuid Martin, revealing as it does a criminal reluctance on the part of the Catholic Church to conform to the norms for child protection which it has itself espoused.

Martin described his decision to fully co-operate with the Murphy commission and the flak he received from colleagues over his lack of criticism of the report and his refusal to say that, had he been in Ireland during the period reported on, he would have done the same as the rest. He responded:

Perhaps I would have acted as those in responsibility did then. It is possible that the advice of lawyers and psychiatrists and media advisors may not have been the best advice. It may also have been that the lawyers and the doctors had been asked the wrong questions or were not given the correct information. In the face of the disastrous situation revealed in the Murphy report, however, I felt that this was not the time for finding faults within the report . . . I still cannot accept a situation that no one need assume accountability in the face of the terrible damage that was done to children in the Church of Christ in Dublin and in the face of how that damage was addressed. The responses seemed to be saying that it was all due to others or at most it was due to some sort of systems fault in the diocesan administration . . .

What was documented in the Murphy report is horrendous. The Archdiocese of Dublin got it spectacularly wrong. All I found I could say on the publication of the report was that the Archdiocese of Dublin got it spectacularly wrong; spectacularly wrong 'full stop', not spectacularly wrong 'but'. That decision of mine was, I was told, 'a catastrophic media strategy'.

He also spoke of the consistent lack of remorse on the part of offenders: 'Without wishing to be unduly harsh, I feel that I can honestly say that with perhaps two exceptions I have not encountered a real and unconditional admission of guilt and responsibility on the part of priest offenders in my diocese. Survivors have repeatedly told me that one of the greatest insults and hurts they have experienced is to see the lack of real remorse on the part of offenders even when they plead guilty in court. It is very hard to speak of meaningful forgiveness of an offender when the offender refuses to recognize the facts and the full significance of the facts.'

We know, in part because the second most senior figure in the Catholic Church in Ireland has told us so, that Church authorities still refuse to face the truth about clerical abuse or to conform to their own or society's norms relating to child protection. It is thus hard to hold out much hope that Diarmuid Martin's vigorous efforts to improve the situation will bear fruit.

The Economist and the Crash

MICHAEL LEWIS (2011)

When the author of *Liar's Poker* and *The Big Short* turned his attention to Ireland, in a *Vanity Fair* piece in March 2011, Ireland took notice. The hero of Michael Lewis's article was Morgan Kelly, an academic economist who turned his hand to journalism in 2006 when he realized what almost everyone else seemed unable to comprehend: that the Irish property market was facing a crash on a staggering scale.

When I flew to Dublin in early November 2010 the Irish government was busy helping the Irish people come to terms with their loss. It had been two years since a handful of Irish politicians and bankers had decided to guarantee all the debts of the biggest Irish banks, but the people were only now getting their minds around what that meant for them. The numbers were breathtaking. A single bank, Anglo Irish, which, two years before, the Irish government claimed was suffering from a 'liquidity problem', confessed to losses of 34 billion euros. [. . .] As the sum total of loans made by Anglo Irish Bank, most of it to Irish property developers, was only 72 billion euros, the bank had lost nearly half of every dollar it invested.

The two other big Irish banks, Bank of Ireland and, especially, Allied Irish Banks (AIB), remained Ireland's dirty little secret. Both older than [the state of] Ireland itself (the Bank of Ireland was founded in 1783; Allied Irish was formed in a merger of three banks founded in the 1800s), both were now also obviously bust. The Irish government owned most of the two ancient banks, but revealed less about them than they had about Anglo Irish. As they had lent vast sums not only to Irish property developers but also to Irish home buyers, their losses were obviously vast – and similar in spirit to the losses at the upstart Anglo Irish. Even in an era when capitalists went out of their way to destroy capitalism, the Irish bankers had set some kind of record for destruction. Theo Phanos, whose London hedge fund has interests in Ireland, says that 'Anglo

Irish was probably the world's worst bank. Even worse than the Icelandic banks.'

Ireland's financial disaster shared some things in common with Iceland's. It was created by the sort of men who ignore their wives' suggestions that maybe they should stop and ask for directions, for instance. But while the Icelandic male used foreign money to conquer foreign places – trophy companies in Britain, chunks of Scandinavia – the Irish male used foreign money to conquer Ireland. Left alone in a dark room with a pile of money, the Irish decided what they really wanted to do with it was buy Ireland. *From each other*. An Irish economist named Morgan Kelly, whose estimates of Irish bank losses have been the most prescient, has made a back-of-the-envelope calculation that puts the property-related losses of all Irish banks at roughly 106 billion euros. At the rate money flows into the Irish treasury, Irish bank losses alone would absorb every penny of Irish taxes for the next four years.

In recognition of the spectacular losses, the entire Irish economy has almost dutifully collapsed. When you fly into Dublin you are traveling, for the first time in fifteen years, against the traffic. The Irish are once again leaving Ireland, along with hordes of migrant workers. In late 2006 the unemployment rate stood at a bit more than 4 per cent; now it's 14 per cent, and climbing toward rates not experienced since the mid 1980s. Just a few years ago Ireland was able to borrow money more cheaply than Germany; now, if it can borrow at all, it will be charged interest rates 6 per cent higher than Germany, another echo of a distant past. The Irish budget deficit – in 2007 the country had a budget surplus – is now 32 per cent of its GDP, the highest by far in the history of the euro zone. Professional credit analyst firms now judge Ireland the third most likely country in the world to default. Not quite as risky for the global investor as Venezuela, perhaps, but riskier than Iraq. Distinctly third world, in any case.

Yet when I arrived, Irish politics had a frozen-in-time quality. In Iceland, the business-friendly conservative party had been quickly tossed out of power, and the women had booted the alpha males out of the banks and government. In Greece the corrupt, business-friendly, every-Greek-for-himself conservative party was also given the heave-ho, and the new government is attempting to create a sense of collective purpose, or at any rate persuade the citizens to quit cheating on their taxes. (The new Greek prime minister is not merely upstanding but barely Greek.) Ireland was the first European country to watch its entire banking system fail, and yet its business-friendly conservative party, Fianna Fáil, remained in office up until February 2011. There's no Tea Party movement, no Glenn Beck, no serious protests of any kind. The only obvious change in the country's politics has been the role played by foreigners. The new bank regulator, an Englishman, came from Bermuda. The Irish government and Irish banks are crawling with American investment bankers and Australian management consultants and faceless Euro-officials, referred to inside the Department of Finance simply as 'the Germans'. Walk the streets at night and, through restaurant windows, you see important-looking men in suits, dining alone, studying important-looking papers. In some new and strange way Dublin was now an occupied city: Hanoi, circa 1950. 'The problem with Ireland is that you're not allowed to work with Irish people anymore,' an Irish property developer told me. He was finding it difficult to escape hundreds of millions of euros in debt he would never be able to repay.

Ireland's regress is especially unsettling because of the questions it raises about Ireland's former progress: even now no one is quite sure why the Irish did so well for themselves in the first place. [. . .] By the start of the new millennium the Irish poverty rate was under 6 per cent, and Ireland was the second richest country in the world, according to the Bank of Ireland. How did that happen? A bright young Irishman who got himself hired by Bear Stearns in the late 1990s and went off to New York or London for five years returned feeling poor. For the better part of the past decade there's been quicker money to be made in Irish real estate than in American investment banking. How did that happen? For the first time in history people and money longed to get into Ireland rather than out of it. The most dramatic case in point are the Poles. The Polish government keeps no official statistics on the movement of its workforce, but its Foreign Ministry guesstimates that, since their admission to the European Union, a million Poles have left Poland to work elsewhere – and that, at the peak, in 2006, a quarter of a million of them were in Ireland.

[. . .] A few months after the spell was broken, the short-term parking lot attendants at Dublin Airport noticed that their daily take had fallen. The lot appeared full; they couldn't understand it; then they noticed the cars never changed. They phoned the Dublin police, who in turn traced the cars to Polish construction workers, who had bought them with money borrowed from the big Irish banks. The migrant workers had ditched the cars and gone home. A few months later the Bank of Ireland sent three collectors to Poland to see what they could get back, but they had no luck. The Poles were untraceable. But for their cars in the short-term parking lot, they might never have existed.

Morgan Kelly is a professor of economics at University College Dublin, but he did not, until recently, view it as his business to think much about the economy under his nose. He had written a handful of highly regarded academic papers on topics regarded as abstruse even by academic economists ('The Economic Impact of the Little Ice Age'). 'I only stumbled on this catastrophe by accident,' he says. 'I had never been interested in the Irish economy. The Irish economy is tiny and boring.' Kelly saw house prices rising madly, and heard young men in Irish finance to whom he had recently taught economics try to explain why the boom didn't trouble them. And the sight and sound of them troubled him. 'Around the middle of 2006 all these former students of ours working for the banks started to appear on TV!' he says. 'They were now all bank economists and they were nice guys and all that. And they were all saying the same thing: "We're going to have a soft landing."'

The statement struck him as absurd on the face of it: real estate bubbles never end with soft landings. A bubble is inflated by nothing firmer than people's expectations. The moment people cease to believe that house prices will rise forever, they will notice what a terrible long-term investment real estate has become, and flee the market, and the market will crash. It was in the nature of real estate booms to end with crashes – just as it was perhaps in Morgan Kelly's nature to assume that if his former students were cast on Irish TV playing the financial experts, something was amiss. 'I just started Googling things,' he said.

Googling things, Kelly learned that more than a fifth of the Irish workforce was now employed building houses. The Irish construction industry had swollen to become nearly a quarter of Irish GDP – compared to less than 10 per cent or so in a normal economy – and Ireland was building half as many new houses a year as the United Kingdom, which had fifteen times as many people to house. He learned that since 1994 the average price for a Dublin home had risen more than 500 per cent. In parts of Dublin rents had fallen to less than 1 per cent of the purchase price; that is, you could rent a million-dollar home for less than $833 a month. The investment returns on Irish land were ridiculously low: it made no sense for capital to flow into Ireland to develop more of it. Irish home prices implied an economic growth rate that would leave Ireland, in twenty-five years, three times as rich as the United States. ('A price/earnings ratio above Google's,' as Kelly put it.) Where would this growth come from? Since 2000, Irish exports had stalled and the economy had become consumed with building houses and offices and hotels. 'Competitiveness didn't matter,' says Kelly. 'From now on we were going to get rich building houses for each other.'

The endless flow of cheap foreign money had teased a new trait out of a nation. 'We are sort of a hard, pessimistic people,' says Kelly. 'We don't look on the bright side.' Yet since the year 2000 a lot of people had behaved as if each day would be sunnier than the last. The Irish had discovered optimism.

Their real estate boom had the flavor of a family lie: it was sustainable so long as it went unquestioned and it went unquestioned so long as it appeared sustainable. After all, once the value of Irish real estate came untethered from rents, there was no value for it that couldn't be justified. The 35 million euros Irish entrepreneur Denis O'Brien paid for the impressive house on Dublin's Shrewsbury Road sounded like a lot until the real estate developer Sean Dunne's wife paid 58 million euros for the four-thousand-square-foot fixer-upper just down the street. But the minute you compared the rise in prices to real estate booms elsewhere and at other times, you reanchored the conversation; you biffed the narrative. The comparisons that sprung first to Morgan Kelly's mind were with the housing bubbles in the Netherlands in the 1970s (after natural gas was discovered in Holland) and Norway in the 1980s (after oil was found off its coast), but it almost didn't matter which examples he picked: the mere idea that Ireland was not sui generis was the panic-making thought. 'There is an iron law of house prices,' he wrote. 'The more house prices rise relative to income and rents, the more they will subsequently fall.'

The problem for Kelly, once he had these thoughts, was what to do with them. 'This isn't my day job,' he says. 'I was working on medieval population theory.' By the time I got to him Kelly had angered and alienated the entire Irish business and political establishment, but he was himself neither angry nor alienated, nor even especially public. He's not the pundit type. He works in an office built when Irish higher education was conducted on linoleum floors, beneath fluorescent lights, surrounded by metal bookshelves, and generally felt more like a manufacturing enterprise than a prep school for real estate and finance – and likes it. He's puckish, unrehearsed, and apparently – though in Ireland one wants to be careful about using this word – sane. Though not exactly self-denying, he's clearly more comfortable talking and thinking about subjects other than himself. He spent years in graduate school, and collected a doctorate from Yale, and yet somehow retained an almost childlike curiosity. 'I was in this position – sort of being a passenger on this ship,' he says. 'And you see a big iceberg. And so you go and ask the captain: Is that an iceberg?'

His warning to his ship's captain took the form of his first ever newspaper article. Its bottom line: 'It is not implausible that [Irish real estate] prices could fall – relative to income – by 40 to 50 per cent.' At the top of the market, he guessed, prices might fall by a staggering 66 per cent. He sent his first piece to the small-circulation *Irish Times*. 'It was a whim,' he says. 'I'm not even sure that I believed what I was saying at the time. My position has always been, "You can't predict the future."' As it happened, Kelly had predicted the future, with uncanny accuracy, but to believe what he was saying you had to accept that Ireland was not some weird exception in human financial history. 'It had no impact,' Kelly says. 'The response was general amusement. It was *what will these crazy eggheads come up with next?* sort of stuff.'

What the crazy egghead came up with next was the obvious link between Irish real estate prices and Irish banks. After all, the vast majority of the construction was being funded by Irish banks. If the real estate market collapsed, those banks would be on the hook for the losses. 'I eventually figured out what was going on,' says Kelly. 'The average value and number of new mortgages peaked in summer 2006. But lending standards were clearly falling after this.' The banks continued to make worse loans, but the people borrowing the money to buy houses were growing wary. 'What was happening,' says Kelly, 'is that a lot of people were getting cold feet.' The consequences for Irish banks – and the economy – of the inevitable shift in market sentiment would be catastrophic. The banks' losses would lead them to slash their lending to actually useful businesses. Irish citizens in hock to their banks would cease to spend. And, perhaps worst of all, new construction, on which the entire economy was now premised, would cease.

Kelly wrote his second newspaper article, more or less predicting the collapse of the Irish banks. He pointed out that in the last decade the Irish banks and economy had fundamentally changed. In 1997 the Irish banks were funded entirely by Irish deposits. By 2005 they were getting most of their money from abroad. The small German savers who ultimately supplied the Irish banks with deposits to re-lend in Ireland could take their money back with the click of a computer mouse. Since 2000, lending to construction and real estate had risen from 8 per cent of Irish bank lending (the European norm) to 28 per cent. One hundred billion euros – or basically the sum total of all Irish bank deposits – had been handed over to Irish commercial property developers.

By 2007, Irish banks were lending 40 per cent more to property developers alone than they had to the entire Irish population seven years earlier. 'You probably think that the fact that Irish banks have given speculators €100 billion to gamble with, safe in the knowledge that the taxpayers will cover most losses, is a cause for concern to the Irish Central Bank,' Kelly wrote, 'but you would be quite wrong.'

This time Kelly sent his piece to a newspaper with a far bigger circulation, the *Irish Independent*. The *Independent*'s editor wrote back to say he found the article offensive and wouldn't publish it. Kelly next turned to the *Sunday Business Post*, but the editor just sat on the piece. The journalists were following the bankers' lead and conflating a positive outlook on real estate prices with a love of country and a commitment to Team Ireland. ('They'd all use this same phrase, "You're either for us or against us,"' says a prominent Irish bank analyst in Dublin.) Kelly finally went back to the *Irish Times*, which ran his piece in September 2007.

A brief and, to Kelly's way of thinking, pointless controversy ensued. The public relations guy at University College Dublin called the head of the Department of Economics and asked him to find someone to write a learned attack on Kelly's piece. (The department head refused.) A senior executive at Anglo Irish Bank, Matt Moran, called to holler at him. 'He went on about how "the real estate developers who are borrowing from us are so incredibly rich they are only borrowing from us as a favor". He wanted to argue but we ended up having lunch. This is Ireland, after all.' Kelly also received a flurry of worried-sounding messages from financial people in London, but of these he was dismissive. 'I get the impression there's this pool of analysts in the financial markets who spend all day sending scary e-mails to each other.' He never found out how much force his little newspaper piece exerted on the minds of people who mattered.

It wasn't until almost exactly one year later, on September 29, 2008, that Morgan Kelly became the startled object of popular interest. The stocks of the three main Irish banks, Anglo Irish, AIB, and Bank of Ireland, had fallen by between a fifth and a half in a single trading session, and a run on Irish bank deposits had started. The Irish government was about to guarantee all the obligations of the six biggest Irish banks. The most plausible explanation for all of this was Morgan Kelly's narrative: that the Irish economy had become a giant Ponzi scheme, and the country was effectively bankrupt. But it was

so starkly at odds with the story peddled by Irish government officials and senior Irish bankers – that the banks merely had a 'liquidity'
problem and that Anglo Irish was 'fundamentally sound' – that the
two could not be reconciled. The government had a report newly
thrown together by Merrill Lynch, which declared that 'all of the
Irish banks are profitable and well-capitalized'. The difference
between the official line and Kelly's was too vast to be split. You
believed either one or the other, and up until September 2008, who
was going to believe this guy holed up in his office wasting his life
writing about the effects of the Little Ice Age on the English population? 'I went on TV,' says Kelly. 'I'll never do it again.' [. . .]

The Best Supporters in Europe

DONALD MAHONEY (2012)

> Even more so than at previous major soccer championships, where
> Ireland fielded competitive teams, at Euro 2012 the Irish story was all
> about the supporters: the team was hopeless. Donald Mahoney's
> account of events in Poland captured the double-edged nature of
> glorious failure, Irish style, against a backdrop of economic ruination
> at home.

I never expected to spend my thirties attending pointless sporting
occasions in drab places. On the 17th of June, I travelled from
Dublin to Thurles to watch a middling game of hurling between
Clare and Waterford at a dozy Semple Stadium. I'm not from Clare,
not from Waterford, not even from Ireland. Confronted by exis-
tential solitude and the certainty of death, some people find succour
in the idea of God, others embrace nihilism. I had gone crazy for
sports.

I woke at around five the following morning after four hours of
restless sleep. I got out of bed, finished packing my rucksack, cooked
an omelette. I had a ticket for an early flight to Poznań to attend
Ireland's match against Italy in the European football champion-
ships, which would be played that evening. It was the sporting
equivalent of a funeral: Ireland had been eliminated from Euro 2012
after being thrashed in their first two matches. The Italy match
would bring their tournament to a merciful end, regardless of the
result. I had no ticket for the match, no accommodation and no plan
other than to drink beer all day with friends and travel to Berlin at
some point afterwards. Once, I'd considered myself immune to the
lies Ireland tells itself, but as I waited for the 16 bus on O'Connell
Street and envisioned the day ahead, I accepted that I was just
another sucker.

To counteract the frivolity of the occasion, I'd purchased Timothy
Snyder's *Bloodlands*, a historical account of the murder of fourteen

million people in eastern Europe by Hitler and Stalin between 1933 and 1945. Over half of those murders had been perpetrated in the two countries that were hosting the tournament, Poland and Ukraine. It seemed like worthy reading, but as I read the first paragraph of the prologue while sitting beside a female fan drinking a morning can of Carlsberg, the concept of genocide felt beyond me.

The boozy somnolence of the Ireland supporters who constituted almost all of the plane's cargo lifted somewhat as we stepped off and boarded an awaiting bus. People started singing right away, not lustily but because they seemed to think it was expected of them. Fearsome security guards watched us parade into the airport, and attractive young women distributed pastries in 'Poland Loves Food' boxes as we walked out of it.

The people who made the journey to Poland were inheritors of the hallowed legacy of blissful, non-violent inebriation that had inspired Irish supporters to anoint themselves 'The Best Fans in the World'. Ireland had qualified for just five international football tournaments in its history, the first in 1988. One extremely tenuous slice of boom-time pop economics posited that the Irish nation gained the confidence to become a (temporary) economic powerhouse after watching its national soccer team reach the quarter-finals of the 1990 World Cup. (I was a ten-year-old in New Jersey when that tournament took place, and I watched the penalty shootout victory against Romania with my mother, an Irish emigrant. She has forgotten those fifteen minutes, I know, but I consider it to be among the meaningful experiences we have shared.) The late Irish sportswriter Con Houlihan once wrote ruefully that he had missed Italia '90 because he was covering the World Cup in Italy: the real action, from an Irish perspective, was away from the pitch. The supporters had become an entity unto themselves.

It had been ten years since Ireland's last appearance among the elites of global football – at the 2002 World Cup – and there was an element of pent-up demand in the tens of thousands of Irish people who defied the economic ruination at home to travel to Poland. Much of the Irish support consisted of twentysomethings who had never been old enough to attend one of these events. The drawn-out

drunken revelry that preceded Ireland's matches escalated into a performance for a global audience. Something strange had happened
between the fans and the Irish team in that week before I arrived in
Poland, something that was in keeping with the baffling logic that
prevails over Irish life: the worse Ireland fared on the football field,
the more Ireland's supporters enjoyed themselves. This phenomenon reached a crescendo during the seven-minute-long keening of
'The Fields of Athenry', arguably the most mawkish dirge in the
Irish songbook, towards the end of Ireland's four–nil defeat against
Spain. The fans had been liberated by their team's abjection. My
inner American bristled at the thought, even as I travelled to join the
party.

I found my way to Stary Rynek, Poznań's old market square, by
around two o'clock. The square functioned as an open-air bar for
the duration of Euro 2012. Touts carried signs revealing themselves,
and as soon as I bought a ticket for €30 I was offered a free one via
a text from a friend in the Irish media. I quickly sold the €30 ticket
to a young woman from Kerry. 'I don't care where the seat is,' she
said. 'I'm just here for the craic.' The touts were also buying up
Irish supporters' tickets for the quarter-finals. Young women
walked around the square advertising car tyres, mobile phones and
strip clubs.

From the west end of the square, a group of Polish teenagers in
green T-shirts streamed past, carrying inflatable bananas in the Irish
colours. They were led by a girl with a megaphone who was pleading
with the Irish supporters to follow her. I joined the back of the procession. At the far end of the square, on the steps of the old town hall,
beside a restaurant advertising full Irish breakfasts, these teenagers
staged a goodbye ceremony for the fans. If it was unusual to hear
Ireland supporters sing 'A Team of Gary Breens' – a toast (to the tune
of 'Yellow Submarine') to the moderately talented defender who
retired from international football in 2006 – it sounded even more
bizarre when delivered by Polish youths. The Poles seemed most
enamoured of a chant that involved everyone sitting down (for the
Boys in Green), then standing up (for the Boys in Green), removing a
shoe (for the Boys in Green) and waving it in the air. I assumed the

locals were politely expressing their gratitude to the Irish for not raz-
ing their city; but a month later, billboards would appear in Dublin
thanking the 'kings of craic' for visiting Poznań, and the mayor of
the city commissioned an exhibition of photos of Ireland fans that
were mounted alongside one of the paths in St Stephen's Green in
August.

At a Jim Morrison-themed bar, The Lizard King, I met my friend
Myles and his friend Declan, who'd taken a bus over from Berlin
that morning; then Jiggy and his friend Barry, who'd flown from
Dublin via Stockholm for the Spain match on Thursday; Jiggy's
brother Mick, who'd arrived from London on Friday; and then my
friend Eoin. We met friends of friends who were on their tenth consecutive day of drinking. They'd survived the squalid campsites. We
spent lavishly on pints of beer at the bar before realizing we could
buy cans of Tyskie and Zywiec and sickly-sweet miniature bottles
of lemon vodka from a nearby shop and drink them in the square.
Men in green jerseys walked by us carrying framed portraits of Pope
John Paul II, newly purchased. Grown men wore tricolour afros,
tricolour punk-rock mohawks, tricolour hard hats and tricolour
spandex body suits. Each corner of the square featured a fountain,
and these served as plinths for particularly vocal supporters when
organizing call-and-response sessions and group choruses. Along
the west side of the square, the famous 'Angela Merkel Thinks We're
At Work' flag that made the cover of German tabloid *Bild* was on
display. Beside it were other flags with messages like 'Sharon Curley's
Pregnant' and 'That's Limerick Citayyy'. Some advertised towns
and villages, others described how social welfare had financed the
trip. The Irish were like a conquering army; if only there had been
something to celebrate. Back home the country was a shambles, and
the Irish team had disappointed everyone who'd travelled to Poland.
Hold that thought a moment too long and the entire experience
might be derailed.

John McGahern gets close to capturing the essence of the Irish
preoccupation with sport in his short story 'The Creamery Manager'.
The titular character, Jimmy McCarron, takes two local policemen,

the Sergeant and Guard Casey, to the Ulster final between Cavan and Tyrone. McCarron has been stealing money from his workplace and hopes the investment might buy the loyalty of the guards, especially the Sergeant, who played a few times for Cavan in his youth. After he is arrested a month later, McCarron feels genuine guilt about the stunt, though not about his crime. The naïve Guard Casey refuses his apology: 'You gave us a great day out, a day out of all our lives,' he says. The carnival in Poznań that afternoon was the euphoric last act of an extended holiday from reality.

It was during one of my numerous visits to the port-a-loos that afternoon that I first saw a poster seeking information on the whereabouts of a 21-year-old Irish supporter, James Nolan. He'd been separated from friends in the fan zone in Bydgoszcz, a city on the road to Gdansk from Poznań, 130 kilometres away, and hadn't been seen since early Sunday morning. I tried my hardest to remember the face on the poster, but I'd forgotten it within fifteen minutes. Two days later, his body was pulled from the Brda river, only 500 metres from one of the pubs he'd been drinking in. Nolan's death was ruled accidental. 'He was loving it over here, making up loads of songs,' his travelling companion Aaron Eustace told the *Irish Sun*.

As the light of the day began to fade, the Irish supporters lit out en masse for the stadium, which was six kilometres from the centre of town. I felt gripped by a vague sense of panic. I was starving and drunk. Trams were the most direct route to the stadium, but the station was mobbed. We'd need to find an alternative route. I nominated myself as navigator and led us down the one road in Poznań I knew, in the opposite direction from the Irish support. Within five minutes we'd lost Jiggy's brother Mick. We tracked back for him, but he was gone. There wasn't much time until kickoff; we had to go on without him. Further down the road, Eoin spotted a Subway. I learned that 'tuna' is a word that transcends European linguistic divides. Eventually we spotted a taxi and worry turned to exuberance. We made up songs about Enda Kenny, our taxi driver and ourselves along the way.

The taxi dropped us a half mile from the stadium. When the majestic shell of Stadion Miejski came into view, Barry addressed me emphatically: 'Donny, you have to get an Irish flag for your face.' I didn't argue. The face paint cost as much as the cab ride.

Our tickets were in different parts of the stadium, and so we made a plan to reconvene outside Beverly Hills Video near the tram stop after the match. I stashed the rest of our drink in the gutter of a one-storey shed next door, fully expecting it to be gone when we returned. There was a beautiful pallid light around the stadium as night fell. We trekked across a sandy field, slugging the remnants of our cans, before passing through a number of security cordons and going our separate ways. I found my seat about a minute after the national anthems had been completed. It was the only part of the match I actually wanted to witness in person: 'Amhrán na bhFiann' always stirs something deep from the sentimental pit of me.

A football match was played. Ireland lost again. There were no recriminations from the supporters. They stood up and sang through-out the entire match, adding an obligatory, if half-hearted, 'Fields of Athenry' after the final whistle. Buffon, the Italian captain, made a point of saluting the Ireland supporters after the game and the Italian sitting in the row ahead of me shook my hand after the match had ended.

'You Irish are the best supporters in Europe,' he said.

I left the stadium and headed for Beverly Hills Video, which had converted itself into an off-licence for the tournament. None of my friends were around and our beer had been taken. Night had fallen, and supporters milled about aimlessly. One guy was wearing the boot of Irish centre-half Sean St Ledger. Forked lightning began to illuminate the night sky. Lightning is a rare sight in Ireland. We all stared at the intermittent flashing in disbelief.

'Let's get out of here,' I remember someone saying. 'There's rain coming.'

I heeded that advice and boarded the first tram I could squeeze onto. The result of the match, though entirely predictable, had wiped the ecstatic sheen from the drunkenness of the Irish fans. The tram passed the city-centre Sheraton, but no one had a clue how to get back

to the square and most people took the tram all the way to the termi-
nus. Somebody ascertained that we'd gone eight kilometres beyond
Stary Rynek. Eventually I got in a cab with three other Ireland fans.

It was after midnight when I reached the square. I passed about a
hundred riot cops casually talking amongst themselves. Rain was
falling now and the cops seemed confident the Irish fans would drink
themselves to sleep. I found Myles and Declan outside the Lizard
King. They said that scores of local women had just been working
their way around the square, chatting up any Irish man in their path.
The square was full again and the Irish were still drinking. There
were queues outside the strip clubs. The singing continued, though it
was more muted. Hours ago, when the sun shone, this collective
seemed capable of some grand subversive gesture. But, of course,
there would be no cathartic release, just another hangover. It was
only football that brought us here, after all.

Myles and Declan were taking a 3 a.m. bus back to Berlin. They
said the bus had been full on the way over, but there might be room
on the way back. I saw sleeping Irish supporters scattered across the
square, on barstools and on benches, and caught a glimpse of my own
fate if I didn't get on the bus.

The bus turned out to be a pair of minivans. Myles and Declan
boarded one. There was a single empty seat on the other.

'Two hundred zloty,' the driver said. That was about fifty euros,
double what Myles had spent on his fare, but I didn't think twice. I
sat down in the van, closed my eyes and woke up outside Berlin's
Schönefeld Airport.

'Get out,' the driver said.

'City centre?' I said.

'No city centre,' he replied. 'I have to go back to Poland to do
another run.'

The sun was shining. It was around 5.15 a.m. I looked for Myles
and Declan but there was no sign of them. I trudged into the airport
and saw a few other zombified Ireland supporters with tricolours
hanging from their necks. I was surprised to be alive. I asked a
woman at an information desk for directions to the toilet. She
pointed at a door five feet away. Maybe it was her dour German

countenance, or perhaps just the hour, but she seemed disgusted by the sight of me.

In the toilet, I caught a glimpse of myself for the first time since I'd touched down at Poznań airport. Each of my cheeks featured an Irish flag in immaculate condition. A voice in my head reminded me I was in Germany, financial overlords of the Irish state, and that it was Tuesday morning. I used ample amounts of hand soap, but could not completely erase the green and orange paint.

The Strange Career of Thomas McFeely

SUSAN MCKAY (2012)

A large estate of new homes on the northern outskirts of Dublin had to be evacuated in 2011 because it was discovered that many of the buildings were so substantially in breach of fire regulations that they were uninhabitable. They had been built by a firm owned by Thomas McFeely, a developer with a colourful political past in Northern Ireland. Susan McKay's profile appeared in the *Guardian*.

Thomas Bernard McFeely could not have been more indignant. The Irish woman who has become the bane of his life, Theresa McGuinness, had challenged his UK bankruptcy. 'As a British citizen I have always objected to being forced into bankruptcy in a foreign jurisdiction,' he informed the high court in London in June. 'I maintain this is a breach of my human rights.'

The foreign jurisdiction in question is Ireland, where hollow laughter greeted McFeely's sudden declaration of Britishness. After all, this is a man who once believed so fiercely in his Irishness that he fought in the IRA. He refused to recognise the British court that sentenced him in Northern Ireland in the 1970s, went on hunger strike and was prepared to die in the notorious H blocks in 1980. He later broke from Sinn Féin to join the League of Communist Republicans. Then he became a multimillionaire property developer.

McFeely is bankrupt in Ireland now and will be out of business for 12 years. He is embroiled in numerous other court proceedings. His Victorian mansion on one of Dublin's most expensive avenues has been repossessed by the state. He says it's because he's a 'Nordie'; that he is a victim of southern Irish prejudice against northerners, exacerbated by the global economic crisis. Few, however, see him as a victim. McFeely needn't worry about a roof over his head. His creditors, on the other hand, include several hundred people who bought apartments from him in Priory Hall, a development deemed so dangerous it was evacuated with fire crews standing by.

One Irish newspaper editorial recently said of McFeely that he lives on a 'different moral planet to the rest of us'. However, McFeely's planet is entirely recognisable as contemporary Ireland. His dramatic rise to wealth was encouraged and facilitated by successive governments of a Republic that each year commemorates the egalitarian ideals of the 1916 Easter Rising. A Republic that is, according to the findings of the recent Mahon tribunal, endemically corrupt.

McFeely's spectacular fall is mirrored by those of dozens of other developers and bankers, many of whom are queueing up to take advantage of more lenient bankruptcy laws in the UK and the US. Some have hidden billions abroad. Those paying for the excesses of the Celtic Tiger are ordinary Irish people, such as the former residents of Priory Hall, who took out inflated 20- or 30-year mortgages just before the bubble burst.

Ireland, puffed up for a decade on the success of its peace process and the booming of its economy, is now bust, a land of zombie banks, ghost estates and empty monster hotels. Irish sovereignty, fought for by generations, has largely been forfeited to the so-called troika of the International Monetary Fund, the European Central Bank and the European Commission.

McFeely regards journalists as 'scum'. We meet at the headquarters of his main Irish company, Coalport. The building is on the edge of one of Dublin's grandest Georgian squares, but its large boardroom is as sparse as a prison cell. Grubby white walls, a basic table and chairs, a single poster of the Manhattan skyline. He takes the seat at the head of the table. He tells me he used to have antiques in the boardroom, but the sheriff took them. He fields calls. One, he says, is from a bank manager in Portugal, where he also has property problems.

He was born in 1949, the eldest son in a Catholic family of 13, in Parkland, County Derry. His grandfather joined the British army and was injured in the first world war. His uncle was in the British marines and was killed in action. 'My grandmother never forgave the

British army for taking her son. She was one hell of a lady. She had presence. Her daughter, my mother, was fairly militant.' His father was a cattle dealer and more of a nationalist than a republican.

McFeely says he will never forget the family home being wrecked during a raid by 'the B men', members of the notorious unionist Special Constabulary. 'You'd have thought a bomb had hit the place.' The 'B Specials' were usually local men; the poet Seamus Heaney, also from Co. Derry, called them 'neighbours with guns'.

McFeely went to school in Derry. 'There were houses that were semi-derelict. It was primitive to say the least. I remember seeing roofs with the slates in a big hollow in the middle.' He left school at 14 and worked with a farmer until he was old enough to get on to a building site. When he was 15, there was an election. He was sent out to vote for the nationalist candidate, but voted instead for the republican: 'I had a mind of my own.' He served his time as a bricklayer, working from 7 a.m. till 9 p.m. 'Everything I've done, I was diligent at it. I was "on the grip", paid by the brick.'

He went to England in 1968 and got work straight away. 'The 5th of October brought me back. It was typical of what I had learned all my life – we were a people to be put down in our own country,' he says. He is referring to the violent attack by the police on a civil rights march through Derry. Discrimination was institutionalised in Northern Ireland but was particularly acute in Derry, shortly to be dubbed 'the capital city of injustice' by Bernadette Devlin (then a leading civil rights campaigner and soon to become Britain's youngest ever woman MP). Housing was at the heart of it, with disenfranchised and unemployed nationalists living in poverty in desperately overcrowded slums.

The Troubles had started, and McFeely pitched in: 'I would always have been up at the front of the riots where the hand-to-hand fighting went on.' Though he has boasted of wielding a hatchet, he says he also listened to the speeches and particularly admired Devlin and Eamonn McCann. 'I was taken by the socialism. We were all downtrodden, even a lot of the Protestants, though they thought they were aristocracy.' He stopped practising Catholicism in 1971. 'As Lenin said, it is the opium of the people.'

His activism quickly 'morphed into' IRA involvement. 'It was a way of getting back at the state.' Facing six months in jail, he went on the run in the Republic, but missed the action and his fiancée: 'I couldn't stay away.' He got married and had two daughters. He set out to bomb the new dole office in Antrim, where he had bought a house. There was a chase, he was cornered, punched a policeman in the face, escaped, went on the run in the Republic, got caught, was jailed, escaped again. 'I went back to the North,' he says, 'which was hot and heavy.'

He knew Martin McGuinness, who admits he led the IRA in Derry at the time of Bloody Sunday in 1972, but claims to have left by 1974. 'Martin was game. Martin was all right. It's not like him to leave in the middle of a good row,' McFeely says with heavy sarcasm.

McFeely was not, he says, involved in the 1972 bombing of Claudy, a few miles from his childhood home. Nine people were killed, with no warnings given. 'But if I'd been there I would have planted the bombs. It is the reality of war. I only regret I wasn't able to do more.'

After carrying out an armed robbery on a post office, he and another IRA man took over a rural house, which was put under siege by the security forces. 'It was a bit Wild West, to be honest. The idea was to go out and take as many of them out as possible.' He shot a policeman (who survived) and when he eventually gave himself up, he expected to be shot dead. He got away with 'a fair decent beating' but was sentenced to 26 years in 1977 by a judge who called him 'an extremely dangerous, intelligent and vicious young man'.

McFeely puts his head in his hands when asked about his prison years. 'What do you tell? You got booted around, the screws would come in with drink on them and raid the cells, they'd spit on your food, you'd to walk naked, they'd set the dogs on you . . . There was fear, humiliation. I was in for the fight – I'd give the screws a damn good kicking.'

Screws were prison officers, mostly Protestants. He names one, 'the only evil man I ever met', and says he is still glad he 'died a horrible death, a bomb under his car – he was mangled'. McFeely's violence meant he spent a lot of time 'on the boards' (in solitary confinement).

After the British ceased to recognise IRA members as political prisoners, McFeely was the OC (officer in command) of those who refused to wear the prison uniform and went 'on the blanket'. This escalated into the 'dirty protest'. The prisoners stopped washing; they urinated in their cells and smeared excrement on the walls. Soon the cells were crawling with maggots and prison officers wore gas masks against the stink.

McFeely, described by another IRA prison leader as 'a very, very strong character', was one of seven chosen to go on hunger strike, and was regarded as probably the most determined of them all. His face, gaunt, young, rakishly handsome back then, was on the posters that were carried on demonstrations in Belfast, Dublin and London. Halfway through, another prisoner described seeing McFeely: 'It was frightening. He looked like a skeleton with skin pulled over him.' After 53 days, with one man about to die and rumours of a deal with the British, the hunger strike was called off. McFeely was blind, and furious. He vehemently opposed the decision.

He is still full of rage about what happened. The deal was useless – the hunger strike had failed. When a new one began, the leadership refused his offer to go on it. 'I had no role after that.' The demoralisation was 'absolutely terrible'. Violence inside the prison and out on the streets continued. Ten men died on the hunger strike. Along with another ex-hunger striker, Tommy McKearney, McFeely split with Sinn Féin to set up the League of Communist Republicans.

Essie Kealing was a working-class hero. She lived in a flat in a complex that had been built for Dublin's poor by one of the 1916 revolutionaries. The flats were sold in the 1970s and Kealing led an eight-year rent strike to stop the landlord from evicting the tenants. In 1999, when she was 76 and had lived in her flat for 40 years, she received several visits from the new landlord, who attempted to persuade her to move out in terms that can be guessed at from her description of him as a 'rough merchant'. This was Tom McFeely, ten years after his release from Long Kesh prison.

Though he had not recognised the court, McFeely had appealed against his sentence and was released in 1989. His marriage had broken up. He moved to Dublin. He likes to tell the story of his first night, sleeping in his small car, almost penniless. Hired initially by other former IRA prisoners, he went back 'on the grip', intent upon building up his fortune brick by brick.

He was just in time to avail himself of minister Padraig Flynn's new light-touch regulatory regime which allowed 'self-certification' of compliance with the law by architects, engineers and builders. Local authorities were empowered to carry out inspections, but in reality the pace of building was soon such that they lacked the resources to do so in more than a token number of cases.

Successive Fianna Fáil governments laid out a range of tax breaks and schemes which, along with low interest rates and a striking absence of regulation, were designed to encourage speculators. A government minister praised the Irish 'frontiersmen' mentality. The *New York Times* said Dublin had become known as 'something of the Wild West of European finance'. Many of those who profited bankrolled the party. McFeely says he did not. 'But if I'd been asked, would I have done it? Yes. I don't know anybody with a halo.'

Within a couple of years, McFeely had enough money to buy a pub back home in Dungiven. He had no fear of authority. His modus operandi, if there was a finding against him in one court, was to appeal to a higher one. There were long-running legal battles with other major developers. 'I pushed it all in front of me. I never kept money,' he says.

He didn't part with it readily, either. Following a Criminal Assets Bureau investigation in 2006, he had to pay out more than €8 million in unpaid taxes, dating back to his arrival in the Republic. The following year, Coalport was the subject of no fewer than eight high court proceedings. He took out a loan of €10 million for his house, the former German embassy, but stopped paying the mortgage. In 2009 he was ordered to repay €6.2 million to a bank, as well as a further revenue payment of €580,000.

McFeely's companies built houses, apartments and commercial units all over Ireland, as well as in England. He maintained the tradition of employing ex-prisoners. An absence of building experience was not a barrier. During the boom, he freely admits, 'Everything was done in a rush. The attitude was get it up, get it off, get on to the next job. Come back and finish it later.'

In 2002, Theresa McGuinness liked what she saw of McFeely's plans for a small development in County Dublin and paid a cash deposit of €35,000 on a house. It was a decision that would come to dominate her life for at least the following decade. Within two years she was suing McFeely. 'You could see the house was a disaster by its roof,' she said. 'It was literally sagging in the middle. Inside, you'd have thought someone had taken a hammer to the place.'

The signs were bad for Priory Hall right from the start. The development was part of the much-vaunted new Northern Fringe. 'The idea was to develop an extension to the city of Dublin with high-density housing and good public services and transport,' says local TD Tommy Broughan. Many of the top developers obtained sites. McFeely's was at the southern end of what was to have been the main boulevard through the new towns of Clongriffin and Belmayne. 'They call it the boulevard of broken dreams now,' Broughan says.

In 2004, a woman had just dropped her children at school and was driving home along the edge of McFeely's building site when her car was crushed by steel mesh grids weighing over a tonne. She was described as having narrowly escaped death. Two years later, another woman had a narrow escape when her car was hit by a section of scaffolding falling from the same site. A health and safety inspector said this was 'one of the most unsafe' sites he had ever inspected. The high court ordered the site to be temporarily closed because of 'systemic' breaches of regulations.

In the years that followed, there were complaints about estates left in an 'appalling state', roads unfinished, 'wires sticking out of the showers', fire hazards. After Dublin city council brought McFeely to court over problems in an estate in west Dublin, the president of the high court said there had been 'clear unwillingness' and 'foot dragging' by the developer.

Clongriffin today is a sorry sight. There's a forlorn railway station, but most of the promised facilities were never developed. Some

estates are half-empty, while others have been half-built, then abandoned. Roads end in hoardings. One has 'Drug dealers out' scrawled
on it.

One public housing tenant at Priory Hall was taken to hospital
because of the damp soon after it opened. Just before Christmas in
2009, the council moved its tenants out after fire inspectors deemed
the buildings dangerous. Broughan demanded a debate in the Irish
parliament about the 'outrageous situation', pointing out that 'key
planning and building regulations' had obviously been ignored.
McFeely undertook to do works.

One owner agrees to take me round and talk about what happened on condition that I do not use his name. McFeely's reputation
as a 'rough merchant' has not diminished. (In May, a London high
court judge found there was a 'strong suggestion' that, based on a
sham lease he had helped to devise, McFeely had received almost
€4m in rents for a building near the Olympic Village in Stratford,
and that he and others had intimidated the directors of the leasing
company.)

'My wife and I bought off plans in 2005,' the apartment owner
says. 'It was our first home together. The apartments were expensive
but this was the peak of the boom and the banks were throwing
money at people. We brought in a surveyor but he was refused access.'

The security man on the locked-up site lets us in and we climb
stained, carpeted stairs to the apartment. The living room window
looks out over the abrupt end of the road and a mound of grassed-
over rubble at the edge of waste ground where the boulevard was
meant to be. 'We kind of knew from the start the place was blighted,'
the man says. 'The car park was always flooded. The place was damp.
One morning we were woken by a knock on the door and it was the
young couple downstairs. Their ceiling had fallen in. Sewage pipes
went nowhere – just ended. We were paying a management fee but
nothing was getting done.'

Then, one morning in October 2011, the man was driving to work
when he heard on the news that the city council had gone to court to
get an order for the apartments to be evacuated. Insurance companies
ceased cover. Fire crews stood by as residents packed cars and vans,

and moved to hotels, spare rooms and rented apartments. The high court ordered the council to pay for their accommodation – it has since appealed against this.

'Self-regulation is outrageous,' the man says. 'It turns out McFeely declared the complex to be "in substantial compliance" with all the rules and regulations, and the council just accepted that. It was crazy – we first set eyes on McFeely in court. He called us begrudgers and "jumped-up little Hitlers".' One resident shouted back at the builder that he 'couldn't build a snowman'.

At first, it was agreed that setting things right would take five weeks. Then a dispute blew up between McFeely and Dublin city council, which led to McFeely being arrested and briefly jailed, before he appealed to the supreme court, which found in his favour. When the council made public its enforcement order, the owners knew the place was doomed. 'There were 18 pages of items, most of them very serious. Basically, nothing was right.'

'They crucified me,' McFeely says of the massive tax settlement he had to make with the Criminal Assets Bureau. Having paid, he went straight out and bought a Bentley for nearly €50,000. 'I stuck my two fingers up at them. They thought they could destroy me. I'm getting hammered because I had the audacity to come down here and live on Ailesbury Road. It's the Free State mentality – I'm a Nordie with a republican reputation.'

It is certainly true that the wealthy of Dublin tend to be snobbish and that the huge made-in-the-H-blocks Celtic cross in McFeely's drawing room window looks incongruous. He is far from being the only local resident to be familiar with the inside of a courtroom, but is one of the few who has been in jail. His fleet of vehicles is normal for the area – though the Bentley has gone. 'I paid a lawyer with it.' In fact, the McFeelys have been ordered to leave the house after his second wife failed to persuade the high court to let her remain there in her own right.

McFeely says his building practices and standards are normal, and that he has co-operated with attending to any 'snags' as required, though he disputes others' assessments of these. There is mounting evidence that he is right about standards – one large apartment block built by another developer has recently been evacuated as unsafe and it is likely that more will follow. 'A lot of the other developers are bad-mouthing me because they think I'm bringing the heat on them,' McFeely says. 'But I'm no tout.'

He makes no apology for his British passport. 'I am still a republican, but I was born a British subject and I'm smarter than the rest of them. I fought for a socialist republic and I still believe in that. Blame the peace processers for copper-fastening the border. And by the way, you get better justice in the British courts.'

There is still a framed poster on the staircase of Sinn Féin's offices in Dungiven, near McFeely's old home, showing him among the 1980 hunger strikers. The museum upstairs is full of Troubles memorabilia, including a glass case containing a couple of AK47s and a 1977 poster demanding 'Break the connection with England – the source of all our evils.' But all has changed. Downstairs, at the front desk, there's the order of business for the Assembly at Stormont, where Martin McGuinness is now deputy first minister. The day I visit, the front pages have photos of McGuinness and the Queen shaking hands.

McFeely's old IRA comrades are loyal. They speak of the 'rare bond' that exists between ex-prisoners. They say they don't know much about what he is accused of in the Republic. Sean McGlinchey, now Sinn Féin mayor of Limavady, says McFeely, still a good friend despite their political differences, 'never got over' the end of the hunger strike. 'He is no angel, but we all have our faults, we all make mistakes.' He admits McFeely was always aggressive. 'He wouldn't go around a thing – he'd go through it. He's a bull.'

Down the road in Derry, Eamonn McCann, who inspired McFeely all those years ago, is still a campaigning socialist. 'McFeely represents something almost stereotypical,' he says. 'A republican who is a property developer and a landlord. There is a great deal of resentment against the political establishment in the Republic. Men like McFeely feel they have done intense things "for Ireland" and they are entitled to some return. Of course, you have Fianna Fáil ministers who have also acted as if the state is something to be treated with contempt.'

Theresa McGuinness has no interest in any of this. She has spent the past decade fighting through the courts, representing herself, to get McFeely to pay her back the money he owes her for the house she never got. She has been more assiduous than any state agency in her pursuit of him. 'This man has put me through a pure nightmare,' she says. 'Why should I let him get away with it?' [. . .]

Acknowledgements

This collection has its origins in a conversation with my colleague Michael Foley of the Dublin Institute of Technology a decade or more ago. Since then, this selection has also benefited from many conversations with, and advice from, among others, Joe Lee, Maurice Walsh, Mary Maher, Mary Kenny, Mike Freeman, Sinéad Gleeson, Mark O'Connell, David Waddell and Tom Garvin. Not all of the articles shortlisted made it over the final fences, but all had their unique attractions nonetheless.

Olivia O'Leary not only provided a typically stylish and insightful Foreword, but made me aware of several articles whose claims would otherwise have been overlooked, and that made it easily into the final set of choices. I am grateful to her on both counts.

I am particularly grateful to those copyright holders, many of whom are also journalistically active today, whose permission to use their work has been recorded elsewhere. The work of tracking down original texts and the present whereabouts of copyright holders is not always as easy as is imagined and, in this context, I am particularly grateful to many of my former colleagues in Irish journalism, to Nicholas Furlong and his staff in the National Library of Ireland; Terry McDonald in the Library of Trinity College, Dublin; Patrick and Slaney Devlin of London; Antony Farrell of Lilliput Press; Ulick O'Connor, Vincent and Malachy Browne of *Magill*; and to Maurice Earls, John Logan, Angela Bourke, Felix Larkin, Clair Wills, Jonathan Williams, Dennis Kennedy and John Boland.

Many of the older texts have had to be digitized. In this context I warmly thank Miriam Laffan, Sarah Keating, Maria Dunne, Paul O'Mahony, Erin Flanagan, Ciara McDermott and Niamh Cassidy.

I would like to thank, also, Brendan Barrington of Penguin Ireland, who contributed his enthusiasm to this project over the long period of its gestation and, in due course, added his exceptional editing skills.

Last but not least, I owe my wife, Mary Jones, ever-lasting gratitude for the support she has given, not only for this project but for many others over the years, and for tolerating many journalism-related, deadline-induced absences and other forms of antisocial behaviour with never-failing patience and generosity.

Sources

The editor and the publishers would like to express their gratitude to the writers and publishers who have given permission for the republication of these pieces.

Binchy, Maeve: *Irish Times*, 15 November 1973. Permission granted by the Estate of Maeve Binchy and the *Irish Times*.

Bowen, Elizabeth: National Archives, Kew, DO 130/28, 31 July 1942. Permission granted by Curtis Brown, as agents for the author.

Brennan, Maeve: *New Yorker*, 12 June 1962; republished in *The Long-Winded Lady* (New York: Houghton and Mifflin, 1998). Reprinted by permission of Russell & Volkening as agents for the author.

Browne, Harry: *Dublin Review* 8, Autumn 2002. Permission granted by Harry Browne.

Browne, Vincent: *Magill*, 1 February 1998. Permission granted by Vincent Browne and Emdee Productions.

Butler, Eoin: *Mongrel*, August 2007. Permission granted by Eoin Butler.

Butler, Hubert: *The Twentieth Century*, January 1958; republished in *Escape from the Anthill* (Dublin: Lilliput Press, 1985). Permission granted by the Estate of Hubert Butler and Lilliput Press.

Comfort, Alex: *Horizon* 3:2, April 1943. Permission granted by Nicholas Comfort.

Cronin, Anthony: *Magill*, 1 September 1978. Permission granted by Anthony Cronin.

Crowe, Catriona: *Dublin Review* 43, Summer 2011. Permission granted by Catriona Crowe.

Cummins, Mary, *Irish Times*, 24 February 1972; republished in *Changing the Times*, ed. Elgy Gillespie (Dublin: Lilliput Press, 2003). Permission granted by the *Irish Times* and Lilliput Press

Dunphy, Eamon: *Magill*, 1 September 1984. Permission granted by Eamon Dunphy.

Gaffney, Gertrude: *Irish Independent*, 7 May 1937. Permission granted by the *Irish Independent*.

Geary, Frank: *Irish Independent*, 12 August 1922. Permission granted by Patrick Geary and the *Irish Independent*.

Healy, John: *Irish Times*, 18–19 November, 1965. Permission granted by the *Irish Times*.

Holland, Mary: *Irish Times*, 23 March 1988. Permission granted by Kitty Holland and the *Irish Times*.

Houlihan, Con: *Evening Press*, 25 September 1978. Permission granted by Harriet Duffin on behalf of the Estate of Con Houlihan and by the *Irish Press*.

Hourihane, Ann Marie: *Dublin Review* 23, Summer 2006. Permission granted by Ann Marie Hourihane.

Johnston, Denis: *The Bell* 16:6, March 1951. Permission granted by Rory Johnston.

Kavanagh, Patrick: *The Standard*, 12 June 1942; republished in *A Poet's Country: Selected Prose*, ed. Antoinette Quinn (Dublin: Lilliput Press, 2003). Permission granted by the Jonathan Williams Literary Agency as Trustees of the late Katherine B. Kavanagh.

Kenny, Mary: *Irish Press*, 30 September 1969. Permission granted by Mary Kenny and the *Irish Press*.

Kerrigan, Gene: *Magill*, 1 September 1983. Permission granted by Gene Kerrigan.

Kimmage, Paul: *Sunday Independent*, 3 July 2000. Permission granted by Paul Kimmage and the *Sunday Independent*.

Leahy, Pat: extracted from *Showtime* (Dublin: Penguin Ireland, 2009). Permission granted by Pat Leahy and Penguin Books.

Levine, June: *Magill*, 1 December 1983. Permission granted by Ivor Browne.

Lewis, Michael: extracted from *Boomerang* (London: Allen Lane, 2011). Permission granted by Penguin Books.

Liebling, A. J.: *New Yorker*, 6 December 1941. Reprinted by permission of Russell & Volkening as agents for the author.

MacAnthony, Joe, and Paul Murphy: *Sunday Independent*, 23 June 1974. Permission granted by Joe MacAnthony, Paul Murphy and the *Sunday Independent*.

McCafferty, Nell: *In Dublin*, 24 February 1984; republished in *The Best of Nell* (Dublin: Attic Press, 1984). Permission granted by Nell McCafferty and Cork University Press (for Attic Press).

McDonald, Frank, and Kathy Sheridan: extracted from *The Builders* (Dublin: Penguin Ireland, 2008). Permission granted by Frank McDonald, Kathy Sheridan and Penguin Books.

McKay, Susan: *Guardian*, 10 August 2012. Permission granted by Susan McKay.

MacNeice, Louis: *New Statesman*, 5 July 1963; republished in *Selected Prose of Louis MacNeice*, ed. Alan Heuser (Oxford: Clarendon Press, 1990). Permission granted by the Estate of Louis MacNeice, through David Higham Associates.

Maffey, John: National Archives, Kew, PREM 1/340, 20 September 1939; republished in *Documents on Irish Foreign Policy*, Vol. VI: 1939–41, ed. Catriona Crowe, Ronan Fanning, Michael Kennedy, Dermot Keogh and Eunan O'Halpin (Dublin: Royal Irish Academy, 2008).

Maher, Mary: *Irish Times*, 6 June 1973. Permission granted by Mary Maher and the *Irish Times*.

Mahoney, Donald: *Dublin Review* 48, Autumn 2012. Permission granted by Donald Mahoney.

Myers, Kevin: *Irish Times*, 19 December 1987. Permission granted by Kevin Myers and the *Irish Times*.

na gCopaleen, Myles: *The Bell* 1:2, November 1940. Permission granted by the Estate of Myles na gCopaleen.

O'Brien, Conor Cruise: *Irish Times*, 24 August 1982. Permission granted by the Estate of Conor Cruise O'Brien.

O'Brien, Kate: *Spectator*, 24 September 1948. Permission granted by the Estate of Kate O'Brien.

O'Clery, Conor: *Irish Times*, 18 August 1980. Permission granted by Conor O'Clery and the *Irish Times*

O Connor, Fionnuala: *Irish Times*, 26 November 1984. Permission granted by Fionnuala O Connor and the *Irish Times*.

O'Connor, Joseph: *Sunday Tribune*, 26 June 1994; republished in *The Secret World of the Irish Male* (Dublin: New Island Books, 1996). Permission granted by Joseph O'Connor and New Island Books.

O'Hagan, Andrew: *Dublin Review* 10, Spring 2003. Permission granted by Andrew O'Hagan.

O'Kane, Maggie: *Guardian*, 21 May 1992. Permission granted by Maggie O'Kane and Guardian News and Media.

O'Leary, Olivia: *Spectator*, 29 May 1982. Permission granted by Olivia O'Leary.

O'Reilly, Emily: *Sunday Tribune*, 12 June 1983. Permission granted by Emily O'Reilly and the *Sunday Tribune*.

O'Toole, Fintan: *Irish Times*, 18 February 1989; republished in *A Mass for Jesse James* (Dublin: Raven Arts Press, 1990). Permission granted by Fintan O'Toole.

Patterson, Glenn: *Guardian*, 5 August 2005; republished in *Lapsed Protestant* (Dublin: New Island Books, 2006). Permission granted by Glenn Patterson and New Island Books.

Pritchett, V. S.: *Christian Science Monitor*, 22 May 1923. Reprinted by permission of Peters, Fraser & Dunlop on behalf of the Estate of V. S. Pritchett.

Purcell, Deirdre: *Sunday Tribune*, 9 October 1988. Permission granted by Deirdre Purcell and the *Sunday Tribune*.

Raftery, Mary, and Eoin O'Sullivan: extracted from *Suffer the Little Children* (Dublin: New Island Books, 1999; republished 2013). Permission granted by the Estate of Mary Raftery, Eoin O'Sullivan and New Island Books.

Ronan, Sean: National Archives of Ireland, DFA 96/2/17, 1965–66.

Smyllie, R. M.: *Irish Times*, 4 November 1936. Permission granted by the Estate of R. M. Smyllie and the *Irish Times*.

Tóibín, Colm: extracted from *Bad Blood: A Walk Along the Irish Border* (London: Vintage, 1994; first published as *Walking Along the Border*, 1987). Permission granted by Colm Tóibín.

Tracy, Honor: *Sunday Times*, 14 May 1950. Copyright © Honor Tracy.
Viney, Michael: *Irish Times*, 27 April 1966. Permission granted by Michael Viney and the *Irish Times*.
Waters, John: *Hot Press*, 14 December 1984. Permission granted by John Waters.